Crawford Howell Toy

Judaism and Christianity

A Sketch of the Progress of Thought From Old Testament to New Testament

Crawford Howell Toy

Judaism and Christianity
A Sketch of the Progress of Thought From Old Testament to New Testament

ISBN/EAN: 9783337009915

Printed in Europe, USA, Canada, Australia, Japan

Cover: Foto ©Lupo / pixelio.de

More available books at **www.hansebooks.com**

JUDAISM AND CHRISTIANITY

A SKETCH

OF

THE PROGRESS OF THOUGHT FROM OLD TESTAMENT TO NEW TESTAMENT

BY

CRAWFORD HOWELL TOY

PROFESSOR IN HARVARD UNIVERSITY

BOSTON

LITTLE, BROWN, AND COMPANY

1890

University Press:
JOHN WILSON AND SON, CAMBRIDGE.

PREFACE.

THE present volume was begun as a continuation of my " Quotations in the New Testament," with the purpose of giving an orderly view of the development of religious thought apparent in the way in which Old Testament passages are interpreted and used by New Testament writers. On further consideration of the subject, however, I came to the conclusion that this end would be better gained by a general historical survey of the period reaching from the distinct legal organization of the Jewish people to the close of the New Testament Canon. In so large a field I have been obliged to confine myself to the discussion of general ethical-religious ideas, omitting many details which might properly have been introduced but for lack of space; and this condensation will not be without advantage if it helps to secure clearness of outline without the sacrifice of anything essential to the discussion. For the same reason — namely, lack of space — I have not gone into full critical examination of the Biblical and Apocryphal books which

have furnished the material for my discussion, but
have contented myself with brief indications of
the grounds of my chronological classification. For
details on this point I refer to the well-known
works of Reuss, Kuenen, Stade, Weiss, Meyer, and
others. I felt doubtful about inserting so meagre
an outline as I have given of the subject of the
Introduction, — a subject that richly deserves a
separate treatise; but on the whole it seemed
better to treat it even very briefly than to
omit it altogether. Among works bearing on
this subject may be mentioned Bagehot's "Physics
and Politics," Kuenen's "National Religions and
Universal Religions," and W. Robertson Smith's
"Religion of the Semites."

I need hardly say that I do not claim absolute
correctness for my results. In the treatment of so
long a period of history, for the construction of
which the data are sometimes lacking and often
uncertain, one can hope only for an approximation
to the truth, and I shall be grateful for any criticisms which may lead to a correcter or completer
interpretation of the facts.

C. H. T.

Cambridge, Mass.,
    October, 1890.

TABLE OF CONTENTS.

INTRODUCTION.

PAGE

On the General Laws of the Advance from National to Universal Religions 1–46

I. THE SOCIAL BASIS OF RELIGION 1–6
§ 1. Social Character of Religion 1, 2
1. Religion a product of human thought, 1. — 2. Content of the religious consciousness, 2.

§ 2. Growth of Society 2–6
1. General laws of growth, arrest, retrogression, and decay, 2, 3. — 2. Application of these laws to society, 3, 4. — 3. Relation of size of community to law of growth, 4, 5. — 4. Religion subject to the laws of social growth, 5, 6.

II. GENERAL CONDITIONS OF RELIGIOUS PROGRESS 6–39
§ 1. Formation of Communities 7–11
1. Organized social life the condition of the development of a religion, 7–9. — 2. Nations formed by combinations of smaller communities, and national religions by aggregation of tribal faiths, 9–11.

§ 2. Internal Development of Ideas 11–21
1. Constant refashioning of religious ideas in a growing community, 11, 12. — 2. Interaction between the different elements of social thought; influence of art and politics on religion, 12. 13 — 3. Religion modified and developed by science, 14–16. — 4. Religion and ethics, their independent developments and mutual influence, 16–20. — 5. Content of the religious sentiment determined by science and ethics, 20. 21.

§ 3. Great Men 21–26
1. Great men a necessity in social progress, 21, 22. — 2. They are the product of their times, 22. 23. — 3. There is something inexplicable in them, 23,

PAGE

24. — 4. They give a new unity to thought and society, 24, 25. — 5. The part they have played in the establishment of religions, 25, 26.

§ 4. EXTERNAL CONDITIONS 26–30
1. The extent of the religious influence exerted by one nation on another depends in part on closeness of intercourse, 26, 27. — 2. Such influence reciprocal, and the more developed the religious culture the greater its influence, 27, 28. — 3. Effect of excitement of thought, 28. — 4. Borrowing of ideas is direct or indirect, conscious or unconscious, 28, 29. — 5. It is determined by a nation's capacity for assimilation, 29, 30.

§ 5. THE GENERAL LINES OF PROGRESS 30–36
1. Abandonment of local usages, 30–32. — 2. Broadening of ideas, 32. — 3. Selection of a new idea as basis of organization, 32–34. — 4. Response to the demands of the times, 34, 35. — 5. An absolutely universal religion has not yet appeared, 35, 36.

§ 6. EXTRA-NATIONAL EXTENSION 36–39
1. There is necessary an idea broader than national areas, 36, 37. — 2. There must be a wide social unity, 37. — 3. And religious emptiness in the areas conquered, 37, 38. — 4. The conquering religion must offer what is needed, 38, 39.

III. THE ACTUAL HISTORICAL RESULTS 39–46
§ 1. THE UNIVERSAL RELIGIONS 39, 40
Conditions to be fulfilled numerous. Number of universal religions small. Rise of Buddhism, Christianity, and Islam.

§ 2. STUNTED AND ARRESTED GROWTHS 40–41
1. Stoicism and other philosophical systems, their lack of theological framework, 41, 42. — 2. Confucianism. — 3. The old Egyptian religion, bound to the soil. Mazdeism, its lack of clearness, 42, 43. — 4. National and international churches, 43, 44.

§ 3. NATIONAL AND TRIBAL RELIGIONS 44
Inertness of the great mass of the religions of the world.

§ 4. THE OUTLOOK 44–46
1. Signs that a few great religions will in time control the world, 44, 45. — 2. Superiority of Christianity, 45. — 3. Improbable that other religions will survive as systems, 45. — 4. Probable modification of Christianity in the future, 45, 46.

JUDAISM AND CHRISTIANITY.

PAGE

RESULTS OF ISRAELITISH THOUGHT UP TO EZRA'S TIME . . 47–51
Practical Monotheism. Sound system of practical social ethics.
Organization of public worship. Messianic hope.

CHAPTER I.

THE LITERATURE 52–76
§ 1. THE LITERARY DEVELOPMENT 52–68
    1. Prophetic writings. Decline of prophecy, 53. Malachi
       ritualistic, 53. Zechariah and Joel predict the revi-
       val of nationality, 54.
    2. Rewriting of history from the ritualistic point of view:
       Chronicles, Ezra, Nehemiah, 55.
    3. Chronicles; its embellishments. The romances: Jonah,
       Esther, Judith, Tobit. 55–58.
    4. Wisdom-books; their practical character. Proverbs.
       Ecclesiastes; its philosophical scepticism. Wisdom
       of Solomon; its Platonic and Stoic elements. Wisdom
       of the Son of Sirach; its Jewish tone. 58–60.
    5. Liturgical literature. The book of Psalms. Enig-
       matical character of the Song of Songs. 61, 62.
    6. Apocalypses; their origin and form. Daniel. Enoch.
       Sibylline Oracles. Baruch. Assumption of Moses.
       Psalter of Solomon. Book of Jubilees. Second
       Esdras. 62–67.
    7. Historical and theological works. Maccabees. Jo-
       sephus. Philo. 67, 68.
§ 2. THE CANONS 68–76
    1. Origin of the canonical idea. 68, 69.
    2. Beginning of canonization. The Tora or Law, its his-
       torical development. 69–71.
    3. The second or prophetic canon. 71–73.
    4. The third or non-prophetic canon, the grounds of choice
       of its content. Palestinian and Alexandrian canons.
       Uncanonized books. 73–76.

CHAPTER II.

THE DOCTRINE OF GOD 77–140
    The monotheistic idea firmly established in fifth century B. C.,
       but not theoretically complete. Elements of the theistic
       conception. 77, 78.

1. Governmental side: supremacy of God, — his providential care for men, and for inanimate and brute nature; his special relation to Israel; his justice, how defined by theological theories in O. T. and N. T. 78–83.
2. Love as a divine attribute, — historical growth of the conception; Greek influence. 83–86.
3. Spiritual relation of God to the individual man; conception of God as pure spirit. 86–89.
4. Hypostatic differences in the divine nature. 89–121.
    Hypostatizing tendency in O. T.: angel of the presence; angel of the name; angel of Yahwe. 90, 91.
    Hypostatical development of spirit, 92–96; of wisdom, 96–103; of word: Philo, N. T., 103–121.
5. Relation of God's self-manifestation to natural law; N. T. miracles. 121–127.
6. Authority of the Scriptures: inspiration; attitude of N. T. writers toward O. T.; Jewish critical methods; use of O. T. in N. T.; quotations. 127–140.

CHAPTER III.

SUBORDINATE SUPERNATURAL BEINGS 141–172
1. Survivals from early animistic beliefs: teraphim; demons; magic; Azazel. 141–144.
2. Spirits, — their origin; their subordination to God. 144–146.
3. Angels, — their origin; historical development; Persian influence; position in N. T. 146–154.
4. Evil spirits: Satan; his appearance in O. T. and apocryphal books; his rôle as tempter. Fallen angels. Leviathan, Behemoth, Rahab. The Satan of N. T. Origin of the figure of Satan; later Persian influence. Historical development of evil spirits; demoniacal possession. 154–172.

CHAPTER IV.

MAN 173–290
1. Constitution of man: body and soul. O. T. use of terms body, soul, spirit, heart, reins. N. T. use of body, flesh, heart, spirit, mind. Not a trichotomy. 173–182.
2. Nature and origin of sin. 183–220.
    O. T. conception of sin; general development of the idea. Two elements of consciousness of sin. Historical development: period of Judges and David; of pre-exilian

prophets; of Jeremiah; of the Levitical law; of the Book of Psalms. Consciousness of righteousness. Gradual deepening of the sense of sin. 183–193.

O. T. view of origin of sin. Its reticence. Narrative in Gen. iii.,—its date; its design; assumes human inclination to sin. The serpent in the narrative,—a rational beast; probably mythical in origin; identified with Satan, not in O. T., but in Wisdom of Solomon. The narrative in Genesis not an allegory. Its representation of death. 193–205.

Conception of sin in apocryphal books and Philo. 205, 206.

N. T. representation of sin; its practical interest produces reticence as to questions of origin of sin and of consequences of Adam's transgression; Paul's treatment of this last point; rôle assigned to the woman. 206–211.

N. T. view of corruption of human nature : Synoptic Gospels, James, Pastoral Epistles, Paul, Ephesians and Colossians, Fourth Gospel. No gnostic asceticism. 211–220.

3. Removal of sin. 220–233.

Prophetic view of expiation. Sin atoned for by the sinner's suffering. Vicarious human suffering: origin of the idea; its treatment by the exilian Isaiah. 220–225.

Formulation of idea of ceremonial atonement in the Law; its restricted character. 225–227.

Appeal to the mercy of God. Human mediation for sin. Negative attitude of prophets toward sacrificial ritual. 227–231.

Teaching of the extra-canonical books. 231.

Point of view of Jesus that of the pre-exilian prophets spiritualized. The early disciples. Paul's conception of the sacrificial nature of the Messiah's death. 231–233.

4. O. T. conception of righteousness. 233–246.

O. T. conception of moral goodness : prophetic standard ; Deuteronomy; the "new heart;" two tendencies ; idea of inward purity in the Psalms. Twofold view of the source of righteousness : man's will and God's help. 233–237.

Nomism. Introduction of the complete Law. Internal and external causes of the Jewish nomistic organization. Strength and weakness of nomism: precision of religious life ; pride ; externalism ; casuistry ; depression of spirituality. General moral influence of the nomistic system in Judaism and in Christianity. 237–246.

5. Succeeding development of the idea of righteousness. 246–266.

Synagogues; their origin and influence. 246–248.

Parties. Tendencies formulated in the Greek period.

The Pharisees,—their origin; representatives of broader nationalism; acceptance of new doctrines; possible Greek influence. The Sadducees; their origin, beliefs, and influence. The Essenes, — their peculiarities; their effect on the general Jewish life; traces of the party in the N. T. The Zealots. 248–258.

The Sanhedrin. The legal schools; greatness of their influence. Sayings of Simon and Antigonus; Stoic influence. Rivalry between Pharisees and Sadducees represents in one aspect the struggle between progressive nomism and conservative nationalism, in another aspect the conflict between Jewish and foreign ideas. Hellenism, though it could not crush the Jewish religion, impressed itself on Jewish thought. Illustrations from the teaching of the lawyers, especially Hillel and Shammai. Religious breadth of Hillel. 258–266.

6. N. T. conception of righteousness. 266–290.

Teaching of Jesus: he recognized the Law; spiritual character of his nomism; source of righteousness in the soul itself. The early Church, — stress laid on sincerity rather than on spirituality; relation of Jesus to man's righteousness scarcely touched on. 266–271.

Paul's doctrine of imputed righteousness, — recommended to him by his own experience; not alien to the thought of the time. O. T. basis of the doctrine; application to Jesus suggested by Paul's high conception of the functions of the Messiah. Paul's doctrine of faith. 271–275.

Opposition to Paul's apparent antinomianism. His reply brings out the spiritual side of his idea: disappearance of desire to sin; faith not merely intellectual belief; appeal to the power of an ideal; indwelling of God in the soul; the death of Christ the condition of salvation. Summing up of Paul's doctrine. 275–281.

Subsequent history of the idea of righteousness in the N. T.: Ephesians, Colossians, and First Peter substantially Pauline; O. T. point of view in Hebrews; universality of First Timothy; Pauline tone of Second Timothy and Titus; in the Fourth Gospel and First John righteousness is a divinely created light-nature. Three conceptions in N. T. idea of righteousness: personal goodness, imputed goodness, transformation of soul. 281–285.

The insufficiency of the Jewish national nomism. Effect of the teaching of Jesus, and of the systems of Paul and the Fourth Gospel. Later history of Jewish nomism. Mingling of nomistic and antinomistic elements in Judaism and in Christianity. 286–289.

Contrast between the outward method of attaining righteousness through a vicarious sacrifice, and the inward method of transformation of soul. 290.

CHAPTER V.

ETHICS 291–302

Ethical discussion in the Bible practical, not philosophical. 291, 292.

1. Jewish moral code of 5th century B. C. purely national. 292, 293.

2. Greek period. Broader ethical tone of Wisdom-books. 293, 294.

3. Ethics of Jesus; its religious sanctions. The golden rule. 294–297.

4. Ethics of the Epistles. Attitude toward unbelievers. Cosmopolitan tendency. 297, 298.

5. Biblical view of the aim of life. Egoism. Ethical defect of N. T. speculative rather than practical. 298–300.

6. Distinctive spirit of N. T. ethics. Ethical power of the Church. Influence of Christianity on the ethical life of the world. 300–302.

CHAPTER VI.

THE KINGDOM OF GOD 303–371

The conception of the kingdom of God a characteristic of Jewish thought; its four stadia. The Jewish national hope; its origin in Jewish power of persistence and of religious organization. The idea of a national covenant with God; its growth and its consequences. The history of the national hope is the history of the national thought. 303–308.

1. The pre-prophetic, non-ethical period; its preparatory character. 308, 309.

2. The pre-exilian and exilian prophetic period. Hope of political and moral-religious prosperity in Amos, Hosea, Isaiah, Micah, Nahum, Zephaniah, Habakkuk, Jeremiah, Ezekiel, the exilian Isaiah, Mic. vii., Deut. xxviii.–xxx., 1 Kings viii. 309–312.

3. The post-exilian prophetic period. Ritual tinge in Haggai, Zechariah, Malachi. Cosmopolitan spirit of Isa. ii. 2–4, xix. 18–25. 312–314.

4. Legal period. Joel, the second Zechariah. The king as national deliverer, in Ezekiel, Jer. xxxiii., 2 Sam. vii.,

Zech. vi., Mic. v. 2–6, Isa. xi. 1–9, ix. 6, 7, Zech. ix. 9. This prophetic national hope traceable in the later literature down to the beginning of our era. 314–319.

5. Greek and Roman period. Desire for deliverance intensified by national suffering. Apocalyptic works : the national future in the early Maccabean period (Daniel, Sibylline Oracles, Enoch); in the Roman period (Psalter of Solomon, Sibylline Oracles, Enoch-Parables); in later literature (Assumption of Moses, Jubilees, Philo). Moral progress visible in non-apocalyptic writings. Summing up of Messianic material in pre-Christian literature. Condition of membership in the new community. Other points of popular belief mentioned in N. T. Deep Messianic feeling in Palestine at beginning of first century of our era. 319–331.

6. Profounder view of the political-religious situation at beginning of first century, — weakening of desire for political sovereignty ; recognition of necessity for moral reform. Appearance of John the Baptist, — his prophetic character; nature of his reform. Desire for reform felt throughout the Græco-Roman world. Peculiarity and advantage of the Jewish reform-movement of this period. 331–339.

Work of Jesus. He begins apparently as disciple of John. Moral-spiritual character of his movement, — it was the summing-up of O. T. and N. T. His teaching stands apart from the current political and ecclesiastical Messianic ideas of the time : stress laid by him on moral-spiritual side of the kingdom of God ; the public entry into Jerusalem ; he was looked on as politically unimportant by Roman and Jewish authorities ; doubtful whether he intended his teaching to be limited to the Jews ; conflicting nature of the testimony ; he attempted no separate organization of his disciples. 339–350.

His conception of the outcome of his movement. First, did he regard himself as the promised Messiah? The incident at Cæsarea Philippi. How he looked on his own death. Conception of his mission suggested by the title " Son of Man." 350–355.

His idea of the destiny of the world. Representation in the Synoptics that he would come in person to hold a final judgment. Facts going to show that he held such a view. Facts opposed to such a supposition. His moral power independent of his opinions on this point. The eschatological discourses in the Synoptics. 355–362.

Christian conception of the kingdom of God in the first century : James, 2 Thessalonians, 1 Corinthians. Gradual

disappearance of the old Israelitish conception. Attempts
to define the time of the second coming of Christ. Destruction of Jerusalem looked on as turning-point. Overthrow of the Roman empire regarded as necessary. Representation in the N. T. Apocalypse; in 2 Thessalonians.
362–366.

Outward organization of the Church; change in the
principle of membership introduced by Paul. Paul's
creative dogmatic work. Dogma inevitable; its unspiritual influence. Christianity the fusion of two great masses
of human thought; how far it achieved unity in the world.
366–371.

CHAPTER VII.

ESCHATOLOGY 372–414
Value and interest of eschatological ideas. 372.

1. Final form of earthly kingdom of God in N. T. Apocalypse.
Its sources: Ezekiel, Isaiah, Enoch. Origin of the conception of two judgments. Whether Persian influence is
recognizable. The details belong to the thought of the
times; the Jewish idea adopted by Christianity, but gradually modified. Its moral influence. The Church's conception of the reign of Christ. 373–377.

2. The doctrine of immortality. O. T. idea of the future life.
Decline of necromancy; indifference of the shades. O. T.
passages supposed to teach immortality. O. T. idea of
the other life belongs to the old-Semitic conception; this
perhaps explicable from the character of the Semitic mind.
Whether the rise of the Jewish belief in immortality can
be referred to the growth of spiritual feeling; first distinct statement of the belief is found in Wisdom of Solomon; contrast between this book and Ecclesiastes and
Ecclesiasticus; probable Alexandrian Jewish-Greek origin
of the doctrine. 377–388.

3. The doctrine of resurrection. Examination of O. T. passages supposed to teach it. Egyptian and Hindu ideas.
Persian doctrine; probably adopted in modified form by
the Jews; they held at first to a partial, afterward to a
general resurrection. How far the belief in a general resurrection prevailed in the Church of the first century. 388–
395.

4. The doctrine of a final judgment. Idea of divine retribution
universal. Its progress along three lines: (1) ethical;
(2) from individualism to nationalism; (3) from conception
of earthly to that of extra-earthly judgment: the Jewish

idea of an earthly judgment of all nations by Yahwe modified by the introduction of two articles of faith, the expectation of a personal Messiah and the belief in immortality.
Assignment of office of judge to Messiah in Enoch-Parables and N. T.; origin of this idealization, whether
Christian. Immortality in connection with judgment in
Enoch-Parables and N. T.; double sense of the expressions "this age" and "the age to come." Christianity,
in accepting the doctrine of judgment from Judaism, substituted the Church for the nation.   395–404.

5. Reconstruction of the doctrine of the future life. Representation in O. T. and Enoch. Origin of Jewish
conception of rewards and punishments after death. Representation of future punishment in N. T. Duration of
punishment in N. T. The future abode of the righteous:
the earth and the new Jerusalem; the Eden garden of
Genesis; paradise; heaven. Condition of men between
death and judgment, in Enoch and N. T.; annihilation;
future probation. Idea of moral probation in the Bible
modified by that of final judgment.   404–413.

Christian idea of the kingdom of God drawn from
diverse parts of the Western world. The triumph of the
Church was the essence of Christian eschatology. Strenuous ethical basis of the Jewish-Christian conception of the
kingdom of God.   413–414.

CHAPTER VIII.

RELATION OF JESUS TO CHRISTIANITY   415–435
Outline of the preceding sketch of the transformation of Judaism into Christianity. What is the relation of Jesus to
this movement?   415, 416.

1. He announced the germinal principles of Christianity. The
spiritual basis of his teaching. Significance of his silence:
he added nothing to the existing idea of immortality;
whether he represented himself as a sacrifice for sin;
whether he taught the dogma of imputed righteousness;
whether he regarded himself as superhuman.   416–423.

2. The result of his teaching. Did it alone create the Church,
or was it modified by his followers? And if it was so
modified, what was his relation to the new ideas? The
creed of the infant Church was belief in Jesus as the Messiah. Whether there is sign of dogmatic reconstruction
in the earliest Christian records. Concurrence of favorable conditions at the birth of Christianity. The early
Church the creation of Jesus.   423–427.

PAGE

3. Paul; his dogmatic system the result of his conception of
   Jesus.   How the Church came to interpret the death of
   Christ as sacrificial.   The exaltation of Jesus; distinguished from deification.   The conception of Christ's righteousness as legally justifying.   427–431.-
4. The logos-doctrine, in Hebrews, Ephesians, Colossians,
   Fourth Gospel.   431–433.
       The variety of the portraitures of Jesus an indication of
   his power; he is always the centre of life and belief; the
   Church his creation directly or indirectly; his place in the
   succeeding history of the Church.   433–435.

INDEX OF CITATIONS .   .   437
INDEX OF SUBJECTS   445

INTRODUCTION.

ON THE GENERAL LAWS OF THE ADVANCE FROM NATIONAL TO UNIVERSAL RELIGIONS.

I.

THE rise of Christianity out of Judaism is a fact which, though of enormous significance, is yet in conformity with a well-defined law of human progress. The recognition of this law is so important for the proper understanding of these two religions that it will be not out of place to attempt a brief sketch of its working before entering on our main subject. We may begin by pointing out the social basis of religion, and then go on to examine the conditions which determine its advance from lower to higher stages.

§ 1. SOCIAL CHARACTER OF RELIGION.

1. Religion must be treated as a product of human thought. For supposing a supernatural intervention for the communication of truth, it must, in order to be success-ful, conform to human conditions, and have a real genesis in man's mind. And as human thought is developed only in and through society, religion (like language and ethics may be regarded as a branch of sociology, subject to all the laws that control general human progress.

2. A religious consciousness may be spoken of as we may speak of a moral, a literary, or a scientific conscious-ness ; these expressions imply not separate faculties of the mind, but merely the ordinary mental activity applied to

particular classes of objects. The content of what we call the religious consciousness is twofold, — the idea of God; and the conviction that man needs and may obtain the help of God. Each of these elements is the product of reflection. The belief in God rests on the recognition of a non-human, super-human power in the phenomena of outward nature and human life. The desire to secure God's help springs from man's feeling that he is in the midst of an environment which is beyond his control, at the mercy of elements and beasts, disease and circumstances. How he construes these two facts, what comes out of them for his weal or woe, — this is a part of his social history. His thought, which keeps pace, or rather is identical, with his social organization, occupies itself with all the problems of life; and none of these is more important for him than the question of his relation to the mysterious, invisible power which he believes to stand behind all phenomena. Religion must grow as society grows.

§ 2. The Growth of Society.

1. The general law of natural growth is modified by other laws of arrest, retrogression, and decay. Plants and animals have their laws of increase against which they seem to be powerless. The human body, as a whole and in all its parts, reaches, after a time, a point beyond which it cannot advance, and the human soul appears·to have equally definite boundaries marked out for it. Nature seems to have stamped on all living things this tendency toward a condition of equilibrium in which the supply of force is just equal to the waste, the powers of the organism just suffice to make head against external retarding and destructive influences. Does this law hold of communities as well as of individuals? Certainly there are a number of cases in which it seems to show itself, — savage tribes, for example, which appear

not to have made any social advance from time immemorial; and of the greater communities, China is often cited as an example of stagnation. But it need hardly be said that great caution is necessary in such affirmations. It is very doubtful whether the term "arrest of growth" can be used of China in any proper sense; and as for the savage tribes of the world, we are in a state of dense ignorance of their history. Social stagnation is perfectly conceivable : a community like the Fuegans, for instance, may reach a point of content where there is not sufficient inducement to make inroads upon the natural environment; but whether this is actually the case we do not know. We may leave the question undecided whether there is any community which has reached the state of social equilibrium.

2. The same thing must be said of the natural law of retrogression or decay as applied to the inward life of societies. We may admit its possibility, but whether it is to be recognized in any particular case is matter of special examination. Certainly many historical examples are improperly cited to prove its existence. The great empires of the Old World — Egypt, Assyria, Babylonia, Persia, Greece, Rome, and in later times the Califate and the Byzantine Empire — perished, not through internal moral-intellectual decay, but by outward pressure. They fell apart through insufficient political organization, and succumbed to the violence of stronger powers. In our own times the case of Spain is instructive. She has fallen back from the relative position she occupied in Europe in the sixteenth and seventeenth centuries; she has made less advance than her neighbors; but she has really grown in all the elements of the best national life. Christianity did not undergo a decay or retrogression in the Middle Age; its ethical-religious principles passed over from civilized Greeks and Romans to groups of barbarian tribes which, at first incapable of grasping them,

nevertheless entered on a career of steady growth. Seeming decay is sometimes only a form of growth. An organism rids itself of some part in order to substitute for it a higher form. A growing society is constantly changing its institutions; the institutions decay, the society lives. Medieval chivalry and monarchy, though no doubt admirable in their day, have given way to something better. The transition from the old to the new may be attended with evil: steam takes the place of human labor, and thousands of people suffer till society has accommodated itself to the new arrangement; the rule of the few is succeeded by that of the many, which brings with it a host of inconveniences and corruptions till the community has been trained to use its powers aright. In all these cases we have to await the result before deciding whether the new scheme means growth or decay.

3. Other things being equal, the larger the community, the more assured is its continuity and duration of growth. This results from the fact that the larger social life calls into being a greater moral-intellectual force; and it is this which furnishes the best safeguard against disintegrating influences. In a large community the elements of life are more numerous, their interactions more frequent, each is developed with more completeness, and is more thoroughly and beneficially affected by the others; just as the more thoroughly developed a man's nature, the broader his sympathies, the completer the activity of each of his powers, the less likely he is to succumb to hostile agencies, physical, intellectual, or moral. The individual and the nation may perish by violence, but of the two the nation is less exposed to decay. It renews its life by a succession of individuals, and if these retain and increase the moral-intellectual power which comes from high social organization, and if there intervene no physical attack from without or within, then we can hardly put a limit to the duration of national life. In a modern nation

like England, we may be slow to predict dissolution from internal decay; her resources of physical food may disappear, or her national existence may be crushed by wars, but so far as her higher life is concerned, we may reasonably expect that it will grow stronger rather than weaker.

4. Religion, as an element of social life, will be subject to all these laws of social development. It will grow or decline with the community in which it exists. The possibility of religious stagnation, retrogression, and decay must be allowed. Whether these have ever actually occurred, must be decided by the examination of the facts in any alleged case. Here, also, seeming decay may be a form of growth. Judaism did not suffer by the destruction of the temple, though it lost its apparatus of sacrifice. The Christianity of to-day is not inferior in vigor and purity to that of the fourth century, though it has discarded many opinions and practices of that period. Religion must be distinguished from any particular organized form of religion. In the bosom of a national church there may arise an impulse which shall ultimately change its outward and inward constitution; and the new form may represent a truer and more beneficent religion than the old. Ideas which seem to many persons fundamental may vanish, and their adherents may believe that an era of impiety has begun; yet out of the ruins of a shattered faith may spring another faith filled with a higher spirit.

The larger the community, the more persistent and vigorous the religion is likely to be. The recognition of religion as a necessary element of life will not become feebler with the intellectual and ethical growth, but the form of the conception of it will be modified. The stress will be laid on the rational spiritual side. So long as the community exists, danger to religion can come only from its failure to respond to man's deepest needs and highest desires. But there is no reason why it should fail to do this ; the natural supposition is that religion will advance with the intellectual life of the community, and come into possession of all its elements of strength. The free individual life, with its diversities and complexities, will preserve religious thought from onesidedness; and the higher social organization which always attends unfettered individuality will guard it against unfruitful shapelessness and license. A small religious sect is in danger of sinking into a useless narrowness from the lack of broad intellectual excitement, and of perishing by the gradual loss of individuals. Such a sect, by withdrawing itself from the community, in so far diminishes the mass of productive thought, and is obstructive and retardative. This is an altogether different thing from the position of a minority, like the Israelitish prophetic circle or that of Luther and his friends, which really represents and expounds the deeper-lying thought of the community, and thus paves the way to a higher and truer unity of thought. It is in this way that all religious revolutions have been accomplished. The realness and the success of such movements depend on the fidelity with which the profounder thinkers interpret the instincts of the mass. The firmer the organization of the community, the freer the intercourse among its parts, the truer will be its feeling, and the more certain the expression of it. A sect is injurious as representing not simply individuality, but individuality cut off from real intellectual communication with the mass of the community.

II.

We come now to inquire into the general conditions under which religious progress, so far as we can trace it in the world, has been made. These conditions may be divided into those which control the formation of nations, and those which determine progress within the nation ; and these last are either inward, springing naturally out of the community itself, or outward, coming from foreign communities. Only the more general laws can be touched on here, but the principles on which they rest will apply as well to the smaller religious bodies as to those great movements which have issued in the formation of national and universal religions.

§ 1. Formation of Communities.

1. A few words on this head will suffice. A large social life, as has already been pointed out, is an essential condition of the development of a great religion. It is only out of a national organization that those large experiences spring without which religious systems are narrow and unfruitful. A religion in the better sense of the term is the organized product of a national thought concerning man's relation to the divine. The more mixed the nation, provided it has reached true social-political unity, the broader and more genial the religion is likely to be, and the greater its power of commending itself to other communities. In general, the religion is coextensive with the nation, or rather with the people; if the latter is extinguished, the former perishes. It is a misfortune, for example, for the comparative history of the Semitic religions that the Assyrian and Babylonian empires were destroyed by violence in so early a stage of their career; for with them perished their religion, and we have no means of deciding, among other things, the question whether it would have advanced sensibly toward practical monotheism. Similarly, the religions of the Hittites, the Lydians, the Phœnicians, the Egyptians, have perished with the nations to which they belonged ; while in Japan, China, and India the maintenance of the national life has preserved very ancient forms of religion.

The continuance of a national-political organization is not always necessary to the maintenance of its system of religion. The essential thing is social organization, — a real unity of thought in a large mass of individuals; if this exists, political independence may be destroyed, the people may be driven from their land and become wanderers in the world, and yet preserve their religion substantially intact. Whether this can be effected will depend on the vigor of character of the people, on the moral-intellectual elevation of the religion as compared with that of other religious systems with which the banished people are brought into contact, and on the isolation in which they live. The most striking case in point is that of the Jews. Driven from their own land, and living in the midst of alien communities in Asia, Africa, Europe, and America, they have held to the religion of their fathers with a very remarkable pertinacity, but only in so far as they have been socially isolated. In the Middle Age, as inheritors of a religion which represented centuries of thought and culture, they were decidedly superior to their Moslem and Christian neighbors, and above the temptation of being influenced by them ; and, further, they were hated and persecuted, and forced into social isolation. But so soon as they came into relation with other communities and felt the influence of a thought higher than their own, they yielded and modified their religion accordingly. Another though less striking example is that of the Parsees, who have preserved the Mazdean faith through twelve centuries of bondage and persecution. Their position, however, differs from that of the Jews. A foreign faith was forced on Persia; Islam expelled Zoroastrianism, and the Persians are Mohammedans. The small body which remained faithful to the old national religion was compelled to leave its native land, and in India the Parsees, isolated by their beliefs and practices, have maintained their religion intact, but have at the same time held themselves aloof from outside thought, and as a consequence have sunk into almost complete stagnation. Neither medieval Judaism nor Parseeism has had any real inward development out of its own resources. Neither has impressed itself sensibly on other communities; both have held substantially (except under impulses from without) to the old traditional faiths which they have worked up more or less mechanically.

A community without national political organization is thus exposed to the double danger of extinction and assimilation. Its members perish and are with difficulty replaced; or under the influence of alien thought its religion is gradually, often insensibly, transformed till it ceases to have anything but the name in common with its old self. And so, while admitting a certain vitality in some politically unorganized communities, we may recognize in history the general rule that fruitful religions have arisen in societies characterized by a true national life. And it is always possible that from such a national religion an idea may spring so simple and broad that it shall commend itself to other communities, and clothe itself with an organization which ignores and transcends national lines.

2. In what has been said above, it is assumed that in any regularly organized society there is a natural law of progress. This is no doubt true of the society after it has received definite shape; but it must be borne in mind that its final shape is usually the result of a process of aggregation. The old genealogical scheme in which one ancestor, by natural increase through a number of generations, becomes the father of a great nation, is not in accordance with the testimony of history. The composite character of the Hindu, Greek, Latin, French, English, and other peoples is well known; and the Old Testament, which is concerned to derive the

Israelitish nation from Jacob, yet gives us hints here and there of the entrance of alien tribes and of a mixed nationality. As far as we can trace the process, nations have come into existence by successive combinations of small communities, and national religions are aggregations of tribal faiths.

Let us suppose that in several small communities dwelling near one another, different though similar religious creeds have grown up. Each community will have its scheme of deities and worship, its vague conception of the relation between the human and the divine. In process of time it may come to pass that these communities shall be united by conquest or otherwise. When a real social-political unity shall have been established, a new faith will have come into existence, comprising all the substantial elements of the old faiths, but probably broader and truer than any one of them. Ideas and customs will have been sifted and massed, the merely local, the comparatively unimportant, rejected, and what remains will be the religious material that commends itself to the intelligence and feeling of the whole body of the resultant large community. This process may be repeated until a nation arises whose thought-material will be the outcome of a long process of experience and reflection, in which only that will be retained which appeals to the presumably higher intelligence and more serious needs of the larger community. A well-known example of this process of religious aggregation is furnished by the pantheons of Egypt, Babylonia, and Greece; the number of parallel and duplicated deities is most naturally explained as the result of the welding together of different communities, and the combination of their religious schemes into one system, in which, of course, divergencies and discrepancies often show themselves. There are traces of the same sort of syncretism in the Old Testament, in the divine names, and perhaps elsewhere.

The same process has been repeated on a larger scale in the greater religious movements of the world. In Islam we have a mixture of ideas from three sources, — the Old Arabian religion, the Jewish, and the Christian. Christianity has blended with the religious and moral ideas of the New Testament much un-Jewish European thought. The Judaism of the two or three centuries just preceding the beginning of our era combined Hebrew and Greek conceptions. Wherever there is intimate intellectual intercourse between nations, this larger religious syncretism must follow. The stage of unity of religious thought which modern Europe has reached is the result of social assimilation; and if the process of assimilation goes on, we may hope for a constant progress toward complete religious unity. We may go farther and discern increasing points of contact in the more cultivated religious thought of Europe and Asia. The early stages of social-religious aggregation are thus the first step in a much wider movement, which, under favorable conditions, may issue in a religious unity that shall embrace the whole world, and shall be broad and high in proportion to the mass of thought which enters into it.

§ 2. THE INTERNAL DEVELOPMENT OF IDEAS.

1. The nation being formed, and the conditions of its life being such as to permit social progress, there will be first within its own limits a constant elaboration and perfecting of religious conceptions. Religion is so prominent and definite an element of social life that it will be the object of constant reflection on the part of the community. Its fundamental ideas and its practices will shape themselves in accordance with the intellectual-moral status of the nation. The religious system of the people will express its attempt to construe the world in accordance with its highest instincts; the national thought will be forever reaching out

after some better definition of the relation between the human and the divine. Old customs and ideas which have become unsatisfactory will be modified or abandoned, and new customs and ideas adopted. Each generation will remodel in its own interests the material of its predecessors, retaining what it can use, and fashioning the whole after its highest ideal. If it retains and reverences old forms, it will nevertheless interpret them in a new fashion. No community can really occupy a religious position which is inferior to that of its intellectual-moral thought; inferior religious ideas, even if they be nominally embraced, will be practically dead. There will be an overlapping of the new by the old, and temporary anachronisms and inconsistencies, but these will be constantly yielding to the pressure of thought, and the moulding power of the religious system will reside in those general ideas of life which meet the needs of the age. There will always be more or less of intellectual confusion and disingenuousness; at any particular moment there will be a conflict in most men's minds between the conservative reverence for the past and the demands of the present. At any given moment also, decided progress will be visible only in the few; the many will seem to be inert and stationary. Nevertheless, a process of leavening goes on, ideas make themselves felt; and after a time it is seen that a change has come over the spirit of the community, there is a chasm between the men of the time and their fathers. Whether this change will be for the better will depend on the character of the general social progress, as to which we must in each particular case decide in accordance with historical fact.

2. In so far as the community is a unit, it will advance as a whole, all its elements moving together, though not necessarily developing to the same extent. Men's thoughts are constantly occupied with all that concerns life; they

devote themselves with greatest assiduity and intensity to what they think most important, but no phase of life can be judged to be altogether unimportant. Religion, social and political organization, morals, art, and science must move hand in hand. They all issue out of the same social life. Each in a sort goes its independent way, yet each influences and is influenced by the others. Examples of such influence readily occur to us, as the way in which art has been affected by religion and by science. We are not here concerned with the full discussion of these interactions, but only with the question how far religion is affected by other lines of social thought. What does it owe to politics, ethics, art, and science?

Besides its general quickening and developing effect on thought, art has aided, by training the constructive imagination, in the formation of all systems of religion; it has played the part of instructor by embodying moral-religious ideals in pictures, statues, and buildings, and thus holding up to men's constant contemplation those ethical and religious conceptions which artistic imagination has adopted or created from current thought; and by its appeal to the emotional nature it has stimulated and intensified the whole of man's religious side.

The social-political constitution of a community usually serves as model for its theistic system. The organization of the clan, the family, the nation, in the relations of husband and wife, parent and child, ruler and subject, is reproduced in the construction of the supernatural powers. In savage tribes the deity is father or husband or chief of the clan; in more advanced communities he becomes king, tyrant, or archon, his powers and qualities being those of his human model. In the Christian Church a resemblance may be traced between forms of church government and the social-political ideas of the periods or communities in which they have arisen.

The influence of science and ethics on religion may be examined somewhat more at length.

3. Religion and science have this in common, that they both attempt to explain the phenomena of the world and of life. They differ in that this explanation is a secondary object for religion, a primary object for science. Religion, recognizing the divine, seeks to enter into relation with it, gain its favor, and secure its aid. It sees intimations of the divine in man and in the world. Men began with assuming that all phenomena were the direct acts of the deity; that they had a direct relation with the existing human life, and were controlled by motives such as men felt in themselves. Rain, drought, sunshine and cloud, wind, thunder and lightning, earthquake and eclipse, were conceived to be expressions of the divine pleasure or displeasure; all the fortunes of life were supposed to be the direct product of the intervention of the deity. Life was thought of as a system of rewards and punishments from without, fashioned by the good-will or anger of the superhuman power, according as man was obedient or disobedient. From the creation of the world to the growth of a blade of grass, from the extinction of a nation to the most trivial bodily pain, all was looked on as the immediate act of a god, friendly or unfriendly, standing outside of and above human thought and effort.

The scientific impulse — that is, the desire to understand phenomena — was coeval with the religious; but as it demanded more exact observation, its development was slower. Little by little, facts were observed in their connections, sequences were established, and the belief in an orderly arrangement of things came into existence. This belief laid the foundations at once of civilization and of spiritual religion. As long as men were ignorant of the natural order of things, on which all effective industry depends, they were at the mercy of superstition and of chance; they began to make progress as soon as they accepted natural law, and yielded themselves to its guidance. As a matter of course, the domain of natural law was subtracted from that of direct divine intervention. The effect on religion of such a view was not to diminish the conception of divine power, but only to modify the interpretation of phenomena as expressions of the will of the deity. Freer play was given to human thought and activity when it was seen that man's inner life sprang from himself, and that outward events, whether in the domain of physical nature or in that of human action, could be in some degree foreseen and controlled in the interests of the individual. More and more it came to be felt that God, though omniscient and omnipotent, had so ordered things that the immediate, practical direction of affairs was in man's hands; the whole might be directed by the divine power for ends beyond man's ken, but the visible nexus of events was committed to the human mind; the world was given over to man to be studied and subdued, and he was intrusted with the care of his own heart, to fashion and train it according to the demands of conscience. But here, in the domain of conscience and spiritual life, he was felt not to stand alone; gradually the conviction gained strength that the divine influence manifested itself in the spiritual sphere, bringing the heart of man into harmony with the divine spirit, and disciplining it into purity. During this period of scientific training, the idea of God was constantly advancing, rising from the warrior or demon of earliest times to the spirit of justice and love.

Science has been the handmaid and friend of religion, relieving it of the burden of superstitions, of false relations between phenomena, and pushing it to the conception of the spiritual relation between man and God. This long-continued process (still going on) might be called a conflict between the two, but it is better to regard it as a single process, in which one element in human life has been constantly influenced by another. There have indeed been sharp conflicts. Religion has identified itself with certain physical beliefs, invested them with divine sacredness, and mercilessly trampled on all who opposed them, — the Galileo episodes of history are not few. Even to-day the purely scientific theories of the evolutionary origin of man and of the Pentateuch seem to some persons anti-religious and destructive, things to be opposed as warmly as if they denied man's moral nature. But on the other hand, there is a constantly widening religious circle which holds that science, being simply the observation of phenomena, can never be hostile to religion properly conceived; can be only beneficial in helping to define the religious sphere; cannot limit the power of God, who stands above or beneath phenomena, but may better our conception of him; can, in a word, result only in the purification of religion, and therefore in its exaltation and strengthening as an element of human life.

4. Ethics, like science, has worked out its results independently of religion, to which, however, it is nearer in its material, and from which it has generally derived its highest motives and sanctions.

We are here dealing with practical ethics, the moral ordering of human life, men's ideas of right and wrong, and the way in which they were arrived at. Our moral codes arise out of the necessity that is laid upon man to live in society.[1] The individual starts with certain instincts (the

---

[1] In some cases social or governmental usages and quasi-ethical rules issue out of religious ideas, notably under the operation of tabu. Such usages are felt in primitive societies to be distinctly religious, — for example, the prohibition of the use of the name of the chief or king, who is regarded as a divine person; the laws relating to food among the Persians, Arabs, Jews, and other peoples (treated in the Levitical codes as religious usages); customs connected with childbirth (these also retain their religious character in the Old Testament law), and special disabilities as to food imposed on women; the stringent prescriptions controlling sacerdotal persons in all

origin of which we need not stop here to ask) which direct his conduct; these instincts are self-assertion and sympathy. How these shall manifest themselves in actual life, how each shall modify and control the other, — this is determined only by the needs of social life, by the conclusions which men reach respecting the well-being of the whole society, or what practically amounts to the same thing, by the individual's opinion of what will secure the best good of himself considered as a member of society, himself including any circle whose interests he regards as identical with his own. Moral rules relating to respect for property and life, and to utterance of truth, spring naturally from experience, which shows that without them society could not exist. Social progress is attended by the formulation of constantly broadening rules of conduct, as men's relations with their fellows become wider and more intimate; as the recognition of the power and value of each human personality becomes more

ancient nations, as, for example, the Roman Flamen Dialis and vestal virgins, and the Jewish priesthood. Such of these customs as concern the general daily life probably rest finally on social conditions; the sacredness or (what is the same thing) the "uncleanness" of the cow, the swine, and other animals (whether totemistic in origin or not) may be supposed to depend on their relation to the life of early man. When the strictly tabu or religious character of these usages begins to fade away, they are brought more and more under the control of ethical principles and judged accordingly; when they cease to be religious they are maintained or set aside by considerations derived, not from religion, but from social life. The canon law against marrying the sister of a deceased wife (based, apparently, on a misinterpretation of Lev. xviii. 18) is now discussed on purely ethical grounds. In some cases religion adopts and enforces social conditions, as in the Hindu caste system, which seems to have arisen from the amalgamation of various tribes. More generally, it may be said to be probable that in most instances of religious-ethical usage, religion makes a special application of an ethical principle already wrought out by society. Thus, if a field is made tabu by a private man, the respect which other men show for his rights rests finally on their recognition of the rights of property. It is, however, often difficult to decide where the religious feeling ends and the ethical begins. It is sufficient for our purposes to accept the fact that the general ethical system of men has arisen from social relations.

distinct; and as the sense of union among all men emphasizes the feeling that the good of one is inseparably connected with the good of all. The final result of the process
is the formation of ethical ideals which . are always in advance of the actual practice, which become more exalted
with each age of progress, are more and more loved for
their own sake, and take their place as a definite and powerful ethical impulse. They are naturally appropriated by
the individual, and form the material on which the instinct
of self-assertion or self-perfecting acts. These two lines of
ethical growth, — the perfecting of self and the perfecting of
society, — inseparably connected from the beginning, and
brought into an ever-growing closeness of alliance, act and
react on each other, and tend to form the absolute subjective
ethical unity, in which the whole nature of man shall be
consecrated to the highest ethical ideals.

Ethics thus belongs essentially to human relations, and is
in itself independent of that sense of the divine which constitutes religion. The instances are well known of deep or
high religious feeling existing along with low ethical ideas:
Socrates, with his pure conception of the deity and his approval of practices now looked on as monstrous; the lofty
theistic creed of the exilian Isaiah, and the unhappy international sentiment of Psalm cxxxvii.; the intense piety and
the relentless cruelty of the Spanish Inquisition; the Geneva of the sixteenth century, religiously serious and strenuous, yet thinking it a desirable thing to put a man to death
for denial of a theological dogma; the piety and pitilessness
of the English Puritans of the seventeenth century, Sanchez
and Xavier in the same religious community; devotion to
the Church and disregard of honesty and truthfulness in
many individuals in all parts of the world to-day. There
are as many examples of the coexistence of little or no religious feeling and pure ethical ideas and practice: Stoics,

Epicureans, Confucianists, Buddhists, Comtists, Agnostics,—
in the ranks of these and other bodies which practically dispense with God are found men inferior to none in strictness
of moral code and practice, in the exhibition of the finest
and most genial ethical feeling. The sense of the divine
may be high, while the feeling of sympathy with one's fellow-
men is low ; or, conversely, the first may be feeble and the
second strong. In like manner a scientific or unscientific
conception of God may coexist with great or small religious
or ethical feeling.

Yet there is a very important relation between religion
and ethics ; they tend constantly to coalesce. God, who is
the religious ideal, naturally becomes the ethical ideal, and
comes to embody the best ethical thought of each period,—
this thought having been developed, however, not by religion, but out of social conditions. It is a familiar fact that
in a growing community — for example, among the Hebrews
of the Old Testament time — the conception of the deity becomes ethically higher and higher ; theology appropriates
the results of moral experience. There is then a reaction on
human life ; man shapes his conduct so as to please the
deity, and the greater the ethical purity of the divine character, the greater the stimulus to man's moral life. In addition to this purely ethical relation, there is the sanction
conceived to be affixed to the moral law by the Supreme
Ruler ; the rewards and punishments in this world and the
next, bestowed by the deity, constitute to some extent a barrier against wrong-doing and an encouragement of right-
doing ; though as a matter of fact it would seem that men's
social conduct is usually determined more by their relations
to their fellows than by their relations to God,— rather by
the visible and immediate than by the invisible and remote.
Scientific thought also modifies this conception ; it discards
anthropomorphic divine intervention, and represents ethical

good and evil as bringing their reward and punishment solely in the way of natural law.

Practical religion is the attempt to propitiate the deity and live in union with him; practical ethics is the attempt to recognize man and live in harmony with him. But out of the idea of ethical obligation naturally arises the conception of absolute right, which must be identified with the idea of God. Right, truth, goodness, these are the will of God; they are the moral order of the universe, the manifestation of the infinite spirit. From this point of view religion and ethics are one; to know God is to know his ethical self-manifestation in the world. This is the highest single conception of the divine; but the complete knowledge of God includes, as far as human thought can comprehend it, the whole of the divine self-manifestation. And this, as is intimated above, has been the underlying idea in all religious history. Men have put their best science and ethics into their conception of the divine, — ethics and science both imperfect in varying degrees, and the conception of God consequently exhibiting what seems to us to be contradiction.

5. Religion is thus primarily a sentiment, the recognition of the relation between God and man, the effort to found life on something higher than man; and its content is determined by science and ethics. To the former is due man's conception of the nature of the divine and the mode of its self-manifestation; from the latter comes the moral ideal of life from which religion can never withdraw itself. Dogma and conduct are the necessary complements of the religious sentiment, the material which the religious consciousness assimilates, and by which it grows; and the history of religion consists in the development of these two elements. Ritual is merely a form of expression of dogma.[1] The ab-

---

[1] This is true even in those early systems in which ritual may be said to form the whole of religion.

solute power of any given religion will be in proportion to the purity — that is, the spirituality — of its dogma, and the elevation of its moral ideal; its practical power at a given moment and in a given community will depend on its capacity to commend relatively high dogmatic and ethical conceptions to men's minds and hearts.

§ 3. GREAT MEN.

We have spoken of social-religious progress as continuous, and this it doubtless is when long periods are taken into consideration. But within these longer periods progress is marked by flows and ebbs, elevations and depressions, intervals of calm followed by apparent sudden outbursts of energy. We are not called on here to attempt the explanation of this fact; it is sufficient to note its existence. But there is one feature of the development so important as to call for special mention, — the part, namely, played by individuals in the extension and elevation of human thought. History proceeds by crises, and a crisis implies a great man.

1. We may say in the first place that great men are a necessity in social progress. At intervals of greater or less extent the ideas and institutions of a growing society have to be recast in accordance with advancing thought. For a time men may be able and willing to live under a set of institutions with which they are more or less consciously out of sympathy; there will be a general uneasiness, which for a while, however, will not be sufficient to interfere with the orderly course of life. But there comes a time when a change is imperatively demanded. Conscience, the moral and religious ideal, protests against the existing order; there is an increasingly oppressive feeling that the present is out of relation with the past and the future, a sense of moral-religious uncomfortableness, which drives men to define their ideals and to shape life in accordance therewith. This

sense of the need of social and individual renewal naturally becomes distinct and effective first in the minds of the chosen few, the leaders of thought, those whose souls are aglow with moral-religious excitement and inspiration, the true practical idealists. But even a small body of men find it hard to attain the definiteness and unity which are essential to action; individual divergencies lame practical energy. Some one man must, as a rule, put himself at the head of the movement, called to that position by his gifts, and enforcing recognition by his eminence; and as a matter of fact such an one usually appears so soon as the time is ripe for action. Such crises are continually occurring in life; they are of different degrees of importance, relating to all affairs from the smallest to the largest, from the opening of a new street in a city to a change of the organization of a college, from the introduction of a new fashion in dress to a revolution in science or government, or the restatement of the religious beliefs of a nation or a continent. But great or small, each will have its representative man, who is the embodiment of the current ideas and the mouthpiece of opinion, the concentration of the energy of the circle of interests involved. He is always the great man of the occasion; and when the body of thought which he represents is large and effective, he is one of the great men of the world.

2. It is involved in what is said above that such a man is born out of the thought of his time; he is essentially the child of his age. The material of his thought must come from his own present and past; an absolute break is unthinkable. Thought itself is impossible without material already furnished to the mind. Usually it is possible to discover a man's relation to his past and to his present; this is what we demand from the biographer, and this is what he undertakes to do, whether his subject be Calvin or

Confucius, Zoroaster or Swedenborg. We feel that an idea born out of nothing would be unintelligible and dead.

3. Yet in this process, which we must recognize as orderly, there is always something inexplicable in the achievement of the guiding mind. We may demonstrate the man's relation to his past, exhibit the circle of ideas in which he grows up, and perceive the connection between his thought and that of his times; but in the last analysis, when we reach the creative moment, it is impossible to give the history of the process. There is a mystery in his mental experiences, in the way in which he seizes on the problem, combines its elements, and reaches his result. He himself can commonly give no logical account of his procedure, he can only say that he sees and knows the solution; out of many possible ways of dealing with the questions of life, he has chosen one which proves to be the right one, inasmuch as it commends itself to men and introduces harmony and peace in place of discord and unrest. The larger the problem, the more numerous do the possible solutions seem to men to be, the greater the difficulty of seizing on the one simple thought which shall convert the chaos into a cosmos, and the harder to represent the mental spiritual process by which the transforming discovery is made. It is a mystery that meets us in every department of human life; when we have called it genius, intuition, or inspiration, so far from defining it, we have only labelled it with a name which defies definition. Great artists, statesmen, discoverers of natural law, social and religious reformers, move in a sphere beyond the reach of other men; they are linked with the world by all natural ties, but their thought seems to be born in a sphere above the world. Their fellow-men have naturally thought of them as seized on by a higher power, especially when they had to do with the religious life; the word "inspiration" has been almost exclusively set apart to denote the deep

spiritual knowledge and the transforming religious energy which, it has seemed to men, could issue only from a super-human source. It is the word which expresses for our ordinary conception the mysteriousness of the human soul in contrast with its orderly obedience to law. These two elements of human thought are harmonized when we conceive of it as the creation of the divine spirit working according to natural law.

4. Such an eminently endowed leader of men gives society in a real sense something new; he converts into an established principle and rule of life what was before only a vague conception or desire. The undefined sense of need which for generations had stirred men into an unrecognized uneasiness, and had manifested itself in inarticulate cries rather than in intelligible words, rather by gropings than by organized action, — this he clearly recognizes and formulates, and then offers something which shall satisfy the need, and make rational and happy activity possible. Thenceforward the life of society is changed; there has entered into it an element which did not exist before. The difference between the new and the old is the difference between vision and blindness; there has come the discovery of the disease and the application of the remedy. Men's view of life has changed; their attitude toward the facts of religious experience is different. The proper centre is established; things group themselves more naturally, and are estimated more nearly according to their real nature and importance. The discovery that the Hebrew vowel-points were not given to Moses from the mouth of God on Mount Sinai was a veritable liberation of thought. The declaration of Jeremiah and Ezekiel, that the true divine law was written on men's hearts, must have been revolutionary for the circle of men who believed it; they could not afterward look on religious life in the same way as before. A wider liberation was

effected by the moral-religious principle announced by Paul and adopted from him by Luther, that righteousness is a transformation of soul instead of a string of legal performances. It is a still loftier and more potent principle which is contained in the word of Jesus, that all moral-religious life is summed up in love to God and man. When such principles as these have been announced and accepted, society assumes a new form. What was before shapeless becomes organized and regulated; that which was a dim longing becomes a definite impulse. Life approaches nearer to unity; there is less disharmony between mind and soul, between what tradition and custom sanctify and what reflection approves, — there is the sense of the removal of a weight, a fuller freedom of activity in thought and feeling. The connection with the past is not destroyed, but past and present are renewed into a higher life.

5. The part played by individual men in the establishment of great universal religions is well known. There is no doubt as to the process of origination of Christianity and Islam; and while in regard to Buddhism scholars are divided in opinion, there is a strong disposition to trace it to some one man. In China a great rôle, no doubt, is to be assigned to Confucius; on the other hand, the personality of the Israelitish Moses is dim, and the Persian Zoroaster is probably to be abandoned to the region of legend and myth. Socrates, Luther, and Wesley embody in themselves great religious movements. These men are all the prophets, the spokesmen, of the religious consciousness of their times, and they are no less independent and creative thinkers. It is necessary, therefore, in tracing the history of any religious movement to take into account these two elements, — the religious attitude of the epoch and the personality of the founder. It is only by combining and harmonizing the two that we can reach a clear idea of the evolution of the new religious

principle. It is a misfortune for the history of Buddhism that the person of Gautama is so enshrouded in legend; Mohammed is better known, and the beginnings of Islam far clearer. For Christianity we have records of its founder which, though embarrassed by legendary additions and reconstructions, still enable us to form a tolerably distinct picture of his person and life; and this is the first task of the historian of Christianity.

§ 4. External Conditions.

Up to this time we have been occupied with those conditions and agencies which within the community itself initiate and direct religious progress. But it is possible that a community may be affected by its neighbors. Such international influence is probably the rule in the history of religions; the better acquainted we become with the old religious faiths of the world, the more clearly we see that they are not simple products each of one national consciousness, but have all more or less freely given and received. We cannot, of course, assume in any particular case that such international action and reaction have occurred; the question is to be decided by an examination of the facts.

1. The religious influence exerted by one nation on another depends for its extent in part on the closeness of the intercourse between the two. The relations must be such that there is an exchange of individual opinions by conversation or by books. A very favorable condition for interchange of ideas is contiguity of social groups, when one community, by its local relations to another, is compelled to become acquainted with the customs and opinions of its neighbor; a good example of this is furnished in the early history of the Jews when they had partly conquered Canaan, and Israelitish and Canaanitish communities dwelt side by

side, intermarrying and coming to share one another's ideas in a very definite manner. More general social relations may be maintained by commercial intercourse, such as existed among all the national groups in Canaan and Syria in David's time, or between the Tigris-Euphrates valley and the Greek and other residents in Asia Minor from an early period; or political relations may induce an exchange of ideas, as when King Ahaz of Judah, going to Damascus to meet the Assyrian king, Tiglathpileser, saw there a Syrian altar the pattern of which he sent to his priest Urijah at Jerusalem with orders to make one like it; or as when Manasseh, as it would appear, adopted the Assyrian astral worship; or exile, like that of the Jews in Babylonia, may bring about intimate social relations. After the rise of the Persian empire the Jews in Babylonia and elsewhere must have been constantly in contact with Persian opinions and customs. The Greek conquest of Asia in the fourth century B. C. introduced Greek settlements and ideas into all the Western Asiatic communities, and promoted a contact of mind which was eminently favorable to the adoption of new ideas. For some centuries before Mohammed's time communities of Jews and Christians had been living in Arabia in the closest personal intercourse with the natives. In India, on the other hand, in the period when Buddhism arose, there seem to be no traces of such foreign influence.

2. In such social intercourse we may commonly assume reciprocal influence, — each community will be more or less affected by the other. In which direction the greater effect will be produced, will be determined by the relative impressibility of the two communities; and this will depend on their relative religious development, — the less will be directed by the greater. A higher general social culture, more definite opinions, better elaborated institutions, will impress themselves on that community which stands lower in these

respects. Impressibility will come from the natural desire to know and adopt what is pleasing.[1] The Jews were inferior in general culture and in certain points of religious development to the early Canaanites, the Assyrians and Babylonians, the Persians and the Greeks; the Arabians of the sixth century of our era felt the religious superiority of the Jews and Christians; the direction of the influence was in accordance with these relations.

3. Another favorable condition of international influence (closely connected with the first-mentioned) is the excitement of thought arising from lively social movement. The older civilization was made comparatively stagnant by the fixedness of national lines. At that stage of growth it was instinctively felt that national isolation was a necessity; there could be no brotherhood of nations, no rapid and stirring interchange of thought. But all this was changed by the Greek conquest. The mixture and close contact of different nationalities forced men to recognize one another, partly obliterated the old stiff national lines, and called out a hospitality for new ideas which had never before been seen in the world. Greeks, Jews, and Romans came into close relation with one another, and the result of their interchange of ideas may be traced in the religious history of the time. The interesting point for our discussion is whether the Jews were materially affected by the Greeks.

4. The borrowing of ideas which results from social intercourse may be direct or indirect, conscious or unconscious. There are cases in which a religious reformer has deliberately borrowed institutions and ideas from the books of foreign religious communities; so Mohammed did from the Hebrew

---

[1] It is of course essential that a religion, in order that it may be influenced, should not have reached the point of petrifaction,—that some of its material should be in a fluid state; and in point of fact, a living community never hardens into this insensibility, but always reserves a certain power of self-modification.

and Christian Scriptures.[1] Princes and priests may introduce new forms of worship; the Romans adopted Syrian deities and cults, and the Greeks appropriated Egyptian symbols and ceremonies; possibly in this way it was that the feast of Purim came to the Jews from the Persians.

Perhaps, however, it is the unconscious influence of one community on another that is the more deep and lasting. Ideas represented by the customs and expressions of one people insensibly make their way to others, and commend themselves by their naturalness and utility, by their capacity to satisfy an existing feeling of need. They may at first be adopted by advanced thinkers, and be gradually propagated in the lower strata of society; or they may receive for a long time no definite expression, — they may be simply in the air. Silently they make themselves felt; more and more, generation after generation, they color and control ideas, opinions, and usages. Finally they find expression in books or customs; the community accepts them as something quite natural, and wakes up to find itself in possession of thoughts which were unknown to the fathers, the genesis and authority of which no one is able to trace. After a while comes a period of reflection which seeks to bring the present into logical relation with the past; the new ideas are held to have existed in ancient customs and writings, back to which they are followed in an unbroken line, and the silent influences which produced them pass out of memory and rest unrecorded. Effects of this sort could doubtless be traced in the history of all religions if the data were sufficiently numerous; in later Jewish history the important periods in this regard are the Persian and the Greek.

5. It is obvious that the choice which a community makes in borrowing will be determined largely by the relation of

---

[1] The contents of these writings were known to him, not by his own reading, but through garbled oral communications.

the new ideas to the existing system of thought. A nation does not readily abandon its conception of life and religion; there is a definitely fashioned skeleton, which, however, may be clothed anew and so modify its form; there is a persistent idea, which maintains itself against all assaults from without, yet is capable of assimilating new material, of extending and defining itself by modifications which do not touch its essential nature. A borrowed idea will attach itself to some recognized thought of a community; the borrowing, to be healthy and beneficent, must be a free assimilation, not a mechanical addition, and fulness of life may be measured by the capacity for natural appropriation. We cannot say beforehand how far this process of assimilation may go; forms of religion, like forms of organic life, seem to be capable of indefinite variation without abandoning the type. The question what constitutes the essence of a religion can be answered only after a survey of its complete historical development; it is only then that we can perceive what has remained fixed amid all the modifications of idea and usage.

§ 5. The General Lines of Progress.

The advance which a religion makes under the favorable conditions above described will be in accordance with the general character of social progress. It is a growth from youth to manhood; it signifies a more serious view of life, a deeper conception of fundamentals, a sharper analysis which separates the higher from the lower. The progress may be greater or less, but in so far as it exists at all we can hardly think of it as not involving a change from the less to the more general.

1. One natural result is the abandonment of local usages. This takes place in a nation in proportion as its religion is centralized, and as a civilized unity comes into existence. A national church of to-day imposes its customs on all parts

of the land; and these are broader and more human than those of any particular district. It was a true instinct that led the Jews of the seventh century B. C. to insist that Jerusalem should be the only lawful place of worship; it was the only way to wipe out the unseemlinesses of the local cults. The effect is wider when a nation is forced to judge its customs by the standard of other national usages. The broader international feeling leads men to dispense with those things which are likely to offend the common feeling. At the same time the conviction naturally grows that such things are relatively unimportant. Yet it is impossible to say beforehand how far the outward form will be retained. In all organized systems of religion up to the present time some framework of form has been found to be necessary; and experience only can demonstrate how much of it will prove to be compatible with the life of larger societies. Buddhism began as a mendicant order, a constitution which would have excluded the majority of men; but in time it modified this arrangement, introducing grades which recognized the ordinary social relations, yet always giving greatest honor to the original form. Judaism took the same course with respect to circumcision, not always insisting on it, but still making it the badge of highest religious citizenship; Paul, with the instinct of genius, took the bold step of practically abolishing it. Mohammed showed his wisdom in the simplicity of the forms which he imposed on his followers; the most oppressive of them — the pilgrimage to Mecca — was afterward dispensed with in various simple ways. The Catholic Church has means of lightening its ceremonial burdens under certain circumstances. It is the instinct of the religion which guides it in such matters. The first and most important step is its extension beyond its original national bounds; having passed out into a wider world, it will know how to change its form according to circumstances, and its capacity to do this will be a measure of its success.

2. The more important element of progress is the generalization of ideas, the excision of the local and sensuous, and the emphasizing of the broadly spiritual. The agencies by which this is effected are pointed out above. The growth of national self-consciousness, the development of thought which naturally attends the widening of social relations, advance in ethical feeling, the rise of scientific thought, contact with foreign ideas, — these occasion a constant revision and reformulation of religious ideas in the light of broader knowledge, and the abandonment of such things as offend the finer religious sense. The Jews after a while gave up the national proper name Yahwe, substituting for it the general term God, or some such paraphrase as The Lord, or The Holy One. Islam contented itself with a statement of the divine character and government so simple that it could be understood by all the world. Similar processes might be traced in all the great religions. Here, again, it is impossible to say beforehand what direction the simplification and generalization will take. This will depend on the character and needs of the communities involved, and will always be tentative; that is, the generalization will proceed as far as it is forced by the public thought to go, and will advance only in those societies in which it proves to be an element of success. Although force has been often used in the propagation of religions, yet to explain their success we have always to consider finally their capacity to adapt themselves to the social-religious conditions of human life. Islam, for example, has kept itself pure only in Semitic communities.

3. National advance in breadth and elevation of thought does not, however, account for the rise of the great universal religions. In a national religious system most diverse elements are mingled, — broad and narrow, high and low,

attractive and repulsive. These, according to their characters, commend themselves to different circles. The victory of new ideas is gradual; at a given moment, while the farthest advanced line of thinkers have reached pure conceptions of man's relation to God, a large mass of the people may be buried in superstition, formalism, or indifference. The religious books and creeds will show the same diversities, — masses of noble thought embedded in low, mechanical conceptions. Or, at the best, the national development may be seeking to purify and elaborate some religious element of life which, though not without virtue and potency, is not the highest, and not of a sort to commend itself outside the limits of the nation. In point of fact this is what seems to have occurred in the case of Brahmanism and Judaism; Islam does not here come under consideration, for it was invented at a blow, we may say, out of almost entirely foreign materials. In this mixture of national religious opinions, what is needed, in order to secure a new vitalizing impulse, is just that which happened to the Jews at the conclusion of the Babylonian exile. They went to Babylonia as a motley mixture of good and bad, — a comparatively small prophetic circle which shared the opinions of Jeremiah and Ezekiel, and a large majority whose views and usages are set forth in the naïve speech made by the men and women in Pathros in reply to the prophet Jeremiah's indignant reproof: "As long as we worshipped the queen [or host] of heaven we were happy; since we have left off this worship all this evil has come upon us." The exile sifted this mixed community; only those returned to Palestine who were in sympathy with the prophetic ideas and could begin the national life on a new basis. And in the same way, in Babylonia the idolatrous portion was absorbed in the alien population, and those who were in sympathy with the higher national conceptions formed a separate circle and lived a new life. The starting-point of the new Jewish life was the selection of a new idea as the basis of organization; purified from alien elements, this idea colored and controlled the whole subsequent national development. Some such process is necessary for the transformation of a national into a universal religion. The choice of a central idea will be made by the whole community, under the leadership of individuals. In the exilian and post-exilian history of the Jews, we have glimpses of controlling minds, — Ezekiel, Zerubbabel, Joshua, Ezra, Nehemiah; and if we were better acquainted with the history of the Babylonian Jews of that period, we should no doubt find there also men whose personal influence guided the thought of the community. In the larger religious movements, as is remarked above, the presence of a controlling individual mind seems to be necessary to give unity and effectiveness to the new development, though the leader will naturally gather about him a body of coadjutors.

4. And this leads to the mention of another condition of the transition to a universal religious form which is involved in what has just been said. The revolution must be a product of the times, a response to the demand for change, the outcome of generations of thought. The man or the men who appear as leaders put into shape (as is observed above) what many of their contemporaries had indefinitely thought; they give vitality to the unorganized mass of vague conceptions. They themselves would be impossible without the background of the community, without the accumulation of thought which they inherit from the past. This is obvious in so many cases that we are warranted in assuming it to be probable even when definite facts cannot be adduced in proof. There is evidence that Mohammed arose out of a circle of thinkers who represented a tendency of the times; there are reasons for believing that the founder of Buddhism did not occupy an isolated religious position.

It is clear that Isaiah, Jeremiah, Ezekiel, and Ezra were true prophets of their times, the spokesmen of select groups who were in sympathy with the deeper and more spiritual thought of their periods. There is no reason to suppose that Christianity is an exception to this general principle.

It is true in one sense that the success of a religious revolution depends on the completeness with which its creator responds to the needs of the age. Men will take only what seems to them to be useful; popular approbation is the measure of practical wisdom. But this is a local and temporary criterion; it does not follow that the tendency of an age is the best possible, or its satisfaction the absolute right. A reformer may go far beyond the conceptions of his times, and be unsuccessful because not understood. To be immediately effective he must stand in close relation with his contemporaries, and it is not conceivable that he should be entirely out of relation with them. But it is possible that while one side of his thought is apprehended and accepted, another and higher side may be ignored. In that case, his highest influence will vanish unless it happen that he find a prophet, — an interpreter who shall know how to link his person to the life of the times, and thus preserve the substance of his uncomprehended thought. The interpreter will have his own conception of the person and work of the master, and may initiate a new direction of religious thought, as the Apostle Paul substantially did. It may then happen that succeeding times shall throw off what is local in the thought of the interpreter, and return to the idea of the master, of which the interpreter's system is only the framework.

5. We are here, of course, employing the term "universal" loosely to mean what is endowed with practically indefinite capacity of extension. We know of no religion which experience has shown to be really universal. No religion has yet been accepted by all nations; and we should hardly be war-

ranted in going beyond the bounds of experience and affirming that this or that religion has elements which must commend it to all peoples. It is indeed difficult to see why Christianity in its simplest New Testament form should not prove thus universally acceptable, though on the other hand, it is impossible to say how far this simple faith, in order to commend itself, must be supported by a more elaborate system. And further, even when a religion is accepted in general by a nation, it may be rejected by a considerable circle. In the purest and highest historical religion there must remain something local and temporary; and the question to be decided by time will be how far it can dispense with this local part without losing its essential nature. The absolutely universal religion will be that which satisfies universal human needs, spiritual and intellectual, lacking nothing which is necessary for the practical guidance of human life, containing nothing which offends the most advanced thought, offering and claiming nothing which is not capable of universally acceptable demonstration.

§ 6. Extra-national Extension.

In any social group of nations, as has already been pointed out, there will be a mutual influence of their religions, according to the nature and extent of their social intercourse. In general, the stronger will coerce the weaker. The elements of strength and weakness are various, issuing from all the social phenomena, and these latter change with every age and clime. There are, however, a few conditions of international influence which from the testimony of history we may assume to be common to all those great movements in which a religion extends itself beyond its national lines.

1. The principal condition of this sort of conquest is the fact already mentioned, — the possession of an idea broader than national areas. There must be something that com-

mends itself to the human soul apart from national feelings and customs. Further than this, there must be something that appeals to the age, that satisfies a need felt over a wide space at that particular time.

2. This condition presupposes a certain unity in a section of the world. It assumes that men in different nations, starting from different points and proceeding along different lines, have yet reached the same goal of religious feeling and desire. It is the teaching of history that some such unification as this is essential to the rise of a religion that shall embrace various nationalities. This procedure is most obvious in the history of the rise of Christianity; the Greek and Roman conquests, by their political and intellectual results, had impressed a visible unity on the Western world. The fact is less clear in the histories of Islam and Buddhism; but here also we can see that natural processes of culture had brought a number of peoples or communities to about the same stage of intellectual-religious growth, or it may be better to say, to a point where real sympathy among them in the religious life was possible. The Arabs of the first century of Islam were capable of appreciating the moral and religious ideas of the Christians and Mazdeans with whom they came in contact; of India and the neighboring lands we have less information, but such indications as exist point to a similarity in the social-religious structure of the various nationalities affected by Buddhism.

3. The progress of a religion implies a sense of need in the communities to which it commends itself. It signifies a failure of existing religious systems, especially in peoples alien to the home of the new religion. The people in whose midst a new creed has sprung up have at least the training of the ideas which produced it. This training has not been so fully enjoyed by foreign peoples; their sense of need and emptiness will be all the more pronounced. Such a social-

religious emptiness is distinctly visible in the areas first conquered by Christianity and Islam; the Roman world was
tired of Greek and Latin divinities, and hopeless of anything
better; the Christianity and the Mazdeism of the seventh
century, when Islam appeared, had dwindled into shapeless
masses of shrunken, lifeless dogmas;[1] for the beginnings of
Buddhism we have no such full details, but we may perhaps
infer from the enthusiasm and vitality of Asoka's edicts that
the Brahmanism of the preceding centuries had left a vacuum
in the popular feeling. The national mind, thus emptied of
distinct convictions and hopes, is prepared to accept a well-
defined system of religious thought.

4. The conquering religion offers what is needed in the
way of precision and organization. It will possess not only
a general fundamental religious idea, but also the framework
necessary to give it popular acceptation. A simple ethical-
religious conception, however broad and pure, is usually
neither intelligible nor acceptable to the masses of men;
they demand in addition a drapery of processes and forms,
a certain quantity of machinery, a routine by which life
may be ordered. There is no instance on record of wide
popular acceptance of a religious system whose essence was
merely a principle of the inward life; there is no reason to
suppose that a reformer who should confine himself to this
subjective ethical-religious sphere would be successful unless
his work were supplemented. Mohammed devised a system
remarkable not only for the purity and simplicity of its
dogma, but also for the mingled simplicity and completeness of its ritual; Buddhism initiated a set of forms which
satisfied the demand for guidance; Paul supplied a dogmatic
framework for the ethical-religious ideas of Jesus.

It is from this non-ethical dogma and form that spring the

---

[1] Islam appropriated and infused life into high moral and religious ideas
which were held lifelessly by the neighboring peoples.

organization and the enthusiasm necessary to a career of victory. It is not hard to understand why a purely ethical idea does not lead to organization; it is too individual, has too few points of contact, common to all men, with the external world. A conquering religion must be a church if it is to have a visible organized victory. Purely ethical ideas may spread and get control of men, but their influence is silent, showing itself in the way of coloring thought and deed; they do not clothe themselves with that bodily form which we call "a religion."

III.

We may conclude this sketch of the principles of the progress of religions by a brief mention of the actual results as far as we can trace them. It is on these results that what is said in the preceding pages has been based. Even a bare mention of the facts will suffice to show how largely these laws of progress have obtained, and what different degrees of effect they have had in different nations and under different circumstances.

§ 1. The Universal Religions.

It may at first be surprising that of all the religions of the world only three have grown into universal form, — Brahmanism into Buddhism, Judaism into Christianity, and the old Arabian faith into Islam. It would be more accurate to say that only these three have developed into effective organizations. There may be universal ideas which from their nature are not capable of giving rise to ecclesiastical organizations. It has happened in the case of these three religions that the circumstances of the times supplied both the living ideas and the necessary framework of secondary conceptions. Nothing is more remarkable in the history of the establishment of Islam than the way in which Mohammed fitted his transforming ideas into the existing social system, with what sagacity he recognized popular customs and opinions, and thus made the popular life the receptacle for higher conceptions which were destined to transform it; in a word, he combined an idea and its dogmatic ritual clothing into a unity which answered the demands of his time. So it was with Christianity and Buddhism. The other outward conditions of progress also were fulfilled in the rise of these three religions, — religious vagueness and emptiness around them, distinctness, organization, and enthusiasm within them. We can see, as a matter of fact, that the world was prepared for them. And considering the complexity of the relations, the mass of conditions to be fulfilled, it cannot be surprising that the number of great international religions has been small. The failure of a single condition may be fatal. A lack of completeness in one direction may confine a religion to the bounds of its own nation, though it might seem otherwise to have all the requisite conditions for general extension. That this has been the case will appear from a brief examination of some of the failures.

§ 2. Stunted and Arrested Growths.

It may be said from one point of view that all religions tend to become universal; that is, natural growth is in the direction of the excision of the local and the retention of that only which satisfies more highly cultivated thought and feeling. In fact, however, the conditions of success are so numerous that the probabilities of failure are great. We find a gradation in the history of religions, cases of more or less serious effort to transcend national bounds, with varying degrees of success or failure.

1. The nearest approach to speculative universality was achieved by the Greek philosophy which followed Plato and Aristotle, especially by the Stoics. The conception of the unity of the world was practically established in Greek philosophic thought at the close of the fifth century B. C., about the time when the Jews were beginning to formulate their practical monotheism. The Stoics affirmed the unity of the world in a more thorough manner than the Jews, and rather speculatively than practically. They worked out a system of morals in some respects so complete that it commanded the admiration of the world, and for centuries satisfied the ethical craving of the best minds of Greece and Rome. Here was apparently the foundation for a universal religion, — ideas of life almost completely divorced from local-national conceptions. In fact, Stoicism had a great career. Its ideas penetrated into all parts of the Roman empire, leaving no cultivated community or circle untouched or uncolored by their influence, — not even Jewish Palestine, so much disposed to hold itself aloof from heathen thought. They were in the air, and could not be excluded.

Nevertheless, Stoicism did not become a popular religion; as a system it remained the possession of the cultivated few, and for obvious reasons. It lacked the theologic framework which was essential for wide popular effect. In its thorough-going speculative unification of the world and its determined recognition of rigid natural law, it reduced the deity to a minimum, and it took no practical account of the future life. These were fatal lacks. And further, in its endeavor to realize what it regarded as the absolute good, it undertook to obliterate the emotional side of man and transform him into a machine for the production of right will. This will was made dependent on right thinking; thus resulted an admirable ideal of the perfect man, whose reflections were always just and his decisions rational. But it was an ideal beyond the conception of the people, — practically no God, no life to come, no full flow of passionate human desire. Stoicism remained an idea capable of coloring the world's thought, but incapable of creating an organized religion. It began in speculation, and never as a system advanced beyond speculative circles. Judaism, on the other hand, felt its way cautiously, constantly keeping in touch with human needs and fashioning itself so as to satisfy them.

The same thing is to be said of other Greek and Roman systems of philosophy. They had their universal side, but failed to take account of all the elements of life of their time.

2. Confucianism has labored under a similar onesideness. With a carefully wrought-out ethical system, the object of which is to make the man a beneficent member of society, it has scant recognition of the theological or purely religious side of human nature, it is silent or non-committal with respect to the future life. It is the religion of the learned, but not of the masses in China. Its ethical universality has enabled it to pass the bounds of its own nation and find some footing in Japan and other neighboring countries where Chinese influence has been predominant, but further than this it has not gone and is not likely to go. Not only does it lack universal-religious ideas, so that in fact it can hardly be called a religion at all; its ethical system also is largely colored by national peculiarities. The State-religion, as distinct from Confucius's special teaching, has a defined worship which is not without a monotheistic tinge; but the cult is decidedly national, and the Emperor is the sole ministrant.

3. In the old Egyptian religion we have an example of a steady advance in the direction of both religious and ethical universality, a pronounced monotheism in higher circles of thought, and a very noble moral code. But this broader

religious movement seems not to have become national; there was no such sifting process as took place among the exiled Jews; the people remained polytheists. Egyptian ideas penetrated to some extent into the Greek and Roman empires; in Alexandria they were doubtless amalgamated with Greek and Jewish conceptions; but they were too much bound to the soil by their theologic and ritual clothing, and could offer the world nothing so distinct and satisfactory as that which was brought by Judaism and Christianity. The Isis-cult, though it made its way into Syria, Greece, and Rome, was forced to yield to a more powerful rival.

The Persian religion — a remarkable and noble attempt to embody in religious creed the everlasting conflict of human life — suffered under the double burden of a somewhat complicated theology and a local ritual. That which was universal in its religious conception never found distinct expression, or if it did finally struggle into utterance, this was not till after Christianity had got possession of the field. Manichæism was an attempt to combine the two rival systems, but it had the power of neither, and proved an utter failure. Mazdeism was never able to subordinate, as Judaism did, the evil principle absolutely to the good; it was half-hearted, and therefore without power over foreign peoples. This is a part of the explanation of the inglorious way in which it succumbed to Islam.

4. The tendency to universality is visible, not only in national religions, but also in certain great Christian communities, as the national churches of England and Germany. These churches have for centuries embodied the religious thought of the national mind, and have reflected the national progress. It is always a comparatively small body of thinkers that in any generation represents the advance; but if we take the Church of England, for example, it is evident that it represents to-day, as compared with the Church of the

sixteenth century, an avoidance of the local and particularistic, and an emphasizing of those elements of religion which appeal to all men. The same thing may be said of the Church of Rome, which is becoming more catholic, not only in the extent of its territory, but also in the hospitality it offers to broader religious ideas. A similar progress may be perceived in other great Christian bodies which have no connection with the State.

§ 3. National and Tribal Religions.

The great mass of the religions of the world have failed to pass beyond the communities in which they originated. This remark must be understood, however, as applying to them only in the comparatively advanced stage in which we actually find them. The hundreds of tribes dwelling in Asia, Africa, America, and Oceanica, each with its apparently petrified and motionless religion, have all had their histories; what inward development and outward extension may have taken place in remote times through amalgamations and conquests, we cannot tell. Nor is it possible to say with certainty what changes are now in progress, since we are so slightly acquainted with the condition of the barbarian peoples of the world. Some of them, it is known, have elaborate cosmogonies and mythologies and a great mass of folk-lore, implying a long development in some past period. But granting the possibility of small movements and growths, it is no doubt true that the barbarous religions of to-day are confined within the limits of their own communities, and there is no sign among them of the intellectual activity which is necessary to progress.

§ 4. The Outlook.

1. The present indications are that a few great religions will in time control the whole world. Buddhism, Christian-

ity, and Islam now occupy a great part of the globe, and the last two are advancing in various directions. The majority of barbarous religions have shown themselves unable to hold their ground against the inroads of intellectually and ethically superior faiths. Of the old national religions, those of India, China, and Japan alone show anything like solidity of organization and capacity of resistance, and of these the Japanese seems to be not disinclined to accept European ideas.

2. As between the three great universal religions there can be little doubt as to where the prospect of victory lies. Religion follows in the wake of social progress, and it is this last that determines the relations among nations. Christianity (to say nothing of its moral and spiritual superiority) is the religion of the great civilized and civilizing nations of the world, in whose hands are science and philosophy, literature and art, political and social progress. European and American civilization, in its gradual encroachment on the other peoples of the world, necessarily carries along and plants Christianity.

3. This implies that the other great religions of the world will not be able to adapt themselves as systems to the new social order of things. Some parts of their apparatus of creed may survive, some view of life may commend itself to the new civilization and enter into and color the established European creed ; but if we may judge from the present condition of the Asiatic peoples, their religions must as systems pass away with the civilizations to which they belong.

4. Nor is it probable that Christianity, if it should be the sole survivor of the world's religious creeds, would retain its present form unmodified. It is more likely that it will from generation to generation feel the double influence of territorial expansion and inward development of thought. Having the whole world for its heritage, it will adapt itself to the

world's needs; and standing always in close contact with the world's highest thought, it will throw off from time to time what it feels to be opposed to the purest ethical-religious conception of life, and retain only that which the best thought of the time demands.

The preceding sketch attempts to give the principles of religious progress in general outline. That there will be exceptions to or modifications of such general rules is to be expected. The almost infinitely diversified local conditions will give peculiar turns and colorings to the various developments, and these form the material of special histories. But amid all differences, it is important to recognize the working of those general laws which both explain individual peculiarities, and stamp unity on human religious history.

DEVELOPMENT OF RELIGIOUS THOUGHT

FROM OLD TESTAMENT TO NEW TESTAMENT.

———◆———

IN tracing the history of Jewish religious ideas into the New Testament times, it is proper to begin with the period represented by the name of Ezra. The introduction of the complete Levitical legislation is a most important turning-point in Jewish religious history; it transformed the nation into a church, and gave a new coloring to the whole national life, or to state the fact in more general terms, it was coincident with the beginning of what may be called modern Judaism, the Israelitish life as it appears in the New Testament.

The results attained by Israelitish thought up to Ezra's time may be summed up in a few particulars, which appear with sufficient distinctness in the literature.

First, the nation had reached the point of practical monotheism, the conviction that in general the affairs, not only of Israel, but also of the whole world, were controlled by the God of Israel. This belief appears in the prophetic writings from Amos to Zechariah. The prophets, as the great religious thinkers of the period, are its formulators and expounders. They were not its creators; it grew out of the necessities of the national life, but naturally took distinctest shape and received best expression from the most advanced minds. The approach to monotheism was a gradual one;

idolatry was rife among the people down to and during the Babylonian exile. The captivity sifted the mass of the people; the adherents of the monotheistic tendency in Babylonia were drawn into close relations with one another (this we may infer from the subsequent developments), and those who returned to Canaan shared the same views. It was by no means a theoretical and thorough-going monotheism which was held; we shall see that alongside of the belief in the practical aloneness of Yahwe, the existence of other deities was admitted, and the power of Yahwe therefore represented as limited. But happily this logical inconsistency seems to have had no practical results, and after a time vanished before the increasing firmness of the monotheistic faith.

In the next place the nation had worked out a reasonably sound and satisfactory system of practical social ethics. The moral principles which we find in the prophets and the law books show a high state of ethical culture, culminating in the precept, "Thou shalt love thy neighbor as thyself" (Lev. xix. 18). Only it has to be observed that the "neighbor" here is one's fellow-countryman; it was not supposed that the obligation of love extended beyond the bounds of Israel; international ethics was no more recognized by the Jews than by any other people of that day.

The organization of public worship in the temple was completed by the end of the fifth century; some modifications were afterward introduced, but the sacerdotal system of the New Testament is substantially that of the time of Ezra. The effect of this rigid organization was first to isolate the people from their neighbors, and secondly to confirm and develop the legal conception of life, — the idea that every act is prescribed or regulated by special divine command, and that the perfect man is he who knows and obeys these prescriptions. The system was the essence of national particularism, favorable to intensity in one direction, unfavorable to breadth and catholicity; fortunately it was afterward to some extent modified by the conditions of the national life. We are of course not to look on the Tora (as the Law now came to be called) as something forcibly injected into the national life from without, and intrusively moulding it. The divine instruction (*tora*) had been gathering volume for centuries, and the national feeling had been moving toward the conviction that this instruction was its organic law; but when this function had been distinctly recognized, and the law embodied in a complete code, it entered into the national life as one of its main factors. It was by no means the only factor — other elements, religious and ethical, were potent — but this determined the form of life and the constitution of the State.

One other fact must be mentioned, — the form which the Jewish Messianic hope had assumed in Ezra's time. The term "Messianic" does not properly belong to this period; it was the product of the ideas of a later time. But the hope which it implies had been long in existence; it was a natural product of the conviction of Yahwe's care for Israel, — a sort of belief and hope that have no doubt existed among all nations, but received among the Jews peculiarly definite expression and exerted a peculiarly lasting and profound influence. It had already passed through various phases in Israel. Amos, Hosea, Isaiah, and Micah looked simply for deliverance from Assyrian attacks and the happy ethical-religious maintenance of the existing political organization; Jeremiah and Ezekiel, with the same hope of deliverance from political enemies, perceived also the need of spiritual transformation, and made a new heart the condition of the era; the later exilian prophets (whom we may group under the name of Deutero-Isaiah) were absorbed in the prospect of restoration to Canaan and the vision of the triumph of

Israel's worship over all the nations; the prophets of the return, Haggai and Zech. i.–viii., sinking down from these pictures of glory to the hard realities of their present, confined themselves to the task that lay before them, of rebuilding the temple and securing a feeble foot-hold in the promised land. The form of the expectation of national triumph had varied from time to time according to the condition of the national fortunes.[1] In the fifth century came a lull: the temple had been built, but nothing more had been accomplished; bare existence was all that the colony had achieved. The advent of Ezra and Nehemiah fixed attention on the legal-religious organization of the nation, and for the moment there was neither time nor inducement to follow the glowing pictures which the old prophets had given of the future. The little community was undergoing a transformation, and had to await further developments before it could resume its outlook into the future.

It is at this point that we begin our study. We are to trace the history of the Jewish religious ideas from the fifth century on (going farther back when it seems desirable), and to follow them into the New Testament times. While Palestine is the centre of the movement, we shall have to include also those phases of thought which we find among the Egyptian Jews, and other Israelitish communities, and those Persian and Greek influences which seem to have left their trace on Jewish theology. Instead of taking the history by periods, we may trace the development of each common line of

---

[1] See, for example, the political and religious constitution of the future. Generally the nation as a whole is alone spoken of; Jeremiah (xxiii. 5) and Ezekiel (xxxiv. 23, etc.) include the royal dynasty as a part of the established order. An individual king as leader is mentioned in four passages, — Isa. ix. 6, 7 (*Heb.* ix. 5. 6); xi. 1–9; Mic. v. 2 (*Heb.* v. 1); Zech. ix. 9, — all of which seem to be post-exilian. The priesthood does not receive special mention till the time of Ezekiel (xliv. 15); nearly contemporary is Jer. xxxiii. 14–26, which is an expanded recension of Jer. xxiii. 5–8. The order is prominent in Zechariah, Malachi, and Joel.

religious thought continuously into the New Testament. This plan has the advantage of presenting each doctrine as a unit, and of bringing out under each head more distinctly the continuity of progress.

Before beginning the discussion it will be proper to give a brief survey of the non-Christian Jewish sources of the history.

CHAPTER I.

THE LITERATURE.

§ 1. The Literary Development.

THE period on which we now enter, from Ezra to the beginning of the second Christian century, was one of great mental activity and varied literary productiveness. It offers no such sustained compositions as the second Isaiah and Job, at least nothing that rivals these in imaginative flight and literary skill; we have instead a multitude of larger and smaller writings representing various tendencies of thought, among them one at least, the Wisdom of Solomon, which deserves a place among the Jewish classics. The old isolated life of the nation, with its self-centred calmness, was at an end; the era of closer international relations had begun, and this for the politically unstable little Jewish community meant constant contact with novelties, new intellectual and religious excitements and literary ventures. There are few of the literary products of the period that are not interesting in themselves, but we shall consider them only in so far as they bear on the history of religious thought.

The literary history is by no means formless. We recognize the passage from prophecy through ritual history and romances to philosophy, lyrical poetry, and apocalypse, the return to history especially for the portraiture of the great Maccabean era, and then apocalypse again, with history and theology. A brief sketch of this development will suffice here; the material of the books will be used in the course of the discussion.

1. *Prophetic Writings.* The old prophecy had spent its strength; after the exile it was no longer what it had been, and in our period it is only the shadow of its former self. It had successfully carried through the first great movement of Israelitism, — it had crushed idolatry and established monotheism; and, this foundation laid, the national thought had turned to other things. The great legal movement — the ritual organization of the nation — had superseded the old spontaneous utterance of prophetic men. Religion was becoming more an affair of rule and reasoning; the divine word, instead of issuing in burning words from the souls of seers, was fixed in a book. This was not necessarily a religious retrogression, — it was rather a natural and necessary progress in reflection, — but it gave a new turn and tone to the literature. Yet there still came occasionally the breath of the prophetic impulse, though in comparatively feeble form.

After the building of the temple the maintenance of the worship was naturally the pressing question. About 460 B. C.,[1] the prophet who is known by the name of Malachi was moved to reprove the people for their negligence in bringing offerings to the temple. Seeing in the priests and Levites the hope of the nation, he predicted a coming day of Yahwe which should purify them and usher in an era of complete religious-moral unity for Israel. It is an interesting point in his short prophecy that he records the existence of practical religious scepticism and the beginning of the closer social-religious life (Mal. iii. 14–16).

It is after a considerable interval that we meet with two productions which have the clear stamp of the legal period,

---

[1] A date before the reform of Ezra and Nehemiah is to be preferred on the grounds that the Levites are not definitely distinguished from the priests (Mal. ii. 4 ; iii. 3), and that the strict marriage-regulations of Ezra (Ezra x.) seem not to be in force (Mal. ii. 11).

and probably fall after the Greek conquest of Palestine.[1] Zech. ix.–xiv. is occupied with various local relations, the petty States around Jerusalem, the conflict between the people of the city and the people of the country districts, and looks forward to a great catastrophe, the result of which shall be that Judah shall be ceremonially sacred to Yahwe, and that all the nations of the earth shall come up to Jerusalem to worship. The course of events is marked by the fact that the existing prophetic institution is expected to fall into disrepute (Zech. xiii. 3–9); the writer feels himself to be apart from the prophetic herd, whose inspiration he connects with an unclean spirit. The political and religious condition of the people was lamentable (Zech. x. 12–14; xi. ; xiii. 2), but our prophet, recalling the old form of government, has the vision of a coming king, righteous and devoid of pride, saved by God, and extending the dominion of Judah over all the nations (Zech. ix. 9, 10). Joel also expects a catastrophe from which Judah shall issue in safety to abide forever. It is noteworthy that he mentions, as characteristic of the coming time of blessedness, the universal diffusion of the spirit of prophecy among all classes, young and old, bond and free, male and female (Joel ii. 28–32 [*Heb.* iii.], cf. Num. xi. 29); the prophesying seems to be defined as dreaming dreams and seeing visions, and is introduced as a mark of Yahwe's specific and intimate presence among his people. Zechariah looks at the corruptness of present prophecy; Joel hopes for a revival of the true spirit. In both writers we observe more glow than is found in the prophets of the return. With the firmer organization of the Palestinian colony came a revival of the old hopes and a more strenuous assertion of political nationality. It is sufficient to mention the short polemic against idolatry, entitled the " Epistle of

---

[1] See the references to the Greeks, Zech. ix. 13, Joel iii. 6, and to the developed ritual, Zech. xiv. 12–21, Joel ii. 15–17.

Jeremiah," belonging perhaps to the latter part of the third century.

2. The complete reconstruction of the national life under the control of the Law naturally led to the desire to rewrite the old history from a new point of view. The books of Chronicles, Ezra, and Nehemiah recount the national fortunes from the accession of David to near the end of the fourth century, — Chronicles representing the full Levitical ritual as having been in existence from the first, and describing in a multitude of unhistorical details the constant and visible intervention of Yahwe in the nation's affairs; Ezra and Nehemiah, on the other hand, are sober in their statements. These books belong not far from the year 300 B. C.,[1] and give the first complete historical view of the Israelitish constitution as a theocracy. The Greek 1 Esdras adds no important particulars.

3. Chronicles marks a new tendency in historical composition. The older books, — Judges, Samuel, Kings, — composed in or near the exile, had indeed interpreted the past in the light of their present, and regarded it as an illustration of the truth that national success was dependent on obedience to the nation's God. Chronicles conceives of the history more distinctly as the embodiment of an idea, the illustration of which is the main function of the facts. The chronicler's idea was one which entered into the very essence of the Israelitish thought of his time, and represented in general the outcome of the history. It was Yahwe's guidance of Israel under the government of the Law and the temple-ritual. But it was natural that the idea should coerce the facts. Legendary material there is in abundance

---

[1] The close connection between the three books is generally recognized; see, especially, the genealogical lists in 1 Chron. i.-ix., Ezra ii., Neh. vii. The list of high-priests is brought down, in Neh. xii. 11, to Jaddua, who, according to Josephus (Ant. xi. 8, 4), held the office when Alexander came to Jerusalem, B. C. 332.

in the earlier histories ; but it is a natural growth which has incorporated itself organically into the real history, while a large part of the embellishment of Chronicles has the air of an artificial addition. It may be to some extent a real traditional coloring, but seems in many cases to be due to the imagination of the writer, who could conceive of the past only under the form of the present, and writes the story accordingly. The result at any rate is thorough-going ritual reconstruction, a new nicely rounded history in which the well-known characters of the books of Samuel and Kings play rôles foreign to the prophetic conception. The Chronicler gained his end, — his work is a literary success ; but it is a religious romance rather than a sober history. Such remodelling of the old material under the control of an idea, with free handling of the facts, was made possible by the literary conditions of the time : there was no scientific conception of the value of facts as the only embodiment of human history ; there was no critical public ; manuscripts were few and little read ; they were written for sympathetic circles, and having obtained the approval of the literary minority, might pass on to the general public unchallenged and uncontrolled. The inducement was great to use the past freely as a mere vehicle of moral teaching. Already in the historical parts of the Pentateuch the old stories had been lavishly employed to this end. There was a natural conservative desire to establish the present in and by the past ; and the Jewish mind (it is a Semitic trait) preferred objective historical portraiture to abstract discussion. A century after the production of Chronicles this tendency manifested itself in a group of works of which four have come down to us ; a larger group there probably was, — it is not likely that these four are all that were produced, — and we have perhaps a trace of one such story in the episode of Darius and the three young men in 1 Esdras iii., iv. The romances which have been preserved are Jonah, Esther, Judith, and Tobit; they seem all to belong in the period from 250 to 150 B. C.

The book of Jonah embodies a religious sentiment strikingly broad and lofty in comparison with the reigning Jewish particularism of the time; it represents God as caring for heathen peoples not less tenderly and completely than for Israel. How far this embodies the thought of a wider circle it is hard to say; we find scarcely the trace of such a conception elsewhere in this period.

The sentiment of Esther is precisely the opposite of this. It is fierce, intolerant nationalism. Its principal design seems to be to commend to Palestinian Jews the feast of Purim (cf. "the day of Mardochaeus" in 2 Mac. xv. 36), which it represents as having been established in commemoration of a great national deliverance. The author of the Hebrew work is so absorbed in his picture of the prowess and triumph of the Jews that he makes no mention of God and shows no consciousness of religion ; this defect is remedied in the Greek recension, which inserts among other things prayers offered by Mordecai and Esther, and a vision with theocratic interpretation.

The motive in Judith seems to be merely to comfort and inspire the people in a time of distress by the picture of a remarkable divine intervention, — by the hand of a woman the God of Israel discomfits mighty enemies. The details of the narrative may rest on some obscure tradition, but can be brought into relation with no known facts of history.

In Tobit we have a charming picture of family life, reflecting the political conditions and religious ideas of the author's time. It is the first example of a novel proper, — a tale in which the interest lies chiefly or largely in incidents of every-day life. The moral lesson, however, is not lacking; the religious faithfulness of Tobit is rewarded with family prosperity, and by the victory which his son gains over the fiend Asmodæus.

4. The more definitely reflective tendency of the time appears in the group of philosophical works, books of Wisdom, which seem to have been composed a little later than the romances, about from 230 B. C. to 130 B. C., comprising Proverbs, Ecclesiastes, The Wisdom of Solomon, and The Wisdom of the Son of Sirach. The Jews had no metaphysics, no attempts at organized systems of thought; their philosophy consists of detached, practical reflections on life. The beginning of this species of composition is referred by the tradition to Solomon. Popular proverbs, embodying observation of simple facts of experience, doubtless existed at an early time; and there may have been wise men who uttered pithy, practical sayings as early as Solomon, or earlier. But the form of the books which have come down to us is late; their religious ideas, at least, are those of the legal period. The composition of such works implies a reflective spirit which belongs, in the course of the national development of thought, naturally after the prophetic period.

The book of Proverbs is no doubt the result of numerous collections made at different times. Much of the material in the middle portion of the book, consisting of maxims of experience in common life, may be old, but it has all been worked over under the influence of the late religious thought. Chapters i.-ix., by their broad, rounded style, and by the personification of Wisdom in chapter viii., belong to the latest period of the collections; and the hints of social and political conditions in the concluding chapters suggest the times of Greek control.

The social framework of Ecclesiastes is that of the city-civilization of the Greek period, complicated social relations, political instability, organized social-religious life. The author's negative and indifferentistic conception of life suggests an influence of the Greek Cynical philosophy which was firmly established on the north coast of Africa in the third century B. C. The way in which he combines a distinct theistic faith with a practical scepticism is not entirely satisfactory. One would suppose that his belief in the absolute divine control of things would enable him to look on life with something like cheerfulness and hope; but he sees nothing in the world worth the devotion of the soul; he has no enthusiasm; his highest effort is to enjoy what exists, and refrain from useless longings and hopes. All things, he says, come alike to all; time and chance happen to all; man knows not his time, and is taken like birds caught in a snare. When he does counsel energy and intensity in living, it is from the reflection that there is nothing beyond this life: "Whatever thy hand finds to do, do it with thy might; for there is no work, nor device, nor knowledge, nor wisdom, in Sheol, whither thou goest" (Eccl. ix. 10). Certain variations in the thought might suggest that the book is not a unit; the epilogue, xii. 9–14, is the work of a later hand, but in the body of the book the seeming discrepancies may be satisfactorily explained as the oscillations of thought of a Jew tinged with Greek sceptical philosophy, holding to his faith in God and to his veneration for righteousness and wisdom, but convinced of the emptiness of things, the futility of ambition, and the folly of enthusiasm. The result is that he holds himself aloof from the great world, looking on its feeble struggles and passions with pitying but not unfriendly eye, and reserving to himself a quiet enjoyment of the present, without disturbing thought of the future. The moral tone of the book is high, and its general effect is to give us a large view of life. It seems to have been written in Egypt about the year 200 B. C., and doubtless represented the opinions of a certain circle. It stands, however, outside the general Jewish development; the views expressed by its author can only have colored Jewish thought in a general way.

We find an equally pronounced but entirely different Greek influence in the Wisdom of Solomon, — orthodox Judaism lighted up by Platonic and Stoic philosophy, or Platonism and Stoicism interpreted by Jewish theology. In contrast with Ecclesiastes, the author has warm faith in God and in human life, conviction that all things are ordered by the Divine Providence, that God is the Saviour of all, that there remains for all men life beyond the grave, and in the present life the universal divine love: "Thou lovest all the things that are, and abhorrest nothing that thou hast made; for if thou hadst hated anything, thou wouldst not have made it; . . . thou sparest all because they are thine, O Lord, lover of souls" (Wisd. xi. 24–26). The gist of the book is the praise of wisdom, — divine wisdom, of course, — the insight into life which belongs to God and comes to man through communion with God. Its personification of Wisdom amounts almost to a hypostatic conception; and there are few passages in ancient philosophy more eloquent than those in which the author describes her being and functions. The use of the book is visible in the New Testament (vii. 22, cf. James iii. 17; vii. 26, cf. Heb. i. 2).

The Wisdom of the Son of Sirach is cast in a purely Jewish mould and stands in close relation with the middle part of the Old Testament book of Proverbs, with which it agrees in general in its theology. It seems to have been written in Palestine (or possibly in Egypt), in Hebrew, and to have been translated into Greek in Egypt about B. C. 132.[1] Much of its ethical material is found in the New Testament.

---

[1] The second Prologue gives the thirty-eighth year of Euergetes as the date of translation. The king meant is probably the second of the name, called Physcon, whose thirty-eighth year, reckoning from the time when he first ascended the throne, falls in 132.

5. In the romances and books of Wisdom we can trace the general moral-religious thought of the Jews in the first half of the Greek period. During the same period there had been slowly growing a literature which arose out of the needs of the temple-service, — religious hymns, giving expression to national feeling on various occasions, and constituting our present book of Psalms. The meagreness of the data makes it difficult to trace in detail the history of Hebrew lyrical poetry. There are one or two odes (Isa. xii., Hab. iii.) which may belong to the pre-exilian time, and the book of Job is placed by many critics in the Babylonian exile (though it is probably later). There are some of the Psalms also — as Ps. cxxxvii. — which seem to have been composed at that time. But the theology and the historical conditions of the great body of the songs of our Psalter indicate the Greek period as the time of their composition. In them the ritual is well established; the nation is a church; the wicked are mostly foreign oppressors; the righteous and meek are Israelites; prophecy no longer exists, but the nation is righteous as a whole. Such odes must have come into existence not only after the establishment of the full temple-ritual, but also after the politically annihilated nation had begun to feel the weight of the oppressor's arm. Some of the Psalms (xliv., lxxiv., lxxix., and others) belong to the Maccabean period; and while in many cases there are no certain signs of date, the probabilities are that the body of the Psalter came into existence after the year 350 B. C. The book is a most precious mine of religious thought; out of it the theology of the Greek period may be constructed with considerable fulness and certainty.

It will suffice to mention the Song of Songs as an isolated production of the Jewish literature of the period. All that can be certainly said of it is that it is a poem in praise of love. As it is totally devoid of religious feeling, it throws no light on the history of Jewish religious development. Its claim to our interest lies in its literary charm and in the indication it gives of the cultivation of non-religious literature among the Jews.

6. The preceding sketch has brought the history of the literature down to about the first part of the second century B. C. We come now to a group of works which, beginning about the middle of this century and going on two or three hundred years, embody a remarkable and significant phase of the Jewish national feeling. The apocalypse was a natural product of the times of Greek and Roman oppression, and of Maccabean triumph. It was born of the old prophetic hopes and the present needs; it was the interpretation which the hard reality forced on the glowing promises of the past. The prophets had predicted the glorious establishment of Israel in its own land, under its own rulers, and the triumph of the religion of Yahwe over all the nations of the earth. The prophetic spirit died out; no seers arose to kindle new hope by the free prophetic portraiture of the future on the basis of the present. The old prophetic liberty of thought had vanished; its inward and outward conditions no longer existed. Inwardly there had come hard and unelastic social-religious organization; outwardly the political conditions pressed on the people with relentless reality, — the Egyptian and Syrian Greek kingdoms and the Roman empire were hard facts, not to be dealt with as the old prophets had dealt with Edom, Damascus, Assyria, and Babylon. But the popular imagination necessarily turned to the future; the promised deliverance *must* speedily come. The feeling naturally arose that the best way to comfort and inspire the people in the present suffering was to paint the glorious future in glowing colors. No doubt it seemed to many that the set time had come; prophets had in many places de-clared that the final day of triumph was to be preceded by

a night of oppression, and surely there could be no sorrow greater than this sorrow of Israel in the hands of heathen enemies, its law, its religion, its life, scoffed at and trampled under foot.

The form which these consolatory writings assumed was a development of the old vision. To the pre-exilian prophets the divine revelation came mostly as a clear, intelligible word of rebuke or promise; occasionally there was a brief vision, as in Amos, Isaiah, Habakkuk. In Ezekiel we have a sudden expansion of the revealing picture, — he sees in a vision the whole religious-political constitution of the restored Israelitish State. In the first Zechariah this form of revelation occupies a still greater space; it is in this way that he presents all that he has to say of the future (when a present question is to be solved, chapter viii., he falls into straightforward discourse). The content of the prophetic visions is small, and limited to the immediate future. But when, under the Greek dominion, the Jews came into closer contact with great kingdoms, and became acquainted with the succession of empires, it was natural that the function of the vision should be enlarged; it came to present a philosophy of history, a sketch of the progress of the world-kingdoms under the government of the God of Israel in the interests of his people. Since the exile the history of the world had been wonderful: empire after empire had arisen only to fall before a stronger successor; it was well, so thought the Jew, to point out that this was only God's preparation for bringing on the appointed day of judgment and deliverance. The fashion arose of putting reviews of history into the mouths of seers. It was necessary that the assumed seer should live at the beginning of the period embraced in the vision; according to the starting-point, whether in the patriarchal time, or during the exodus, or in the exile, or later, Enoch or Moses or Daniel or Ezra or some other was selected as the organ of the revelation. This procedure was in accordance also with the taste of the times, which delighted to find authority for its own opinions in the person of some ancient sage or saint. The symbolic form of these writings often makes them obscure; but the author's date may frequently be determined from his historical allusions, and from the general fact that his description down to his own time is apt to be full and vivid, and after that to become meagre and vague.

The book of Daniel, the first in order of the apocalypses, traverses the period from the Babylonian kingdom of Nebuchadnezzar to about the death of Antiochus Epiphanes, B. C. 164. The seer is a Jewish prince, brought a captive to Babylon, educated in Chaldean astrological science, and elevated to posts of trust under Nebuchadnezzar and Darius; he is probably an old legendary figure (see Ezek. xiv. 14). In different visions he portrays the four world-kingdoms of Babylon, Media, Persia, and Greece, coming in the last to a detailed description of Antiochus. His chronology (which irreconcilably contradicts history) is based on the seventy years of Jeremiah (Jer. xxv. 12) which he converts into seventy year-weeks, four hundred and ninety years, for the period from Cyrus's decree of restoration to the deliverance; that is, practically to his own day (Dan. ix. 24, 25). The oppression is to end (xi. 45) with the death of Antiochus; the angel Michael, the guardian prince of Israel, will then intervene, and the wise and pure shall be blessed and the wicked punished. At this point the author, with noteworthy soberness, abruptly closes his description. The book is valuable for its picture of the religious life and thought of the time of Judas Maccabæus. It presents not an individual Messiah, but only a triumphant people (vii. 21–27); it teaches the resurrection of Israelites, — some to glory, some (the apostates) to contempt (xii. 2).

The book of Enoch was composed somewhat later than Daniel, to which it is greatly inferior in literary charm and religious impressiveness. It consists of several distinct parts, belonging to different periods. The original work, which has the form of a revelation to Enoch, describes the sin of the angels (Gen. vi.), their subsequent evil doings and punishment, the places of reward for the chosen and punishment for the wicked (with much astronomical lore), and finally the history of the world from the creation to the Messianic time. A long interpolation, consisting of three Parables, deals with the last judgment of righteous and wicked, which is conducted by the Messiah; in this section is inserted from another hand a revelation to Noah respecting the flood and the evil angels. The book is a rich storehouse of material in the subjects with which it has to do, and not a few of its angelological and eschatological ideas appear in the New Testament (Jude and the Revelation). Its fondness for superhuman machinery comes in part from its subject-matter, and is an evidence of the activity in this direction that prevailed in the second and following centuries, though how much of its contents belongs to the thought of the age, and how much is peculiar to the authors, it is hard to say. In the original portion the Messiah is a man (xc. 37), and appears after the chosen people have returned to the Lord; he is preceded by a great deliverer (xc. 9), who is to be identified either with Judas Maccabæus (B. C. 168–161) or with John Hyrcanus I. (B. C. 135–107). The Parables give a different representation: not only does the Messiah (called the Chosen One and the Son of Man) conduct the judgment and usher in the state of blessedness (xlv. 3, 4), but he is said to have been chosen before the world was created (xlviii. 6). Such conceptions, foreign to all other Jewish pre-Christian thought, suggest a Christian author or editor. The Parables draw largely from Ezekiel and Daniel.[1]

The work which has come down to us under the name of the Sibylline Oracles is a congeries of many fragments of various dates. In imitation of the heathen sibyls, it details the various parts of the history of the world for the purpose of introducing the glorious future of the chosen people. The pictures of this future vary little from those already described; at a given moment, when the oppression has become intolerable, God intervenes, destroys the enemies, and saves his people. In some cases, a personal Messiah is introduced. The more important pieces are found in the third book, vs. 97–210, which are probably to be assigned to the middle of the second century B. C.[2]

The book of Baruch is of uncertain date (hardly earlier, in its present form, than the second century B. C.) and of indefinite content, containing only the prediction that Jerusalem shall be restored. The thought is a reproduction of the older literature, the second part (chs. iii.–v.) following especially Job and Isaiah.

The Assumption of Moses is a prediction of the establishment of the kingdom of God; it was probably composed not far from the beginning of our era.

A more interesting work is the Psalter of Solomon, — a collection of eighteen psalms written apparently not long after the death of Pompey (B. C. 48), in a period of great depres-

---

[1] The book of Enoch was probably originally written in Hebrew or Aramaic, and thence translated into Greek; it now exists only in an Ethiopic translation made from the Greek; the best Ethiopic text is that of Dillmann, Leipzig, 1851. An excellent English translation (with introduction and notes) is that of G. H. Schodde, Andover, 1882. For the critical literature, see James Drummond, "The Jewish Messiah," London, 1877, Schodde's above-mentioned translation, and Schürer's "Hist. of the N. T. Times."

[2] See the editions of Friedlieb, Leipzig, 1852, and Alexandre, Paris, 1869.

sion (ii 30, 31). Modelled after the older psalms, it is full of cries for help, and beseeches God to raise up the righteous king who shall rule over Israel, crush wicked rulers, and purify Jerusalem from the heathen who are trampling it down to destruction. The author's view is clearly limited to the immediate future, and he seems to expect nothing more than the re-establishment of the old royal régime in righteousness and truth.

The book of Jubilees, which describes the primeval times by periods of fifty years, hardly deserves mention here except as an illustration of the delight which the Jews of the first century of our era took in expanding and commenting on the old history. The natural growth of embellishment is clearly seen when we compare the book of Jubilees with the text of Genesis and Exodus, on which it is based.

Second Esdras belongs probably toward the close of the first century of our era, and is of interest as testifying to the existence at that time of the expectation of the kingdom of God. In its present form it appears to have been, if not written by a Jewish Christian, at any rate retouched by a Christian hand.[1]

It will suffice to mention the Testaments of the Twelve Patriarchs and the Ascension of Isaiah, — works which belong in the beginning of the second century of our era, and are of small importance for the history of the genesis of our Christian ideas.

7. The works which go under the name of Maccabees furnish, along with the history, a number of details of the opinions of the times. First Maccabees covers the space

---

[1] The date is doubtful. See a good discussion of this point in Drummond's "Jewish Messiah." The writer (xii. 10–32) identifies his final world-period with Daniel's fourth kingdom (Dan. vii.), which, according to Josephus (x. 11, 7), was the Roman, and his twelve kings are most naturally explained as Roman emperors. A Christian coloring seems probable in the title "Son of God" applied to the Messiah (vii. 28, 29; xiii. 32, 37; xiv. 9).

B. C. 175–135; Second Maccabees B. C. 176–162; Third Maccabees B. C. 221–204; Fifth Maccabees extends from B. C. 176 to the beginning of our era; Fourth Maccabees is a philosophical tract on the Autocracy of Reason, founded on the story of the martyrdom of Eleazar and of the seven brothers and their mother (2 Mac. vi. vii.).

Two other writers remain to be mentioned. The works of Josephus contain a great mass of matter respecting the religious history and opinions of the Jews during the period beginning with the Maccabean struggle and ending with the destruction of Jerusalem by Titus, A. D. 70. It is hardly necessary to say that his statements on these points have to be received, certainly not with scepticism, but with critical examination.

The influence of Philo (first half of the first century of our era) on Christian thought was deep and lasting, though it at first affected a small circle of thinkers.

§ 2. The Canons.

1. During the development of the literature above described a parallel movement of great importance had been going on among the Jews. They selected certain books, which they believed to have been imparted by divine inspiration, collected them into a sacred canon, and invested them with absolute authority. The effect on Jewish thought was, as in all such cases, both limiting and inspiring: it established a fixed rule of life and offered a body of admirable writings for study; but it tended also to exclude all other literature and to enfeeble thought by the pressure of an absolute body of truth beyond which the mind could not permit itself to go. Embryonic canons have existed among other peoples, as the Greeks, Romans, and Chinese; Buddhism, Zoroastrianism, and Islam went further and established definite collections of sacred writings; but no people laid hold of the idea of

canonization with so much precision and carried it out with so much vigor and definiteness as the Jews. The process was a gradual one: those books were first chosen which satisfied the first and most pressing needs of the post-exilian Jews; and gradually, as literary and religious interest widened, other works were included according to the appeal which they made to the national religious consciousness. We have only meagre details of the principles according to which the selection of the canonical books was made. We may gather that the tests were both external and internal: a book to be chosen must come supported by some recognized high authority, prophetic or other; and at the same time it was necessary that its contents should commend themselves to the religious feeling of the best men. A book might be valued for its legal material, for its ethical exhortation, for its edifying emotion, for its historical information, or for its consoling view of the future. Doubtless over many books there were long discussions; such discussions, in the case of Ecclesiastes and the Song of Songs, and one or two other books, the Talmud speaks of as having been carried on up to the end of the first century of our era.

2. The root of the idea of a canon goes back, no doubt, to very early times. Its basis is the conviction that Yahwe announced his will directly to Israel through chosen men, prophets, and priests. The *Tora* was originally the divine word which came to the prophets respecting the moral, religious, and political condition of the nation (Isa. viii. 16 . As society became better organized, the need was more strongly felt for a definite system of regulations of life No distinction was made between the ethical, religious, and political codes; the nation was conceived of as a unity under the guidance of the national deity, whose will was the norm of conduct in all phases of activity. For the king on the throne, the priest at the shrine, and the common man in

every-day life there could be but one rule, namely, to do those things, ethical and ritual, which the God of Israel had declared to be well-pleasing in his sight. At the end of the seventh century came a great outburst of nationalism, one result of which was the compilation of the Deuteronomic code, — a collection of laws (developed out of earlier material) intended to be a complete manual of life. The code was naturally ascribed to Moses as its author. He was the greatest name in the tradition of the olden time, — he had led the people from Egypt to Canaan; he had been at once captain, judge, and priest. The line of legal traditions went back to him, and the fact that there had been constant accretions was forgotten or neglected; according to the historical ideas of the time, it was he who should have announced the organic law of the nation. Such a law in the nature of the case would tend to become finally regulative; the Deuteronomic code was the inception of the canon. Yet that the canonical idea was not then completely established is shown by the freedom with which the prophet Ezekiel (Ezek. xl.–xlviii) deals with the material, advancing beyond Deuteronomy, modifying its prescriptions, and suggesting or announcing new regulations as if he were quite unconscious that there existed a code of final authority. The beginning had been made, but the end was not reached till the time of Ezra and Nehemiah. Then the little church-nation in Babylonia and Palestine, isolated and helpless, feeling more definitely that its national life was bound up with a divinely given code, accepted the fuller Levitical legislation of the time as God's final word to the people. The feeling of need and the law which responded to it had grown up together; and when Ezra and Nehemiah announced to the congregation the new and complete set of regulations, there was no question of forcing an unacceptable law on a reluctant people, — the proposed code seemed natural and necessary, and was accepted with joyful acclamation. It also was of course ascribed to Moses; doubtless to the masses of that time the idea of a break in the continuity of tradition never occurred. Issuing from the mouth of God, having its root in the beginnings of the national life, the *Tora*, based on and sustained by everything that was most sacred in human thought, was an eternal rule on which no profane hand could be laid with impunity. From this time on, the possession of this divinely given code was the source of perpetual joy and exultation to the Jews, who believed that they were thereby forever separated from, and lifted above, all the other nations of the earth.

3. The canonical idea, once introduced, was capable of extension. During the remainder of the Persian period, and especially afterward under the Greek rule, the national consciousness of separateness and sanctity steadily grew, and all that bore on the history and development of the people became constantly more interesting. There were extant writings which narrated the fortunes of the nation from the settlement in Canaan down to the exile, setting forth how the people had prospered in proportion as they had been obedient to Yahwe, and how he had sent his prophets to instruct them and to guide them; and there had also been preserved the discourses of certain of these prophets, in which Israel was rebuked for its sins and threatened with punishment if it did not repent, but also promised a glorious future if it would turn to its God with wholeness of heart. In process of time canonical sanctity came to attach to some of these writings.[1] We have no information as to the grounds which controlled the selection, but we may be reasonably sure that the main consideration was their true national character; those books were chosen

---

[1] The second canon contains Joshua, Judges, Samuel, Kings, and the prophets (including Jonah and excluding Daniel).

for canonization which depicted the national life in accordance with the ethical-religious point of view of the fourth and third centuries B. C.; the prophets who survived were those whose thought was justified by the result. The standard of election was high, in accordance with the lofty view held of the ethical-religious enlightenment, obligation, and mission of the nation; possibly literary considerations also entered. In regard to such men as Amos, Hosea, Isaiah, Micah, Zephaniah, Habakkuk, Jeremiah, Ezekiel, the exilian Isaiah and the post-exilian Haggai, Zechariah I., Zechariah II., and Joel, there could be no ground of hesitation, — their general thought was in accord with the true ethical-religious instinct of the nation. Nahum and Obadiah must have commended themselves purely by their nationalism, since they contain no real ethical or religious thought; the little book of Jonah, not properly prophecy at all, though it embodies a noble religious conception, probably owed its place in the new collection to its religious excellence and its supposed connection with the old prophet of that name in the time of Jeroboam II.

This body of writings was gradually brought into shape during the two centuries that followed the canonization of the Law. The conditions were not entirely favorable to the preservation of the original prophetic words. Manuscripts were copied and recopied by scribes who not only sometimes made errors in letters and words, but permitted themselves to introduce new material into the text, or to combine in one manuscript, without mark of division, writings composed by different men; instances of these sorts of procedure are found especially in Micah and Jeremiah, and the groups of prophecies which go under the name of Isaiah and Zechariah. Scribes and collectors were often, perhaps generally, ignorant of the dates of the writings with which they had to do; they seem, indeed, to have attached little importance to author or time, being more concerned with the thought and its bearing on the edification of the nation.

We have no external testimony as to the time when the prophetic writings were gathered into a canon, except the obscure statement in 2 Mac. ii. 13 (a book of small authority), where it is said that Nehemiah founded a library and gathered together the books concerning the kings perhaps our Judges, Samuel, and Kings), and the prophets and the things of David (possibly an historical book or some collection of psalms), and the epistles of the kings concerning the holy gifts (the letters of Persian monarchs). This statement is valuable only as proving the existence of a tradition respecting the collection of the prophetical books; one might surmise from it that there were various attempts to gather these books before the collection assumed the form of our second canon. From the second prologue to Ecclesiasticus it may be inferred that this canon was in existence before the year 200 B. C., and we may assign it the approximate date of 250.

4. Meantime, writings of a different order were coming into existence, — ethical-religious discussions, proverbs, histories, stories, temple-songs, and apocalypses. As these were not composed by prophetic men, and were not immediately connected with the organic law of the nation, they were relatively slow in acquiring authority. A certain literary training was necessary, and a certain broadening of the national religious consciousness, in order that speculative and emotional works which bore a distinct impress of the personality of the writers should be accepted as part of God's revelation to the nation. It is probable, however, that the national feeling here also entered largely into the decision of the question. The book of Job might be looked on as describing not only the trials of a pious soul, but also the sufferings of the nation; Chronicles, Ezra, Nehemiah, and Esther portrayed

various aspects of the national fortunes, and Ruth chronicled the beginnings of the royal house of Judah ; Lamentations and Psalms expressed the national feeling and uttered the national prayer in various seasons of joy or grief ; Proverbs gave rules of life which might be regarded as a supplement to the law ; Daniel offered much-needed consolation in the shape of a glowing picture of glorious triumph. In respect to Ecclesiastes and the Song of Songs there might be doubt; neither of them is national ; the first is gravely and reservedly sceptical and indifferent, and the second is secular and sensuous. In fact, the opinion as to these books was not unanimous ; up to the end of the first century of our era the question was discussed whether they were edifying and entitled to a place in the canon. The favorable opinion finally arrived at probably resulted from the allegorizing of the Song into a history of Israel, and from an appendix to Ecclesiastes which gave it an air of orthodoxy. Difficulties arose also with respect to other books.[1]

Such was the course of thought in Palestine. It is evident that the choice of books for the third canon was controlled by a somewhat stringent ethical-religious and perhaps literary feeling. But other considerations, sometimes purely local, probably entered into the decision of the question. In Egypt the conditions were different. The Greek translation made in Alexandria in the third and second centuries includes in the third canon not only the books above mentioned, but a number of others : additions to Ezra, Daniel, and Esther ; the Prayer of Manasseh, Baruch, and the Epistle of Jeremiah ; Judith and Tobit ; the Wisdom of Solomon, and the Wisdom of Jesus the son of Sirach ; and the first and second books of Maccabees. The reasons for the acceptance of these works into the Alexandrian canon

---

[1] The books whose canonical character was called in question were Ezekiel, Proverbs, Esther, Ecclesiastes, and the Song of Songs.

are obvious: some of them are merely expansions or theocratic interpretations of recognized canonical books; some are imitations of the prophets; some depict the life of the people, national or individual, as guided by the God of Israel; some give maxims for the direction of life. That these works were not accepted by the Palestinian Jews as canonical was probably due to their stricter standard; the legal-ecclesiastical organization in Palestine was far more definite and effective than that in Egypt, and excluded, on literary and auctorial grounds, much that might commend itself to the freer and looser judgment of the Alexandrians. And it may be added that while the term "canonical" (more precisely "deutero-canonical") may properly be applied to these books (as we may infer from the consideration accorded them by the Christian world), we must suppose that it was understood in general in a looser way in Egypt than in Palestine. The Alexandrian collection was probably closed in the first century before the beginning of our era.[1]

The remaining books, though they enjoyed considerable respect and authority, were never canonized. Some of them, as the Jubilees, the Apocalypse of Baruch, Second Esdras, the Ascension of Isaiah, and the Testimony of the Twelve Patriarchs, were composed too late, and were lacking in definiteness of thought and in literary excellence; of those which fall earlier, the Assumption of Moses and the Psalms of Solomon are destitute of impressive or inspiring qualities, and the Sibylline Oracles, though intensely national in feeling, were perhaps too un-Jewish in form to satisfy the demands of the time. Why the book of Enoch was rejected

---

[1] Second Maccabees, which seems to be the latest book in the collection, closes its narrative with the fall of Nicanor, B. C. 161, and the first prefatory letter bears the date (i. 9) 188 of the Seleucidan era, that is, B. C. 124. As the work is an abridgment of another history (ii. 23), we may allow fifty or seventy-five years for the interval between its appearance and the events it describes.

is not clear. It is quoted in one New Testament book (Jude), abundantly used in another (the Revelation), and is modelled in part after Daniel. Perhaps it was felt that the book really added nothing to the existing apocalyptic material; perhaps its loose and exuberant demonology and astronomy made it unacceptable; and the interpolations show that it circulated for some time uncontrolled by the learned colleges of Palestine.

All these works, canonical and uncanonical, are signs of the times, and must be taken into account in the description of the thought of the period. Perhaps the greater authority in this respect is to be accorded in general to the canonical books on the ground that they received wider and completer recognition. Yet this distinction cannot be absolutely maintained, since other than purely religious or theological reasons helped to determine the fact of canonization, and since it appears that some of the uncanonical books were very generally and highly esteemed.

CHAPTER II.

THE DOCTRINE OF GOD.

AFTER this brief survey of the literature we may enter on the special study of the development of the Jewish religious thought, the conditions that determined it, the phases it assumed, and the forms it presented at the moment when Christianity made its appearance.

As we have seen, the decisive step in the construction of the theistic doctrine had already been taken when the complete Levitical law was introduced in the fifth century B. C. Monotheism was practically established, and the more spiritual elaboration of the theistic conception was only a matter of time. Yet the oneness of the divine person and rule was not held in perfect purity. There were remnants of idolatry among the people down to a comparatively late period; in the coming day of regeneration, says Zechariah xiii. 2 , the names of the idols shall be cut off out of the land. This, however, was apparently only a feeble survival of the old practice; it soon passed away, coerced by the ruling monotheistic spirit, and after the middle of the second century B. C., we hear no more of it.[1] Perhaps the same thing is true of the belief in the existence of heathen deities. In at least

[1] See the curious statement in 2 Mac. xii. 40, that after the defeat of Gorgias there were found on all the slain Jews things consecrated to idols, and the author adds that this is the reason why they were slain. But this devotion to idols, whatever it may mean, was apparently quite isolated. And it is said further that Judas, mindful of the resurrection, sent a sin-offering to Jerusalem and had prayers offered for the dead. There is no other mention of such defection from Israelitish worship except under the political and social pressure brought to bear by Antiochus Epiphanes.

two of the psalms which seem to be late, a part of the government of the world is ascribed to the gods of the nations (Ps. lviii. 2; lxxxii.), and this is of course a curtailment of the power of the one God. So in the book of Daniel, the functions ascribed to the guardian angels of the various nations cannot be quite harmonized with the absolute rule of the God of Israel. The same thing must be said of the power with which Satan was credited. Not only does he lead David astray (1 Chron. xxi. 1) and induce God to heap sufferings on Job, but he is represented (Wisdom of Solomon ii. 24) as having brought death into the world. But the Jews, like other men, were capable of happy logical inconsistency; in spite of heathen deities, guardian angels, and powerful demons, they believed substantially in the aloneness of God. He was held to permit the existence and suffer the activity of subordinate supernatural beings, yet always to stand apart and control them for his own purposes. This is also the theistic conception of the New Testament, where God is clearly supreme, while yet very great power is ascribed to Satan and the demons.

This idea made a great gulf between the Jews and their neighbors, and by means of this sundering, helped to develop nationalism and the whole national life. It imparted to the consciousness of the people a sense of superiority which produced both religious vigor and religious pride. On the national thought monotheism produced its natural effect, — it gave unity to the conception of the government of the world, though it was held in a narrow way so as to exclude all peoples but the Jews from the sympathy and guidance of the deity. We may now proceed to state the elements of the theistic conception a little more in detail.

1. The governmental side of the idea of God was firmly established from a comparatively early period; there is little

difference between Paul's conception of the divine control of things and Jeremiah's. In the literature from Ezra down God is conceived of as practically omnipresent, omniscient, and omnipotent. This doctrine is not held in a speculative or metaphysical way; it was simply believed that God was capable of doing whatever was to be done. He controls all individuals and nations: the Assyrians in Judith, the Greeks in Maccabees, all the races of mankind in Enoch and the Sibyl, all men, good and bad, in the books of Wisdom and the Psalms. This conception is held almost unconsciously throughout the whole period which ends with the close of the first century of our era. There is no attempt at demonstration; there is no sign of doubt; and this shows that the conception had become part of the religious furniture of the time.

There was of course involved in this the general idea of God's providential care for men. The conception of a universal, divine providence in the form which it is now held is not found in the earlier books of the Old Testament. In them it is only for Israel that God really cares; the rest of the world is treated as a mere appendage to the chosen people, to be dealt with solely in its interest. But traces of a broader view are perceptible, for example, in Ps. civ. and cvii., and in Wisdom of Solomon xiv. 3: "Thy providence governs it [a ship at sea]; . . . thou canst save from all danger;" still there is little or no warmth in the picture of God's care for men. In the book of Ecclesiastes, he is sometimes represented as half indifferent to human affairs; he controls, but he feels small interest: "I have seen the labor that God has imposed on the sons of men; . . . man cannot find out God's work from beginning to end; . . . God proves men that they may see that they are beasts; . . . God is in heaven and thou upon earth, therefore let thy words be few; . . . when thou vowest a vow to God defer not to pay it, for he has no pleasure in fools. . . . God gives a man riches and honor, but not the power to enjoy it." But this is the thought of a half-Hellenized Jew of Egypt, who had probably only a small circle of followers. Of theoretical atheism there is no trace; practical doubt of the advantage of serving God is referred to in Mal. iii. 14, Ps. x. 14, 36, — an ethical-religious, not a speculative-theological view. The apparently most general pre-Christian affirmation of divine providence is found in Wisdom xvi. 7, where God is called the Saviour of all (as in 1 Tim. iv. 10); yet from the connection, where the author is speaking of God's care of Israel, it is doubtful whether the phrase can be taken in a universal way.

In the later literature, God's close connection with inanimate and brute nature is brought out in a marked manner; see Pss. xix., xxix., lxv., xciii., xcvi., cii., civ., cxlviii. He watches over and controls the sustenance and life of all plants and animals, and directs immediately all natural phenomena. There is a certain warmth of coloring in the representation of God's relation to nature: " Thou makest the outgoings of the morning and evening to rejoice; . . . thou dost visit the land, making it soft with showers; . . . the hills are girt with joy; . . . the valleys shout for joy and sing (Ps. lxv.); . . . he sends springs into the valleys which give drink to every beast of the field; . . . among the branches sing the birds of the heaven; . . . he causes grass to grow for the cattle, and wine that it may make glad the heart of man; . . . the young lions roar after their prey and seek their food from God; . . . all wait on thee that their food may be given them in due season " (Ps. civ.). It is in the same tone that Jesus speaks of birds and flowers (Matt. vi.), in contrast with the way in which Paul rejects the idea that God takes care for cattle (1 Cor. ix. 9). This ascription of tenderness to the divine feeling for nature was the result of belief in the universal divine providence, unchecked by narrow national feeling.

The Jews (clinging to the old tribal feeling) found it hard to conceive of the God of Israel as thinking kindly of Israel's enemies; but there was no such feeling of hostility toward beasts and birds, mountains and seas, trees and flowers. Doubtless we have here an advance along the two lines, — the unitary conception of the universe and the broadening of ethical feeling in the direction of kindness and love; the supreme God must embrace the world in that sentiment of love which more and more approved itself as an ethical ideal, — the only disturbing element in the Jewish conception being that all other men existed only for the sake of Israel.

This narrowing conception of God's relation to Israel, inherited from the prophets and ingrained in the national constitution, clung pertinaciously to the Jews throughout this period and in all their succeeding history; it is an idea of which they have rarely rid themselves. Even Paul could not shake it off. In spite of his grand theorem (in which he doubtless heartily believed) that the true Israel was characterized not by bodily descent from Abraham, but by ethical-religious faith in God, he returns with natural patriotic illogicalness to the position (Rom. x. xi.) that the promises are to the national Israel; his higher religious instinct leads him to one interpretation of the Old Testament, his patriotic feeling to another. It is only in the Gospels that the highest point of view is attained.

The whole conception of God in the later Jewish literature assumes his justice. This idea was held in a practical, general, and imperfect form. The epithets "just" and "righteous" are freely applied to the divine being, and the doctrine is formulated in Gen. xviii. 25, "Shall not the Judge of all the earth do right?" This quality was assumed to be part of the divine perfectness, but its content is not carefully examined or definitely fixed; or, to speak more accurately, its content was determined by the ethical ideas of the age.

The wicked and the enemies of Israel (terms which are often synonymous) are hardly thought of as having rights. A careful estimate of each human being, with precise apportionment of reward and punishment according to his merits and demerits, entered only in small degree into the mode of thought of the time. Yet, though the ethical details were not definitely fixed, the idea existed. The important point is that the conception of the deity was truly ethical; the devout man could not think that God would ever violate the laws of justice; the fuller elaboration of the content of justice had to be left to the better developed ethical conceptions of succeeding times. Substantially the same representation is found in the New Testament, — the divine justice is taken for granted without being formally defined. The Old Testament division of men into the two classes of "righteous" and "wicked" is retained. The doctrine is summed up by Paul in Rom. ii. 6–11: God, with whom is no respect of persons, renders to every man according to his works. The apostle seems in this discussion to take the broadest ethical point of view, — Jews and Gentiles alike, he says, shall be judged, not by their historical relation to the Jewish law, but by their conformity to right-doing; elsewhere, however (Rom. v. viii.), he makes right-doing dependent on faith in Jesus Christ, and practically divides the world into Christians and non-Christians, the first being necessarily favored and the second necessarily condemned by the divine justice. In this conception, great prominence is given to the ethical element, — the life of the believer, says Paul, must and will be holy; but on the other hand, there is a confusion of the ethical and theological factors of life, and the attitude of the just God toward men is made to depend practically on their acceptance or non-acceptance of the historical fact of the Messiahship of Jesus of Nazareth. In the New Testament Apocalypse the question is treated more brusquely: all men who do not belong to the Church of Christ are regarded as enemies of God to be mercilessly trampled out of existence. The Fourth Gospel conceives of human life more philosophically and ideally as a conflict between light and darkness; but the source of light is the historical person of the Christ, and he makes the line of demarcation between the two classes of men: "This is the judgment, that the light is come into the world, and men loved the darkness rather than the light, for their works were evil" (John iii. 19). The discourses of Jesus in the Synoptics give the purely ethical conception of the divine justice; that is, if we assume the Sermon on the Mount to represent his mature idea. There are passages in which God's judgment of men seems to be represented as determined by theological dogma (Matt. xii. 31), or a peculiar view of the historical kingdom of God (Matt. xvi. 27; xix. 28; Mark x. 23–31), or where the old division of the world into Jews and Gentiles is maintained (Matt. xv. 24. Without undertaking to decide on the genuineness or chronological order of all these passages, it is sufficient to observe that the pure ethical conception is expressed in the Sermon on the Mount: the divine justice in estimating men takes into account only their conformity to the law of right.

2. The conception of God as a being of love was of course later than that which emphasized his governmental attributes; it was possible only at a stage of social development when it was felt that love to man is one of the highest qualities of the human soul. The old Israelitish idea of the divine love was, so far as we can gather from the literature, a purely national one. Yahwe was the father (Hos. xi. 1) or the husband (Jer. ii. 1; iii. 4; Isa. lxii. 5) of Israel. In the later psalms more individual relation is expressed, — Yahwe is said to pity them that fear him as a father pities

his children (Ps. ciii. 13). Gradually the paternal relation, as expressing most completely the combination of guidance and tenderness, came to be employed as the representative of God's relation to man : " He is our father forever " (Tob. xiii. 4); the righteous man is "numbered among the sons of God " (Wisd. v. 5); "that thy sons, O Lord, whom thou lovest might learn that . . . it is thy word which preserves them that put their trust in thee " (Wisd. xvi. 26); " O Lord, father and ruler of my life " (Ecclus. xxiii. 1). The conception of God's fatherly relation to individuals existed therefore a couple of hundred years before the beginning of our era, and we may suppose that it gathered force and fulness as the increasing purity and elevation of ethical ideas was transferred to the divine character. Still, it does not seem to have been a favorite conception; the Jewish national feeling was strong enough to depress it. It was probably held by a select circle of thinkers, but it was kept out of general view by the circumstances of the time, the political excitements, and the religious-ethical tendencies thence resulting. In the Sermon on the Mount, the conception of God as universal father is stated with perfect distinctness and fulness. God's fatherly care is represented as extending equally over the just and the unjust; he feels for men in all conditions of life and phases of experience the sympathy of a tender father. Men may go to him with the assurance that he comprehends and loves them; and he, so far from standing apart and separate from human life, is the model of human action; his perfectness is the goal toward which men must strive; and the completion of human character and life is the attainment of perfect harmony between man and God. This highest conception of the relation of the personal God to men Jesus distinctly formulated as a practical element in human life. How far it entered into the current Jewish thought of the time when he began his public career we cannot say. The religious literature of that period is jejune and uninspiring, mostly occupied with unspiritual national questions; but on the other hand, the ethical thought, as is remarked above, had attained considerable purity.

We must also ask how far the Jewish thought at this time had been influenced by Greek conceptions. That Paul, some years later (Acts xvii. 28: "We are his offspring", should quote the Cilician Stoic poet Aratus, seems natural from the apostle's surroundings; it may appear more doubtful whether the Galilean community in which Jesus grew up could be acquainted with the thought of a Greek who spent the greater part of his life at the court of Macedon in the third century B. C. It is not probable that Aratus was known in Galilee; but doubtless he did not stand alone in the affirmation of the fatherhood of God. The Stoic Cleanthes had expressed the same conception about the same time; it is hardly doubtful that it was adopted by many followers of the Stoic philosophy, adherents of which we may suppose were found among the Greeks and Romans who lived in Palestine during the two centuries preceding the beginning of our era. Such an idea, once announced, would naturally harmonize with Jewish thought and find acceptance in the more deeply spiritual circles of Palestinian Jews. Galilee was not cut off from the intellectual life of the land; in its numerous cities there were to be found educated men of all the nationalities then represented in Palestine; and the intercourse with Jerusalem was easy and large enough to allow the Galileans to appropriate the best thought of the capital. A profound thinker, master of the religious ideas of his own people, keenly sensitive to all religious impressions, would inevitably recognize what was lofty in the current ideas of his surroundings. There are hints in the Gospels that Jesus came into contact not only with the Jewish schoolmen, but also with educated Greeks and Romans (Matt. viii. 5 ff.; John xii. 20). The influence of Hellenists, of proselytes, and of the Alexandrian Jewish thought, must also be considered; every year there came to Palestine from all parts of the Roman Empire men who brought with them a breath from the outer world, and presumably left their traces in the religious ideas which they expressed. We have no direct information as to how far this was the case. But Galilee must have been sharply isolated if it remained unaffected by the lines of religious thought then existing in the world. Taking into account all the circumstances, it seems probable that the idea of the fatherhood of God was, in the beginning of the first century of our era, not unfamiliar to advanced religious circles. It had been slowly developing by independent ways among Jews and Gentiles; the former reached it through the conception of the nation as the son of God, the latter through the unitary view of the world, and the conception of God as the ethical ideal. But however widely it may have been recognized in religiously cultivated circles, it had not become the possession of the world. It was the profound spiritual instinct of Jesus which led him to make it the central point of his theistic teaching. He discerned its dominant relation to other sides of the conception of God; he infused into it the warmth and coloring of human feeling and the practicalness of every-day life, and therefore he is to be regarded in a true sense as its author.

3. While the conception of God as governor and father was thus taking shape, there was a parallel development of the idea of his personal spiritual relation to the individual man. This is expressed abundantly in the later lyrical literature, the Psalms, and the Wisdom books: God bestows on his servant a clean heart (Ps. li. 10); delivers him from sin (Ps. xxxix. 8, 11; li. 1, 2); sets him apart for himself

(Ps. iv. 2); watches over him (Ps. xxxiv. 20; xl. 11); teaches him his ways (Ps. xxv. 4); chastens him (Ps. vi. 1; xxxviii. 1); is his salvation (Ps. xxvii. 1; xxxv. 3); manifests to him loving-kindness and mercy (Ps. lxix. 16; ciii. 12–14; cviii. 4; cxi. 4; cxii. 4; cxvi. 5; cxxxix. 17; cxlv. 8, 9; Wisd. i. 2; xv. 1; Jud. ix. 11). The righteous man on his part feels joy in the presence of God (Ps. xvi. 11). The relation of the divine being to the wicked is equally personal (Ps. l. 16–21; lxxiii. 18–20). In the same direction is the saying attributed to the first great Rabbinical teacher, Antigonus of Socho: "Be not like servants who wait on the master in the hope of receiving reward." This was the natural growth of the feeling of human individuality. In the earlier Old Testament literature the individual exists wholly or mainly as a member of the nation, and the divine procedures are almost exclusively national. A distincter individual tone appears in the book of Nehemiah, and with continually increasing prominence, until in the New Testament we find each individual man expected to recognize his personal relations with God.

There was a corresponding advance in the conception of God as pure spirit, the abandonment of the old anthropomorphic representations of his nature and activity. In a great part of the Old Testament he is bound by conditions of time and space; he is attached in an especial manner to the Jerusalem temple or some other shrine, and his favor is gained by definite modes of sacrifice. The Babylonian exile no doubt greatly helped to throw off this local conception by forcing the Jews to adopt a worship which was independent of the temple. The general religious growth led to the establishment of synagogues about the beginning of the second century B. C.; here was the minimum of form; the sacerdotal element was excluded; the essence of the worship was the individual appropriation of the divine word. The temple furnished the framework of the traditional, collective, national divine service; but for his own edification, day by day, the pious man looked to the synagogal worship, where the visible machinery was of the slightest, and he was brought face to face with God. Reverence for the temple continued; but the sentiment of ethical-religious independence had established itself at the beginning of our era. The Law had become a rival of the temple. The great Rabbinical teachers exerted an influence second to none in the land; the conception of the national life was no longer chiefly that of devotion to the temple ritual, but rather that of conformity to divine law.

No doubt the progress in this line of thought was gradual, — the purer view was for a long time tainted with the old local conception; in fact, the mass of men have never got rid of the lower earthly way of regarding God. Nationalism clung to the Jews almost like the essence of their religious life. The earliest Christians — Jews who accepted Jesus of Nazareth as their Messiah — shared this nationalism (Acts i.–v.), and appear not to have separated the divine being perfectly from the old traditional limitations of time and space. The entrance of the Gentiles into the Church necessarily brought about a change in this regard; Palestine and the Jerusalem temple lost their peculiar sanctity; Christian worship was performed without respect to outward conditions, and the feeling came into existence that the supreme God entered immediately into communion with the heart of man. This is the spirit of the Sermon on the Mount and of the New Testament epistles, and is formulated in John iv. 24: "God is a spirit, and they that worship him must worship him in spirit and in truth." This idea may be found in substance in Stoic writings, but in connection with a theistic conception not definite and personal enough to commend itself to the mass of men. Stoicism reached this view by philosophical reflection, Christianity by the influence of social-religious conditions on the Jewish national thought. The national Judaism found it next to impossible to discard national localism; Christianity, starting from the national Judaism, found itself forced by the influx of other nationalities to abandon the merely national point of view and to regard divine worship and the divine presence as divorced from human limitations. This divorcement was best expressed, in the language of the time, by the declaration that God was a spirit, — a designation which ascribed to him the sum-total of the highest side of existence. The idea, once announced, became a possession for mankind destined to be fruitful of best results. It has not always retained its purity, but it has never completely faded from men's minds; and it is to early Christianity that we owe its definite formulation and its establishment as an element of human life.

4. We come now to follow in the pre-Christian Jewish thought the tendencies toward the establishment of hypostatic differences in the divine nature. In all religions the complexity of the phenomena of the world and of life has led to the differentiation of the supernatural power into a variety of persons or agencies, — the creation of a more or less distinct and developed Pantheon. Such was the natural conception reached in polytheistic societies.[1] But where polytheism had been discarded and a substantially unitary view of the supernatural power adopted, this tendency toward differentiation of function could show itself only in

[1] In the Semitic religions the feebleness of differentiation makes many of the deities appear as undefined hypostases of the Supreme Power. It is doubtful, however, whether we are to attach any such meaning to the Phœnician titles "name of Baal" (given to Ashtoreth in the inscription of Eshmunazar) and "face of Baal" (an epithet of Tanit frequent in the Carthage inscriptions). They seem to signify some sort of identification or connection of these goddesses with Baal, but their precise force is not clear.

a more or less complete personification of the parts and functions of the divine being.

Add to this the natural disposition to introduce a mediating power between the deity and the world. In polytheistic systems certain subordinate deities subserved this end, and the Jews gained the same result in part by the ministration of angels. But as the supreme God became grander and farther removed from visible things, there remained the feeling that an intermediate power was necessary to account for his relations with the universe, to explain its creation and maintenance. Greek philosophical systems felt the same necessity, and whether theistic or pantheistic, constantly strove to bring the processes of cosmal production nearer to man.

The later Judaism absolutely excluded polytheism from its own conception of God, but nevertheless recognized this necessity of differentiating his functions, and bringing him into closer contact with man's life.

We have first to notice in the Old Testament certain expressions which may be considered to indicate an hypostatizing tendency, but never develop into anything definite. The face or presence of God is a natural representation of his power and being, and in the Old Testament is embodied in the form of an angel (Ex. xxxiii. 14; Isa. lxiii. 9); but this angel, though invested with divine authority, is regarded as a subordinate being distinct from God. The conception did not become very prominent in the Old Testament, and did not find a place in Christian thought.[1] The same thing may

---

[1] It attained greater prominence in the Targums and the Talmud under the name of the Shekina, the glorious divine presence. In the earlier Targumic literature it does not denote an activity (see, for example, Targ. of Jonathan, Hab. iii. 4), and may be considered to be throughout impersonal. In the Talmud it stands sometimes more definitely for God, but this is the free, poetical representation of the schools, and can hardly be regarded as a theological dogma. Here, as elsewhere, the movement toward an hypostasis did not assume definite shape in pure Jewish thought.

be said of the expression "the name," which is so generally employed in the Old Testament as equivalent to the sum-total of the divine attributes or to the divine essence and glory. The later Jewish thought made the "Name" a synonym of God, a hint of which view is found in Lev. xxiv. 11. The angel who is charged with the task of guiding Israel from Sinai to Canaan (Ex. xxiii. 21) is the bearer of the divine name and authority; but he appears nowhere else in the Old Testament, and was not adopted in succeeding theological systems. As little can we ascribe a hypostatic character to the angel of Yahwe, who in so many places seems to speak and act as if he were God (Gen. xvi. 7, 13; xxxii. 24, 30; Judg. xiii. 13, 18; Zech. iii. 1, 2); the name "angel" distinguishes this being from God, and his apparent separateness from other angels was not maintained in Jewish thought. The Old Testament angel is a development out of the Elohim-beings of the polytheistic period; inferior divinities, put into a distinctly subordinate position under the influence of monotheism, became messengers of God. It is not surprising that in some instances the messenger retained a part of the old polytheistic coloring and acted as if he were an independent deity.[1]

These three representations may be regarded as cases of arrested growth; they were efforts at differentiation which did not commend themselves to the general feeling, mainly because they were rendered unnecessary by other more fortunate attempts. We may examine a little more fully the

---

[1] It is only necessary to mention the Metatron of the Rabbinical literature, apparently an exaggeration of the biblical "angel of Yahwe." He stands nearest to God's presence and will, is his supreme agent and interpreter, sometimes almost his other self, yet never ceases to be a creature, absolutely dependent, like other creatures, on the Creator. He may be regarded as a scholastic effort to establish an intermediary between God and the world; but the conception did not definitely affect Jewish theology, and came too late to influence the doctrine of Christianity. See Weber, "System der palästinischen Theologie," p. 172.

expressions, "spirit," "wisdom," and "word," which made a much deeper impression on Jewish and Christian thought.

In the Old Testament the term "spirit" is employed, often in a vague and general way, to set forth the seat of the inward divine energy. It is a perfectly simple anthropomorphic conception : as in man the spirit was the place and source of life, thought, courage, energy, so these same qualities in the essence of God were ascribed to the divine spirit. It was this that entered especially into relation with the soul of man ; bodily affairs, such as the guidance of a nation or an individual, the infliction of a plague, or the overthrow of an army, were committed to angels, while the infusion of courage into the breast of a hero, or of the word of truth into the mind of a prophet, was the work of the divine spirit.[1] It was natural that the spirit should tend to stand forth as an independent power ; but in the Old Testament it never attains the form of a distinct personality, — it is always explicable as the simple representation of the divine influence. In the pre-Christian Jewish literature outside of the Old Testament, there is an advance in the direction of personality. In the Wisdom of Solomon (i. 7), it is said that the spirit of the Lord fills the world, and is in all things (xii. 1), and it is substantially identified with wisdom. Philo thinks of the divine spirit as the image of God (i. 207),[2] and as the indivisible source of understanding and knowledge (i. 255, 256). The precise force of these expressions will appear more clearly when we come to speak of Philo's doctrine of the Logos ; but it seems evident that

---

[1] In the earlier literature these effects are produced by a spirit (Hebrew, *ruach*) sent from Yahwe (Judg. xiv. 6 ; 1 Sam. xvi. 13, 14 ; xix. 20), and it is sometimes hard to decide whether the term means such a spiritual agent or the inward being of God. The latter sense it seems to have in some exilian and post-exilian passages, as Isa. xxxii. 16 ; xlviii. 16 ; Job xxvi. 13 ; Ps. li. 12 (14) ; civ. 30 ; Dan. iv. 8.

[2] The references to Philo follow Mangey's edition.

he is inclined to treat it as something more than a mere name for divine power.[1]

This is about the stage at which we find the expression in the earliest New Testament writings. For Paul the spirit is more than mere divine energy, yet not quite a definite, separate personality. In the eighth chapter of Romans, for example, there is a certain vacillation in his use of the term; it is sometimes hard to say whether he means by it a definite person or a personification or a mere influence. Thus in verses 4–8 the spirit, represented as the opponent of the flesh, seems to be man's higher as opposed to his lower nature; but in the next verse, believers are said to be in the spirit if the spirit of God dwell in them, where the signification of the first "spirit" is doubtful. On the other hand, the divine spirit is said to bear witness with the believer's spirit that he is a child of God (v. 16), and to make intercession for men (v. 27), and it is added that God, who searches hearts, knows the mind of the spirit. Here there is a clear distinction between God and the spirit. In another passage (1 Cor. ii. 10–13) there seems to be a blending of the Old Testament conception and a more developed view: God reveals his mystery to his servants by his spirit, for the spirit searches into and comprehends God's deepest thoughts. In explanation of this fact, Paul goes on to say: "Who of men knows the things of a man save the spirit of a man, which is in him? So the

---

[1] In the Targums the expression "spirit of God" is avoided, and "a spirit from God" substituted for it, the purpose being to eliminate the anthropomorphic representation of the divine being as possessing a spirit. The spirit, thus separated from God, takes on a certain personality. In the Talmud it is described as the source of all human enlightenment (as in the Old Testament), as the guide of Israel,—an advance on the Old Testament in distinctness of conception, yet not necessarily an hypostasis. The development appears to be almost identical with that in the New Testament. If the later Jews had hypostatized the Memra (the Word), they would probably have hypostatized the spirit also. Compare Weber, "System der pal. Theol." § 40.

things of God none knows save the spirit of God," where the divine spirit is represented as bearing the same relation to the divine being as the human spirit to the nature of man ; yet the spirit as the investigator of the divine thoughts seems to stand apart from God. In 2 Cor. iii. 17, 18, the spirit is represented both as a part of the Lord and as identical with him. The most natural explanation of this variation of thought is found in the supposition of an incomplete hypostasis of the spirit. The strong disposition, inherited from the Old Testament thought, to isolate, personify, and hypostatize the divine spiritual energy in the heart of man leads Paul sometimes to speak of the spirit as almost a distinct divine entity; at other times, the original conception of the spirit as simply a part of the divine constitution, thought of as analogous to that of man, suggests expressions which make the spirit little more than a divine influence. In other passages (as Gal. iii. 14 ; iv. 6) there may be the survival of the Old-Testament conception of a spiritual agent sent by God. We find a similar difference of conception in the Synoptic Gospels. The Sermon on the Mount does not mention the spirit, and such statements as that of Matt. x. 20, "It is not ye that speak, but the spirit of your father that speaketh in you," leave the significance of the term undecided. The same thing may be said of the Epistle to the Hebrews : God endows the disciples of Jesus with gifts of the holy spirit (ii. 4) ; it is the voice of this spirit that is heard in the words of the Old Testament (iii. 7) ; believers are made partakers of the holy spirit (vi. 4) ; Christ offered himself to God through the eternal spirit (ix. 14); an apostate from Christianity does despite to the spirit of grace (x. 29). All these expressions may be understood of a simple divine influence, but they more naturally suggest a hypostatical conception not fully developed. On the other hand, the representation in Matt. iii. 16, Luke iii.

22, where the spirit is described as descending in the shape of a dove, involves a distinct idea of personality. The incident mentioned in Matt. xii. 24–32 contrasts the spirit of God on the one side with Beelzebub, and on the other with the Son of Man, and appears therefore to ascribe to it as distinctive a personality as belonged to them. This is also the natural interpretation of the baptismal formula (Matt. xxviii. 19) where the spirit is mentioned along with the Father and the Son, and apparently as a separate person ; though we cannot certainly infer the equality of the three, we must understand the writer as ascribing distinct personal existence to the spirit. The passages last cited all belong to a later stratum of the Gospel narrative, and represent a hypostatic conception more definite than that which is found in the utterances of Jesus himself. In the Fourth Gospel, in which we have, not only a later, but a more speculative theological system, the spirit appears as a distinct person, but in a relation of subordination to the Father and the Son : " I will ask the Father and he shall give you another paraclete ; . . . the spirit of truth whom the cosmos cannot receive" (xiv. 16, 17) ; "if I go not away the paraclete will not come to you. . . . When he, the spirit of truth, is come, he will guide you into all the truth, for he shall not speak from himself, but what he hears he shall speak " (xvi. 7–15).

There is thus an evident advance of the hypostatic conception of the spirit within the New Testament itself. This is to be referred mainly to the natural growth of the tendency, but we must also take into consideration the influence of the distincter hypostasis of the Messiah. Paul's idealized, exalted Jesus was necessarily a distinct person, resting on and identical with the historical Jesus ; and later the author of the Fourth Gospel gave distinct form to the logos by making it one with the historical Jesus. The hypostatic conception thus established might be the more easily transferred to the spirit. Yet a difference continued to exist between the two, — there was no historical person with whom the spirit could be identified; and it is perhaps largely for this reason that the third person of the Christian Trinity has never in the history of Christianity assumed so definite a shape as the second person, nor played so prominent a part. In the Christian consciousness the spirit has commonly been a somewhat undefined, divine influence, which it was almost impossible to distinguish from the workings of the human soul. And this is the general effect which the New Testament representation makes upon us, — a mighty, divine influence, tending to take shape in a person, yet for the most part standing undecidedly between the two conceptions.

The hypostatizing process seems to have come mostly from Gentile Christianity. It is feeble in the purely Jewish books of the New Testament, such as Hebrews, James, and the Apocalypse; it is most completely elaborated in the Fourth Gospel, the ideas of which are controlled by Greek thought. Paul, on whom a Gentile influence must be recognized, stands midway between these two extremes. In the more developed statements of the Synoptic Gospels, we may recognize the influence of the church-thought which had grown up out of these conditions of the times. We may sum up by saying that the hypostatical conception of the spirit of God, having its roots in Old Testament thought, took more definite shape in the Christianity of the first century, partly by natural growth and partly urged on by the more complete hypostatization of the glorified Messiah and the Word of God.

The most striking and distinct of the personifications of the Old Testament is found in the representation of wisdom, which approaches the very verge of hypostasis without, however, reaching it; and its relation to the conception of the divine word is so close that the two should be considered together. To the philosophical Jewish school of the second century B. C., wisdom seemed the crowning attribute of deity. This view rested on a conception of life entirely distinct from the sacerdotal and the legal; the former of these looked on God as a power to be placated by sacrifice and ritual, and the latter construed human life as a mass of actions to be controlled by divinely given rules. Jewish philosophy, always holding more or less firmly to the national life, yet overstepping national bounds, preferred to conceive of the world as a gracious, beautiful unit, the product of the divine mind, bearing the impress of God's perfect wisdom. Human life, in its ideal shape as a rounded, orderly scheme, was viewed as an element of the divinely ordered cosmos, partaking of its constitution and governed by its laws. The same spirit of perfect knowledge that filled the universe had its abode in man's soul and fashioned it into the likeness of the supreme goodness. For the explanation of this new direction of Jewish thought we must look to the widening of general culture under the influence of the new social conditions. Through contact with the great Egyptian-Greek world the Jews had come to a better knowledge of the physical and moral sciences of the time. A certain portion of the nation (probably not a large one) came into closer sympathy with these broader ideas and were charmed by the conception of the world as a unit pervaded by a divine fashioning spirit. It was the orderliness of the universe and its obedience to law that most impressed the imagination of these thinkers; and since such conceptions are not found in pure Jewish literature and were foreign to Jewish modes of thought, we must recognize in them the influence of the reigning Greek philosophies of the day, especially the Platonic and the Stoic. In Jewish hands the Platonic idealism and the Stoic rule of law suffered a certain transformation; they had to be brought into direct connection with the God of Israel, whose thought had produced the wondrous uni-

7

verse ; and this highest thought was naturally conceived under the form of wisdom, as the highest intellectual, moral, and spiritual attribute of being. Wisdom being thus conceived as the all-potent factor in the physical and moral world, it needed only one step further to personify it as an individual and universal energy, to ascribe to it functions of physical and spiritual creation and maintenance, the guidance of the worlds and the purification and perfecting of the human soul. Similar functions were ascribed also to the divine spirit and word ; the three conceptions, standing in so close relation one to another, were interwoven one with another and sometimes apparently identified and confounded. We are not to expect here sharp psychological and cosmological analysis and hypostatic differentiation. The new conception of a divine energy filling and fashioning the world took hold of these men with power ; and whether it were spirit or wisdom or word that most appealed to the imagination of the thinker, each of these ideas would for the moment dominate his thought, and assume the proportions of a universal energy. We shall not be surprised, therefore, to find word and wisdom playing the same part in the world, the functions of each being ascribed to the other ; and we shall have to ask how it was that one of these conceptions faded away, while the other advanced steadily in Christianity to the fulness of hypostatic form.

We may perhaps regard the description in Job xxviii. as the earliest example in the Old Testament of a philosophical conception of wisdom.[1] The writer confines himself to de-

---

[1] The body of the book of Job cannot be put earlier than the Babylonian exile, and there are strong grounds for giving it a later date. Its elaborate discussion of facts of human experience, its developed doctrine of Satan, and its Aramaisms, would suggest rather the fifth century than the sixth, if indeed we must not come still further down to find its true place. The book is not a unit ; the Elihu episode, chs. xxxii.-xxxvii., is manifestly an interpolation, and chapter xxviii. is clearly out of place where it stands. It interrupts

claring the mysteriousness of it, — it cannot be found, he says, in earth or sky or deep, and only God knows its place; finally, it is identified with the fear of the Lord (Adonai). Here is elaborate description, which shows that the writer was impressed by the idea; but there is only a feeble personification, and no attempt at representing it as an energy. Only it is to be noted that that which in the divine mind is connected with creation and government is conceived as the ethical-religious directive principle in the life of man. In Prov. iii. 13–20 we have a similar personification, only in verse 19 a closer connection with God's work of creation: " Yahwe by wisdom founded the earth." The fuller description, viii. 1–ix. 6 introduces a far distincter personification and an ascription of personal energy which shows a considerable advance toward hypostatizing. The most striking passage is viii. 22–31 : wisdom, it is said, was brought forth before the world was made, and was present during the work of creation; she stood by the side of God as architect or master-workman, being daily his delight. and sporting continually in his presence. The epithet " master-workman " seems almost to ascribe to wisdom the direction or performance of the work of creation. The foundation of the representation is of course the idea of the divine wisdom ; but this attribute is so boldly isolated and personified as almost to take the form of an independent energy. Its moral function is indicated by the statement that its delight is with the sons of men. We can scarcely avoid regarding this as a dis-

Job's argument, introducing a line of thought quite foreign to the subject of his discourse in a style different from that of the remainder of the book. It is an addition by a writer of a different school, but we have only the most general considerations for determining the date. There seems to be nothing in the history of Jewish literature to prevent our putting it in the third century n.c.; this would bring it into intelligible connection with other Old Testament passages. If we may be guided by the nature of the thought, we should place it in the same category with the canonical and apocryphal Wisdom-books.

tinct effort at hypostatization, not completely successful, but a very clear indication of a tendency of thought; and the passage on general critical grounds is to be placed not earlier than the third century.[1]

The point of view of the Son of Sirach (xi. 1–20; xxiv.) does not differ substantially from that of Proverbs; he gives a vivid personification which does not quite reach the form of an hypostasis. Wisdom is said to have been created before all things (i. 4, cf. Prov. viii. 22); she was poured out on all the works of the Lord (i. 9), and covered the earth as a cloud (xxiv. 3); she dwelt in high places, her throne being in the cloudy pillar (xxiv. 4); her habitation was with the sons of men (i. 15, cf. Prov. viii. 31); she was commanded by the Creator to make her dwelling in Israel (xxiv. 8). The resemblance to Proverbs is obvious; the son of Sirach probably imitated the biblical book, on whose ideas he makes no advance. A bolder conception is found in the Wisdom of Solomon. Wisdom is almost identified with God: " Wisdom is a philanthropic spirit, and will not acquit the blasphemer of his words, for God is a witness of his reins; . . . for the spirit of the Lord fills the world " (i 6, 7). She is a source of immortality: " Obedience to her laws is assurance of incorruption, and incorruption brings us near to God " (vi. 18, 19). In the magnificent description contained in chapters vii. and viii. the author, inspired with fervid enthusiasm for his grand conception, seems to be on the verge of a real hypostasis; he ascribes to wisdom all conceivable lovely qualities and beneficent activities, so that in certain passages it might be doubtful whether he does not conceive of her as an independent power and being. She is a breath of the power

---

[1] The introduction of the book of Proverbs, chs. i.–ix., is distinguished from the rest of the book by its continuous discourse and flowing style. The social evils on which stress is laid (i. 10–14; ii. 16–19; v. vi. 1–5 ; vii. ix. 13–18) point to the later city-life. The prominence given to wisdom suggests a period posterior to that of the prophetic thought.

of God, a pure effluence from the glory of the Almighty, a reflection of the everlasting light, the image of God's goodness; though only one, she can do all things, and remaining in herself, makes all things new. There are some striking points of contact between this description and certain New Testament passages. There is in her, says the author, a spirit intelligent, holy, only begotten, manifold, subtle, lively, clear, undefiled, plain, not subject to hurt, loving what is good, penetrating, unrestrained, beneficent, philanthropic, steadfast, trustworthy, free from care, having all power, overseeing all things, and permeating all intelligent, pure, and subtlest spirits (cf. Jas. iii. 17). The tone and wording of Heb. i. 2, 3, resembles that of Wisd. vii. 26, 27, where wisdom is described as the reflection of the everlasting light, a mirror and image of God, omnipotent for good. This may be said indeed to mark the extreme point in the advance toward the hypostatizing of wisdom. Philo does not appear to go beyond this. It was natural that wisdom should play a prominent part in his conception of life, since it is so prominent in the Old Testament, from which he takes the greater part of his phraseology. He was also doubtless acquainted with the Alexandrine Wisdom-books. and there is little in his thought on this point that may not be found substantially in Proverbs and the Wisdom of Solomon. It has already been remarked that his conception of a directing intermediary power between God and the world leads him in many cases to a practical identification of wisdom, spirit, and logos; only he treats the last of these most elaborately, dwells on it with preference, and pushes its personification to the farthest point. A few citations may suffice to indicate the way in which he treats the conception of wisdom. In his discussion of Eden in the Allegories (i. 56) he regards the four rivers as representing the four cardinal virtues, — prudence, sobriety, courage, and justice, — and adds that the

greatest river whence the four flow is generic virtue, goodness in general, which arises from Eden, the wisdom of God.
Wisdom is here the source of human virtue and goodness,
delighting itself in God alone, — a representation which is
identical with that of the book of Proverbs. Elsewhere
(ii. 385) he calls wisdom the eldest in the creation of the
whole world, whom it is neither lawful nor possible for any
but God to judge. A distincter personification is given in
the passage (i. 202) in which she is termed the mother of the
world, through which everything was completed, God being
the father. It is evident that wisdom here performs substantially the function elsewhere ascribed to the logos, it
being natural, indeed, to assume the identity of the divine
reason and the divine wisdom. In fact, the difference between Philo's representations of the two seems rather to be
one of degree and circumstance than of essence, as will be
pointed out more fully below. The conception of wisdom
lent itself naturally to the process of hypostatizing; it could be
looked on as the largest and noblest of the divine attributes;
but it lacked certain conditions which were fulfilled by the
conception of the logos. In the New Testament the conception of wisdom appears in the form of distinct personification, but goes no farther. Wisdom is said to be justified by
her works (Matt. xi. 19) or by her children (Luke vii 35) Of
Christ it is declared not only that in him are hid all the
treasures of wisdom (Col. ii. 3), but also that he is the wisdom of God (1 Cor. i. 24), and is made unto believers wisdom
from God (1 Cor. i. 30). Here the apostle, in his polemic
against the worldly wisdom of Greek philosophy, is naturally
led to identify the only true and saving divine wisdom with
the glorified Messiah, through whom God had ordained that
redemption should come to men. But it is still nothing
more than strong personification. Under favorable conditions, we may suppose, the conception would have advanced

to the form of full hypostasis as it did in some of the Gnostic systems, but it has played no such part in Christianity.

We come now to the idea of "the word," and must attempt briefly to trace the process by which it attained a complete hypostatical form. As the distinctest expression of human thought, the word naturally represented reason, to which it owed its being, and was looked on as the intermediary between man and the world, — the instrument by which his designs were accomplished. This representation was at an early period transferred to the divine being. His word was conceived to be the expression of his thought; and thought and word were easily identified. His word was the embodiment of his purpose and law, and might be regarded as the agent which called his dispensations into being; it might even be looked on as identical with the things which itself produced. So mighty is the effect of the spoken word[1] that the natural tendency was to personify it more and more distinctly, and such we find to be the case in the Old Testament. Throughout the prophetic writings the word of God is the divine message sent to Israel to keep it in accord with divine law; it is the transcript of the divine reason. Though the prophet might sometimes be conscious that it was the expression of his own religious feeling, he nevertheless always looked on it as a powerful, objective, divine utterance. Is not God's word, says Jeremiah (xxiii. 29), like fire, and like a hammer that breaks the rock in pieces? The word here is merely the expression of the divine thought. In one prophetic passage (Isa. lv. 11) there is an approach to personification: "My word shall not return to me void, but it shall accomplish that which I please, and it shall prosper in the

---

[1] According to primitive ideas the uttered word had an independent, objective existence and power; a charm once spoken must work its effect. So in Gen. xxvii. the blessing which Isaac bestows by mistake cannot be recalled (vs. 33–37).

thing whereto I sent it." Activity and efficiency are ascribed to the word of God in Deut. viii. 3 : Man does not live by bread alone, but by everything that proceeds out of the mouth of God, — human life is controlled by the divine word. Still more distinct is the personification in certain psalm-passages : he sent his word and healed them (Ps. cvii. 20), where the logos is despatched as a messenger on a mission of healing ; by the word of the Lord were the heavens established (Ps. xxxiii. 6), where the logos is the agent of creation. In none of these passages is there anything more than personification ; but there is the sign of a disposition to isolate the spoken word as God's instrument in doing his work, and as the representative of the divine reason. We may here mention the development which the idea of the word received in the later Judaism. In the Targums the divine activity is habitually referred to the Memra, especially where the Old Testament expressions are anthropomorphic, where the text speaks of God's face, eyes, mouth, voice, hand, or of his walking, standing, seeing, and speaking. It may be assumed, therefore, that the expression Word of God was used in order to avoid what seemed irreverent in the human representation of the Divine Being. But the choice of the term was no doubt fixed by the Old Testament usage, especially from such a passage as Isa. lv. 11, where, as we have seen, an almost independent existence and objective activity are ascribed to the divine word. The usage of the Aramaic paraphrases may therefore be regarded as a natural growth out of the Old Testament thought. The personification in the Targums approaches very near an hypostasis. The Memra is creator and lord of all things, the guide, punisher, and rewarder of Israel, and the source of the prophetic inspiration, not an angel and not the Messiah, but a representative of the immediate divine activity. The conception did not keep its hold on Jewish thought; it was discarded in the later literature. Yet it probably helped the formulation of the Christian doctrine of the word. The oldest of our present Targums, indeed, hardly dates farther back than the third century of our era; but we must suppose that the germs of their ideas existed some time before, and it will not be rash to assume that in the first century Jewish thought had already come to look on the Memra as a sort of substantial activity, intermediate between God and the world. For the Jews the conception did not prove to be a fruitful one; it was coerced and ejected by their strict monotheism, but it maintained itself in Christianity for reasons to be hereafter mentioned.

The Wisdom of Solomon does not advance beyond personification when it represents the word as the instrument of the divine creation: "O God, who didst make all things by thy word" (ix. 1). The author may have had in mind the account of creation in the first chapter of Genesis, where the recurrence of "God said" naturally associates creation with the spoken word (and so in the psalm-passages cited above); but the spoken word necessarily expresses and involves the divine reason. In xvi. 12 there is an expansion of the idea of Ps. cvii. 20: "Thy word heals all things." Here, as the connection shows, the word is identified with God, who delivered his people and tormented their enemies, who leads down to the gates of Hades and brings up again, from whose hand escape is not possible. In v. 27 of the same chapter is an allusion to Deut. viii. 3: "Thy word preserves them that trust thee." In the description of the death of the first-born of Egypt, the author introduces a striking poetical personification: "While all things were clothed in deep silence, and night was in the midst of her swift course, thine almighty word leaped down from heaven from the royal throne like a fierce warrior into the midst of the doomed land, bearing as a sharp sword thine unfeigned commandment; it stood and filled all things with death; it touched heaven and planted itself on earth." In this figure there is no advance toward an hypostasis, nor do we find anything more definite in the succeeding literature up to Philo, to whom we must now turn.

In the space at our command it will not be possible to give more than a bare sketch of Philo's many-sided and intricate doctrine of the logos. That it should involve many different elements and shades, and that these should in some cases be hard to reconcile with one another, and sometimes even contradictory, is what we might expect. The Stoic doctrine of the logos, reason or word, as the formative or directive power in the world including human life, combined with the Old Testament and later Jewish representation of the energy of the divine word, had taken a strong hold on his imagination. Imbued equally with the love of Greek philosophy and with reverence for the Scriptures of his people, he felt the necessity of uniting the two in one system of thought. He had to hold to the rational, orderly unity of the world, the predominance of law and reason, and at the same time maintain the supremacy of the one Almighty God. The cosmos stood out before him as the embodiment of reason and as its creation, and at the same time as the work of God alone. This view was supplemented in his mind by the Platonic theory of ideas, archetypal forms which existed in the divine mind from all eternity, and took shape under the directive hand of reason in the visible world of nature and man. It is easy to see that in so vast a scheme his attention might be fixed on different points at different times, and that his representation of reason or word would vary with the material with which he was employed, especially as his particular line of thought was often determined by the Bible passage which he was expounding. We have here only to ask whether in his various representations of the logos there is one that reaches an hypostasis.

We need not stop with the passages in which he employs the term as merely equivalent to abstract reason or to law, as in ii. 46, i. 456; let us turn to those in which there is a more or less distinct personification. One of the simpler conceptions is that in which the logos is the primeval type of things. " It is evident," he says (i. 5), " that the archetypal seal also, which we call the intelligible cosmos, is itself the archetypal pattern, the idea of ideas, the logos of God," where the logos is nothing more than the divine thought ready to express itself in deed. In his comment on Gen. xv. 10, " the birds he did not divide," the logos occupies the same position in the universe as the soul in human nature; the two intelligible and logical natures — that in man and that in the All — he declares are necessarily each an undivided whole, the logos of God standing alone, apart from the crowd of created and destructible things (i. 505). This representation approaches very near an identification of the logos with God, — a step which it would seem impossible for a monotheist to take if the logos were thought of as a personal being. It is conceivable, however, that the latter might partake of the divine nature without being equal to God, and something like this Philo seems to say in his allegorical exposition of the bite of the serpent (i. 82): " Those who partook of the manna were filled with that which was most generic, for the manna is called ' what?' [or 'something' according to a possible etymology in Ex. xv. 16] which is the genus of all things ; and the most generic thing is God, and second is the logos of God." It is evident that by the term "generic" he here means universal, and that in ascribing the second place in this category to the logos, he separates it from all other things, brings it into a peculiar relation with God, and confers on it a very definite personality. The same inference might be drawn from those passages in which he speaks of the logos as the image of God. In his treatise on Moses' account of the creation of the world, remarking on the superiority of the intelligible[1] world over the visible, he compares it to the superiority of mind over things of the senses, and adds: "He [Moses] says that the invisible and intelligent divine logos is the image of God" (i. 6). And again: "And if we are not yet worthy to be esteemed sons of God, we may be children of his invisible image, the most holy logos, for the eldest logos is the image of God" (i. 427). A still stronger statement is found in his exposition of the cities of refuge, 19: "But the divine logos who is over these [the cherubim] attained no visible idea, being similar to no object of sense, but himself the image of God, the eldest of all ideal things, the nearest copy, without interval, of the only one" (i. 561). Though such language might conceivably be used of the abstract divine reason, the impression made on the mind is rather that the author, with his intense conception of the logos as the shaping power of the world, thinks of it as a distinct personality, not one with God, yet not to be separated from him in nature and essence. The logos is the very stamp and image of deity, and between the two there is no interval; if this is not a true hypostasis, it contains all the elements in solution, waiting only for the occasion which shall precipitate them into an objective and concrete form. In other passages Philo attempts to define the nature of the logos in its relation to the divine. Speaking of its position midway between God and man, he describes it as "neither uncreated like God nor created like you, but midway between the two extremes, in contact with both" (i. 502). To the same effect in the treatise on dreams, ii. 28, where he regards the high-priest as the symbol of the logos: "He, few when reckoned

---

[1] That is, the ideal world as it existed in the divine mind before creation.

with others, becomes when he stands alone many, — the court, the whole council, the whole people, the crowd, the whole race of men, rather, if the truth is to be said, a nature bordering on that of God, less than he and greater than man. For 'when,' it is said, 'the high-priest enters the Holy of Holies, there shall not be a man' (Lev. xvi. 17). Who is he, then, if not a man? Is he God? I would not say so; . . . nor is he man, but touches both extremes as base and head" (i. 684). That Philo thinks it necessary here to affirm that the high-priest as symbol was not man, points to a very definite personal conception of a power midway between God and man and partaking of the natures of both.[1] The definiteness of the representation in this passage is due in part to the fact that there was a human personage with which this intermediary conception could be identified. The priest was in the form of man as the representative of man, yet, standing for the whole human race, must be universal, a divine man ; nothing else than such a being could act as medium between the two extremes of deity and humanity. It will be sufficient in this connection to mention the title "first-born son," which Philo in a number of passages gives to the logos (i. 308, 415, 427, 502 ; the significance of this name will depend on the connection in which it occurs. Philo goes still farther and finds in the Scripture an ascription of divinity to the logos, though he holds that the word "God" is in such cases used in an improper (catachrestic), that is, an accommodated sense. Remarking on Gen. xxxi. 12, 13, according to the Septuagint text, he says: "Let us examine carefully as to whether there are really two Gods, for it is said 'I am the God who appeared to thee' not in my place, but 'in the place of God' [so the Septuagint renders Bethel], as if another deity were referred to. How are we to treat

---

[1] That the high-priest here represents the logos appears from such passages as i. 653, 452, where his symbolic character is definitely expressed.

this statement? The explanation is that the true God is one, but those improperly so called are many. The sacred Scripture, therefore, denotes the true God by the article, saying, ' I am God ' [$\acute{o}$ $\theta\epsilon\acute{o}\varsigma$], and in the other case omits it: 'Who appeared to thee in the place,' not of the God, but merely 'of God.' Here he calls his oldest logos God, having no superstitious feeling about the application of names" (i. 655, 656). It is significant that in spite of the protest of Philo's monotheistic feeling he here finds himself able to apply to the logos a predicate of divinity which is evidently, in his apprehension, not an empty sound. It is improper, he says ; yet that he uses it and that he supposes the Scripture to use it shows that he regarded it as not wholly improper. How can we understand his anxiety to distinguish the logos from God and guard the supremacy of the latter, except as an indication that the former was assuming in his mind some sort of personality which partook of the divine nature ? We may close this statement of Philo's view of the nature of the logos by referring to what he says (Life of Moses, iii. 13) of its twofold character: " The logos is dual both in the All and in the nature of man ; in the All it relates to the incorporeal and typical ideas from which springs the intelligible world, and to the visible things which are copies and images of those ideas, from which this perceptible world was established. And so in man the logos is internal and uttered,[1] the former being, as it were, a spring, the latter that which flows from it" (ii. 154). He adds that the cosmic logos has the two virtues of manifestation and truth (the Urim and Thummim of the high-priest) ; the same qualities belong to the two forms of the human logos, — manifestation to the uttered and truth to the internal. This old Stoic double conception of the human logos, the inward reason, and the uttered word which is the expression of

---

[1] Endiathetos and prophorikos.

this reason, is simple and natural. How are we to understand its application to the divine logos? The most natural explanation is that Philo takes it in a perfectly simple way: the divine reason, in its nature purely reflective, necessarily utters itself in words or deeds. But so strong is Philo's conception of the unity and divinity of the logos that he cannot permit himself to divide it into two parts and to assign to these parts severally the qualities of manifestation and truth; these two virtues he represents as belonging to the whole logos, which is thus the divine reason thinking and acting,—a single conception, the personalization of the divine energy which mediates between God and the world.

Philo's representation of the function and work of the logos is in accordance with his conception of its nature. The universe, he says, is, as it were, a flock, guided by God, the shepherd and king, who has set over it his right logos, his first-born son (i. 308). Here the logos is director of the life of the world; elsewhere he is presented as its actual maker: "This oldest son the father of beings brought into being, whom elsewhere he named the first-begotten, and who, though begotten, yet imitating the ways of his father, and looking to his archetypal norms, gave shape to species" (i. 414, 415). He is further described as putting on the world as a garment and as the bond which holds all things together (i. 562), as the driver of the powers which control the world (i. 560, 561). In a striking passage in the tract on The Heir of Divine Things, 42, the logos is distinctly portrayed as mediator between God and man: "On the archangel and eldest logos the father, who begat all things, bestowed this choice gift, that he should stand on the border and separate the created from the Creator. He is a suppliant in behalf of the mortal for immortality, and the ambassador of the king for obedience, ... being neither unbegotten like God nor begotten like you, but midway between the two ex-

tremes, bordering on both, appealing to the Creator in faith
that he will never destroy the world, and offering to the
creature the hope that the merciful God will never disregard
his own work" (i. 501, 502). Such representations may no
doubt be understood of the abstract divine reason; but their
frequency and distinctness rather suggest a desire and effort
after a separate personality.

It must be added that Philo has other representations of
the logos. He declares that God needed no assistant in
creation (i. 5), that in this work he stood alone (i. 66). The
world is said to be founded on the divine word (i. 7, 8), and
indeed to be the word (i. 4, 5, 630). The distinctness of the
logos from God is affirmed in a number of passages (i. 6, 128,
625, 655). Its functions are sometimes nearly identical with
those of the spirit and of wisdom. There may be many
logoi, — the laws of God (i. 128). Philo's use of the term
is so various that one may construct from his works any
logos-theory that one pleases. This variety of use, as is
remarked above, is just what we should expect from the
vastness of the conception with which the philosopher's
mind was filled, and the diversity of the sources from which
he drew his material. A Jewish monotheist expounding the
Hebrew Scriptures after Platonic and Stoic principles might
well occasionally differ from himself. Yet in spite of diversities, there is a very serious and persistent unity in his portraiture of the logos as the divine shaper and director of all
things, — the mediator between God and the world. To this
conception the author ever returns with greatest fondness.
There is a certain pantheistic element in his thought: the
world is the logos, for it is nothing but the utterance of the
divine reason, a view which resulted from the author's determination to grasp the unity of the universe. Again, the
logos, though all-powerful, is the creature of God and subordinate to him, — a Jewish monotheist could take no other

view. All through these variations of the theme the central idea of the logos as a substantially divine personality makes itself heard with greater or less distinctness. This is the idea which is constantly striving to take shape in Philo's mind, though it is often jostled or excluded by other conceptions held with equal firmness. He was not in position to conceive a complete hypostatization of the logos. If there had been any visible historical person to which to attach the idea, it might have been different; it was hard to elevate an abstract conception to the position of a person.[1] The same difficulty existed in the case of wisdom, and to a less degree in the efforts at hypostatizing the spirit. Philo seems to have gone as far as was possible for him under the circumstances; his feeling of the necessity of an intermediate power between God and the world led him to treat the logos as much more than an abstract conception, though it is not possible to say that he made it an absolutely distinct personality.

His preference for this expression for the mediating power

[1] It does not appear that Philo identifies the logos with the Messiah, or even that he mentions a Messiah; the passages cited as referring to the Messiah (ii. 423, 436) hardly bear this interpretation. The first (which occurs in a description of the final defeat of evil men) reads: "For a man shall go forth, says the oracle [Num. xxiv. 7], at the head of an army . . . and shall conquer great and populous nations." But this "man," as Oehler (quoted by Drummond) remarks, is immediately explained as a symbol of courage and strength, and in fact is not again mentioned. He does not play the rôle of a Messiah, and he is by no word brought into connection with the logos. The second passage, describing the return of the scattered Jews to their own land, says that they shall be led "by a certain appearance ($\delta\psi\epsilon\omega\varsigma$) more divine than human," which shall be invisible to all but those who are being saved. This can hardly mean the Messiah, who would certainly not be invisible to his enemies; nor is it in this way that Philo speaks of the logos The "appearance" seems to be an allusion to the pillar of cloud and fire (Ex. xiv. 20), a general guidance by God; there is no mention of a person, human or divine, as leader. He goes on to say that the people will have three intercessors with God, — the goodness of God himself, the holiness of their ancestors, and their own improvement; this assumes the ordinary national life, and does not favor the supposition of salvation by Messiah or logos.

was doubtless determined by the usage of the Stoic philosophy. The Old Testament offered other terms which might have been chosen, such as wisdom, glory, spirit, presence. But Philo's philosophic studies would naturally fix his attention on this particular expression, which, besides, best accorded with the tendencies of the Greco-Jewish philosophy of the time. That which most appealed to one part of the thought of the age was not so much the divine power or goodness, or the spiritual relation between man and God, as the conception of law and reason in the government of the world. The term "logos" offered a fulness of meaning which could not be found in any other expression. It represented the absolute reason, and at the same time the utterance or objective expression of this reason. It was anthropomorphic and in a sort anthropocentric, but in the grandest and purest way. It glorified reason, but attached it inseparably to the ideal divine. It gave unity to the world without impairing the aloneness of God or the independence of man. It was, in addition, an expression of the Hebrew Scriptures, invested with peculiar sacredness by prophets, psalmists, and Law. It would not be a matter of surprise, then, if the idea got a strong hold on those Jews who were acquainted with Hellenizing philosophical thought. We are not informed how far Philo's writings were known outside of Egypt, but such ideas could not easily be kept within the limits of one land ; in their general outline, indeed, they belonged to a school of thought, and would be likely to have their representatives all over Hellenized Asia. But so far as we know, it was he who fused the Stoic conception with the Old Testament thought into a theological system which might commend itself to orthodox monotheists. It was he who made the rational word the only begotten Son, the image and the agent of the one only true God and Father, standing midway between the extremes of the divine and the human, in contact with both.

Within a century after the composition of Philo's works there appeared a Christian book in which Jesus of Nazareth was identified with the logos.[1] The resemblances between the representations of the word in Philo and the Fourth Gospel lie on the surface. If we leave out the fact of incarnation, there is nothing in the latter that is not found in the former. The Gospel describes the logos as having existed in the beginning in the presence of God, partaking of the divine nature, and as having been the sole agent in the divine creation; he is declared to be the only begotten Son of God, the source of life to men. Reference to the quotations above given will show that all these elements of the conception are contained in Philo's representation. The distinction which the latter makes, by the insertion or omission of the article, between the absolute divine being and the divine nature possessed by the logos is made also in the first verse of the Gospel. The evangelist seems to be concerned, like Philo, while ascribing the largest divine powers to the logos, yet to keep intact the substantial aloneness of God himself. He declares, according to one reading of the text (John i. 18): "No one has ever seen God; the only begotten Son who is in the bosom of the Father, he has declared him," a state-

---

[1] This is a sufficiently definite statement of the date of the Fourth Gospel for our purposes. It is impossible here to go into a discussion of the numerous and intricate questions connected with the investigation of the origin of this Gospel. The church tradition assigns the work to the closing years of the first century, and Justin Martyr appears to have been acquainted with it. From these data we might place it between the years 100 and 130, and there is nothing in the book itself to make such a date improbable; at the distance of nearly a century from the death of Jesus, such an idealizing portrait of him would be not unnatural, and the existence of the Grecizing tendency of thought among the Jews at that time is vouched for by the works of Philo. We are not here called on to decide how far the author of the Fourth Gospel used the other gospels, or in general how far an historical tradition lay at the basis of his work; we have to accept the book simply as a product of the first part of the second century, made up of Christian material shaped under the influence of Jewish-Greek philosophy.

ment which forms the gist of Philo's description, in which the logos is the utterance and declaration of the invisible God. Another reading of the Gospel passage has "the only begotten God" instead of "the only begotten Son;" as to this (which on its face and in the connection is less likely than the other) we can only say that it still makes a clear distinction between this only begotten divine person and the absolute "God," who is invisible,—a distinction likewise found in Philo.

The decisive difference between the Alexandrian philosopher and the Gospel is that for the latter the logos is incarnate in the person of Jesus of Nazareth. We have seen that Philo did not identify the logos with the Messiah or any other man. It is no doubt the failure of such an identification that gives a wavering and indistinct character to his conception, and deprives it of the roundness and objective power which resides in a visible historical form. This was the great advantage enjoyed by the Christian writer over the Jewish philosopher,— the presence of a man in whom the logos could be seen; this was the condition necessary for the final and complete hypostatization of the conception.

We cannot trace in minute detail the steps by which the historical Jesus became one in Christian thought with the divine Word, but we may discern the broad outlines of the movement. The two elements of the process of identification are: the gradual idealizing of the person of Jesus, and the acceptance by a part of the Christian world of the Greek philosophy as adapted to monotheistic ideas by the Alexandrian Jews. The latter of these elements we may consider to have begun with the establishment of the Philonic system. As has already been remarked, there is nothing to prevent our supposing that its central point — the conception of a divine, rational word mediating between God and the world, — had obtained a footing in Asia Minor, where the Fourth

Gospel is described by the tradition as having originated. There Philo's works may have been known, or the substance of them may have been discussed in philosophizing circles. To a Christian work embodying this conception a certain definiteness and simplicity would be given by the historical personage of Jesus. There would be no need of metaphysical subtlety or indistinctness. The divine word, spoken of in the Old Testament, and elaborated in Alexandria out of Old Testament material, had appeared in visible form. The author of the Fourth Gospel, after in the beginning of his work identifying Jesus with the logos, does not return to the subject; he contents himself with the portrayal of him as the principle of light and life in the world, combating darkness and death. The evangelist necessarily treats his subject with freedom and independence. What especially interests him is to point out how Jesus, in the midst of the darkened, unbelieving world, asserts himself as the absolute truth, as the manifestation of the Father with whom he is one, to whom, nevertheless, he is subordinate, without whom he can do nothing, by whom he has been sent on a mission of eternal life, through whose power and direction they who have been chosen come to the Son and believe on him unto eternal life.

But while in the choice of the term " logos " we must recognize the connection between the Fourth Gospel and the Alexandrian philosophy, it is also true that in other Christian circles during the first century the person of Jesus had been steadily growing in dignity. We have no means of tracing the development of Paul's thought between his conversion and the first of his epistles; but from the beginning he seems to have conceived of Jesus as the glorified Messiah invested by God with supreme authority for the salvation of men. On Christ's earthly life Paul laid little stress. A few times he mentions his birth as a man (Gal. iv. 4; Rom. i 3), his sacrificial death (Gal. i. 4; 2 Cor. **v.** 21; 1 Cor. **v.** 7), and very often his resurrection from the dead. On this last point he dwells with preference; it is his real starting-point for Christ's work. The glorified Jesus is the Son of God, who dwelt from the beginning with the Father, who laid aside his riches and glory that he might become the Saviour of men (2 Cor. ii. 9; Phil. ii. 6–9); he is the power of God and the wisdom of God (1 Cor. i. 24), the Saviour and Lord of believers. On the other hand, he is distinguished from and subordinated to God; there is one God, the Father, and one Lord Jesus Christ (1 Cor. viii. 6), and at the end he shall deliver up his kingdom to God and be subjected to him who subjected all things to him, that God may be all in all (1 Cor. xv. 24–28). Paul's view doubtless arose from the combination of his Old Testament monotheism with his exalted conception of the spiritual function of the Messiah. Jesus he believed had been raised from the dead to reconcile men to God; such a task demanded the noblest personality and the largest authority compatible with the aloneness of God. Jesus is supreme in the Church, but he derives all his authority from the Father. This view may have so leavened Christian opinion as to prepare the way for the preciser statement of the Fourth Gospel. It is, in fact, itself a long step toward a complete hypostatization. Jesus, according to Paul's view, is far above all other beings except God, one with him in purpose and act, only less than he in the universe.

In this connection we must mention the representations of Jesus given in Hebrews, Ephesians, and Colossians, in which the influence of the Greek thought seems recognizable. The expressions in Heb. i. 2, 3, in which the Son is God's agent in creation, the effulgence of his glory and the image of his substance, remind us of the Fourth Gospel and Philo;[1]

---

[1] And see Wisdom of Solomon, vii. 26.

and here also the Son receives this glory by the appointment of the Father, that he may become the Saviour of believers. In Ephesians and Colossians Christ, while his function in the Church is substantially identical with the teaching of the Pauline epistles, is conceived in a more philosophical and ideal way; in him all things in the universe are summed up (Eph. i. 10); he is the image of the invisible God, the firstborn of all creation; through him all things were made, and in him they consist; he possesses all the treasures of wisdom and knowledge, and in him dwells all the fulness of the Godhead bodily; he is seated at the right hand of God; he is the life of believers, who shall share in the glory of his manifestation. These expressions we are warranted in interpreting in accordance with the spirit of Paul and of Hebrews: Christ, being the sum of the universe, and having in him all the fulness of the Godhead, is yet to be distinguished from God, from whom he derives his authority, and on whose aloneness he does not impinge. These epistles we may regard as having been composed in sympathy with the Pauline doctrine, but under the influence of the Alexandrine philosophy. Possibly they form the transition from the earlier to the later conceptions of the person of Jesus. Indeed, the statement in the proem of the Fourth Gospel, though more succinct and scientific in form, is not more decided than what we find in Hebrews and Colossians.

There is no lack of unity in this portrait of Jesus. There are no inconsistencies and discrepancies in the utterances of Jesus respecting himself or in the introduction to the Fourth Gospel, if we look on the evangelical logos as substantially identical with that of Philo, the divine reason and word, the divine manifestation of God, one with man and one with God, Maker and Lord of all things, yet always under the control of the only one God, the Son having the glory of the only begotten of the Father, the one source of life and salvation, the one power able to regenerate the world.

In contrast with these representations, the picture of the Word of God in the New Testament Apocalypse (xix. 13–16) follows the Jewish Old Testament conception. The Word, who is King of Kings and Lord of Lords, smites the nations with the sharp sword which proceeds out of his mouth, rules them with a rod of iron (Ps. ii. 9), and treads the wine-press of the fierceness of the wrath of Almighty God (Isa. lxiii. 3). This may be called the purely Jewish-Christian conception.

Paul's view was determined by his intense and lofty moral-spiritual earnestness, which led him to construe the glorified Messiah as the saviour from sin, the creator of righteousness, and the reconciler of God and humanity. We have no need to call in the Alexandrian philosophy in order to understand his position. The case is different with the other New Testament writings cited above, in which so many of the expressions are identical with those of systems based on Greek thought.

We conclude from this survey that there are in the New Testament two distinct lines of advance in the construction of the person of Jesus, — the one Pauline, the other Alexandrian. The first was soteriological, the second philosophical; the first magnified the person of the Messiah so as to bring it into harmony with the great function assigned him, — a function the conception of which Paul seems to have reached by spiritualizing the Old Testament view of salvation; the second identified Jesus, the Messiah, with the grand mediatorial figure which, first presented by the Stoics, was elaborated in Alexandria, and perhaps elsewhere, in accordance with Jewish monotheism. The blending of these two lines of thought is visible in Hebrews, Ephesians, Colossians, and the Fourth Gospel, in which we have the culmination of the effort made by the early Christian thought to idealize the person of the Messiah in the loftiest spiritual way. Yet, as we have seen, the New Testament, with all the grandeur of character and function that it ascribes to the Christ, maintains the unique supremacy of the one God. The demand for a mediating power between God and humanity is pushed to the farthest point which thought can occupy consistently with the maintenance of the absoluteness of the one Supreme Deity.

5. In connection with the development of the theistic idea, we must consider the conception of the relation of God's self-manifestation to the laws of the natural world. In the early times of Israelitism, as in all primitive systems of religion, there was no sharply marked distinction between the natural and the supernatural. The scientific idea of the orderly constitution of nature according to law did not exist, or at least had not been so formulated as to exercise a controlling influence over human thought; it was easy and natural to regard the deity as interposing at will in the affairs of life. We may distinguish two stadia in the conception of divine intervention. There was the primitive, naïve feeling that the deity was everywhere, showing himself in all occurrences of life, but especially recognizable in great calamities and blessings and other stupendous events. Survivals of this feeling in the Old Testament may be seen in the familiar intercourse between God and the patriarchs in Genesis, and in such occurrences as the appearance of the angels to Gideon and Manoah (Judg. vi. 11 ; xiii.). The second stage belongs to the more highly developed theocratic feeling, according to which the whole life of Israel was under the direct and constant supervision and guidance of its God; and all things, great and small, simple and involved, were his doing. Whether it were the appointment of a king, or the overthrow of an enemy, a message of encouragement or reproof through the

mouth of a prophet, or the revelation of a law of worship and conduct, the bestowal of bounteous crops, or the infliction of pestilence or famine, the decision of a lot between two men, the overthrow of a nation or its restoration to its own land, —all was the immediate work of Yahwe, God of Israel. From this point of view there was no great distinction between ordinary and extraordinary. divine action; the latter only served to call man's attention more sharply to the divine presence.[1] The Old Testament writings abound in angelic appearances, prophetic messages, and other indications of the constant readiness of Yahwe to take part in the affairs of his people.

At the same time there are indications of another popular view which looked on life simply as a sequence of events, the natural progression of which it described without feeling called on to recognize in it a divine element. The stories of Micah and Samson in the book of Judges, much of the history of David in Samuel, and of the annals of the monarchy in Kings, are mere records of natural occurrences from the human point of view; and in the story of Esther, in the form in which it occurs in the Hebrew Scriptures, the divine agency is completely lost sight of. This non-religious conception of life was as natural to the Israelites as it is to our own times, when even persons distinctly or fervidly religious describe social or political occurrences without ever thinking of introducing divine agency; the belief in God exists, but the attention is absorbed by the events described.

The tendency of social growth is to favor this non-religious mode of conceiving history; the presence of law and order is more and more recognized, and it is felt more and more strongly that recognition of and obedience to this order in human life is a prime condition of success. The conviction

---

[1] Cf. the modern popular distinction between general and particular providence.

of divine supremacy remains; but the impression of the natural order of things becomes more and more powerful. Men learn to depend on themselves; and self-reliance is harmonized with dependence on God by the belief that he manifests himself in accordance with natural law. There is perhaps a hint of this feeling in the story told in Isa. vii. 10–12, where Ahaz, engaged in preparing the defences of Jerusalem, declines to ask a sign from Yahwe; the ground he assigns for his refusal is that he does not wish to tempt the God of Israel, but his real reason perhaps was that he relied more on fortifications than on divine signs. Whether this was the case with Ahaz or not, we find in certain late post-exilian books, as Ezra and Nehemiah, a very decided non-miraculous view of life. Toward the close of the exile, the return to Canaan had been painted in glowing colors by the second Isaiah; Yahwe, said the prophet, would prepare the way for his people, bring them with joy and gladness to their land, and there establish them in never-ending blessedness as the centre and head of all the nations. The actual event formed a bitter contrast to the brilliant anticipations of the prophet. All the energies of the little community of returned exiles were devoted to wringing a bare subsistence out of the soil, and painfully building a temple greatly inferior to that of Solomon. Life dragged on slowly till Ezra and Nehemiah came, and gave a new impulse by restoring the fortifications of the city and introducing the elaborate ritual law which had been developed in Babylonia. Still, the hard reality of the situation forced itself on the consciousness of the people; the Persian empire embraced all the territory of the earth known or accessible to the Jews, and its overwhelming power made independence for the smaller nations impossible. Nehemiah felt himself to be simply a Persian governor, and trusted for success to the arts of a skilful politician; he and Ezra lived in the consciousness of God's presence, but they looked for no physical aid from that source. At least, in the books which bear their names, which a century and a half later narrated the history of their mission, there is no trace of supernatural intervention, nothing but a purely human course of events.

The same characteristic is found in the remaining historical literature down to the beginning of our era, which records contemporary events. It is otherwise with Chronicles, the Apocalyptic books and 2 Maccabees;[1] but Chronicles deals with a remote, transfigured past, the Apocalypses with an ideal, glorified future, and 2 Maccabees was written long enough after the events it describes for a halo of embellishment to gather about the history.

In the first century of Christianity we come again on a period of miracle. We have not, it is true, contemporary accounts of the lives of Jesus and his disciples; the Gospels and Acts were composed a generation or two after the events with which they are concerned, and tradition would naturally increase the mass of supernatural material. But the tradition testifies to the existence of the belief in miracle; and we can hardly avoid the conclusion that it had a basis in fact; that is, that the apostles and other prominent disciples did claim to work miracles. Their miraculous activity was not, as is true in a great part of the Old Testament, and a great part of the Apocalyptic books, directed to national ends; it was individual in its aim. The apostles went about doing good, and using their deeds of healing as the occasion of announcing the principles of the new kingdom of God. For a parallel to this in the Old Testament we must look to the quiet, beneficent activity of Elisha. The New Testament miracles are, however, not simply individual or physically beneficent in their aim; they look also to shutting the mouths of opponents, and demonstrating the divine origin

[1] iii. 24; v. 2, 3; x. 29, 30; xv. 12-16.

of the new religion. The Messianic kingdom of God has taken the place of the old national Israel.[1]

The ground of this outburst of miracle in the New Testament times must be sought first in the belief that the Messianic age, as the final era of prosperity for Israel, would be ushered in and maintained by the direct intervention of divine power. So soon as it was believed that Jesus was the Messiah, the memory of the disciples, dwelling fondly on the history of his blessed life, would naturally fill it up with these special signs of the divine presence; and in the same way a later generation would clothe the grand figures of the apostles with supernatural glory. This feeling continued to exist in the Church for many centuries; every great saint was credited with miraculous power, and this in a perfectly simple and sincere way. The legends of the saints were not invented, but grew up out of the conviction that to such eminent servants of God must be vouchsafed the impartation of special power from on high. It is in the historical books of the New Testament that the miraculous element is most prominent. There is a difference in the portraiture of supernatural activity between the three first Gospels and the Fourth: in the former, the work of Jesus is one of simple beneficence; in the latter it is the outstreaming of his divine nature and the manifestation of his glory (John ii. 11); in this respect Acts resembles the Synoptics. The attitude of the Epistles toward the supernatural is different. Paul recognizes it almost exclusively in the fundamental facts of Christianity, the resurrection and ascension of Jesus, the

---

[1] Whether Jesus himself claimed to perform miracles, the data, as it seems to me, do not enable us to decide. The Gospel accounts which ascribe miraculous powers to him may be explained as the product of reverent tradition. His lofty spiritual simplicity is against rather than for the supposition that he assumed such powers. On the other hand, it was the manner of the time to believe in miracle, and he might have shared this belief without impairing his ethical and spiritual purity.

divine origin of the plan of salvation, and in his own special call to the apostleship and instruction by the divine Spirit in the principles of Christ.   He dwells on his own experience, his conversion (Gal. i. 11–24), and his visions and revelations (2 Cor. xii. 1–4) ; but he does not claim the power of working physical miracles,[1] and describes his own work among the churches in purely human terms, except that a general divine guidance in his life is always presupposed.

It appears, therefore, that the New Testament view of miraculous divine intervention in the affairs of men is substantially the same with the second or theocratic stage of the Old Testament representation.   The Church has taken the place of the nation, and God intervenes in a special way when the interests of the Church require it.   The primitive view which saw the deity in every fact and act has passed away, — a natural sequence of events is recognized in ordinary occurrences ; but the life of the kingdom of God is not only to be maintained by constant impartation of the divine Spirit, — it is to be guarded from attacks of enemies, human and superhuman, by supernatural intervention.   The growing feeling in favor of natural order is modified by the conviction that the Church, as a special creation of God, is marked off from the rest of the world, stands, indeed, in sharp contrast with the world, and demands the special protection of God.   This conception (which maintained itself many centuries) gave a natural color to miracles within the Church ; it underlies the whole of the New Testament scheme of thought.   It was the subtraction of a definite segment of life from the domain of natural law.   The subsequent thought of the Church has constantly tended (though with exceptions) to limit the agency of the supernatural to the New Testament times.   The feeling is that while the establish-

____

[1] He mentions, however, the working of miracles as one of the charismata (1 Cor. xii. 10).

ment of the Church was an event of such magnitude as to demand the immediate intervention of God, its maintenance is left to the working of natural or invisible-spiritual powers.

6. In this connection a word may be said as to the authority accorded to the Scriptures from the time of Ezra to the end of the first Christian century. The solemn description of the introduction of the Law in Neh. viii. indicates that it was looked on as the divinely given guide of life. If this narrative be supposed to be colored by the feeling of a later time, it still appears from Chronicles that in the latter part of the fourth century B. C., the Levitical Code was recognized as an authoritative standard. In a work of the second century (1 Mac. iii. 48), we find testimony as to the estimation in which the Law was then held; the canonical character of Jeremiah and therefore, as we may infer, of all the prophets, is involved in Dan. ix. 2, and all three canons are mentioned in the second prologue to Ecclesiasticus. Numerous quotations from the Old Testament in the later books show that its contents were familiar to the writers, though nothing is said of a specifically divine authority, except in relation to Moses and the Law (Ecclus. xlv. 17); see Wisd. xvi.–xix., Ecclus. xliv.–xlix. (a list of Old Testament worthies, but in chapter l., the non-biblical high-priest Simon, the son of Onias, B. C. 219–199, is also mentioned), 1 Mac. iii. 18, 19 (cf. Ps. xxxiii. 16, 2 Chron. xiv. 11); iv. 9; 2 Mac. ii. 8; i. 20. The schools of law, which existed from the second century down, are a proof of the peculiar position held by the Pentateuch. That this reverence for the Scriptures existed in Egypt as well as in Palestine is shown by the Alexandrian-Greek translation, which was probably begun in the early part of the third century, and finished about the end of the second. There was no attempt at this time to define the precise nature or extent of the authority of the Scripture; this subject was first touched on by Philo, who ascribed to

the Old Testament writers an inward clearness of vision bestowed by God, and held the prophets to be interpreters of the divine will, Moses being at their head, the interpreter of God in the highest sense (i. 511; ii. 163). Though he regards all biblical books as in a peculiar sense authoritative, he makes a marked distinction between the Law and the others; and it must be added that he claimed a sort of inspiration for himself, — he sometimes felt his soul suddenly filled with ideas from above; he was seized with enthusiasm, and believed himself to be in direct communication with the divine spirit (i. 441, 692).

This view of the inspiration and authority of the Old Testament accords in general with the indications of the New Testament and the Talmud, and may be accepted as the prevailing Jewish opinion in the first century of Christianity. There is no definition in the New Testament of the authority of the inspired writings; the most express statement respecting their value is found in 2 Tim. iii. 16: "Every Scripture which is inspired by God is also profitable for teaching, for reproof, for correction, for righteous instruction, that the man of God may be complete, fully equipped for every good work." They are abundantly cited in proof, or illustration, or as prediction of facts and doctrines, generally without mention of author or place, with the formulas, — "as it is written," "which was spoken by the Lord through the prophet," "the Scripture says," sometimes "he says to Moses," "Isaiah cries," "David says," "one has somewhere testified," "the Holy Ghost says," sometimes without introductory formula. But we also find citations or insertions from other than Old Testament books; as, for example, from the book of Enoch in Jude and Revelation, and possibly from 2 Mac. vii. in Heb. xi. 35; and even late Jewish traditions are introduced in the same way as biblical citations: Paul speaks of the rock which followed Israel through the wilderness to supply them with water (1 Cor. x. 4), Acts (vi. 22) represents Moses as instructed in Egyptian wisdom, and 2 Tim. iii. 8, gives the names of the Egyptian magicians who withstood Moses. It is evident from these examples that no such sharp discrimination between canonical and uncanonical books, and no such detailed theory of inspiration existed in the first century as were afterward elaborated in the Christian Church. We must suppose a more fluctuating conception of inspired writings. The Old Testament, in the form in which we now have it (the Palestinian Canon), was looked on with peculiar reverence as the fountain of divine truth; but all the books of the Greek Canon were also held in high estimation, and still other books, which never became canonical, were regarded not only as historically trustworthy, but as valid religious guides. It is probable, as is said above, that a peculiar pre-eminence was assigned to the writings ascribed to Moses; but beyond this, we have little to guide us in determining the reigning opinion respecting the degrees of authority of inspired works.

When we turn to the Scriptures themselves, we do not find in the later books of the Old Testament a specific claim to be regarded as infallible religious standards and guides. The Law purports to be a direct verbal revelation from God, and the prophets affirm that they speak what is put into their mouths by the divine spirit; but the books of the Third Canon are conceived in purely human style, as the utterances of historians, sages, and poets who chronicle facts and express their reflections and emotions purely out of the natural impulse of authorship. There is no consciousness in Chronicles, Ecclesiastes, Proverbs, Psalms, of the right to be regarded as standards of faith, no expectation of being received into a third division of inspired Scriptures.

The New Testament writers in like manner (with the exception of the Apocalyptist) lay no claim directly to divine inspiration. In the First and Second Gospels, the writers say nothing of their mode of composition; the author of the Third Gospel describes his procedure as that of the ordinary historian (Luke i. 1–4, and cf. Acts i. 1); the passage at the end of the Fourth Gospel (John xxi. 24), which speaks of the writer and his composition, says nothing of divine guidance. Paul affirms that he received directly through revelation of Jesus Christ the gospel which he preached (Gal. i. 12; 1 Cor. i. 23); but he does not claim supernatural guidance in the penning of his epistles, and as a rule relies for his effect on the appeal to the Old Testament, or to the religious consciousness or the common-sense of his readers. In one passage (1 Cor. vii. 25) he declares that on a mooted point he gives his judgment as one who has obtained mercy of the Lord to be faithful; that is, as a pious man using his common-sense in a question pertaining to the conduct of life. In none of the other epistles is there indication of consciousness that the writer is under divine direction, except that he believes himself to be expounding the truth as it was revealed through Jesus Christ. All, conscious of the possession of truth, write out of the fulness of the heart, as men write to friends, to counsel or comfort them. In what concerns the fundamental principles of the gospel they admit no deviations from their teaching, but on other points they ask only for the respect due to persons of age and experience. They speak as witnesses to a divine historical fact, rather than as formulators of a dogma. The consideration accorded to their words was sometimes dependent on local circumstances. A strong party in Corinth showed antagonism to Paul, admiring his letters as weighty, but declining to obey his commands and suggestions (2 Cor. x. 10, 11; xi. 12; xii. 20, 21; xiii. 2, 3). The Apocalypse is in the form of vision, a direct revelation, as is the case with all apocalypses; and it is precisely in these books that the elaborate literary form makes the hypothesis of vision, except in a very general sense, impossible. It is clear that Ezekiel, Zechariah, Daniel, the Sibyl, Enoch, and the author or authors of the New Testament Apocalypse worked up their material with the greatest care, for the purpose of enforcing a duty or a doctrine, or guiding and inspiring their people in times of doubt and suffering. The author or final editor of the Apocalypse appends to his book an imprecation on the man who shall add to or take from its contents, from which we may infer that he wished them to be regarded as divinely imparted and authoritative; this is perhaps a feeling peculiar to the last Christian redactor of the work. Christianity was in process of organization. The first century felt the throb of a great, uplifting religious idea; the apostles and other church-leaders were conscious (more deeply and persistently than Philo) of the impulse of a divine inspiration, which they believed was to change the current of the world's religious life. But as yet the line of inspiration was not sharply drawn; there were many teachers, and they were not always at one among themselves; their authority depended largely on their personal influence; there was no collection of Christian sacred books. It was reserved for later generations to sift the material, gradually to make a canonical collection of Christian writings, and to invest it with absolute authority in matters of faith and conduct.

As to the attitude of the New Testament writers toward the Old Testament, it has already been remarked that they accept it in general as authoritative, without distinct definition of the character and extent of its inspiration. As Jews they had been trained from infancy to regard it as the word given from God to Israel, handed down from the fathers through the generations. There was no reason why a Jew should question the validity of this transmission. There was no critical discussion. The Talmud decides on date and authorship of Old

Testament books in the most mechanical way. Moses was held to have written the Pentateuch and Job, and Joshua the book that bears his name; Judges, Samuel, and Ruth were ascribed to Samuel, and Kings to Jeremiah; Chronicles, Ezra, and Nehemiah were referred to Ezra, and Esther to the Great Synagogue; the prophets and Daniel were held to have been written by the men whose names they bear; Solomon was regarded as the author of Proverbs, Ecclesiastes, and the Song of Songs; in the Psalter, the titles of the psalms were regarded as authoritative, and certain untitled psalms were provided with authors, none of whom were later than David.[1] The critical-historical method of investigation did not exist. It would no more have occurred to a Jew of that time to doubt the Mosaic authorship of the Pentateuch than to call in question the generally accepted opinion that the sun moved around the earth. We have no reason to suppose that the Jews of the first century of our era knew any better than we why any particular psalm, as the 68th or the 110th, was ascribed to David; they knew only that it so stood in the titles. It probably occurred to no one that the book of Isaiah was a collection of writings by different men. There was little or no curiosity on such points, and so far as it existed, it was easily satisfied by such simple solutions as we find in the Talmud. The New Testament shares the traditional opinion of the time on these points.

If we go back some time to the period when the Old Testament books were edited and collected, it is not impossible to understand the methods by which they were assigned to certain authors. It is tolerably clear how Moses came to be regarded as the composer of the Pentateuch; he was the

---

[1] See L. Wogue, "Histoire de la Bible," Paris, 1881, pp. 15 ff. The psalm-authors besides David (who is held to have written the greater part of the Psalter) are stated to be: Adam, Melkisedek, Abraham, Moses, Heman, Jeduthun, Asaph, and the three sons of Korah.

heroic figure of the formative period of the nation, and the natural traditional author of its legislation and primitive history.[1] But, it may be asked, supposing the ritual to have grown up after the exile, how could the men who developed it ascribe it to Moses? The answer is, first, that in an uncritical age a generation or two of use would suffice to create the opinion that a usage had existed from time immemorial; and further, when a book had been written, the scribes of that day felt no hesitation in making additions to it, — they were innocent of suspicion that they were encroaching on the integrity of the book or the rights of the author, and their additions were accepted without question by an uncritical public as parts of the original work. In this way, from a small body of tradition, believed to go back to Moses, might arise in process of time a great mass of law; and there is no need to suppose deliberate deception, — it was a process of traditional expansion, in which the successive accretions might not unnaturally be regarded as belonging to the original legislation.[2] We can also see how the titles of the prophetic books arose. The prophets lived in comparatively late times, after the beginning of the literary period; manuscripts of their writings and traditions of authors' names might be handed down from the regal period and the exile to the fourth or third century; to such a tradition a certain historical value has to be allowed, — we may feel tolerably sure that we have writings of Amos, Hosea, Isaiah, and the other prophets, down to Malachi, Joel, and the second Zechariah. It does not follow that we have all

---

[1] Compare above, pp. 70, 71.

[2] Ezekiel, it is true, says nothing of Moses (Ezek. xl.-xlviii.), but derives his legislation from an immediate divine revelation. But the orderly development of the Deuteronomic code may have gone on during and after the exile in the way above described; and it is to be noted that Ezekiel's scheme is not incorporated into the Pentateuch. The possibility of deliberate deception in the unknown framers of the Levitical Code may be admitted, but it does not seem to be necessary.

of their writings, or that all the material that we have belongs to the men whose names are attached to the books. The freedom which the scribes of those days allowed themselves was great. The preciousness of parchment led to the custom of writing the compositions of different authors on the same roll; the best example of this composite character of a manuscript is found in our book of Isaiah, which, starting with the discourses of the prophet of Hezekiah's time, has appropriated material from the seventh century, the exile, and the early post-exilian time; handed down through the generations, it was accepted as wholly the work of the son of Amos. The same sort of growth is visible in our books of Micah and Zechariah. The book of Jonah, a late religious apologue, was placed among the prophetic writings because it bore the name of a prophetic man, said in the book of Kings (2 Kings xiv. 25) to have lived in the days of Jeroboam the Second (toward the middle of the eighth century B. C.); the author made the ancient seer the hero of his work, possibly on the basis of a tradition (for in Jeroboam's time the Assyrians and the Israelites had known each other for a century), but chiefly to give dignity and authority to his religious lesson, and probably unconscious of literary and historical sin in ascribing to this old prophet the ideas of a much later time. The historical books of the Second Canon — Joshua, Judges, Samuel, Kings — bear no authors' names; they were gradually compiled from traditions and written documents, and received their final shape from editors (during the exile and later) who did not feel their share in the work to be of sufficient importance to call for the mention of their names. It does not appear that the pre-Christian Jews felt it necessary to know the authors by name; the later rabbis, with greater literary and religious but quite uncritical curiosity, sought the authors of these books in prominent men who were supposed to be contemporaneous with the last events described in them. Of the books of the Third Canon, Job, Lamentations, Daniel, Esther, Chronicles, Ezra, Nehemiah, are anonymous. Job, from its appearance of antiquity, was naturally referred to Moses Chronicles, Ezra, and Nehemiah were with equal naturalness assigned to the eminent man who played so prominent a part in the establishment of the law. To the Great Synagogue [1] or to Mordecai was given the book of Esther, while Ruth, by its subject matter, went with the earlier historical works. The Lamentations over the fall of Jerusalem suggested the sad prophet, Jeremiah; and no other than Daniel could be thought of as the writer of the book which bears his name. As early as the exile, perhaps earlier, the tradition had made Solomon the ideal of intellectual greatness, not the religious wisdom of the later conception, but knowledge of men and things (1 Kings iv. 29–34, *Heb*. v. 9–14). There existed collections of apothegms ascribed to him (Prov. xxv. 1); these were gradually added to down to a late period, and the whole of the resulting book of Proverbs was looked on as his work. It was natural also for the author of Ecclesiastes to select the wise king as the expounder of his philosophy of life; it is less clear how his name came to be attached to the Song of Songs unless it be merely from the statement in 1 Kings v. 32, that his songs were a thousand and five; in both these cases the writer's ascription of his own production to the ancient king was made possible by the unscientific feeling of the times to which reference has already been made. The designation of the writers of the psalms was determined by similar considerations. The tradition pointed to David as

---

1 The Great Synagogue, that National Academy of the Tora which Jewish tradition created for the time of Ezra, is not mentioned in any work earlier than the Talmud, is foreign to the spirit of the fifth century B. C., and must be regarded as an attempt of later Jewish thought to bestow a consecrating antiquity on that official interpretation of the Law which was believed to be the breath of the national life.

the writer of religious odes; in the eighth century he was thought of as the inventor of instruments of music (Amos vi. 5), and he was speedily idealized into the sweet singer of Israel. From time to time collections of hymns were formed bearing his name; an allusion was found to some fact in his history, or, as in the case of Ecclesiastes, a writer would seek to give dignity to his production by ascribing it to the ancient and famous king. Other psalms, composed by Levitical singers, were referred, probably on the basis of a good tradition, to a late organization known as the sons of Korah, or, without authority, to supposed ancestors of similar organizations, as Asaph, Heman, and Ethan; the majestic ninetieth psalm was ascribed to the revered law-giver, of whose wisdom it was doubtless felt to be a worthy monument. These were doubtless the opinions as to date and authorship of Old Testament books held by Jews and Christians in the first century of our era.

The use made of the Old Testament Scriptures by the New Testament writers is such as might be anticipated from the state of opinion just described. On the one hand, the national sacred writings are treated as authoritative; on the other hand, on account of the absence of historical-exegetical feeling, the greatest liberty was assumed in the interpretation and application of Scriptural passages. Small regard was paid to context. Words were made to mean anything which they might suggest. Quotations were taken, not from the Hebrew, but from the Septuagint, or from a current Aramaic version; the Hebrew language had long since ceased to be the spoken tongue of the nation, and had been replaced in Palestine by Aramaic, in Egypt by Greek, and elsewhere by Greek or Latin. The feeling which we find afterward so definite in the Talmud, that the separate words of Scripture had an independent, objective force, was already in existence. The Epistle to the Hebrews, for example (ii. 13), illustrates the oneness of Jesus and his people from Isa. viii. 18, taking a clause out of its connection (herein following the punctuation of the Greek), and entirely changing the sense of the original. The prophet had said: "Behold, I and the children whom Yahwe has given me [who had symbolical names pointing to the fortunes of the nation] are for signs and for wonders in Israel;" the epistle quotes: "Behold, I and the children whom God has given me," and makes the Messiah the speaker, and the "children" those who believe on him. The central motive of the New Testament quotations is the kingdom of God set up by Jesus Christ, — the good news of salvation to the world. This grand and inspiring idea filled and controlled the Christian consciousness of that day. In the fulness of time, it was held, God had visited his people and performed the promises made to the fathers. It could not but be that the prophets, the Psalmist, and Moses in the Law had looked forward to and spoken of this wondrous event. For most Jews of that time there was no literature but the Old Testament, and it was more than a body of ancient literature, — for them it comprehended all truth. The Talmud finds in it everywhere allusions to the current events of the Talmudic period. The Christian reader of the first century, aglow with the inspiration of God's latest manifestation of himself in the gospel, could not fail to find the evangelical history, the history of the kingdom of heaven, in the words of the ancient saints. The life of the Christ, the doctrines of the new dispensation, the fortunes of the Church, would stand out clearly to the Christian eye on the pages of Scripture; the old congregation of Israel was felt to be a preparation for and a prediction of the new congregation of Christ; the chief interest for the Christian lay in the discovery of references to the gospel times, and in a thousand Old Testament passages he might find prophecies and illustrations of what was going on around him. There is, however, a difference in different New Testament books and persons in respect to simplicity and naturalness of citation. The quotations made by Jesus himself are almost exclusively of ethical or general religious import, and bear their validity on their face. The same thing may be said of the Catholic and the Pastoral epistles. The Apocalypse has few direct citations, but a large mass of Old Testament material (together with much from Enoch) interwoven into its text in a free manner. The predictions of the life of Christ given by the evangelists themselves are also marked by uncritical freedom, but are confined to passages whose wording naturally suggests a prediction of the actual experiences of Jesus. Paul's method of procedure betrays his rabbinical training; he not only gives to general Old Testament expressions the technical senses of his own theology, but he allegorizes incidents and words into meanings remote from their original intention. Hagar and Sara he represents as signifying respectively the old Israel held in the bondage of the covenant of Sinai and the Church of Christ freed from the bondage of the law. In his discussion of the glossolaly (1 Cor. xiv.), wishing to prove the superiority of prophecy over the speaking with tongues, he declares that the former benefits those who believe, while the latter is serviceable to those only who do not believe; this he proves from Isa. xxviii. 11: " By men of strange tongues, and by the lips of strangers will I speak to this people," where all that the prophet says is that God will teach the Israelites a lesson through the foreign Assyrians. The height of arbitrary quotation is reached in the Epistle to the Hebrews, in which the free Alexandrian method of treating the Old Testament is visible. There are no bounds to the writer's ability to extract from his Greek version the sense which he desires; he goes so far as to find a demonstration of the necessity of the sacrifice of Christ (Heb. x. 5–10) in a psalm-passage (Ps. xl. 6–8) which affirms that God desires not sacrifice, but obedience to his will.

But while we are forced to admit an uncritical and arbitrary element in New Testament quotations from the Old Testament, we must recognize the power of the new spirit which created this sort of exposition. The circumstances of the time being what they were, it was a necessity that the spirituality of the religion of Jesus should stamp itself on the Jewish Scriptures. The divine revelation to Israel was a standard of faith for the Church of the first century, but a new revelation had appeared in Christianity, and it was essential that the two should be brought into harmony. For that generation it was more important that a higher spiritual feeling should be impressed on the Old Testament than that its meaning should be investigated in a critical, historical way. With us the case is different; the ideas of Christianity have embodied themselves in history, and we can look quietly at the Old Testament religion as one step in the development of Judaism. It was not so in the first century. Christianity was engaged in a struggle for life, and one of its most powerful weapons was the demonstration of its harmony with the book which contained God's revelation to Israel in the olden time. This was the instinctive feeling which prompted the scriptural exegesis of the New Testament writers. And it must not be forgotten that there is a basis of exegetical truth in their procedure. The Old Testament thought is controlled by a true spiritual feeling which found fuller expression in the more developed ideas of Christianity. From this point of view the mechanical predictive element is of small importance. No Old Testament writer foresaw the times of Christianity, though many a prophet and many a psalmist had in his own soul the germs of the teaching of Jesus. The early Christians were conscious of this substantial identity between the two revelations. If they carried the correspondence of form too far, seeing circumstantial agreements where none existed, this is what is to be expected. Christianity, by adopting the Old Testament, established the unity of the whole Jewish development, and thus initiated a study of the Scriptures which was destined after varied exegetical fortunes to lead to a separation between the essential and the unessential, and a recognition of the real spirituality of Old Testament and New Testament alike.

CHAPTER III.

SUBORDINATE SUPERNATURAL BEINGS.

WE have now to inquire into the Jewish doctrine of supernatural intelligences inferior to the divine being. Beginning with the Old Testament, we must then ask whether the doctrine received accretions in the post-biblical period, and in what form it is found in the New Testament.

1. It will suffice merely to mention the survivals from early animistic beliefs which occur in the Old Testament, but do not maintain themselves in the later religious development. That oldest system of thought, according to which every object of nature, animate or inanimate, was inhabited by a spirit, seems to have vanished. We cannot, indeed, be sure on this point, — our existing Hebrew literature has been carefully worked over by monotheistic writers, who have probably omitted or transformed many of the lower popular beliefs. Such beliefs, as we know from the history of other peoples, often survive a long time even in the presence of higher culture. Yet, judging from the few hints given in the Old Testament, it seems probable that the Hebrews, as early as the fourteenth century B. C., had already left behind them, or greatly modified, the old vague fetishism of which traces appear only in a few objects of popular worship.[1] Among these the teraphim may perhaps be included, — household protecting spirits, possibly a developed

[1] On remains of totemism in the Hebrew folk-religion see J. G. Frazer, "Totemism," Edinburgh, 1887 ; W. R. Smith, "The Religion of the Semites," London and New York, 1889.

survival of the primitive divine tree or stone or animal.[1]
More definite instances of demons[2] are found in the *sa'ir* and
lilit of Isa. xxxiv. 14; these creatures (called "satyr," or
"he goat," and "night-monster," in the Revised English Version) seem, like the Arabian *jinn*, to have been originally wild
animals, thought of as hostile to man. They were probably
Canaanitish objects of worship (Lev. xvii. 7); whether they
belonged to the original Hebrew system, or were adopted by
the Hebrews from their neighbors, it is hard to say.[3]

Magic art, of which traces appear in the Old Testament,
was no doubt originally connected with demon-worship; that
is to say, it issues out of that primitive stratum of thought
in which it was believed that man could coerce the extra-
human supernatural powers. This has proved itself to be
one of the most obstinate and persistent of man's primitive
beliefs; it maintained its place down to the New Testament times (with ever-changing forms); it appears in the
Talmud, and exists to-day all over the world. It is founded
on a vague idea that the supernatural is somehow under the
control of law, and that unlimited power and happiness belong to him who can discover this law. It is a curious
example of the survival, in a period of high culture, of the
crude faith of primitive savagery.[4]

---

[1] General analogy would suggest a totemistic origin for the teraphim,
though in the Old Testament they have probably passed beyond the primitive
form and seem sometimes to have been human in shape (1 Sam. xix. 13); in
any case we must suppose that they represent the old family-cult.

[2] The word "demon" is here used not in the later sense of "malignant
spirit," but in the signification (to which the etymology points) of a supernatural being who has not been raised to the rank of a tribal or national god.

[3] For the Babylonian demon *lilit*, cf. Lenormant, "La Magie chez les
Chaldéens," and for the use of the term in the Talmud, see Weber, "System
der pal. Theol.," p. 246. The term *shedim* is employed in the Old Testament
of foreign deities only (Deut. xxxii. 17, Ps. cxxxvi. 37); in Babylonian it signifies "bull-deity," and seems therefore not to express a class of demons.

[4] Necromancy is a well-defined fact in the Old Testament, and was doubtless employed abundantly by the Hebrews (Isa. viii. 19). The demon of necro-

The demon-figure of the Old Testament which is most clearly defined, and which made the most serious effort to maintain itself in the national thought is Azazel (Lev. xvi.). In the solemn rite of the day of atonement he appears as a wilderness-power to whom pertains the domain of evil; the world is, as it were, divided between Yahwe and Azazel. So distinct is the personality and so great the power of the demon that some have thought of identifying him with Satan. But though the two personages are in some regards identical, their historical developments are so different that they must be treated as separate conceptions. Of the early history of Azazel we know nothing; he makes an abrupt appearance in a late post-exilian document and is never mentioned elsewhere in the Old Testament; he plays a great rôle in the book of Enoch (viii. ix.), where he is the leader of the evil spirits, and is condemned to imprisonment till the day of judgment, when he is to be cast into the fire (x.). Here certainly he seems to play the part of Satan; yet in the succeeding literature it is Satan that keeps the first place, and Azazel practically vanishes. It is to be noted that in Leviticus he is spoken of as a well-known person; he is a wilderness-demon, somehow connected with the goat. It seems a natural inference that he was originally a satyr-like or goat-like figure, — a hostile desert-power to be placated by an offering, and by some means singled out from the mass of demons and elevated to a controlling position. The similarity between his rôle and that of the Persian Ahriman is obvious; and it is not impossible that this isolation of Azazel was due to an impulse derived from Persian thought. Satan and

mantic art is called *ob* (1 Sam. xxviii., Isa. xxix. 4, cf. Isa. viii. 19), a word of uncertain origin. Of ancestor-worship there is no direct trace; the teraphim, as household deities, may point to such a cult through a fusion of totems and human ancestors. The plural form of the word may refer to the mass of tereph-objects in a family or clan. Jer. ii. 26, 27, deals with a late form of idolatry.

Azazel may be looked on as rivals; of the contest between them we do not know the details. It appears only that victory fell to the former on probable general grounds which will be pointed out below. That the Azazel-cult had no little hold on the popular feeling is evident from the fact that it was incorporated into the advanced Levitical ritual.[1]

2. Alongside of these demon-forms we find a more advanced conception in the host of spirits who are represented as forming Yahwe's heavenly court. The fullest and most striking description of this court is given in the story of Ahab and Micaiah (1 Kings xxii. 19–23) : " I saw Yahwe sitting on his throne and all the host of heaven standing by him on his right hand and on his left. And Yahwe said, Who will entice Ahab that he may go up and fall at Ramoth-Gilead ? And one said one thing, and another another, and there came forward a spirit,[2] and stood before Yahwe and said, I will entice him. And Yahwe said, How ? and he said, I will go forth and will be a lying spirit in the mouth of all his prophets. And he said, Thou shalt entice him, and also thou shalt succeed ; go forth and do so." Here we have an apparently homogeneous mass of spirits without distinction of grade and authority; the whole body forms a sort of council, whose advice on this important occasion is asked by Yahwe. There is no question of right or wrong; the spirit of falsehood is the agent of Yahwe acting by his direction and assured of his support. The prophet Micaiah, wishing to account for the predictions of Ahab's prophets, thinks

---

[1] Azazel seems to be a Hebrew word, possibly connected with the stem *azaz*, " strong ; " the significations " he from whom one withdraws," or " he who withdraws himself [from God] " (from *azal*) do not accord so well with the probably primitive character of the demon-figure. But the origin of the idea and the name is uncertain.

[2] Literally, " the spirit ; " namely, the one who had just manifested himself in Ahab's prophets, — not the spirit of prophecy in general, but the inspirer of this special prediction.

it necessary to ascribe them to a direct influence from God.
Other examples are found in the evil spirit which, sent by
God, broke up the friendly relations between Abimelech and
the Shechemites (Judg. ix. 23), and the evil spirit from
Yahwe (or from God), which disturbed the soul of Saul
(1 Sam. xvi. 14–23).[1]

These spirits doubtless issue out of old animistic material.
The peculiarity of the conception is that the spirit-being is
completely isolated from the object to which it was attached
in primitive times. The *sa'ir* (and perhaps also Azazel)
seems to have been thought of as possessing an animal form,
as was probably the case in earliest times with most spirits.
It was, however, a primitive belief that the soul or spirit
could detach itself from the body in which it resided, and go
its independent way. We may suppose that the progress of
reflection gradually led men to isolate the spirit from its
bodily connections, and this is a great advance in the organization of the supernatural world. In the Old Testament,
further, the spirits appear as completely subordinated to the
supreme God, and this monotheistic constitution points to a
comparatively late period in religious development.[2] From
the non-appearance of this body of spirits in the prophetic
writings it may be inferred, indeed, that they belonged rather
to the popular than to the prophetical religious scheme; still,
however this may be, and whatever may have been the
looser popular ideas on the subject, the actual spirit-system
of the Old Testament is cast in a monotheistic mould.

[1] Cf. also Job iv. 15, where in a night-vision the announcement of a great
religious truth is ascribed to a "spirit," for so apparently we must render the
Hebrew, and not "wind," or "breath."

[2] Yet here also we find traces of magic, in the exorcism, for example, of
Saul's evil spirit by David's music (1 Sam. xvi. 23), and in the musical invoca-
tion of Elisha's spirit of prophecy (2 Kings iii. 15). This survival of the old
idea seems not to have interfered with the practical supremacy of Yahwe.
At the present day there is found in the Christian world a similar combination of belief in God and reliance on magic.

The subordination to the supreme God is complete,—there is no independence of action in the spirits. Nor is there, so far as appears, any differentiation of moral character among the members of the body. All dwell in the presence of Yahwe, are his servants, carry out his commands whether for good or for evil. If the epithet "evil" is applied to one of them, it is rather from the nature of the work assigned him than from his moral character. They thus represent a stadium in religious development in which a substantially unitary conception of the world has been reached, but the demand for separation between good and evil moral supernatural agencies has not yet shown itself. God is absolutely all,—the creator of light and darkness, peace and evil (Isa. xlv. 7). There came a time when the Israelitish ethical feeling was offended by the imputation of moral evil to God; but apparently down to and during the exile the best thinkers of the nation were satisfied with the acknowledgment of his supreme control of all things. The sharp struggle to establish the monotheistic idea left little time for this sort of ethical elaboration of the theistic scheme.

3. Still another form of supernatural agency is found in the angels. They stand alongside of the spirits, resembling them in some respects, differing from them in others; no attempt is made in the Old Testament to define the relations between the two classes,—both are growths out of the old folk-faith, with different starting-points and paths of development. The angels of the older Hebrew literature (down to the second century B. C.) are like the spirits in having no functional or ethical differentiation among themselves; they are all ministers and messengers of God, executing his designs, benevolent or harmful, saving or destroying without respect to circumstance. They differ from the spirits in the nature of the commissions intrusted to them, appearing often in bodily shape, and performing bodily actions, such as deliver-

ing messages to persons and inflicting plagues, while the spirits act directly on the minds of men.

The ground of this difference between the two categories of being is to be sought in their origins. Both doubtless go back to the spiritual essences which were believed to reside in objects; but the Old Testament spirits seem to be merely the isolation of these essences, while the angels appear to be derived immediately from forms of old deities. For between angels and "sons of God" or "sons of the Elohim" in the Old Testament there does not seem to be any difference of nature. These last occur by name on three occasions: they intermarry with human beings and become the fathers of old heroes (Gen. vi. 2); they form a heavenly court, and report their procedures to Yahwe (Job i. ii); they are present at the creation of the world (Job xxxviii. 7,. It is they also with whom God takes counsel respecting the creation of man, and in whose image man is created (Gen. i. 26); they are consulted by Yahwe as to the coercion of the tower-builders (Gen. xi. 7); they are the Elohim-beings with whom man is compared by the Psalmist (Ps. viii. 5,; with two of them (afterward called "angels") Yahwe descends to earth to inquire into the alleged iniquities of Sodom (Gen. xviii. 19).[1] They carry us back to a theistic scheme in which Yahwe was only the first among a host of equals. In time the rest were subordinated to him, becoming in part the inferior deities of other nations, in part the ministers and messengers

---

[1] In the form of heathen deities, Elohim-beings to whom the nations have been assigned (Deut. xxxii. 8 in the Greek), they appear in Ps. lxxxii. (v. 1: "Yahwe judges in the midst of gods" [*elohim*]; v. 6: "I have said, ye are gods, and all of you sons of Elyon" [the most High]), Ps. xxix. 1 (where the "sons of gods," *elim*, are called on to give honor to Yahwe), Ps. lxxxix. 7 ("sons of gods," *elim*), Ps. xcvii. 7 ("Do homage to him, all gods," *elohim*), and perhaps Ps. lviii. 1 (2), by a slight change of text: "Do ye indeed utter justice, O gods?" This conception of heathen gods, which is inconsistent with monotheism, seems to have maintained itself after the exile, but does not impair the practical supremacy of the God of Israel.

of Yahwe. It is in this latter character that they are termed "angels" in the Old Testament; the expression "sons of the Elohim" (that is, members of the Elohim-class) or "sons of God" designates them in the Hebrew theology rather as the attendants of the supreme deity, while the angels are active agents, and intermediaries between God and the world. Their creation is nowhere mentioned; their existence from the beginning is assumed.

The oldest angelic representation in the Old Testament seems to be that of a being who is apparently charged with the whole divine authority, and acts as if he were an independent divinity (the angel of the Lord or of God). Such is the tone of the being who appears to Hagar (Gen. xvi. 7–13), to Joshua (Josh. v. 13), and to Manoah (Judg. xiii. 18). This figure is perhaps a real survival of an ancient deity; it is thus that an independent deity, transformed in a monotheistic faith into a messenger of the supreme God, would act; and it is to be observed that the title "angel" distinctly and completely differences such a being from God himself, — Yahwe could never be called his own messenger. In this way, also, we are to understand the vision in Zech. iii., where the titles "the angel of Yahwe" and "Yahwe" are interchanged; the divine authority resides in the angel, but he is not identical with the divine being. Closely allied with this angelic form are the angels of the face or presence (Isa. lxiii. 9, cf. Ex. xxxiii. 15) and of the name (Ex. xxiii. 21), who represent the divine power in a very special way. From these passages it may be concluded that this conception of special angelic intermediaries retained its hold on Jewish thought down to a comparatively late period; it appears in an altered form in the book of Daniel. It arose from the demand for an actual divine presence among men, coupled with the feeling that God could not appear in person.

This representation of the intercourse between man and

God was, however, gradually modified by the monotheistic feeling. The increasing exaltation of the divine being tended to reduce all subordinate supernatural intelligences to the same level; more and more he was withdrawn into absolute aloneness, and all his ministers were as one in his sight. Some time before the exile the angel appears as a simple messenger and agent of God; so we may probably understand the horses and chariots which surrounded Elisha (2 Kings vi. 17), and such is the character of the being who acts as interpreter to the prophet Zechariah (Zech. i. 9). This is the view which became more and more prominent in the post-biblical Judaism, and passed into the New Testament; it is found in Daniel, Tobit, and Enoch, and in the Talmud.[1]

At this point we have to notice an extraordinary development of the scheme of the angelic world which appears in the Jewish literature a couple of hundred years before the beginning of our era. In the body of the Old Testament no one of the angels receives a special proper name, nor is there any definite gradation among them. In the books of Tobit, Daniel, and Enoch, we are suddenly introduced to a well-organized angelic society, the individuals of which have their

---

1 Weber, "System der pal. Theol ," §§ 34, 35, and Kohut, "Jüdische Angelologie und Dämonologie." Angelic appearances are rare in the later historical books; doubtless the apparition which struck down Heliodorus (2 Mac. iii. 24 ff.) was thought of as an angel. In the Old Testament writings down to the end of the exile, angels occur almost exclusively in folk-stories. About one fourth of the occurrences are found in the narrative books of the Pentateuch · (15 in Gen , 6 in Ex., 11 in Numb., of which 10 are in the Balaam-story); Judges has nearly one fifth (22, the story of Manoah, ch. xiii., containing 10); Samuel and Kings show a somewhat smaller number (14), and Chronicles nearly as many (10); the prophets are almost silent (1 in Hosea, and 1 in Isaiah). The angel in pre-exilian times thus seems to belong to the popular rather than to the prophetic religion. Immediately after the exile the angelic figure becomes very prominent in Zechariah (20 occurrences), but differs from the earlier form somewhat, in being more intimate and confidential with the prophet. Later in Job (twice) and in Psalms (8 times) the conception of angelic agency is loftier. The word "angel" is found only twice in Daniel, but angelic beings play a very important part.

own proper names and exercise functions unknown to the earlier writings. In Tobit, Rafael is the affable companion and mentor of the young Tobias, occupies himself with domestic matters in a genial human way, and shows himself to be a clever man of affairs. Two other names appear in Daniel: Gabriel is interpreter to the seer (Dan. viii. 16); Michael is the guardian angel of Israel (Dan. x. 13); guardian angels of other nations are spoken of, but not named; mention is made of holy "watchers" who are sent down as agents of God. Enoch details the angelic history at great length, with long lists of names and much specialization of function. The question arises, How is this great expansion of the angelic scheme to be explained; may it be regarded as a purely native development? or must a foreign, especially a Persian influence be appealed to?[1] In the first place, it is to be observed that the existence of a Persian influence on the Jewish pneumatology of this time is vouched for by the name of the evil spirit in Tobit; Asmodeus is confessedly the Persian Aeshma daeva. It is also to be noted that the Persians probably had at this time a well-developed system of supernatural intelligences which was not borrowed by them, since the greater part of it can be traced back to the old Aryan material.[2] Alongside of the supreme God, Ahura-Mazda, stood the six Amesha-çpentas and a host of other deities and spirits who were invested with various functions in the government and maintenance of the world. A special position as guardians was assigned to certain star-deities (Tistrya and three others), who presided over the four quarters of the world, and to the Fravashis, who, whatever their origin, were charged with the control of various departments of human

---

[1] See Kohut, "Angelologie und Dämonologie," and C. de Harlez, "Des Origines du Zoroastrisme," Paris, 1879 (originally appeared in the "Journal Asiatique," 1878).

[2] Spiegel, "Eranische Alterthumskunde," ii.

life. It must be borne in mind that the Jews would probably take such ideas from popular beliefs rather than from
books ; for example, the character of the Asmodeus of Tobit
does not correspond exactly with that of the Aeshma of the
Persian sacred books, and the more natural explanation of
this difference is that the popular mythology diverged a little
from the theological standards, as has been true to a great
extent among Christian peoples. It is quite conceivable that
the Persian popular doctrine of guardian spirits was fuller
than that of the books (supposing, as is likely, that books
existed at this time), or differed from it in some details ; or
we may suppose that the idea of angels as guardians of particular nations originated among the Jews under Persian
influence.[1] Abundant opportunity for borrowing such conceptions was afforded by the long residence of the exiles in
Babylonia after it became a Persian province. Ezekiel and
his successors showed themselves quite ready to adopt certain
Semitic-Babylonian ideas, and there was no reason why there
should not have been a similar willingness to receive suggestions from the Persians. The scenes of the books of Esther,
Tobit, and Daniel lie in the Persian region. A general influence, therefore, is not at all improbable. All that need be
supposed is an expansion of existing Jewish ideas in the
direction of organization and specialization of function. The
supposition of borrowing is made more probable by the fact
that the angelic system in Daniel is not entirely in the line of
the preceding Old Testament development. Angels do not
appear as national guardians in the later post-biblical books.
In the New Testament there is one apparent reference to the
belief in the angelic guardianship of individuals (Matt. xviii.

---

[1] An Old Testament point of attachment for this idea is found in the
Greek text of Deut. xxxii. 8: "The Most High set the boundaries of the nations
according to the number of the angels of God," or, as the emended Hebrew
text would read : " The number of the sons of the Elohim," where the reference would be to the gods of the nations.

10); the Michael of the New Testament Apocalypse has a somewhat different coloring from the angel of that name in Daniel, — he is the prince and leader of the people of God, but his conflict with the dragon connects him rather with the old Babylonian myth of the fight between Bel and Tiamat than with the function of guardianship. The names of the biblical angels are Hebrew, which is what we might expect on the supposition that the Jews took general suggestions from the Persians, and worked them up in their own manner.

The position of angels in the New Testament is in general the same as in the Old Testament, but with noteworthy modifications in some books. They are immortal (Luke xx. 36), and neither marry nor are given in marriage (Matt. xxii. 30); their special ordinary function is to minister to God's people, particularly in times of doubt or distress, and it is thought to be not unnatural that they should speak to men (Acts xxiii. 9, a Pharisaic opinion, shared, no doubt, by Christians); they take a lively interest in men's spiritual experiences (Luke xv. 10); they conduct the souls of the righteous to paradise (Luke xvi. 22); they inflict disease on wicked men (Acts xii. 23); they form a sort of heavenly society, before which Christ will acknowledge his servants, in order that they may be admitted to the privileges of this blessed companionship (Luke xii. 8; Rev. iii. 5); they are to be the attendants of the Son of Man when he shall come to judge the world, it is they who will gather the elect, and remove the wicked (Matt. xiii. 41; xxv. 31; 2 Thess. i. 7); they are themselves called "elect" (1 Tim. v. 21), chosen by God for his service in distinction from those "angels" who pertain to the Devil (Matt. xxv. 41; Rev. xii. 9), — Satan, however, can assume the form of an angel of light, for the purpose of deceiving men, just as his ministers, false teachers of religion, present themselves as apostles of Christ (2 Cor. xi. 14, 15); believers

are attended by angels, who have special access to God (Matt.
xviii. 10; Acts xii. 15); the natural inference is that each
believer has a guardian angel, who represents him in the
divine presence and cares for his interests, — an extension
of the conception in the book of Tobit.

Some peculiar representations are found in Paul's Epistles.
Believers, it is said (1 Cor. vi. 3) are to judge angels (whether
good or bad angels is not clear) to be superior to them in
dignity, doubtless in consequence of their near relation to
Christ, — a view which may be compared with that of Luke
xx. 36, where they are thought of as equal to the good
angels; cf. in 1 Pet. i. 12 the statement that these last
desire to understand the things of the gospel, the inference
being that they are not completely enlightened therein.
More difficult is his opinion that women in the church-
gatherings, or while praying or prophesying, should be veiled
" on account of the angels " (1 Cor. xi. 10). The veil, as the
sign of subordination, is understood to symbolize man's
authority over woman — but what has this to do with
angels ? It cannot be intended simply to express respect for
them ; this would be equally obligatory on men. It cannot
be to teach them, whether they be holy or unholy, a lesson
of subordination , this seems a forced idea. Nor is it natural to regard the expression as meaning that the angels will
report the conduct of the women to God ; the apostle would
hardly thus refer to a general angelic function in connection
with a particular custom. His intention seems to be to
insist that the woman shall wear the badge of subordination
or ownership in the presence of beings who represent, having
had a part in establishing, that order of creation in which
the woman was made subject to the man. In that case we
infer that he understood the " let us make " of Gen. i. 26 as
including the angels. In Rom. viii. 38 a hierarchical constitution of the angelic world is hinted at in the expressions

" angels, principalities, powers," the two last terms being not further defined. These beings are, however, here presented as hostile to the Christian life, as in Eph. vi. 12, Col. ii 15 ;[1] while in Eph. i. 21, iii. 10, Col. i. 16, ii. 10, they are obedient servants of God. It appears, therefore, that these expressions are used by Paul and the authors of Ephesians and Colossians in a twofold sense, of both good and bad supernatural powers.

This later angelic scheme appears thus to be the Old Testament system, organized under Persian influence into a double hierarchy (good and bad), and in the Colossian heresy (Col. ii. 18) tinged with the gnostic thought which represented the angels as being, both ontologically, and as objects of worship and instruments of salvation, the connecting link between God and man. In the Christian scheme proper they were subordinate to Christ, and probably in general to the divine spirit, though in one place (Acts viii. 26, 29) the same act is ascribed at one time to an angel, at another to the spirit. On this point there was doubtless fluctuation of view, by reason of the fluctuating conception of the spirit.

4. Coming now to the doctrine of evil spirits, we take for our starting-point the general Old Testament representation of the spirit-world which is referred to above. This somewhat colorless mass of beings seems to have been gradually differentiated in accordance with the advance of Jewish ethical thought stimulated by outside influences. One might suppose that the highly developed Babylonian pneumatology would have measurably affected the Israelitish exiles; but the literature hardly favors such a supposition, — evil spirits proper do not appear in the Old Testament. The earliest postexilian evil being is Satan; for the explanation of the later

---

[1] The case is different in Gal. i. 8, where the preaching of another gospel by an " angel from heaven " is stated as a mere, and in fact impossible, supposition in hyperbolical fashion.

demoniacal system we are rather led to look to the contact of the Jews with Persian (and perhaps with Greek) ideas. The Mazdean religion had a large machinery of evil spirits, to which was ascribed the production of evil effects on the body and the soul of man, though there seems to have been no well-defined belief in demoniacal possession; the long residence of the Jews on Persian soil may have given them familiarity with this spiritual apparatus. Of direct Greek influence on this doctrine there is no proof; but that it was not wholly ineffective may perhaps be inferred from the usage of the Septuagint translators, who have given us our word "demon." They employed this familiar Greek term[1] to render Hebrew expressions for heathen deities, idols, and wilderness-spirits (Deut. xxxii. 17; Ps. xcv. 5; cvi. 37; Isa. lxv. 11; xiii. 21; xxxiv. 14); that is, for supernatural powers in general hostile to the God of Israel. This sense of the word maintained itself into the New Testament times; it is found, for example, in a passage (1 Cor. x. 20, 21) in which Paul appears to say that the eating of things offered to Gentile deities was having communion with demons.[2] The related sense of evil, indwelling spirit also attached itself to current Greek usage. But before examining this point, we must look at earlier Hebrew developments of the world of evil spiritual agencies.

[1] *Daimon*, used by Homer (Il. i. 222) and the tragic poets in the sense of "god," "divine being," sometimes also with the idea of hurtfulness, came to be employed specifically to signify secondary deities, and finally the shades of the dead. Plato (Apol. i. 5) distinguishes between gods and demons, suggesting that the latter are children of gods. *Daimonion* is likewise equivalent to "deity;" the charge against Socrates was (Xen. Mem. i. 1, 1) that he refused to acknowledge publicly the gods (*theous*) of the city, and introduced other new deities (*daimonia*). Socrates' own *daimonion* was a genius or guardian who told him what he ought and ought not to do (Mem. iv. 8, 1). From this conception in part came the later Jewish use of the term, on which see below

[2] This statement seems to rest on the old idea that sacrifices were acts of communion between the god and the worshipper, both partaking of the flesh of the animal offered.

We have already seen that before the exile no one figure
stands out prominently from the mass of spirits who do the
bidding of Yahwe; he is absolutely supreme, and his ministers perform whatever good or bad offices he assigns them.
But just after the return from Babylon, a new spiritual actor
in the affairs of Israel appears in the shape of an "adversary," a Satan, whose function it is to oppose the welfare of
the chosen people. The prophet Zechariah pictures the high
priest Joshua, the representative of the nation, as pleading
his people's cause before the angel of the Lord; he is opposed
by "the Satan," whose object is to prevent the rebuilding
of Jerusalem; the Satan is rebuked, and Joshua is promised
that if he will faithfully keep God's commands the nation
shall be established. The figure of the great spiritual adversary of the nation seems here to be in the act of taking
shape. He is the embodiment of all of Israel's difficulties
and enemies. Israelitish thought, constantly grappling with
the problem of the suffering of Yahwe's people, had apparently reached the conviction that the opposition to the national well-being must come from a spirit hostile to God.
This is a great advance on the pre-exilian conception of the
constitution of the spirit-world; we can only suppose that
the conditions of Jewish life in Babylonia had induced rapid
progress in this direction. In the book of Job we may recognize further progress in the elaboration of the idea of Satan.
In the prophet, his relations are with Israel; in Job, with
humanity. He traverses the earth with no benevolent in-
tent; he discusses Job's character with cynical acuteness; he
induces God to subject his servant to severest tests simply
to try his integrity. He is a malignant and powerful being,
but he is not detached from the person and service of God;
on the contrary, he is a member of the divine court, presents
himself among the sons of God before the divine throne, is
called on by Yahwe to make report of his doings, and re-

ceives from him his commission to test the character of Job. Such also is probably his position in Zechariah.[1] The representation in Job is an imaginative one ; Satan appears only in the court of heaven, in the dwelling-place of God and his ministers. In 1 Chron. xxi. 1 he is introduced in a more commonplace manner as tempting David to number Israel. The progress involved in this statement may be seen by a comparison of 2 Sam. xxiv. 1, where, in the description of the same incident, it is Yahwe who incites the king to the act of disobedience. Between the two statements (an interval of probably two or three hundred years) the feeling had grown up that instigation to evil could not properly be referred to God ; an evil spirit becomes the agent of temptation to sin. The advance in this representation consists, as is intimated above, in the completer introduction of Satan into man's every-day life. In Zechariah, he is the adversary of the nation ; in Job, his rôle is that of slanderer of righteous men (the nation also being perhaps had in mind); in Chronicles, while the event in question is a national one, it may probably be inferred that he is regarded as a general inciter to evil, entering into the conduct of man's spiritual life.

After 1 Chron. xxi. 1, Satan is mentioned no more in the Old Testament, and rarely in the extra-biblical books; the two works in which he appears treat him in very different ways. The first attempt at a spiritual interpretation of the serpent of Gen. iii. occurs in the Wisdom of Solomon

---

[1] It is difficult to fix the chronological relation of Job to Zechariah precisely. Even if we regard the man Job as the representative of Israel, and the thought of the book as springing out of the exilian suffering, it is not necessary to place its composition during the exile. The condition and feeling of suffering doubtless continued after the return. The elaborate argumentation of the book rather points to a later period. The portraiture of Satan in Job seems to be more developed than that in Zechariah, and the prologue seems to belong to the original scheme of the work. It may be added that the interpretation of the person of Job as a representative of Israel does not accord with the evident non-national coloring of the book.

(ii. 24). The narrative in Genesis recognizes in the tempter of Eve only an animal form, endowed with intelligence and speech.[1] This account, apparently the survival and reconstruction of an old Semitic myth,[2] stands isolated in Genesis; it is mentioned nowhere else in the Old Testament. But after the fifth century B. C. (when the narrative probably assumed its present shape) the feeling would naturally arise in some circles that so tremendous an event as the introduction of sin and death into the world could not be referred to the agency of beast; the serpent-form would come to be regarded as the vehicle chosen by a great spiritual adversary to vent on the first man the hate which according to the earlier books inspired his attempts on Israel and Job. The name given in Wisdom to this wicked spirit is Diabolos, the accuser or adversary (the Greek translation of the Hebrew name Satan). It can hardly be doubted that in the mind of the writer this being was identical with the Satan of the Jewish books. "Through envy of the Devil," so the passage runs (that is, envy of man's immortality or happiness), "death came into the world." Here the activity of the Adversary assumes the largest proportions, — he has succeeded in inflicting the greatest evil on the human race. The book of Enoch, with its fondness for hierarchical organization, makes Satan the head and ruler of evil spirits (liii. 3), and places under him a herd of satans who do his bidding in wicked ministrations.

That the progress of the idea of Satan as tempter was slow seems probable, not only from the infrequency with which he is introduced (he does not appear between Enoch and the New Testament), but also from the fact that neither Enoch

---

[1] Josephus also, who, as belonging to a priestly family, was probably well instructed in the orthodox Jewish theology of the time, here recognizes only the animal serpent (Ant. i. 1, 4).

[2] The conflict of the dragon Tiamat with the gods.

nor Josephus connects him with the serpent of Genesis. Possibly this identification began in Egypt in a Jewish circle influenced by Greek speculation (represented by the Wisdom of Solomon), and only gradually penetrated into Palestine. The data are, however, insufficient for determining to what extent this view was held by Palestinian Jews before the beginning of our era. It is certain that Satan appears as a well-developed figure in the earliest parts of the New Testament, and we may hence conclude that in the preceding two centuries he had formed a distinct part of the Jewish belief. The strenuous Jewish monotheism may have been unfavorable to the easy recognition of so powerful an opponent of God.[1]

Alongside of the development of the conception of a great spiritual adversary, there grew up a history of fallen angels, the starting-point of which was the account in Gen. vi. 1, 2. The origin and date of this passage are doubtful. The "sons of the Elohim" are in general angels (this expression never meaning anything else in the Old Testament), or more exactly, they are members of the class of Elohim-beings, the Israelitish representatives of the old divinities. Intermarriages between deities and human beings abound in all mythologies; such alliances, surviving in a monotheistic system, would naturally take the shape of the Genesis-story. This may be the remnant of a mythical narrative brought by the Hebrews from Mesopotamia to Canaan, or it may have come to the Jews from the Babylonians during the exile, or from the Assyrians before the exile. For our present purposes, it does not greatly matter which one of these explanations we adopt. The incident is not elsewhere mentioned in the Old Testament, and had no perceptible influence on the Jewish thought of the Old Testament time. The story appears to be introduced in Genesis, not to account for

---

[1] The later Jewish Satanology also seems to have been somewhat uncertain in tone. See Weber, "System," §§ 48, 54.

the increasing wickedness of man, and thus as a partial explanation of the flood (for the writer does not condemn the procedure of the angels), but to set forth the origin of the ancient heroes, the men of renown; the incident is narrated with the utmost impersonality, simply as an historical fact. The book of Enoch, which takes this material and expands it at great length, adopts an altogether different tone. It denounces the conduct of the angels as the height of impiety, gives the names of their leaders, and ascribes to them the beginnings of all the wickedness of the world. They are said to have taught men the science of war, the art of writing, and other hurtful things (ch. lxix.). Their leaders are Azazel and Semyaza; their fate is to be bound, hand and foot, and imprisoned till the day of judgment, when they are to be cast into the fire (ch. x.). This elaborate narrative is an attempt at a philosophical history of civilization, following and expanding the idea of Gen. i.–xi.; it undertakes to give the beginnings of the arts of life, which it thinks it necessary to refer to a supernatural origin, and, curiously enough, to antigodly agency.[1] So primitive and malistic a view, one would suppose, could have had no wide currency. The whole angelological scheme seems not to have made any great impression on the Jewish mind; part of the description in Enoch is adopted in the New Testament Apocalypse (xx. 1–3); the fate of the angels who came down from heaven is briefly summed up in Jude 6; and there is perhaps an allusion in Luke x. 18 to the same occurrence in the statement that Satan fell like lightning from heaven; but the body of the New Testament thought ignores this episode. It was re-

---

[1] How the author construed the parallel but dissimilar account of the origins of civilization in Gen. iv. 16–24 is not clear. The descent of the angels is put in the days of Jared (Gen. v. 18, cf. Irad, Gen. iv. 18) in the book of Jubilees (4), and in the Greek text of Enoch (vi. 6), — a bit of folk-etymology ("Jared" means "descending"); the author of Enoch probably held that the Cainites learned the arts from the angels.

served for post-biblical Christianity to elaborate the fall of the angels into a dogma. In the Old Testament neither their fall nor their creation is mentioned; their existence is simply assumed, as in Job xxxviii. 7, where it is said that at the creation of the world the morning stars sang together and all the sons of God shouted for joy. This reticence respecting their creation is easily understood if we consider the angels to be a survival and development out of the old deities, or Elohim-beings, whose participation in the work of the creation of the world is involved in the "let us make man" of Gen. i. 26. The Hebrews, receiving and accepting these beings as coeval with Yahwe, might naturally not think of them as included in the created world; there was an old Babylonian myth (given in the cuneiform creation tablet) which derived all the gods from two primitive water-beings, but there is no clear trace of this in the Old Testament.[1] Those who insist on seeing the creation of the angels in the biblical history of creation either prefer to insert it between the first and second verses of the first chapter of Genesis, and find in the angelic apostasy and rebellion the explanation of the chaos which they hold to have supervened on God's first good creation,[2] or they hold it to be included in Gen. ii. 1, where, however, the "host of them" refers to the physical creation (as in Ps. cxlviii. 5.[3]

In this connection we may note the curious figures of Leviathan, Behemoth, and Rahab, which appear in the Old Testament in several different senses. In Job xli. 1, Levi-

---

[1] The abyss (*tehom*) of Gen. i. 2 is the primeval earth-covering, out of which (vs 20, 21) come marine creatures. If there is a faint survival in verse 2 (the "wind" or "spirit" of God moved or hovered over the waters) of the old conception of the plastic water, it has been quite transformed by the monotheistic feeling. On Leviathan, Behemoth, and Rahab, see below.

[2] Compare the Talmudic statement that the present successful creation was only accomplished after several failures, Weber, "System," § 43.

[3] In Neh. ix. 6, the "host of heaven," which worships God, is different from the "host" which he is said to have made.

athan[1] seems to be the Egyptian crocodile, or else a mythical beast, and in Ps. civ. 26 some huge sea-animal; it occurs twice as a symbol of Egypt in Ps. lxxiv. 21, apparently under the form of the crocodile, and in Isa. xxvii. 1, where it is pictured as a winding serpent. The use of the term in Isaiah connects itself with the mythical reference in Job iii. 8 (cf. xxvi. 13), where the Leviathan is apparently the celestial serpent who swallows or otherwise obscures the sun and the moon, and who may be roused by enchantments; in this late form it is a mythical embodiment of the black storm-cloud or the eclipsing shadow regarded as a hostile demon. It is probable that the portraiture of the dragon in the New Testament Apocalypse receives its coloring in part (see Rev. xii. 4, 13) from this source. An earlier conception is found in Enoch lx. (a Noachic fragment), where Leviathan is a female monster dwelling in the depth of the sea; in 2 Esdras vi. 49–52, the creation of this beast is assigned to the fifth day; and it is stated that it is to be devoured by them whom God shall choose. With Leviathan is associated Behemoth (Enoch lx. 8, where it is masculine), after Job xl. and xli., and in the Talmud it is declared that these creatures are to be the food of Israel in the coming age of blessedness. There is a singular resemblance between this conception of two great water-monsters and the Babylonian myth above-mentioned of the two primitive water-principles, — Apsu and Tiamat, male and female,[2] from whom proceeded all other beings. The resemblance between Leviathan and Tiamat can hardly be accidental; both are female, and both are marine and celestial dragons which make war against the good powers. The Rahab of Job ix. 13, xxvi. 12 (cf. Isa. xxx. 7),

---

[1] The origin of the name is obscure; it may signify any long beast, and so be equivalent to "serpent," or "dragon" (Isa. xxvii. 1).

[2] Cf. Enoch liv. 8, where the water in the heavens is masculine, and the water on the earth feminine.

is a similar demonic conception. These three figures are interesting as instances of the manner in which the Jewish religious thought dealt with the old mythical material, gradually humanizing it, and more and more holding it aloof from the essential spiritual framework of theology. A vindictive dragon, originally the destructive waters of ocean or sky, becomes finally a beast whose flesh is to furnish food to the people of God.

The Satan of the New Testament is substantially identical with the pre-Christian figure, only modified, more sharply marked off, and more highly elaborated, in accordance with the characteristic moral-spiritual ideas and intensity of Christianity. He is the chief of the kingdom of evil spirits and angels (Matt. xii. 26; xxv. 41); he has power to inflict disease on the bodies of men (Luke xiii. 16; 1 Cor. v. 5; 1 Tim i. 20); he tempts to sin (Matt. iv. 1–11; Eph. vi. 11), and may be resisted (Jas. iv. 7); he enters into and controls bad men (Luke xx. 3, 31; John viii. 44); he is the opponent of the truth (Mark iv. 15; Matt. xiii. 39; 1 Thess. ii. 18; Rev. iii. 9; 1 Pet. v. 8); his hatred is said in one passage (Jude 9) to extend to the dead body of Moses;[1] he is identified with the dragon and with the serpent (Rev. xii. 9; xx. 2, 7, cf. John viii. 44; 1 Tim. ii. 14), and the names Satan and the Devil are used interchangeably; he is to be cast into hell (Matt. xxv. 41, and cf. Luke x. 18; Rev. xx. 10). He is, in a word, the prince and god of this world (2 Cor. iv. 4; John xiv. 30), the head and embodiment of all those influences in human life which are hostile to heavenly godliness. He includes in himself the Satan and the Azazel of Enoch and the prince of the demons, Beelzebub (Matt. xii. 24); he unites in his person all morally evil qualities; he is the leader of all those spiritual bad powers whose development has been traced above. In the New

---

[1] On this story see my "Quotations in the New Testament," New York, Scribner, 1884, pp. 250 f.

Testament, as in the pre-Christian literature, his position and functions, and especially his relation to God, are not clearly defined.[1] No attempt is made to show how his enormous power and wicked activity are to be brought into harmony with the divine omnipotent goodness. He is no mere symbol or personification of the wicked elements of life; he is an objective being, acting apparently without limitations of time and space. In some cases his power appears to be represented as co-ordinate with that of God. If God chooses those who are to believe unto salvation, it is Satan who blinds the minds of the unbelieving, that the light of the gospel of the glory of Christ, who is the image of God, should not dawn upon them (2 Cor. iv. 4). The title, "God of this world," implies vast power, and reminds us of the Persian rival of Ahura-Mazda. But on the other hand, the New Testament has a perfectly distinct conviction of the absolute supremacy of God. He is the sole fountain of power in the universe; at the end, the kingdom is to be his, death being swallowed up (1 Cor. xv. 24, 54), and in the Apocalypse (xx. 10), Satan is to be tormented forever and forever. He represents the evil of the world, and is to endure till evil shall be blotted out by the perfecting of the righteous and the imprisonment of the wicked. There is no hint of a possible change in Satan's moral character. The New Testament leaves him, at the beginning of the new dispensation, as the embodiment of evil, to abide forever, but in chains and darkness, shorn of his power, impotent any longer to disturb the moral order of the universe. Its solution of the problem of evil is practical, not logical or philosophical.

---

[1] There is no distinct chronological development of his person in the New Testament. His activity is in general more physical in the Apocalypse and Jude and in the demoniacal representations of the Gospels, more mental and spiritual in the Epistles and the Fourth Gospel, — a difference, that seems to result chiefly from the subject-matter and the religious point of view of the writers.

While we may thus trace the general line of progress of the figure of Satan, it is less easy to account for its origin. It appears suddenly in Zechariah and Job, apparently without preparation. The only individualized evil form of which we read in the earlier literature is the spirit of 1 Kings xxii. 21, and that differs from Satan in two important respects: it belongs to a different class of beings, and it has no distinct ethical character; Satan is not a "spirit," but one of the " sons of the Elohim " (Job i. 6), and he is distinctly malevolent. Both these points have significance in the Israelitish religious development: the Elohim-beings have their own history; and the ascription of moral evil to an Israelitish supernatural form seems to mark a turning-point in the national conception of life, — it is the beginning of the attempt to separate the domain of evil from that of God. When the figure of Satan appears abruptly, just after the close of the exile, we naturally ask whether it is a product of the unassisted Israelitish religious consciousness or the outcome in part of foreign influence. But foreign influence competent to produce such a result in whole or in part, it does not seem possible to discover. The Jews with whom the prophet Zechariah returned to Palestine were in contact with the Persians too short a time to borrow a great religious idea from them, even if the latter then had the Ahriman of the Avesta. Among the Babylonians, with whom the Jews had lived half a century, we know of no great spiritual adversary; they had evil spirits, as the Jews had, but no such idea as that of Satan. It is to be noted that the Satan, when we first meet him, is distinctly incorporated into the well-developed monotheism of the time; he is a servant of Yahwe, though an enemy of Yahwe's friends. Such a conception presupposes a considerable period of development; and in spite of the absence of earlier details, it seems most in accordance with the facts to regard it as a native Jewish growth.

We know that the sons of the Elohim had formed part of the national-religious material, probably of the folk-religion ; this element may have been ignored by the pre-exilian and exilian prophets, as having for them no spiritual significance. But the national history during the seventh and sixth centuries called up serious problems and stimulated ethical-religious thought. In particular, men's minds were occupied with the question of Israel's suffering, — why, it was asked, had Yahwe permitted hostile hands to bear so heavily on his people ? The prophets had their answer, — it was the punishment of the nation's sin. But after a while this answer became unsatisfactory to certain thinkers who held that the nation was not all sinful; why should the righteous be involved in the deserved suffering of their unrighteous fellow-countrymen ? To one man at least it seemed (Isa. liii.) that the affliction of the righteous Israel was vicarious, — that the end in the divine procedure was to bring not only all Israel, but also the Gentiles, to himself (Isa. xlix. 1–6). This exalted view of the situation did not, however, commend itself to all the prophet's contemporaries ; it was too lofty and broad, and perhaps too natural. The larger human question also — why good men in general suffered — was pressing for a solution ; and the idea of individual moral-religious discipline seems not to have presented itself, or, if considered, to have been held to be insufficient. The explanation in both cases was sought in the unfriendly activity of a great supernatural power, — one of those beings who, allied in nature to Yahwe and associated with him, though in a subordinate way, in the control of the world, wielded an important influence over the affairs of men. How such a being came to be unfriendly is not told in the Old Testament: Zechariah introduces the Satan without a word of comment ; the book of Job accounts for the possibility of his procedure by the purpose of Yahwe to test and demonstrate the integrity of his servant. Both books seem to assume that the person of the Adversary was well known ; how long it had been known it is impossible to say. We can only hold in general that the conception of a supernatural being hostile to good men was forced on the Jewish religious consciousness by the circumstances of the time, and that such a being would naturally be looked for in the ranks of the sons of the Elohim, — the companions and servants of Yahwe from time immemorial ; alongside of the good "angel of Yahwe" might stand an equally powerful being with a tinge of malevolence in his nature, possibly the dim survival of an old hurtful deity, more probably the product of a reflective age, which wished somehow to isolate evil from good. The general parallelism between this and the Persian scheme is obvious, — both arose out of the same ethical-religious necessity, — but there seems to be no sufficient ground for supposing an historical connection between the two at this stage.

It is otherwise with the later Jewish development of morally evil supernatural agencies. After the Jews had been a hundred years subjects of the Persian empire and resident in Persian communities, they may easily be supposed to have adopted ideas from their neighbors. The possibility that the rôle assigned to Azazel in Lev. xvi. was in part determined by Persian influence has already been suggested.[1] As to the times of Tobit and Enoch there can be no doubt. The Asmodaeus of Tobit is Persian ; and the elaborate angelology of Enoch is most naturally explained (as in the case of the book of Daniel) as due to an impulse derived from the Persian system. The description in Enoch is based on the account in Gen. vi., and the "sons of God" are identified with angels. The foundation is old-Semitic ; but the organiza-

---

[1] A similar suggestion might be made in regard to the identification of the serpent of Gen. iii. with Satan. For the objection to this view see above, pp. 158 f. It is possible, though hardly probable, that Wisd. of Sol. got its interpretation from a Persian source.

tion of the angels, and their individualization by names and by the assignment of individual functions in the development of human civilization, is foreign. That the names are Hebrew (in contrast with the Persian name Asmodaeus) results from the fact that the figures are Hebrew. The book of Enoch never attained canonical authority; and its angelic names seem not to have been adopted by succeeding generations, — its details were too bizarre for the sober Jewish thought. The idea of the organization of the evil angels under the leadership of Satan commended itself, and is found in the New Testament; but it has little prominence, except in the Apocalypse; in the practical religious life the evil supernatural activity is concentrated in the person of the chief, and his subordinate angels practically disappear. The part which they might play in the infliction of evil on men is assigned to the spirits.

The history of the class of evil intelligences called "spirits" is no less remarkable than that of Satan and his angels. It culminates in the idea of demoniacal possession, — a conception which has its roots in the Old Testament, but suddenly assumes enormous proportions in the first century of Christianity. According to the old Israelitish belief, as we have seen, all mental affections (as in the case of Saul, 1 Sam. xvi.) were ascribed to the agency of spirits sent from God; and these remain throughout the Old Testament morally undefined, — they work good and evil alike. The later differentiation into two classes was effected by Jewish advance in distinctness of ethical thought, and by the influence of foreign ideas, — Persian, Greek, and other.

It is in the book of Tobit that we find the first mention of a definite relation between an evil spirit and a human being (Asmodaeus and Sara); in Enoch the fallen angels appear in human shape, and affect men rather by ordinary human intercourse than by direct influence on the soul. The Greek idea is visible in the passage of Josephus ("War," vii. 6, 3) which assumes that sickness is produced by demons who are no other than the spirits of the wicked. We have no further details on this point in Jewish literature earlier than the New Testament; but that the belief in demonic influence continued among the Jews is evident from the Talmud, which makes abundant mention of evil spirits and magical processes, expanding the Old Testament spiritual material, and dressing out the old narratives with exuberance of picturesque legend (Weber, "System," § 54). The Jews had in the mean time become members of the Roman Empire, in which the belief in magic and exorcism was general. There was, about the beginning of our era, a sort of revivification of the primeval faith. The old machinery of gods had almost disappeared in cultivated circles. Men ridiculed the Olympian deities and even the patron gods of the Roman State, and took refuge in those occult powers and processes which were credible because they were at once visible and unintelligible; they satisfied the demand for the marvellous without offending the science and philosophy of the day.[1] Whether this foreign belief affected the Jews cannot be definitely determined; it seems probable that from so wide-spread an opinion some influence made itself felt in Palestine. The Palestinian belief was in its general material old-Israelitish; but it had received the important modification of the differentiation of the spirits into good and bad. The good, however, seem partly to have been merged in the body of the

[1] Cicero, in the introduction to his work on divination, declares that there is no nation that does not believe in the possibility of foretelling the future. Juvenal (Sat. vi.) testifies to the devotion of the Roman women to Chaldean and Judean supernatural arts, and Apuleius, in the Golden Ass, speaks of magic arts (by which, for example, a woman transforms herself into a bird and the hero into an ass) as a familiar thing in his time (second century of our era). See on the Greek and Roman doctrine of demons of this period the remarks of L. Friedländer, "Sittengeschichte Roms," (Leipzig, 1881), pp. 486—488, and on the belief in miracles, pp. 517 ff.

good angels as the ministers of God's beneficent dealings with men, and partly to have been absorbed in the divine spirit, which came more and more to be regarded as the source of ethically good spiritual influence on the soul. We read of no organization of good "spirits"; in the New Testament the normally sound life is attributed to the spirit of God, while it is certain peculiar abnormal evil phenomena, especially those connected with mental aberration, the explanation of which is held to lie in the agency of bad powers.

The representation of insanity as demoniacal possession was not a new one. It is found in the Old Testament (Saul); the ecstasies of prophets, seers, and priestesses were sometimes akin to madness (1 Sam. xix. 24, Mic. i. 8, and the Pythia). Such a frightful distortion of the human soul was not unnaturally looked on as the result of supernatural influence. The unhappy victims of possession were driven out from among men and forced to dwell in tombs and desolate places; it was natural that Jesus, in his mission of mercy, should meet these unfortunates and try to alleviate their misery and restore them to their right minds; doubtless many of them needed only sympathy and care, and few of them were without a trace of humanity which might be successfully appealed to.

In the New Testament, demoniacs form a separate class, being distinguished from the sick, epileptic, and palsied (Matt. iv. 24); they appear to abound everywhere, and their healing forms a prominent part of the work of Jesus and his disciples. The demons inhabit the bodies and souls of men, so identifying themselves with human spirits that the two personalities are not always distinguished. They are conscious of their subordinate relation to God; they believe in him and tremble (James ii. 19), while they pursue their anti-godly career. They acknowledge the authority of the name of Christ (Matt. viii. 29). They are identified with heathen deities (1 Cor. x. 20, 21; Rev. ix. 20; Acts xvi 16); Satan, their prince, receives the name of the old Philistine god, Beelzebub (Matt. xii. 24). Processes of exorcism are mentioned in Acts xix. 13–16 (cf. passage cited above from Josephus); but Jesus and his disciples expelled the spirits by a word. No account of their origin is given in the New Testament; they are numerous (Mark v. 9); they belong to the kingdom of Satan, — beyond this nothing is said. They are the evil spirits of the Old Testament, organized under Persian and other influence, and developed into sharper antagonism with the kingdom of God by their contact with Christianity.

The belief in demonic possession long remained in the Christian world, passing after a while into the theory of witchcraft, then slowly disappearing. The established belief in the orderly processes of nature makes it impossible for the present day; the Christian world no longer holds to it as an existing phenomenon. It was the product of an unscientific age, — a part of the general attempt to construct a system of intermediate powers between God and man, and to disjoin the realm of evil from the immediate divine activity. This latter purpose it did not really accomplish, since in both Old Testament and New Testament God either enjoins or permits the activity of the wicked spirits. But the religious thought of the biblical times found in this scheme a satisfactory solution of the problem of evil, confronting the fact of present mal-arrangement with the hope of future regeneration. The New Testament thus presents the final shaping of the old animistic material. The ancient spirits are in part transformed into wicked demons which, suffered by God for a time, are eventually to be brought to naught. In the general history of religious thought they may be looked on as a temporary embodiment of that evil which in the Christian conception is finally to succumb to the higher ethical power which belongs to the essential constitution of things.

A general review of the doctrine of evil spirits in Old Testament and New Testament exhibits an influence of the Persian religion on the Jewish, but brings out at the same time the difference between the two faiths.[1] Both sought to account for certain forms of evil in the world by the introduction of intermediate agencies in some sort independent of the righteous and benevolent God. But in one the sense of evil was so strong as to give birth to what was practically an evil deity; in the other the sense of the aloneness of God was so deep as to keep the evil powers practically subordinate to him. In both, the natural ethical feeling imposed limitations on the influence assigned to the evil supernatural agencies; the conviction of man's moral independence gave tone, in spite of all other theories, to the ethical-religious life. This is evident in the prophets and Psalms, in the discourses of Jesus and the Epistles; it is only in the folk-stories and apocalypses that evil spirits play a very important part. It would be fruitless to ask what the Jewish demonological development would have been without foreign influence. We can hardly doubt that the pre-exilian material would have maintained itself and suffered the modifications which growth of ethical feeling would render necessary.

---

[1] Much uncertainty rests on the early history of the Mazdean religion. The origins are discussed by Spiegel, "Eränische Alterthumskunde" (Leipzig, 1871–1878); Darmesteter, "Ormazd et Ahriman" (Paris, 1877); "The Zend Avesta," Parts I., II. (Oxford, 1880, 1883); De Harlez, "Des Origines du Zoroastrisme" (Paris, 1879); "Avesta" (Paris, 1881); Mills, "The Zend Avesta," Part III. (Oxford, 1887); Meyer, "Geschichte des Alterthums" (Stuttgart, 1884); Geldner, article "Zend Avesta" in "Encycl. Brit.," and others. The relation between the Persian and Jewish demonologies is treated by Nicolas, "Des Doctrines Religieuses des Juifs" (Paris, 1860); Kohut, "Angelologie, etc." (in Vol. IV. of the "Abhandlungen für die Kunde des Morgenlandes"), and De Harlez. It seems not rash to infer from the traditions and from the tone of the materials of the "Avesta" that the leading ideas of Mazdeism were in existence as early as the fourth century before the beginning of our era.

CHAPTER IV.

MAN.

WE have now to inquire into the Jewish and Christian views of the moral-religious history of man, the constitution of his nature, his attitude toward right and wrong and toward God, and the means by which he is to attain perfection.

1. The Old Testament idea of the constitution of man is a perfectly simple and popular one, without scientific analysis and distinctions, and without philosophical or theological theories. Common observation teaches that man is a creature composed of a visible bodily frame informed by an invisible something which is believed to be connected with thought, feeling, will, with all that makes up life. Such is the conception given in the second account of creation, Gen. ii. 7: God "formed man of the dust of the ground and breathed into his nostrils the breath of life, and man became a living soul;" the same expression for the totality of human being is found in Isa. x. 18. This duality of being is given throughout the Old Testament, never demonstrated or commented on, but always assumed as common opinion. In the first account of creation, Gen. i. 26–28, it is not even mentioned; man is created in the likeness of the Elohim-beings ("our likeness"), and is invested with dominion over all the earth, — his constitution is taken for granted.

In the Old Testament, the term "body" means only the physical mass of bones and flesh and blood; it is never employed in an ethical sense. Nor do we find such a sense given to the word "flesh;" in Ezek. xi. 19, its physical peculiarity of softness is used to denote figuratively tenderness and impressibility of heart. It is sometimes identical with "body": "My heart is glad and my glory rejoices, my flesh also dwells in security" (Ps. xvi. 9); or it is physically distinguished from the body, probably as part of it: "When thy flesh and thy body are consumed" (Prov. v. 11); or it means the human personality: "My flesh trembles for fear of thee" (Ps. cxix. 120); and so in combination with "heart": "My heart and my flesh shout to the living God" (Ps. lxxxiv. 2). It is used also to express animal nature in contrast with spiritual: "Their horses are flesh, and not spirit" (Isa. xxxi. 3); or human nature in contrast with divine conceived of as pure spirit: "In God I have put my trust, I fear not what flesh can do to me" (Ps. lvi. 4), "The gods whose dwelling is not with flesh" (Dan. ii. 11); and "all flesh" is an expression for all mankind: "O thou that hearest prayer, to thee shall all flesh come" (Ps. lxv. 2). To flesh as the characteristic of the human in distinction from the divine, attaches the idea of weakness: "With him [the king of Assyria] is an arm of flesh, but with us is Yahwe, our God" (2 Chron. xxxii. 8); but no ethical element is involved. Body and flesh were not conceived of as impure, for the flesh of animals was used in sacrifices and regarded as holy. They contained no inherent tendency to sin, though their weakness and their association with the appetites might cause them to be thought of as an occasion of temptation. "Bone" is combined with "flesh" to express the whole physical structure in Gen. xxix. 14, 2 Sam. v. 1; and "bones" is equivalent to "body" in Ps. vi. 2 (1). Blood, in accordance with general observation, is everywhere regarded as the seat of life (Gen. ix. 4; Lev. xvii. 11).

The soul, according to the Old Testament conception, is primarily that breath which common observation shows to be the universal and inseparable accompaniment of life with all its functions. It is sometimes, therefore, simply the animal life, as where Elijah stretches himself on the dead child and prays that his soul may come into him again (1 Kings xvii. 21); or where it is said of the king that he saves the souls of the needy (Ps. lxxii. 13); and such probably is the representation in Gen. ii. 7. In this last passage we have the more developed view of the soul as the breath of God breathed into man; in which, of course we are not to see a pantheistic idea, but only the simple belief that the life of man is the immediate creation of God, — a belief perhaps connected with the statement in the first history of creation that man was made in the image of the Elohim-beings. The word "soul," as synonymous with life, naturally comes to mean "person," as in Lev. v. 1, Gen. xii. 5, Ezek. xiii. 19; and the expressions, "my soul," "thy soul," "his soul," become equivalent to "myself," "thyself," "himself" (Gen. xii. 13; Job x. 1; Ps. lvii 4; 1 Sam. ii. 16; Jer. xxxviii. 17; Ps. lxxxix. 48; Eccles. ii. 24; Mic. vi. 7; Isa. liii. 10); and it may even be used for a dead body, inasmuch as this suggested personality (Lev. xxi. 11). The more important ethical-religious sense of the word is to express the whole inward nature, as in Deut. xiii. 3, Ps. lxii. 5, and many other passages. Whatever man feels, thinks, or wills, is attributed to the soul. It is the organ of all spiritual-religious thought; it is the part of man which comes into contact with God, which constitutes the essence of the personality. So completely does it include all human functions that while it is said to be restored by the perfect law of God (Ps. xix. 7), it also stands for the inward spirit which may be discouraged in work (Num. xxi. 4), and for appetite: " As when a hungry man dreams, and behold, he eats, but he awakes and his soul is empty; or as when a thirsty man dreams, and behold, he drinks, but he awakes, and behold, he is faint, and his soul has appetite" (Isa. xxix. 8).

The use of the word "spirit" in the Old Testament as part of human nature is very nearly identical with that of "soul." It signifies life, or the inward, invisible seat of life: "Who knows the spirit of the sons of men, whether it goes upward, and the spirit of the beast, whether it goes downward to the earth?" (Eccles. iii. 21.) It is the intellect: Daniel is said to have had an excellent spirit and knowledge and understanding (Dan. v. 12); it is courage (Josh. v. 1). It represents the whole inward nature: Pharaoh's spirit was troubled by his dream (Gen. xli. 8); Elisha asks that a double portion (the portion of an oldest son) of Elijah's spirit (that is, of his whole inward power, intellectual and religious) may rest on him (2 Kings ii. 9); the Psalmist begs for a steadfast spirit, a nature wholly attached to God (Ps. li. 10); and he that rules his spirit, that is, himself, the totality of his inward powers, is said to be better than he who takes a city (Prov. xvi. 2). It is the seat of ethical-religious life: "Happy is the man to whom Yahwe does not reckon iniquity, and in whose spirit there is no guile;" "the sacrifices of God are a broken spirit: a broken and a crushed heart, O God, thou dost not despise" (Ps. li. 17).

Nor is there any different statement to be made in respect to the use of the word "heart," which signifies in the Old Testament not especially the emotional nature, but the whole inward being: "Hope deferred makes the heart sick" (Prov. xiii. 12); "If I have purposed iniquity in my heart, the Lord will not hear" (Ps. lxvi. 18); and God is called the "tryer of the hearts and reins" (Ps. vii. 10); and so the term comes to signify the personality, as in Gen. viii. 21, when Yahwe smells the sweet savor of Noah's sacrifice and says "in his heart" that he will not again curse the ground, and Ps. x. 6: "He says in his heart, I shall not be moved," that is, says to himself. The phrase "heart and flesh" also,

as is remarked above, is used to express the whole being
(Ps. lxxiii. 26; lxxxiv. 2); it is equivalent to "mind (or
soul) and body."[1]

The New Testament has all the uses of these terms above
mentioned, and adds others which flowed naturally out of its
higher spiritual conception of human life and its sharper
antithesis between opposing elements. "Body" is the physical structure of flesh and bones (Matt. x. 28; 1 Cor. xii.
14), and so the natural physical life in this world, the taber-
nacle of the soul, the locus and vehicle of earthly activity
(2 Cor. v. 6, 10); and then by a natural transition it is employed by Paul to represent the unregenerate, sinful nature,
as opposed to the higher life of the spirit: "If by the spirit
you kill the deeds of the body, you shall live" (Rom.
viii. 13).

"Flesh" occurs in the simple physical sense (1 Pet. iv.
1), and then as equivalent to humanity, that is, human nature: Christ was an Israelite "as concerning the flesh" (Rom.
ix. 5); the Word became flesh and dwelt in the world (John
i. 14), the combination "flesh and blood" having the same
sense (Matt. xvi. 17; Gal. i. 16); "all flesh" means the whole
human race (John xvii. 2, and the similar expression "no
flesh" in 1 Cor. i. 29). As the instrument of the appetites,
and distinguished by its grossness from the spirit, it is used
by Paul and his school to signify the animal life as the seat

---

1 "Reins" is similarly employed (Jer. xi. 20; Ps. lxxiii. 21; and once in
the New Testament, Rev. ii. 23, the expression being quoted from the Old
Testament). The bowels are the seat of love and the desire, compassion, and
sorrow that spring from love (Song of Songs v. 4; Gen. xliii. 30; Jer. iv. 19;
Phil. ii. 1), or even (in the New Testament, 2 Cor. vi. 12) of the affections in
general; they are regarded also as the source whence life issues (Gen. xv. 4),
and so the loins (Gen. xxxv. 11; Heb. vii. 10). "Liver" (in Babylonian-
Assyrian equivalent to "heart") is used once (Lam. ii. 11) for the seat of
the inward life. It was the prominent organs of the trunk that the ancients
connected with life; the word "brain" does not occur in the Old Testament;
in Arabic, *madmuġ*, "struck on the brain," is "stupid."

of sin, the unregenerate nature: in Rom. viii, it is termed "sinful," is contrasted with the spirit as the seat of the higher life; the mind of the flesh is said to be enmity against God, and they who live after the flesh must die; the "works of the flesh," all sorts of wrong-doing, are detailed in Gal. v. 19-21; the spirit and the flesh are described as antagonists one to the other (v. 17), and "they that are of Christ Jesus have crucified the flesh with its passions and desires" (v. 24); all unbelievers live in the desires of the flesh and of natural human thought (Eph. ii. 3; Col. ii. 11); Paul uses the word also of an unspiritual religion, especially of the Jewish reliance on the Law: "Did you receive the Spirit by the works of the Law or by the hearing of faith? Are you so foolish? Having begun in the spirit, are you now perfected in the flesh?" (Gal. iii. 2, 3.)

"Heart" is the whole inward nature: the Evil One snatches away the word of the kingdom, which has been sown in the heart (Matt. xiii. 19); the Devil put into the heart of Judas to betray Jesus (John xiii. 2); men, after their hardness and impenitent heart treasure up for themselves wrath in the day of wrath (Rom. ii. 5), and with the heart man believes unto righteousness (Rom. x. 10), the act of believing involving all the powers of the mind, — thought, feeling, and will.

"Soul" is equivalent to "life" in Matt. x. 39: "He that finds his soul shall lose it, and he that loses his soul for my sake shall find it;" and Matt. xvi. 26: "What is a man profited if he gain the whole world and forfeit his soul?" and to "person" in Rom. xiii. 1: "Let every soul be in subjection to the higher powers." It signifies the whole inward nature in James i. 21: the word is able to save men's souls; and in John xii. 27: "Now is my soul troubled, and what shall I say?"

"Spirit" is the breath of the natural life (Luke viii. 55), or a disembodied existence (Luke xxiv. 37-39). It represents the inward nature in Mark viii. 12: "He sighed deeply in his spirit" (or it may here mean the personality itself), and 1 Cor. v. 3: "Absent in body but present in spirit;" in the eighth chapter of Romans it is used frequently for the inward spiritual life created by Christ and the Holy Spirit; the spirit and its mind are put over against the flesh and its mind (vs. 4. 5, 6, 9, 10).

The New Testament uses the word "mind" ($\nu o\hat{v}s$) in the same general sense for the reflective faculty, or for the whole inward being. It is the intellect in Luke xxiv. 45, where Jesus opens the minds of the disciples to understand the scriptures; in 1 Cor. ii. 16, it signifies the thought-content of the intellect: we, says the apostle, have the mind of Christ; that is, we have come into possession of his thought, which is the expression of his complete comprehension of the divine purpose. In the quotation from the Septuagint in the same verse, the "mind" is the rendering of the Hebrew word for "spirit," the two being here identical in meaning. Paul employs the term usually in a moral-religious sense for the reason and will, tainted or untainted by sin. Thus in Rom. vii. 23, 25, it is the normal human judgment, which approves the right, and the normal human will, which desires to obey it, though both are overpowered by the "flesh," the corrupt nature, in which dwells the love of evil: he delights in the law of God, but there is another law in his nature warring against this law of his "mind" and bringing him into captivity to the law of sin. Elsewhere the mind is described as reprobate (the heathen, Rom. i. 28), fleshly, — that is, reason and will controlled by the lower nature (Col. ii. 18), — defiled (Tit. i 15, where it is combined with "conscience," as if the two were practically identical).

It is evident from this survey that the terms "body" and "flesh" are practically synonymous in both Testaments, and the same thing is true of "heart," "soul," and "spirit." The number of passages in the New Testament in which the expressions "soul and body," "spirit and body," "spirit and flesh" are employed to denote the whole of human nature shows that its constitution was conceived of as dual; and further it is evident that " spirit " and " soul " are used interchangeably, each as standing for the whole inward nature. With this usage so clearly defined we can hardly accept the supposition of a trichotomy of spirit, soul, and body in the sense that the spirit forms a distinct essence from the soul. It is true that Paul employs the terms " spirit " and " spiritual " in a peculiar way to express the regenerate nature, — the soul of man after a new life has been breathed into it by the divine spirit. It is a distinction which seems to be confined in the New Testament to him and his school. His choice of the word " spirit " to express the higher life which was informed by Christ may have been suggested by his conception of its relation to the divine spirit; it is possible, however, that some distinction between the terms " spirit " and " soul," though not one of essence, had already sprung up and was adopted and applied by him in this peculiar way.[1] The distinction in his mind is brought out in 1 Cor. xv. 44, 45 : " It is sown a psychical body, it is raised a pneumatical body; if there is a psychical body, there is also a pneumatical; so also it is written, the first man Adam became a living soul [psyche], the last Adam a life-giving spirit [pneuma]." The psychical body is that wherein dwells the natural, unregenerate soul; the pneumatical body is that which is prepared to be the dwelling of the regenerated soul, — the spirit which has been touched by the hand of God. The difference between Adam and Christ is that the former was created as a soul endowed with life, the latter was a spirit capable of giving life. The distinction of soul and spirit is not one between

---

[1] On the use of these and the related terms in the Septuagint and by Philo, see E. Hatch, " Essays in Biblical Greek " (Oxford, 1889), Essay III.

different parts of human nature: Adam's soul was capable of becoming spirit; Christ's soul was spirit. It is a moral-religious, not a substantive distinction that the apostle has in mind. The same distinction is found in 1 Cor. xiv. 15: " The psychical man does not receive the things of the Spirit of God, for they are foolishness to him; and he cannot know them because they are pneumatically judged, but the pneumatical man judges all things." He has been speaking of the wisdom of the Gospel as contrasted with human science and philosophy, declaring that the knowledge of the truth of God comes to believers not by their own reflection, but by revelation of the divine spirit, and he then adds the words quoted above; it is evident that he uses " psychical " in the sense of unbelieving or unregenerate, and " pneumatical " in the opposite sense. The one phase passes into the other through the influence of the spirit of God; a transformation is effected in human nature, but there is no change of essence.

When, therefore, we find the nature of man described as " spirit and soul and body " (1 Thess. v. 23), the natural understanding is that the distinction between the two first elements is religious-rhetorical and not one of essence; the soul is first thought of as the seat of the inward life, and then the word " spirit " is added, not as an independent component of human nature, but as expressing clearly that transformed state of the soul in which it comes into the higher relation with God through faith in Jesus Christ. It might seem, however, that a substantive distinction between the two is expressed in Heb. iv. 12: " The word of God is living and active and sharper than any two-edged sword, and piercing even to the dividing of soul and spirit, of both joints and marrow, and a discerner of the thoughts and intents of the heart." But it is to be observed that this passage is rhetorical in its tone, and is therefore not to be interpreted in a strictly scientific way. It is easily supposable that the writer had in mind the idea of Paul, whose theology he so largely adopts, and thought of the soul and spirit as different phases and states of mind ; from this point of view, he would naturally speak of a division made by the divine word of the Gospel between the natural, unregenerate life and thought and that higher perception and feeling which arise from the transforming power of God. Since these two passages admit of a natural explanation on the basis of a dual conception of human nature, it is hardly safe to deduce a trichotomy from them against all other New Testament usage.

This is, however, a point of secondary importance in the statement of Christian doctrine. What is essential and characteristic in the Christian view is the idea of a new perceptive power in man, the development of his nature into a capacity for comprehension of God and fellowship with him. This idea has its roots in the Old Testament, but receives its perfect shape only in the Christian literature of the first century. The completer organization of the inward nature flowed naturally from the strict Pauline Christian conception of divine truth and man's individual independence. Not only, it was held, had God revealed himself in a peculiarly definite manner in the person of his Son, but, in contrast with the national coloring of the Jewish faith, the divine spirit informed and communed with each believer's soul and impressed on each its own personality (Gal. iii. 3 ; 1 Cor. iii. 16 ; Rom. viii. 2) This intimate association between the human soul and the divine demanded in the former an instrument fit to receive the influence of the latter.[1]

---

[1] The immediately preceding Jewish literature offers little material for tracing the history of this conception. A divine influence on the mind is fully affirmed in Wisdom viii., but nothing is said distinctly of a higher faculty of the soul. The classic writers of the Augustan period employ "spirit" in the senses of "life, soul, courage;" the New Testament writers think of a mental power that apprehends divine things.

2. The question of the constitution of man's nature may be said to be chiefly a scientific and non-moral one; the principle of the division of human nature into its parts is not in itself ethical. The more important inquiry is, what is man's natural moral condition, his attitude toward right, his capacity for right-doing? What is the Jewish conception of sin?

That wrong-doing is natural and universal is matter of common observation, — an opinion that has doubtless been held among all communities of men with greater or less distinctness. Wherever a standard of right exists (and we may assume that it exists among all men, even in the most undeveloped societies), deviations from it must occur and be known; and these deviations constitute sin. In themselves, considered as violations of human rule, they are only ethical wrongs; but inasmuch as the deity is identified with the ethical ideal of the community and becomes the judge of right and wrong, moral offences are considered to be committed against him, and in this character are termed sinful. The offences are at first of the simplest sort, violation of customs among men, or of ritual duties toward God. The progress of ethical thought involves a corresponding progress in the conception of sin. Duties are more clearly defined, the higher qualities of the soul — sympathy, love, self-sacrifice, inwardness — become more and more prominent, and their absence is more distinctly noted as a lack, an offence against the command of God. The conception of the divine perfectness goes hand and hand with that of human goodness. The purer and more spiritual the idea of God, the deeper the sense of the violation of his will, which is one with man's highest conception of right.

The two elements in the content of the feeling of sin are, first, the ethical standard, and secondly, inwardness or spiritualness; that is, the feeling of the necessity of purity of soul, of the elevation and renewal of the inward nature so that it shall be in complete sympathy and harmony with the good, and with God as the ideal and source of the good. Jewish thought of the period after Ezra shows a great advance in this direction. The time of the Judges and of David is one of moral rawness: the ethical standard is low; the rules of right conduct are outward and mechanical; and of a sense of sin, in the higher meaning of the expression, there is no trace.[1] The prophetic writings, from the eighth century on, are ethically strict and high, except that they do not recognize claims of foreigners, but confine the circle of their moral obligations to Israel, and that little prominence is given to the inward life; the rebuke of the prophets is directed against idolatry, neglect of Yahwe, drunkenness, the oppression of the poor by the rich, and other external sins. Their point of view is national; they look on the individual almost exclusively as a member of the nation, and are roused to anger by those offences which violate the compact between God and the people, deprive them of his favor and protection, and retard their progress toward the condition of complete, blessed prosperity. A turning-point is marked by the Deuteronomist, Jeremiah, and Ezekiel, who announce the principles of individual responsibility and inwardness of obedience. The incompleteness of the notion of sin which had prevailed up to this time is exhibited in the principle of solidarity which so largely controlled men's moral ideas: children's teeth were set on edge because their fathers had eaten sour grapes; Achan's family was involved in the punishment of his sin (Josh. vii. 24, 25); and the Decalogue declares that Yahwe is a jealous God, visiting

---

[1] The episode given in 2 Sam. xii. 1-14, the rebuke of Nathan and David's repentance, is so out of keeping with the tone of the context that it must be put into the same category with 2 Sam. vii., and regarded as a production not of David's time, but of a later, perhaps the Deuteronomic period.

the iniquity of the fathers upon the children and on the third and fourth generation of them that hate him (Deut. v. 9). And this theory of punishment was held not in the modern form, according to which children by the operation of natural law inherit the consequences of the sins of ancestors, but in a mechanical way which represented God in his capacity of judge as arbitrarily punishing the descendants of evil-doers. It was the survival of a primitive conception of society in which the unit was the tribe or the family;[1] it was banished by the better development of the moral sense which recognized the rights and responsibilities of the individual (Ezek. xviii. 2–4). In the same way, the external and mechanical conception of obedience and sin which belonged to the national point of view disappeared before the rise of a higher estimation of the individual soul. It was just before the destruction of Jerusalem by the Chaldeans that this purer conception found expression in Israelitish literature; from which we may infer that the ethical progress since David's time had been continuous, in spite of the religious oscillations and defections described in the book of Kings, whose narrative, it must be remembered, reflects the ideas of the exile rather than the exact historical course of events. The national conception continued to exist for a long time, but the new ideals had effected an entrance into Jewish life and held their place.

The principal ethical fact in the post-exilian period is the introduction of the complete Levitical legislation. In Pales-

---

[1] As all the members of a family or clan were held to be literally of the same blood, the principle of solidarity was logically conceived in a thoroughgoing literal sense; from this point of view it was natural that all the tribesmen should share the fortunes of a brother, and especially of a chief. This idea survived in religion after it had vanished from the legal codes; an exilian or post-exilian editor represents the whole Israelitish nation as suffering for the sin of its king (2 Sam. xxiv.), and in certain systems of Christian theology the human race is involved in the condemnation of the first man.

tine the interval between the return from Babylon and the advent of Ezra and Nehemiah was almost entirely colorless, so far as our information goes, in regard to the progress of morals and religion. The Jews in Palestine were absorbed in other things, struggling for bread, lacking in high literary and religious stimulus; the flower of the nation was in Babylonia, and Palestine was in a state of comparative stagnation. No doubt there was some progress; but there is little or no sign of it. With Ezra and Nehemiah came a new impulse. It might seem doubtful, however, whether the introduction of the finished Law was an unmixed good from the ethical point of view. The code was largely ritualistic; it fixed men's minds on ceremonial details which it in some cases put into the same category and on the same level with moral duties. Would there not thence result a dimming of the moral sense, and a confusion of moral distinctions? The ethical attitude of a man who could regard a failure in the routine of sacrifice as not less blameworthy than an act of theft cannot be called a lofty one. If such had been the general effect of the ritual law, we should have to pronounce it an evil. But in point of fact, the result was different. What may be called the natural debasing tendency of a ritual was counteracted by other influences, by the ethical elements of the law itself, and by the general moral progress of the community. The great legal schools which grew up in the second century, if we may judge by the sayings of the teachers which have come down to us, did not fail to discriminate between the outward and the inward, the ceremonial and the moral; and the conception of sin corresponded to the idea of the ethical standard.

It is in the book of Psalms that we find the fullest picture of the inward religious experiences of this period from the exile on. We are not, indeed, to understand every expression of suffering and every cry for help in the Psalter as an indication of a sense of sin. Nor can we always say certainly what that iniquity is which a psalmist imputes to himself. The author of Psalm xxxi. regards his misfortunes apparently as the result of his sin: "My life is consumed with sorrow and my years with sighing; my strength fails because of my iniquity; and my bones are wasted away" (v. 10); but at the same time, he can declare that he has trusted in God (v. 14), that he hates those who regard lying vanities (v. 6), and that he belongs in the category of the righteous (v. 18). The same seeming contradiction occurs in Ps. xxxviii. 3, 20, and Ps. lxix. 6, 8, 14; the psalmist acknowledges his sin, yet claims to follow what is good. In Ps. xxv. 7, the "sins of youth" are apparently half-unconscious, unmalignant offences, perhaps opposed to the more conscious and definite "transgressions." In some cases the external, national point of view is obvious, as in lxxxv. 1, 2: "Thou wast favorable to thy land, didst bring back the captivity of Jacob, didst forget the iniquity of thy people." Yet with all these elements of doubt, it is hard to resist the impression that we have in some of the Psalms a true spiritual conception of sin as an impurity of soul which makes a barrier between it and God. In Psalm li. we have a complete combination and fusion of the religious and ethical sides of the consciousness of sin: the writer, in his overwhelming sense of the divine presence and purity, isolates himself from his human surroundings and looks to God as the sole being concerned with his sin: "Against thee, thee only have I sinned, and done that which is evil in thine eyes, that thou mightest be justified when thou speakest and be clear when thou judgest. . . . Hide thy face from my sins and blot out all my iniquities" (vs. 4, 9);[1] at

[1] That is, his feeling is not that he is absolutely innocent with respect to men, but that he is blameworthy with respect to God, — such is the suggestion of the context.

the same time, he longs for purity and inward truth as the result of banishment of sin; he desires to be whiter than snow when his heart shall have been made clean (vs. 2, 6, 7). The psalm is apparently a cry out of the time of the exile (or perhaps later), laden with the sense of suffering of that period; yet the writer, though he may speak as a member of the downcast nation, has nevertheless an individual sense of sin, is persuaded that his own affliction has its roots in his deep-seated transgression; he is so profoundly conscious of his moral weakness and his shortcomings before God that he turns from the outward fact of suffering to fix his attention exclusively on the impurity of his own heart. This humble consciousness of imperfection he declares to be the best sacrifice that can be offered to God (v. 17); but this fact does not diminish the reality of his sense of personal sin. The sentiment of Psalm xxxii. is less clear: "I acknowledge my sin to thee, and cover not my iniquity; I said, I will confess my transgressions to Yahwe, and thou tookest away the guilt of my sin" (v. 5). It is the physical suffering which follows sin that the psalmist seems to be thinking of (v. 6), in reference to which he says: "Happy is he whose transgression is forgiven, whose sin is covered; happy the man to whom Yahwe does not reckon iniquity" (v. 1), — happy because he escapes the consequences of sin; but the ethical side is present in his mind, for he describes this happy man as one in whose spirit there is no guile (v. 1).

By the side of this consciousness of sin in the Psalms, there is, curiously enough, a pronounced consciousness of righteousness. "Continue thy loving kindness to them that know thee, and thy righteousness to the upright in heart; let not the foot of pride come upon me," says a writer who evidently regards himself as upright in heart (xxxvi. 10). Another psalmist, assailed by mighty enemies, declares that it is for no sin or transgression of his (lix. 3). The author of Psalm xviii. formulates this view very distinctly: "Yahwe dealt with me according to my righteousness, according to the purity of my hands he recompensed me; because I kept the ways of Yahwe and did not wickedly depart from my God, for all his ordinances were before me, and his statutes I did not put away from me; and I was perfect with him, and kept myself from iniquity; and Yahwe recompensed me according to my righteousness, according to the purity of my hands in his eyesight" (vs. 20–24). This seems to be an extraordinary assumption of moral perfectness, hard to reconcile with any true sense of sin. The difficulty seems to be increased when the writer proceeds to formulate a general theory respecting God's relations and dealings with men: "With the merciful thou showest thyself merciful, with the perfect, perfect, with the pure, pure, and with the wayward, wayward" (vs. 25, 26). It is a natural conception that God's attitude toward man should be determined by man's moral character; but this complete assimilation of the divine and human attributes, unless it be a poetical exaggeration, seems to be based on a somewhat mechanical conception of the relation between God and man. But the explanation is given in the next verse: "Thou savest lowly people, and haughty eyes thou dost abase" (v. 27). It is the nation Israel that the writer has in mind; it is of it and of himself as belonging to it that he affirms righteousness. Similarly in Psalm xliv. 17, 18: "All this is come upon us, yet we have not forgotten thee nor been disloyal to thy covenant; our heart has not turned back, nor have our steps swerved from thy way." This explanation, however, brings us face to face with the fact of a national consciousness of innocence. The Forty-Fourth Psalm belongs to the latter part of the Greek period, — a time when national feeling was at its height. Syrian oppression had intensified the national sense of religious isolation and superiority in contrast with the heathen cults; the temple-worship assumed especial prominence and importance; the chief duty and mission of the nation seemed to be the maintenance of the worship of the God of Israel according to his ordinances, in the face of and as a protest against heathen beliefs and ceremonies. From this point of view, it was easy to feel that so long as the temple-ritual was observed with precision and sincerity, the people might justly claim to be righteous in the sight of God and to deserve his protection and blessing. Such a national sense of innocence might also become individual; any man, especially if he stood in close connection with the temple, might hold himself, as a part of this exemplary nation, to merit the divine favor. In such cases there may have been also the sense of individual shortcomings, but it would without great difficulty be swallowed up in the conviction of national innocence.

We have thus two especially prominent aspects of the Jewish consciousness of sin. There was, doubtless, a third, —a superficial, indistinct sense of wrong-doing, which did not greatly afflict the soul or color the life. The psalmists represent the intenser, more exalted feeling of the nation; the masses of the people were comparatively indifferent, if we may judge from our general knowledge of human nature and from hints in the Old Testament. But it is with the higher and better-formulated feeling that we are here concerned. What was the advanced Jewish view respecting the nature of sin and its relation to man's inward being? The literature offers no complete answer to this question. Sin is taken for granted. In the earlier prophetic writings it is regarded as a habit, or as a mass of actions. Even Ezekiel's "new heart" (Ezek. xxxvi. 26) is concerned chiefly with external things: "I will give you a new heart, and put a new spirit within you; I will take away the stony heart out of your flesh and give you a heart of flesh; and I will put my spirit within you and cause you to walk in my statutes, and you shall keep my ordinances and do them; and you shall dwell in the land that I gave to your fathers, and you shall be my people, and I will be your God" (vs. 26–28). It is again to the Psalter that we must come for the deeper conception of sin. But even here we have no detailed explanation or distinct theory. "I was shapen in iniquity, born in sin," says the author of the Fifty-First Psalm (v. 5); this is the consciousness of a tendency to wrong-doing from the beginning of life, and in so far implies a weakness, a moral taint in human nature. Such is also the conception in Jer. xvii. 9: "The heart is deceitful above all things, and it is desperately sick; who can know it?" And yet, in spite of the universality of the expression, the prophet seems not to have meant to affirm a total depravity incapable in itself of doing right, for he adds immediately (v. 10): "I, Yahwe, search the heart, try the reins, to give every man according to his ways, according to the fruit of his doings." The possibility of right-doing and of consequent reward from God is here assumed. This presupposition that man is capable of achieving righteousness, of attaining perfectness, runs throughout the Old Testament; human nature is portrayed as weak, as inclined to evil, but not as morally impotent. Ezekiel, in his great appeal to Israel to return to God and to righteousness (ch. xviii.), assumes the ability of the sinner to put away his sin: "If the wicked turn from all the sins he has committed, and keep all my statutes, and do that which is lawful and right, he shall surely live, he shall not die; none of his transgressions that he has committed shall be remembered against him. In his righteousness that he has done, he shall live" (vs. 21, 22). There is no mention of special divine help here; it is assumed that the man by his own inward power changes his moral status in the sight of God. Such is the prevailing view in the Old Testament: sin is universal, but not uncontrollable. Even in the greater part of the Psalter, the root of man's righteousness is in his own heart; and the same thing is true of the reflective literature, — Job, Proverbs, Ecclesiastes. The exception is found in the Fifty-First Psalm. It is the utterance of a man who felt that sin was ingrained in his inner nature, that God, who desired truth in the inward parts, must make him to know wisdom, that he had need of a clean heart and a steadfast spirit, and that the condition of his true life was the presence within him of that holy spirit which God only could bestow. There is still no distinct affirmation in this psalm of a total depravity of the soul. There is a deep sense of inward corruption and of dependence on God for righteousness, which might logically lead to the position that man is incapable of achieving a righteousness of his own; but we cannot assume complete logicalness in emotional religious thought, nor suppose that this psalmist meant to announce a general theory. He stands alone in the Old Testament in his conception of the sinfulness of human nature; no prophet and no other psalmist has expressed this spiritual view of the inward religious life.

We must here recognize a progress in the Jewish idea of sin; the Fifty-First Psalm contains the germ of the New Testament teaching. But the psalmist appears to have been in advance of the thought of his age. The conception of sin in the later Jewish books — such as Ecclesiastes, the Wisdom of Solomon, Ecclesiasticus, Tobit, Daniel, Enoch, the Sibylline Oracles, Maccabees — is the old one, which may be called, by comparison, external,[1] and this view is found also in the New

[1] Ecclesiastes disapproves of sin as irrational (viii. 12; x. 3); Wisdom contemplates the violence of the wicked (ii.) and the wrong-doing condemned in Ecclesiasticus (*passim*) is of the outward sort; Tobit and Daniel are mainly national, or, when individual, ritualistic (Tob. i. 10; Dan. i. 8); Enoch and the following books also deal with sins against the national law and well-

Testament; for example, in the Epistle of James, though here it is somewhat modified by Christian teaching. We must, therefore, regard the Old Testament as teaching not that sin is a nature, but that it is a tendency. It is described as a weakness, a failure, a violent outbreak, a perverseness, or as blindness and folly. It is a disposition or inclination which constantly impels or allures men to wrong-doing; it is not an utter incapacity to do right. It is an enemy ever present, watchful, alert, but not invincible; it can be overcome by man's own effort. Such was the teaching of common experience. But deeper natures, like the author of Psalm li., felt that this perpetual conflict with temptation was unsatisfactory, and that what man needed was freedom from evil inclination, a heart in harmony with the right. This was the view of the minority; the mass of the people was controlled by the nomistic idea; sin was conceived of as the infringement of particular laws, and was avoided by obedience in details.

A careful analysis of the nature of sin would naturally be attended, one would suppose, by an inquiry as to its origin. But on this point the greater part of the Old Testament is profoundly silent. National sin is assumed by the prophets to have existed from the beginning, and no attempt is made to account for its introduction; the necessity for an explanation of so common a fact was not felt by the practical Jewish mind. The traditions of the forefathers preserved in the Pentateuch tell of wrong-doing in Abraham, Isaac, and Jacob, but assume it as natural, and show no curiosity as to the

being. It must, however, be borne in mind that these works, by their subject-matter and aims, would naturally dwell on the outward manifestations of evil, and may have known deeper inward experiences than they express. Further, the existence of different tendencies and modes of thought in different circles must be recognized; the Psalms probably represent the more spiritual thought of the nation; wisdom-books and apocalypses were more interested in other things.

source of the wrong disposition. Abram and Isaac are guilty of prevarication which amounts to falsehood (Gen. xii. 13; xxvi. 7); Jacob and Rebekah deceive the dim-eyed old Isaac (Gen. xxvii.); and Jacob deals fraudulently with his father-in-law (Gen. xxx.), — the stories are told with perfect simplicity; no explanation is felt by the writer to be needed, and none is given.

There is, however, one passage which appears to offer a history of the origin of human sin; it is the latter half of the second history of creation (Gen. iii.). The date of this passage is doubtful. It occurs in the body of traditions (Gen. i.–xi.), which are sharply distinguished in content and tone from the remainder of the book of Genesis. They contain material identical with what we know existed in Babylonia and Assyria, notably the history of the flood. Perhaps the most natural account of the flood-story in Genesis is that it was borrowed from the Assyrians or Babylonians, during or shortly before the exile; on the hypothesis that it was brought by the Hebrews with them from the Tigris-Euphrates valley when they migrated to Canaan, it would be hard to account for the close similarity between the Chaldean and biblical flood-stories (supposing that the Hebrew account was not committed to writing till many centuries later), since in each nation the tradition would go its independent way, and the two would presumably diverge considerably from each other; and it would be equally hard to explain the absence of all allusion to the great catastrophe in the pre-exilian literature.[1] In the Assyrian-Babylonian remains

---

[1] There are traces of different recensions in the Babylonian-Assyrian account, as in the Hebrew. Our Yahwistic and Elohistic components may represent narratives derived from different districts in Babylonia, or the latter may be in part or wholly a later Jewish redaction of the material. The interval of a hundred and fifty years between the arrival of the exiles in Babylonia and the final redaction of the Pentateuch would allow a considerable re-working of the story. The question, however, is not clear; and it is pos-

there are fragments of other narratives which are parallel with parts of the material in Gen. i.–xi. ; for example, with the cosmogony and the story of the Tower of Babel. It is possible that in the serpent of Gen. iii. we have a survival of the dragon of Babylonian myth, who is the antagonist of the gods, here transformed under the influence of the Jewish monotheistic faith, and woven into the general body of Jewish beliefs. No distinct reference to the story is found elsewhere in the Old Testament ;[1] the earliest mention of the beginning of death is found in the Wisdom of Solomon (ii. 24). These indications point to a late date for the present form of the story in Genesis ; and it may be added that the broad cosmopolitan view of history which it involves belongs more naturally to the time when the Jews came into contact with other nations.

But though the story of the temptation of man by the serpent stands thus isolated in the Old Testament, it nevertheless exists, and was, as we know, accepted by and influential in the later generations of Jewish thinkers. What is its design and significance ? The first human pair have their abode in a delightful land which produces no thorns or thistles, where the beasts are obedient to man, and where human labor is only

sible that the Hebrews brought these stories with them from Chaldea at a very early period.

[1] Ezekiel, who shows elsewhere traces of Babylonian influence, has (xxviii.) a description of the Garden of Eden, in which the king of Tyre, the anointed cherub, dwelt till he sinned : "Thou wast perfect in thy ways from the day that thou wast created till unrighteousness was found in thee" (v. 15). It is an allusion to the story of Adam, but nothing is said of the nature and origin of the sin there committed (in v. 16 he has in mind the commercial city). The prophet treats his material poetically, but his imagery shows that he was acquainted with the outline of the history in Gen. ii. iii. His divergencies in details from the Genesis narrative, and his introduction of the Babylonian sacred mountain of the gods (v. 14) seem to point to a time when the story had not yet taken shape among the Jews ; and this fact would favor the view that the material was borrowed by them during the exile, and so either was not a part of their original folk-lore, or, if formerly known to them, was now taken afresh from their neighbors.

a pleasant activity. There is a tree of life, by eating the fruit of which man would become immortal. One moral test is ordained for him : he is forbidden to eat of the fruit of the tree of the knowledge of good and evil, and death is to be the penalty of disobedience. The animals are all endowed with power of speech, and of them the serpent is the subtlest. For some reason not explained in the text (according to the Wisdom of Solomon, it was his envy of man's happiness and possible immortality) he suggested to the woman that she and the man should eat of the forbidden fruit, offering the inducement that they should thus be made equal to the Elohim-beings. They ate, and sentence of death was pronounced on them ; and lest they should eat of the tree of life and live forever, God drove them out of Eden, at the gate of which he placed the cherubim to guard the approach to the tree. What was the effect, in the conception of the writer of this chapter, of man's act of disobedience ? Was it the corruption of his moral nature, the entrance of sin as a power into the world ? On the one hand, the transgression of the divine command was an act of sin, the first, as far as Jewish records go, in the history of the race. On the other hand, the succeeding history in Genesis makes no reference to this event, and shows no consciousness of a dogma of universal and total depravity. The priestly document (i. v., and parts of vi.–ix.) seems to ignore the story entirely ; see, for example, in ch. v. the continuous development from Adam to Noah (v. 29 is an insertion from another source). And in the prophetic narrative, Abel and Noah are righteous men accepted by God and apparently without taint of sin. In both narratives, indeed, the earth is described as having after a time become corrupt before God, but this fact is not brought into connection with the narrative in the third chapter; it seems rather to be the common Old Testament view of the universality of sin, which is the result of experience. Moreover, it must be observed that in this chapter the stress is laid on certain phenomena of life, which are explained by the punishments inflicted: the serpent is to go on his belly, eat dust, and be worsted in his conflict with man; the man and the woman are driven from a delightful abode; the earth is to bring forth inedible and hurtful things; the woman is to be subject to great bodily suffering, and is to be subordinated to the man; the man is to gain his bread by the sweat of his brow and to return to the dust out of which he was made. The main object of the writer seems to be to account for the existence of these great facts of man's experience, — birth, toil, death; and he appends an account of the origin of clothing (v. 21).[1] Of effect on man's inward life he says nothing; he is apparently concerned only with some outward facts. These facts he brings into connection with the initial act of human disobedience to God, and in so far his narrative may be regarded as a history of the origin of sin. But he, like the other Old Testament writers, really takes the human inclination to sin for granted He does not undertake to explain by what inward process the woman came to accept the serpent's suggestion, or why the man decided to follow the woman's example. There is no hint of inward conflict either in the woman or in the man; and it is not true, as is so often said, that Adam and his wife are represented as in a state of childlike moral weakness or ignorance. It was only by eating the forbidden fruit, in-

---

[1] The awakening of the consciousness of nakedness may be looked on as the birth of shame, the natural accompaniment of the sense of sin; this would be a fine psychological touch in the narrative. But it is doubtful whether the writer had in mind anything more than the unseemliness which every tolerably advanced civilization attaches to nakedness. The first pair, as a result of the knowledge acquired by eating of the fruit of the tree, perceived, he would say, the indecency of their position; whence this sense of indecency comes, he does not say; and we may suppose that our author attempted in thought no precise explanation of its origin, but contented himself with regarding it, like toil, as a part of the heritage of civilized life.

deed, that they attained that high perception of good and evil, that fine power of distinguishing and selecting, which equalled them with the Elohim-beings (v. 22); but before this they had been intrusted with the care of the garden, and are represented as human beings of normal intelligence and development. Morally, also, they appear to occupy the normal position of man. Up to the fatal moment of the woman's colloquy with the serpent, they had not sinned ; but this was because no occasion of transgression had presented itself; at any moment it was possible for them to choose the wrong rather than the right. In a word, the question of the origin of sin was remote from the writer's mind; he chronicled the first act of sin, but it did not occur to him that any psychological explanation of such an occurrence was needed. It was matter of common experience that there was in the human soul an inclination to evil ; and in this respect he did not think of the first man as different from his posterity.[1] A sharp temptation presents itself to Adam and Eve, — there is the prize of equality with the divine beings to be gained by one act of disobedience ; they chose to risk the consequences of disobedience. Many questions of psychological interest present themselves to the modern reader of this story ; but it is not probable that any of these were in the mind of its author. Did he regard the godlike knowledge of good and evil as a misfortune, and the desire for it as a crime ? How could man incur the penalty of death at the moment that he became as one of the Elohim ? Is labor, like knowledge, to be regarded as an evil ? But these questions have really nothing to do with the story. For the explanation of its present form we have probably to go first to the old mythical narrative of which it is the monotheistic elaboration,[2] and

---

[1] For a similar rabbinical view see Weber, "System der pal. Theol." p. 206.

[2] The naïveté of the narrative points to an early stage of society for its origin. Man, the serpent, the Elohim-beings and the cherubs associate, as

then to the writer's special purpose to explain certain universal phenomena of human life. He no more explains the origin of sin than do the prophets and psalmists; he relates its historical beginning, but he takes for granted its psychological ground, and in this sense it seems to have been understood by succeeding generations for a considerable time.

The serpent in the narrative is an enigmatical figure. There is no hint that he is anything but the animal, wise above other animals, acquainted with the conditions of man's life and with his relations to the Elohim, but still simply and wholly the animal; the punishment inflicted on him relates solely to the habits of the beast. But there seems to be a difficulty in supposing that the writer of Gen. iii. could attribute such a rôle to a beast. A serpent endowed with reason, and capable of circumventing the designs of God, is a character which might seem impossible to Jewish thought. It has therefore appeared to many persons necessary to hold that the writer meant to represent the animal as merely the vehicle of a malignant spiritual being. Such was the view taken in later times. But is there any ground for attributing such a view to our author? The opinion that the lower animals in primitive times were endowed with reason makes no difficulty; it was widely held in antiquity.[1] The serpent of our chapter must be regarded as going back to a very early time, — the survival and transformation of an old mythical figure, at first probably a literal snake, then gradually interwoven into more developed myths. Such a malign figure might, in the course of generations, take just the shape and play

it were, on equal terms, — a characteristic of primitive narratives. The central idea is man's loss, not of innocence, but of happy ease.

[1] For the evidence that early peoples in all parts of the world made no difference, in respect of reason and speech, between man and other animals, see Tylor's "Primitive Culture," Lang's "Myth, Ritual, and Religion," and similar works.

just the part of the serpent of Genesis. Given the two
conceptions, — a hostile dragon-creature, and the lapse of
man from a state of primitive happiness, — there might
not unnaturally result the story of the temptation and fall.
The Jews may have received it, with the two facts combined, during or shortly before the exile, and impressed on
it the monotheistic stamp, the relation of the serpent and
the man to God which we now find in the story.[1] It may
seem strange to us, or impossible, that Jews should have
been willing to accept such a history from their heathen
neighbors. But we must recollect that the Jews of the
exilian period were not the Jews of the New Testament
times, or of the second century B. C., or even of the period
of Ezra and Nehemiah. They were far more receptive;
their religious dogmas had not been sharply formulated;
their religious life was not petrified. They found themselves
in the midst of a splendid civilization, a people speaking
a kindred tongue to theirs, with stories of the olden times
whose Semitic impress would deprive them of the appearance of strangeness to the Semitic Jew. Such stories, finding their way into the little community of exiles through
their intercourse with their Babylonian neighbors, might
after several generations come to assume a Jewish shape,
so that their foreign origin might be forgotten. The serpent would be accepted as an instrument of God's dealings

---

[1] There is no mention of the temptation in the Babylonian written remains,
only a possible hint of it in the pictures of the tree with two persons, whose
character is not certain. The figure of the hostile dragon (Tiamat) is prominent in Babylonian epic poetry, but in the shape in which we now have it,
is late and complex. It is certainly connected with the sea, as the name indicates; but how the sea came to be represented as a dragon, and the latter
came to be the enemy of the gods (destroyed in the Babylonian story by Bel-
Marduk), is not clear. Tiamat, for example, is in the first creation-tablet the
mother of the gods and of the world. The figure seems to involve the blending of several different lines of mythical narrative. The humanized and
reflective form of the story in Genesis indicates a comparatively late period
for its final redaction.

with man in those far-away times when all the conditions of life were different from ours. The Jew would think it unnecessary to ask how a beast could do such great things, or why the serpent rather than any other beast should have been the actor. The story would be accepted with the same simplicity with which the prophetic writer of Gen. vi. details the history of the angels who came down to earth and took to themselves wives of the daughters of men. These were all things that lay outside of present experience; but they were believed to belong to a unique period of human history.

We should reach the same view of the serpent if we supposed the story to have been brought by the Jews from Mesopotamia and gradually worked up into its present shape. The difficulties in the way of this supposition have already been stated; but on the other hand, there are some features of the narrative that may seem to favor it. The story abounds in incongruities, as if it were the abridgment of an originally much longer narrative. The representation of the divine being is of that highly anthropomorphic character which we more naturally refer to early times: Yahwe brings the animals to Adam to see what he will call them, and only after a detailed examination is it discovered that there is among them no companion corresponding to man, no help meet for him, and it then becomes necessary to create a special being; Yahwe walks in the garden in the cool of the day, — that is, the evening, — because the heat was insupportable at other times; he cannot at first find Adam, who has hidden himself; he comes down for the purpose of finding out the state of things by personal inquiry, and it is by cross-questioning that the facts are elicited; he fears that the man will eat of the tree of life and live forever, — he does not (apparently cannot) withdraw from the tree its virtue, but drives man from the garden, and stations cherubim to guard it. Similar anthropomorphisms

are found in the stories of the flood and of the Tower of
Babel, and indeed elsewhere (Gen. xviii. ; Ps. lxviii.). In
their origin they belong to an undeveloped state of religious thought; but, handed down by tradition, they might
in much more advanced times be accepted and retained as
sacred lore. Anthropomorphisms and incongruities do not,
however, settle the question of origin ; they may have been
old-Babylonian as well as old-Hebrew.

The rôle of the serpent began very soon to cause difficulty in men's minds. The same sort of doubt arose as
now exists among us. What was this serpent ? Whence his
power and malignity ? It would be natural to connect him
with an evil spirit and to identify him with Satan when
the doctrine of a great spiritual adversary of Israel and
of man had been sufficiently developed. This identification
does not occur in the Old Testament. But we know that
the person of Satan was constantly growing in distinctness. In the book of Chronicles (1 Chron. xxi. 1), Satan
tempts David to number Israel, apparently for the purpose
of bringing misfortune on the king and on the people. It
is a procedure parallel with that of Gen. iii. ; in both cases
the tempter suggests an apparently desirable act which he
knows will excite the displeasure of God. We are not able
to trace the development of Satan further in the Old Testament. The book of Daniel, with its large machinery of
angels, some of whom are unfriendly to Israel, makes no
mention of the great adversary. The Wisdom of Solomon,
however, seems to give a definite interpretation of the serpent of Gen. iii. : "God created man for immortality, and
made him to be an image for his own being [or, his own
eternity], but through envy of the devil came death into
the world" (ii 23, 24). There can be little doubt that the
author here identifies the serpent with the devil ; and as
he speaks of this act of the Evil One as well known, we

must suppose that the identification in question had been made by the Jews some time before, — that is, probably as early as the third century B. C.[1] The thought of the time favored such a view. There was a growing belief in the influence of spirits, good and bad, on human life ; and the literary and scientific culture of the day more and more indisposed men to attribute to an animal the part played by the serpent in the history of the first man's transgression.

But even if, as is pointed out above, the serpent of Gen. iii. is not to be identified or connected with an evil spirit, does it follow that the narrative is to be taken literally ? May it not have been intended as an allegory ? The serpent might represent the lower, animal nature in man, from which comes so largely the inducement to sin.[2] The author would then picture life as a struggle between the opposing tendencies of the human soul, and the experience of the first man would be presented as typical of all succeeding human experience. Such a view is in itself quite conceivable, but is open to various objections. It is entirely without exegetical support. The writer by no word hints that the serpent is to be taken otherwise than literally ; it is the real animal that is cursed ; it must be the real animal that tempts. Further, the narrative does not represent Eve as yielding merely to a solicitation of the lower nature. Such was the opinion of the rabbis, but it is not borne out by the text. What the serpent promises is that man shall be made equal to the Elohim in knowledge of good and evil, — that is, in general moral-intellectual power, — surely

---

[1] It has already been suggested that the sharper isolation of Satan and his identification with the serpent were first effected in Egypt, where Greek and Egyptian ideas were influential. In the earliest part of the book of Enoch (a Palestinian production), i.-xxxvi., lxxii.-cv., it is Azazel who is the chief representative of evil, in the Parables (of later date) he is identified with Satan (liii. 3 ; liv. 5, 6). We have here an indication of the gradual coalescence of different lines of development of the principle of moral evil.

[2] Philo (i. 79) regards the serpent as a symbol of sensual pleasure.

not a despicable prize. As to Adam, his reason for eating the fruit is not given; it is only said that he took it when it was offered him by his wife. In the case of Eve, it is added that she observed the beauty of the fruit; a sensual motive thus existed, but it is not represented as predominating over the higher intellectual reason. Such an allegorical narrative might be possible for the time when this story was put into shape (fifth century B. C.); but if that had been the author's intention, he would certainly have given an indication of it, as we find in Isa. v., Ezek. xvi., Ps. lxxx. The abstract character of the supposed allegory would, however, occasion doubt; such a representation, the antagonism between the higher and lower elements of the soul, seems more appropriate to the first century of our era than to the age of Ezra.

In this connection we may notice our author's representation of death. Death is regarded in the Old Testament as the common lot of men (the teaching of experience),[1] and as the greatest of evils (since existence in Sheol was looked on as colorless and negative, devoid of pleasurable activity). It was viewed vaguely as the inevitable outcome of human weakness, though it might be prematurely inflicted by God in the way of punishment.[2] Except in Gen. iii., no other explanation of its presence is offered; it was accepted as an ultimate fact. In the history in Gen. iii., man is regarded as mortal, yet as capable of earthly immortality. If he had eaten of the tree of life, he would have lived forever; and it does not appear why he did not eat of it

---

[1] Nothing is said of a sentence of death passed on the lower animals; their mortality is assumed (Ps. civ. 29), and is not supposed to need explanation.

[2] In rare cases (Enoch, Elijah) a man was held to have passed out of earthly life without suffering death; he was taken directly to the abode of the Elohim. Parallel instances among other peoples are numerous. Such representations appear to issue out of the primitive conception of the essential identity between gods and men.

while he had opportunity.[1] After his sin the punishment of death was denounced against him, perhaps not as stamping mortality on him, but as declaring that he should not gain immortality by the life-giving tree. The death thus imposed was physical and temporal : " Dust thou art, and to dust thou shalt return." There is no hint of a present spiritual death of the soul, nor of everlasting death hereafter, which did not belong to the writer's circle of ideas. The addition made to the general Old Testament teaching by this story is that the first man (and presumably the whole race) lost the gift or possibility of earthly immortality by an act of transgression. Such is the view given in the Wisdom of Solomon (ii. 23, 24) : " God created man to be immortal, . . . but through envy of the devil death came into the world." The statement in Ecclus. (xvii. 1) — " the Lord created man of the earth and turned him into it again "—is indefinite. According to Ecclus. (xxv. 24) and Philo (i. 79), it was through the woman that sin and death came into the world.

The literature between the Old Testament and the New Testament shows no development in the idea of sin. Different tendencies, no doubt, existed among the Jewish people. The nation as a whole came under the control of nomism ; sin, conceived as the violation of some precept of the external law, tended to assume a mechanical character. Where the conduct of life was ordered by minute regulations, the attention was naturally fixed more on the outward precept and less on the spiritual constitution and temper of the soul. This is the conception which we find in the Wisdom of the Son of Sirach, the Sibylline Oracles, Tobit, and the Psalter of Solomon. On the other hand, the existence of a

---

[1] I here take the narrative as it stands, passing by, as unimportant for the present discussion, the question whether the tree of life belongs to the original form of the story. See Budde, " Biblische Urgeschichte," pp. 46 ff.

more spiritual view is vouched for by Ps. li., and by the conception of wisdom found in the Wisdom of Solomon and in Philo. In the last two works, though there is no explicit statement of the nature of sin, it is assumed to be a contamination, restriction, and violation of the higher nature. The true life of the soul is identified with that wisdom which involves both accurate knowledge and purity of will; and wrong-doing is therefore thought of as an impairment of inward spiritual life. In accordance with this view, Philo holds the body to be the seat of evil and the antagonist of the higher life; it conspires, he says, against the soul; it is forever dead (i. 100); it cannot aid in the attainment of virtue, but rather hinders it (i. 64); and so the flesh is put over against the divine spirit, and the two are represented as opposing principles of life : "Men are of two classes, — those who order their lives by the divine spirit and reason, and those who live by the blood and the pleasure of the flesh " (i. 481).[1]

The New Testament representation of sin varies with different writers, passing from the simple Old Testament view to the conception of evil as the corruption of nature. Its universality is everywhere assumed, as in Luke xiii. 3, Rom. iii. 9–19 ;[2] the teaching of the Old Testament and of general human observation and conviction is accepted without argument. The majority of the New Testament books show no interest in the question of the historical origin of sin. Doubtless the narrative in Gen. iii. was accepted with its later interpretation as given in the Wisdom

---

[1] This is not to be regarded as the ascetic view that the body is in itself sinful, but only as the representation of the flesh as in general the visible locus and instrument of the lower pleasures.

[2] The passages here cited from the Old Testament are Eccles. vii. 20; Ps. xiv. 2, 3; Ps. v. 10 (9); Isa. lix. 7, 8; Ps. xxxvi. 2 (1); Ps cxliii. 2. None of these, except the first and last, affirm sinfulness of all men; the reference, with the exception stated, is to the "wicked," who are simply the enemies of Israel; their point of view is rather national than moral.

of Solomon (ii. 24); the common view must have been that man fell from purity by the temptation of the devil. But it seems to have been felt that for the moral-spiritual life, this historical fact was of small importance; the practical thing was to recognize the present relation of sin to the soul. Jesus lays stress on the fundamental fact that the root of evil is in the heart, whence proceed evil thoughts and deeds which defile the man (Matt. xv. 19, 20) and define the character of his soul, for the tree is known by its fruit, and out of the abundance of the heart the mouth speaks (Matt. xii. 33, 34). So in the Epistle of James, the interest is in the present psychological history of sin: "Blessed is the man who endures temptation, for when he has been approved, he shall receive the crown of life which he has promised to those that love him. Let no man when he is tempted say, I am tempted by God, for God cannot be tempted by evil things, nor does he himself tempt any one; but each man is tempted when he is drawn away and enticed by his own desire. Then the desire, when it has conceived, bears sin, and the sin, when it is full grown, brings forth death" (James i. 12–15). In this connection it would have been not unnatural for the writer to refer to the history in Genesis; but he is concerned with practical life, with the present struggle of man's soul. A universal disposition to sin is here assumed, but the psychological analysis relates to every sinful act. As to the origin of this tendency to evil, its relation to the soul, whether it is to be considered a second nature or an original nature, a divine creation or a human addition and blot, — these are questions that the greater part of the New Testament, wholly concerned with practical life, does not touch. The writings of Paul and his school and the Fourth Gospel contain references to the history in Genesis, but merely repeat its statements, without undertaking anything like the spiritual history of the first man: "By one man sin entered into the world and death by sin, and thus death passed unto all men, for that all sinned" (Rom. v. 12); "Adam was not beguiled, but the woman, being beguiled, fell into transgression' (1 Tim. ii. 14); "Ye are of your father the devil, and you will to do the desires of your father" (John viii. 44)

To the same practical interest we may ascribe the reticence of the New Testament respecting the external and internal consequences of Adam's transgression. Did the death inflicted on him (and on his descendants) extend beyond this life and assume the form of everlasting punishment (of annihilation there is no word in either Old Testament or New Testament)? Did the sentence affect man's moral nature, carrying with it a deadness to higher inward impulses and incapacity for holiness? In the greater part of the New Testament these questions are ignored; there is no consciousness of their existence. The Christian life of the first century consisted partly in the acceptance of Jesus of Nazareth as the Messiah and Saviour, and the expectation of his speedy return to earth, and partly in the ethical struggle against the hostility and moral evil of the world. Christianity was eminently a serious, real life, whose practical concerns absorbed the energies of men. The Gospels and most of the Epistles are occupied with the present as a preparation for the future; of the past they think only in so far as it is a prediction of the new kingdom of heaven which has brought peace and moral stability with hope of a coming unspeakable blessedness. Paul, with his analytic and dogmatically constructive mind, is the only writer who feels called on to treat logically the historical beginning of sin; and even he does it only indirectly. His argument in Rom. v. 12-21 has for its main purpose to set forth the introduction of life-giving righteousness through Jesus Christ. He assumes the historical fact that sin and death entered the world through Adam, but he seems not to think it necessary to define precisely the nature of this death. It is first of all physical in his conception: "Death reigned from Adam till Moses, even over them who had not sinned after the likeness of Adam's transgression" (v. 14). But at the same time he takes for granted that it is everlasting, as appears from the antithesis in v. 21: "That, as sin reigned in death, even so might grace reign through righteousness unto eternal life through Jesus Christ our Lord." Further, the contrast running through the paragraph, between the righteousness achieved by Christ and the sinful condition established by Adam, doubtless involved in the apostle's feeling the elements of moral corruption and purification. In his view, deadness to the law, the result of faith in Christ, was also deadness to sin, — a legal status which could not exist apart from the moral attitude of the soul ch. vi). Thus, though he makes no explicit statement of a connection between Adam's sin and spiritual and everlasting death, it may be inferred that the connection existed in his mind. Traces of this conception of the consequences of sin are found in pre-Christian books. But Paul gives it a new prominence; he was naturally led to this view by his conception of Christ as the centre of salvation and the turning-point in religious history, — the new divine life brought in by him was to be set over against the preceding period of dull subjection to external law. His view was no doubt shared more or less by the body of churches with which he was in special contact, and by its logical symmetry more and more commended itself to the Christian world. So far as regards a connection between universal human sinful-ness, a fact of experience, and the historical incident de-scribed in Gen. iii, this is in itself not an ethical element of life, and Paul uses it, as we have seen, simply to bring out clearly the inward righteousness created by Christ; but, raised to the rank of a fundamental dogma and held in a mechanical way, it is capable of exerting an injurious effect on the religious consciousness.

The narrative in Genesis represents the woman as the immediate agent of the introduction of sin into the world,[1] and this side of the history is followed literally in 1 Tim. ii. 14: "Adam was not beguiled, but the woman was beguiled, and fell into transgression." The lesson which the writer draws from this fact is the subordination of women: "Let a woman learn in quietness, in all subjection; but I permit not a woman to teach nor to have dominion over a man, but to be in quietness; for Adam was first formed, then Eve, and Adam was not beguiled," etc. (vs. 11–13). His interest in the narrative is social and practical. Paul, on the other hand, has nothing to say of Eve, but lays all the stress on Adam as the effective person in the transaction. His is the legal view, which regards the man as the head and representative of the household, alone qualified to take legal action, the woman not being *sui juris*. How far this difference of view existed in Christian circles of that day, it is impossible to say. As we have already seen, the Alexandrian Philo makes the woman the introducer of sin, and the same opinion is expressed in the Wisdom of the Son of Sirach. Whether Philo represents the Alexandrian Jewish view, and Paul the Palestinian, we have no means of determining; if the First Epistle to Timothy be regarded as representing Pauline theological ideas, its usage would go to show that both views were held among Palestinian Jews. Not improbably Paul was led to select Adam as the central figure in the history of the first transgression

---

[1] The rôle thus assigned to woman (and not by the Hebrews alone) is perhaps merely the expression of the ancient opinion of the moral inferiority of the sex (Eccles. vii. 28; 1 Tim. ii. 14, 15), such histories having been composed by men. But the origin of the temptation-story is obscure, and it is impossible to say what other elements may have determined its present form.

in order, by contrast with him, to bring out more clearly the work of Christ; the whole of the Pauline theology is derived from the conception of Christ as the centre of salvation.

But though the precise religious significance of Adam's sin is scantily treated in the New Testament, there is no doubt as to its affirmation respecting the corruption of human nature. Here again it is the Pauline school and the Johannean writings to which we owe the most definite statements. The synoptic Gospels say nothing of a moral depravity inherent in man. On the contrary, Jesus everywhere assumes man's moral capability and independence; his appeal is to the human conscience and will, which he takes it for granted can perceive and do what is right; in his view the difference between men consists in the difference of attitude toward God and right. Men are indeed "evil" (Matt. vii 11); but this does not prevent their recognition and performance of what is morally good: "If ye then, being evil, know how to give good gifts to your children, how much more shall your Father who is in heaven give good things to them that ask him? . . . Every good tree brings forth good fruit, and the corrupt tree brings forth evil fruit; a good tree cannot bring forth evil fruit, nor can a corrupt tree bring forth good fruit. . . . By their fruits ye shall know them" (Matt. vii. 11, 17, 18, 20). The same view is found in the Epistle to James: "Who is wise and understanding among you? let him show by his good life his works in meekness and wisdom. . . . Draw nigh to God, and he will draw nigh to you; cleanse your hands, ye sinners, and purify your hearts, ye double-minded. . . . He who converts a sinner from the error of his way shall save a soul from death and shall cover a multitude of sins" (James iii. 13; iv. 8; v. 20). This is also the conception of the soul found in the Pastoral Epistles: "We know that the law is good if a man use it lawfully, as knowing this, that law is not made for a righteous man, but for the lawless and unruly" (1 Tim. i. 8, 9); "The Lord's servant must not strive, but be gentle towards all, apt to teach, forbearing, in meekness correcting them that oppose themselves, if peradventure God may give them repentance unto the knowledge of the truth, and they may recover themselves out of the snare of the devil" (2 Tim. ii. 24, 25, 26); "To the end that those who have believed God may be careful to maintain good works" (Titus iii. 8). These passages assume independent moral capability in man, a view of life which may be held along with the belief in the renewing grace of God, as in the Epistle to Titus: "The grace of God has appeared, bringing salvation to all men, instructing us that, denying ungodliness and worldly desires, we should live soberly and righteously in this present age, looking for the appearance of . . . Christ Jesus, who gave himself for us that he might redeem us from all iniquity" (ii. 11–14); "According to his mercy he saved us, through the washing of regeneration and renewing of the holy spirit, . . . that being justified by his grace, we might be made heirs, according to hope, of eternal life" (iii. 5–7).

This is substantially the Old Testament point of view,—universal moral weakness and natural tendency to sin, with recognition of man's power to will and to do what is right. Christianity, however, by emphasizing the sinfulness of sin, brought out into sharper relief the moral feebleness of human nature and the necessity for the assisting and sustaining grace of God. Paul, under the guidance of his dogmatic system, went a step further, and formulated the doctrine of the natural man's incapacity to do good. In his view, the fatal religious error was the belief in obedience to law as the ground of salvation; the inability of obedience to save came to rest in his mind on man's inability to obey, and this inability involved or was identical with moral impotency. He represents the flesh — that is, normal human nature — as absolutely antagonistic in ethical tone and works to the divine spirit; each of these elements of life cherishes desires hostile to the other, — they are contrary each to the other. All wicked deeds he characterizes as the "works of the flesh" (Gal. v. 17–21). This antagonism between the natural human soul and the divine spirit of purity assumes the corruption of man's heart; for it is only through Christ that one escapes the dominion of the flesh and comes to walk and live by the spirit. It is essential that the flesh with all its affections and desires — that is, the whole ethical side of the natural man — be crucified (Gal. v. 24); its only hope is death; and they who sow to the flesh shall reap corruption (Gal. vi. 8). Elsewhere, Paul represents the moral unreceptiveness of unbelievers as the result of blinding by the god of this age (2 Cor. iv. 4), the result of which must be absolute inability to see or to do the truth. The doctrine is expressed definitely in the Epistle to the Romans: "Our old man was crucified with him, that the body of sin might be done away, that so we should no longer be in bondage to sin" (vi. 6); "I know that in me, that is, in my flesh, there dwells no good thing" (vii. 18); "The mind of the flesh is enmity against God, for it is not and cannot be subject to the law of God, and they that are in the flesh cannot please God" (viii. 7). And yet, with this thorough-going view of man's inward corruption, the apostle still holds to an indwelling recognition of the good, a will which is capable of desire, but not of performance: "To will is present with me, but not the power to do what is right, for the good which I would I do not, but the evil which I would not, that I practise" (Rom. vii. 18, 19). Thus he reaches the conception of a schism in the soul, a conflict between the true self and the sinful self: "If I do what I would not, it is no longer I that do it, but sin, which dwells in me" (Rom.

vii. 20).[1] This is perhaps an illogical position; for if no good can dwell in the soul, it is incapable of willing what is right. But Paul is the last man to concern himself about illogicalness. The very intensity of his logical demands naturally leads him into inconsistencies. When he is pointing out the need of the righteousness of Christ, he describes in unlimited terms man's natural inability to attain righteousness; but in the examination of his own experience, he finds the most striking proof of his moral incapacity in the helplessness of his will against the corruption of his nature, — that is, he assumes the existence of a will which is on the side of right. What this " I " is, this personality which stands opposed to sin, he does not further explain. Evidently he was conscious of natural good impulses which were overborne by temptations; but instead of viewing such impulses as the germ which might be developed into holiness, he fixes his eye on the weak side of his nature and declares it to be totally depraved. It is this side of humanity — man's moral debility — which the apostle's theological system led him to insist on; the other — man's independent conscience and recognition of and striving after the good — he leaves almost completely out of view. Yet, though he does not elsewhere formulate it, the recognition of man's moral capacity may be discerned in the appeals which he so often makes to the conscience and will; in his portraiture of the moral condition of the heathen world, for example (Rom. i. 18–32), he assumes in the heathen capacity to recognize and to obey God.[2] It will be, perhaps, a not un-

[1] It is clear, from vs. 10, 14, 24, that Paul is in this chapter describing the experience, not of the renewed, but of the natural soul.

[2] It was not unnatural that the apostle's picture of the contemporary Roman world should be a dark one, he was absorbed in the demonstration of his theme that the only possible righteousness is that which is revealed in the gospel, the righteousness that rests on faith in Christ. But it is only a half-view that he gives. In the lives of not a few illustrious men whose biog-

fair account of Paul's view to say that he recognizes both those elements of life which force themselves on our attention, moral weakness and capacity for moral good. It is his attitude toward the law which leads him to affirm at times moral deadness, in order to do away with man's pretensions to achieving his own salvation; he feels that he can prepare the way for the righteousness of Christ only by eliminating the righteousness of the law.

Complete moral incapacity is affirmed in the Epistles to the Ephesians and to the Colossians, whose theology, whoever their author or authors may be, is substantially Pauline: "And you did he quicken, when you were dead through your trespasses and sins, wherein aforetime you walked according to the age of this world, according to the prince of the power of the air, of the spirit that now works in the sons of disobedience; among whom we also all once lived in the desires of our flesh, doing the wishes of the flesh and of the thoughts, and were by nature children of wrath even as others; but God, being rich in mercy, on account of his great love with which he loved us, even when we were dead through our trespasses, quickened us together with the Christ" (Eph. ii. 1–5, and so Col. ii. 13). Yet here also we have to note the recognition of man's moral freedom in the various precepts (Eph. iv. v.; Col. iii. iv.), obedience to which is assumed to be within man's power; the Ephesians are even exhorted to put away the "old man," — that is, the corrupt nature. The transition from one of these points of view to another is natural; at one time the attention is fixed on man's obvious moral weakness, at another time

raphies have come down to us, and, there is ground to suppose, of many an unnamed household, there were examples of shining or quiet virtue, of patience, devotion, and love. An age must not be judged wholly by its examples of shining wickedness. Nor is this sweeping condemnation necessary to show the power of a righteousness that has its basis in steadfast loving trust in a holy God.

on that independence and power of moral action without which no true ethical life can be conceived.

In the Fourth Gospel, we pass to a conception of life different from those above described. The author looks not on the individual, but on the mass of humanity. He does not enter into an analysis of the ethical elements and powers of the human soul, but regards the world, the cosmos, as hostile to God, incapable of apprehending the truth, involved in darkness and death. Into this mass of darkness and death Jesus has brought light and life, whereby a conflict between these opposing powers has been introduced. "In him was life, and the life was the light of men, and the light shines in the darkness and the darkness does not apprehend it; . . . and this is the judgment, that the light has come into the world, and men loved the darkness rather than the light, for their deeds were evil. . . . Jesus spake unto them, saying, I am the light of the world; he that follows me shall not walk in the darkness, but shall have the light of life. . . . I am come a light into the world, that whoever believes on me may not abide in the darkness" (i. 4, 5; iii. 19; viii. 12; xii. 46). In the sixth chapter (vs. 33–63), Jesus describes himself as the bread of life, the true manna from heaven, of which a man may eat and never die. Elsewhere it is explained that his words are the source of truth: "The words that I speak unto you, they are the spirit and they are the life" (vi. 63). The world is thus pictured as dead, capable of attaining life only by believing on Jesus, the Son of God, whose teaching is the expression of the absolute truth, who is himself, therefore, the way, the truth, and the life (xiv. 6). And thus the sin of the world is unbelief: the Spirit convicts the world of sin because it believes not on Jesus (xvi. 9). Those who believe are ushered into a new existence and form a separate community, which stands over against the world in a relation of irreconcilable hostility: "If the world hates you, know that it hated me before it hated you; if you were of the world, the world would love its own, but because you are not of the world, but I chose you out of the world, therefore the world hates you" (xv. 18, 19). So sharp is this separation, so completely removed is the world from the sphere of the divine life, that Jesus, according to the representation of the author, puts it out of the sphere of his intercession: "I pray not for the world" (xvii. 9). Yet it is only by God's choice and drawing that men can detach themselves from the mass of the world and come to Jesus: "No man can come to me except the Father which sent me draw him" (vi. 44). The same antithesis of power and impotency, however, is here brought out as in the Pauline writings: "You have not his word abiding in you, for whom he sent, him you believe not; you search the Scriptures because you think that in them you have eternal life, and it is they that bear witness of me; and you are not willing to come to me that you may have life. . . . If you believed Moses, you would believe me, for he wrote of me; but if you believe not his writings, how shall you believe my words? . . . All that the Father gives me shall come to me, and him who comes to me I will in no wise cast out" (v. 38–40, 46, 47; vi. 37). And as God is thus the creator of the new world of light and truth and life, he stands over against the devil, the author of falsehood: "I speak the things which I have seen with my father, and you also do the things which you have heard from your father. They answered and said unto him, Our father is Abraham. Jesus said to them, If you are Abraham's children, do the works of Abraham. But now you seek to kill me, a man who has told you the truth, which I heard from God; this did not Abraham. You do the works of your father. They said to him, We have one father, God. Jesus said to them, If God were your father, you would love me, for I came forth and am come from God; I have not come of myself, but he sent me. Why do you not know my speech? Because you cannot hear my word. You are of your father, the devil, and the desires of your father it is your will to do. He was a murderer from the beginning, and stood not in the truth, because there is no truth in him" (viii. 38–44). The same general view is given in the First Epistle of John.

The author of the Fourth Gospel, looking at the world from a philosophical point of view, conceives of life as a conflict between the divine and the anti-divine elements. The world is corrupt; but he offers no explanation of the source of its moral evil.[1] It was created by God through Jesus Christ, and yet is out of harmony with God : "He [Jesus] was in the world, and the world was made through him, and the world knew him not" (i. 10). Of the condition of the world before Christ came, the author says nothing, yet he assumes that Abraham was in harmony with God (viii. 39, 40). In his portraiture of the moral corruption of the world, he substantially agrees with Paul. But his interest in the question of sin is not an historical one, — he seeks no points of connection with the past; he is concerned only with the fact that into this great corrupt organism, the world, there has streamed a divine life, embodied in the words and thus in the person of Jesus Christ.

[1] From his reference to the devil (viii. 44; xvi. 11) it may be inferred that he accepted the current opinion which connected the "prince of this world" with the lapse of the parents of the race from innocence. He does not, however, attempt to bring this fact into relation with the original function of the Logos. His fondness for the term *cosmos* (more than one-half the occurrences of this word in the New Testament are found in the Fourth Gospel and the First Epistle of John) suggests the Stoic idea which is adopted by Philo. It would seem, therefore, that on this Philonian conception (Cosmos and Logos) he has simply grafted the Jewish idea of the entrance of sin into the world through an evil supernatural being. But he is so absorbed in the present mission of the Logos that he does not care to account for the fact which makes that mission necessary.

His eye is fixed not on man's inward struggle against sin, but on the transforming power of God, which lays hold of man and brings him into the sphere of light and life.[1]

The idea that sin inheres in the flesh as matter does not belong to the teaching of the New Testament. We have already seen that the Old Testament regards the human body as the instrument of the soul, and therefore as often the occasion of sin, but not in any wise as in itself impure. The transition, however, to this latter view of the impurity of the flesh was natural and easy; the body, being the occasion of evil, would without difficulty come to be thought of as its seat. Such seems to be the idea in Wisdom of Solomon (viii. 19, 20), where the author is describing his own birth : " I was a child of excellent disposition, and I obtained a good soul; yea, being good, I came into an undefiled body." The thought here is not clear; but there is in any case the suggestion that some human bodies are in themselves impure. So in the passages quoted above from Philo, the flesh is identified with evil; but in the New Testament the term is used in a figurative sense for the corrupt nature, and there is no indication that the gnostic doctrine of the impurity of matter is held by any New Testament writer. It is opposed and condemned in the Epistle to the Colossians (ii. 20–23).[2]

---

[1] The peculiar representation in John ix. 34, of the blind man as born in sins, and the idea that the blindness was the punishment of parental sin (ix. 2), belongs to the Old Testament view; we have here a popular conception which does not essentially modify the theory of the Fourth Gospel or of the New Testament generally.

[2] Neither gnosticism nor that asceticism which is allied to gnosticism seems to be a Jewish (or indeed a Semitic) conception. Certainly nothing of the sort is found in the Old Testament, which is rather marked by an intense love of this life and conviction of its goodness. The Rechabite abstinence from wine was a survival of the old nomad life, and the same thing is probably true of the Nazarite vow, — the Nazarites mentioned in the Old Testament are anything but ascetics. The Wisdom of Solomon and the writings of Philo are not of purely Jewish origin, and the same thing may be suspected of the isolated Essenian community.

The New Testament conception of human sinfulness, therefore, differs little from the result of general observation. Men are held to be everywhere prone to evil; and on the other hand, the ethical independence of the conscience and will is recognized. Of the historical genesis of sin in the world almost nothing is said; the main interest attaches to the present problem of life, the annihilation of sin as a power in the soul. Jesus thinks of this destruction of sin as produced by the voluntary attitude of the soul toward God and man; in the Epistle of James we find the Old Testament conception of the overcoming of sin by effort of will; the writings of the Pauline school consider the destruction of sin in the soul to be the result of the death of Christ and the new creation thence resulting. In the Fourth Gospel the celestial light brought into the world by the Son of God dispels the darkness of sin in the hearts of those who believe. The characteristic of the New Testament teaching is its intense conception of sin as the one great evil in the world, as the central fact of life, around which range themselves all the powers of heaven, earth, and hell. All the manifestations of God in history look finally to the annihilation of this malignant power of the human soul.

3. The destruction of sin is the negative side of the divine process of salvation in the Jewish and Christian Scriptures; the positive side is the attainment of righteousness. The two are inseparably connected; but it will be convenient to consider first the methods by which the removal of sin was supposed to be effected.

The legislation introduced by Ezra and Nehemiah, while it contained an elaborate new sacrifice for sin, did not discard the older ideas on the subject. Up to the time of the exile, the theory of expiation corresponded with the general ethical and religious status of the nation; for the prophets, the national sin was the absorbing interest, and they appear as protesting against an earlier opinion, which disposed of sin in an easy, mechanical way by sacrifices. Such was the primitive view respecting offences against God : if the deity was angry, he was to be appeased by a gift ; and this gift, when the sense of the moral guilt of sin was better developed, assumed the form of a vicarious offering. When the offence was against man, forgiveness might be obtained, if it were thought desirable, by repentance and reparation ; in so far as it was conceived also as an offence against God, it was to be atoned for by sacrifice. For the old mechanical idea that the deity was appeased by a gift the prophets desired to substitute the conviction of the necessity for repentance and reformation. This protest of the prophets represents a most important advance in the ethical conception of sin and the deliverance from sin ; it is stated with admirable fulness and clearness by the prophet Isaiah : "Hear the word of Yahwe, ye judges of Sodom ; give ear to the teaching of our God, ye people of Gomorrah. To what purpose is the multitude of your sacrifices to me ? says Yahwe ; I am full of the burnt offerings of rams, and the fat of fed beasts, and I delight not in the blood of bullocks and lambs and he-goats. When you present yourselves before me, who has required this at your hand, to tread my courts ? Bring no more vain oblations ; incense is an abomination to me ; new moon and Sabbath, the calling of assemblies, I cannot endure, — it is iniquity. Your new moons and your appointed feasts I hate ; they are a burden to me ; I am tired of bearing them. And when you spread forth your hands, I will hide my eyes from you ; and when you make many prayers, I will not hear ; your hands are full of blood. Wash you, make you clean ; put away the evil of your doings from before my eyes ; cease to do evil ; learn to do well ; seek judgment, relieve the oppressed, judge the fatherless, plead for the widow. Come now, and let us reason together, says Yahwe ; though your sins be as scarlet, they shall be as white as snow ; though they be red like crimson, they shall be as wool" (Isa. i. 10–18). This is the prevailing view in the prophetic writings up to the time of the return from the Babylonian exile : wrong must be put away by an act of will; the right must be done; the soul must come into an attitude of willing obedience toward God ; then he will pardon the sin, whether of the nation or of the individual, and bestow the blessings of his favor. This simple ethical conception of the escape from sin by an act of the will, corresponding as it does to human experience, maintained itself through the Old Testament times and appears in the New Testament. It is one side of the struggle against sin, — a side that can never be safely ignored, though it may be conceived in a mechanical way, and lead to a depressed and unspiritual religious life.

This double view of expiation for sin continued down to the exile. In the temple and the other sacred places the traditional sacrifices were maintained, and the ethical ideas of the prophets no doubt penetrated the mass of the people to some extent. Alongside of these there was, however, another conception of the way in which sinning man might be reconciled to God. It was a natural feeling that the sinner's suffering atoned for his sin ; suffering was the punishment of sin ; and when the just measure had been reached, the wrong-doer might hold that the ground of the divine displeasure had been removed. This natural view of the subject had no doubt existed all along among the Israelites (as it has always existed among men); but it does not find definite expression till the latter part of the exile, when the grievous affliction of the nation and the hope of coming deliverance led it to take shape in the mind of the second Isaiah : "Speak ye comfortably to Jerusalem, and cry unto her that her time of service is accomplished, that her punishment is accepted, for she has received at the hand of Yahwe double for all her sins" (Isa. xl. 2). Traces of this feeling may be discerned in the later literature, in the frequent cry, "O Lord, how long?" So just after the return from Babylon the angel of Yahwe appeals to God: "O Yahwe of hosts, how long wilt thou not have mercy on Jerusalem and on the cities of Judah, against which thou hast had indignation these threescore and ten years?" (Zech. i. 12.) Such is probably the feeling underlying the laments of Ps. lxxix. lxxx. lxxxv.

It was but a step from this conception to the idea of vicarious human suffering. This idea resides in the theory of solidarity which has always prevailed in the world, and maintained itself in Israel, notwithstanding the larger recognition of individual responsibility, which was a concomitant, or rather an element, of the ethical growth of the nation. The members of any social unit — as the family, the tribe, or the state — were thought of as bound together into a unit of moral responsibility. The sin of the father imperilled the happiness of his children; the nation suffered for the faults of its rulers. But on the same grounds, all the members of the social unit would share the blessings achieved by its head: if he was good, they prospered; if he by suffering wrought out forgiveness of sin, they might share the pardon and its attendant blessing. The idea must have existed in germ from early times, but it could receive full expression only after the moral consciousness had attained a relatively large development. The question of the relation of suffering to sin, which had always been in men's minds, came into new prominence during the exile. The old theory was that all suffering was a punishment for sin: the good prospered; the wicked suffered. So the prophets had explained the destruction of the northern kingdom and the fall of Jerusalem: the people had sinned; the nation must be destroyed. But at the same time there had been growing up a consciousness of righteousness. In contrast with other nations, Israel had been obedient to Yahwe. Under the new conditions of life in Babylonia, where there was probably a sifting of the exiles, one section of the nation had come to feel that it was faithful to the divine law, and the question arose why it should be involved in the dreadful suffering of banishment from home and contact with unsympathizing idolaters. The answer which presented itself to the great prophet of the latter part of the exile was that the suffering was vicarious. Through it, he said, the body of the nation was to be brought back to obedience and the favor of the God of Israel. The pious, faithful kernel of the nation was the true servant of Yahwe, despised and rejected of men, esteemed to be stricken, smitten of God, and afflicted. Yet in truth it was for the iniquities of the nation that he was bruised; Yahwe laid on him the iniquity of them all. He was oppressed; yet in the land of exile, in the midst of enemies, he humbled himself and opened not his mouth. For the transgression of his people he was cut off from the land of the living, though he had done no violence, and there was no deceit in his mouth (Isa. liii. 1–9). Such is the picture which the prophet gives of the suffering of pious souls in the midst of alien enemies. And what was the explanation? Would Yahwe arbitrarily involve the faithful in the punishment of the unfaithful? Would he be insensible to the claims of his obedient sons? Such a supposition was impossible. The prophet rises to a grand conception of the destiny of the nation. As the bearer of the divine word, Israel was to become the centre of illumination for the nations, the standard-bearer of truth and purity. But to fulfil this mission, Israel must first itself be purified, its sin must be punished and removed; yet it was not necessary that the needful purifying suffering should be

borne by the sinners themselves. It might be laid on innocent heads ; and the greater the purity and dignity of the
vicarious sufferer, the greater the efficacy of his suffering,
and the larger the blessing which would issue from the favor
of God thus obtained. The prophet idealizes the faithful of
Israel into a personality of perfect innocence (and it does
not matter, for the development of the doctrine of vicariousness, whether he has in mind the contemporary body of the
faithful, or a contemporary or future individual conceived
as a representative and ideal Israelite). Out of this suffering was to arise the highest blessing. It pleased Yahwe to
bruise his servant ; but when the sufferer's soul should have
been made an offering for sin, then he should taste the fruit
of his self-sacrifice, — he should see of the travail of his
soul and should be satisfied (Isa. liii. 10–12). Israel should
become righteous ; and further, the world should share its
righteousness : "It is too light a thing that thou shouldst
be my servant to raise up the tribes of Jacob and to restore the preserved of Israel ; I will also give thee for a
light to the Gentiles, that my salvation may come unto the
end of the earth" (Isa. xlix. 6) ; "Strangers shall build up
thy walls and their kings shall minister to thee ; . . . that
nation and kingdom that will not serve thee shall perish"
(Isa. lx. 10, 12).

It is only an external effect that is here described ; nothing is said of an inward conflict of soul produced by the
contemplation of unmerited suffering. It is only the objective idea of vicarious human suffering that is brought out in
the exilian prophecy ; and it appears to have been an isolated product of this period, a special flight of the pious
imagination of one great thinker. There is no reference to
it in the post-exilian literature. After the great crisis of the
exile and the introduction of the law, it fell into the background, not to be revived till the rise of Christianity. The

external, ceremonial idea of atonement for sin was definitely formulated by the Law in its system of sacrifices. As has already been remarked, the element of vicariousness enters into sacrifice as a result of deeper moral consciousness. Sacrifice was at first a gift to the deity, which a profounder sense of moral unworthiness converted into a victim bearing the guilt and punishment of the offerer. The Levitical law is not to be looked on as a mere extension and organization of the ritual. It did, indeed, continue and expand the old sacrificial usage, but it embodied also the profounder moral feeling of the later period. Its ritual was in great part the organized expression of the consciousness of sin. The ancient mind, Jewish and Gentile, saw the most definite and satisfactory atonement for sin in the blood, that is, in the life, of a victim. There were, as we have seen, other conceptions of expiation, as through the suffering of the offender, or of some human being with whom the offender stood in close social relation; but the visible surrender of a life answered most completely to the existing ideas of social-religious order. It is not surprising, therefore, that the Law embodied this conception as the national form of deliverance from sin.

But the Jewish Law made no attempt to provide an atonement for all sins; its restriction in this respect is noteworthy. The offences for which it does provide are, first, sins of ignorance (Lev. iv.); and secondly, certain slighter ceremonial offences, failure to testify in a court of justice, and false dealing in money-matters (Lev. v. vi.). To this must be added the expiation of the great day of atonement (Lev. xvi.), which, however, was of a purely national character, and could have had no bearing on individual sins. Offences other than those above mentioned were regarded by the Jewish Law as committed against society, and were punished accordingly. So far as they were regarded also as committed against God, they were expiated only by the punishment inflicted by the state, the whole law, civil and religious, being the enactment of God. The regulations respecting expiation belonged only to visible sins; the Law is in fact substantially a civil code, the religious ceremonial itself being looked on as part of the outward, social life. Of inward sins, transgressions of the law of purity and love, which belong to the heart, nothing is said; this was a domain which the national legislation did not undertake to enter. Yet it recognized the idea of vicarious atonement, and this idea had a wider range than the book of Leviticus would indicate; it practically included intercession. Job is said to have offered burnt offerings for all his children, fearing that they might have sinned (Job i. 5); the wrath of Yahwe against the three friends is turned aside by a similar sacrifice (Job xlii. 8). The author of the Epistle to the Hebrews (ix. 22) declares that according to the Law there is no remission without shedding of blood; and this statement, though it is to be taken with the restrictions above mentioned, yet accurately represents the prevailing ancient idea of a connection between forgiveness of sin and the blood of an animal-sacrifice.

But the Law had larger consequences than its mere details would suggest. It cultivated the moral sense of the people into results above its mechanical prescriptions. It developed the sense of sin, as Paul points out (Gal. iii. 19), and therewith a freer feeling which brought the soul into more immediate contact with God. Apart from all legal prescriptions, the pious heart cast itself on the mercy of God: "Yahwe is merciful and gracious, slow to anger and plenteous in mercy. He will not always chide, neither will he keep his anger forever. He hath not dealt with us after our sins, nor rewarded us according to our iniquities. . . . As far as the East is from the West, so far hath he removed our transgressions from us" (Ps. ciii. 8–10, 12). Sometimes the appeal to God's mercy was based on the feeling of human weakness : "What is man, that thou shouldest magnify him and set thy heart on him, that thou shouldest visit him every morning and try him every moment? . . . If I have sinned, what can I do to thee, O thou watcher of men? . . . Why dost thou not pardon my transgression and take away mine iniquity? for now I shall lie down in the dust, and thou shalt seek me diligently, but I shall not be" (Job vii. 17–21); "Wilt thou harass a driven leaf? wilt thou pursue the dry stubble?" (xiii. 25.) "Man that is born of a woman is of few days and full of trouble; he comes forth like a flower and withers, he flees as a shadow and continues not; and dost thou open thine eyes on such an one, and bringest me into judgment with thee?" (xiv. 1–3.) "Remember not the sins of my youth nor my transgressions; according to thy lovingkindness remember me for thy goodness' sake" (Ps. xxv. 7); "Like as a father pities his children, so Yahwe pities them that fear him, for he knows our frame, he remembers that we are dust" (Ps ciii. 13, 14). This direct appeal to the divine mercy is connected with a deeper consciousness of sin, such as appears in Ps. xxxii. and li : "I said, I will confess my transgressions to Yahwe, and thou forgavest the iniquity of my sin" (Ps. xxxii. 5); "I acknowledge my transgressions, and my sin is ever before me" (Ps. li. 3).

To this broader conception of the relation between God and man belongs also the idea of human mediation for sin (the connection of which with the Law is referred to above), as when Job is directed to pray for his three friends (Job xlii. 8), or when Samuel says, "Far be it from me to sin against Yahwe in ceasing to pray for you" (1 Sam. xii. 23); or the prophet Jeremiah declares that even the intercession of Moses and Samuel would not avail for Israel (Jer. xv. 1). Such mediation, however, was not confined to men, if we may understand Elihu's interpreting angel (Job xxxiii. 23, 24) as interceding with God for the afflicted man. This idea of mediation for the sinner by men or angels, though a perfectly natural one, does not find frequent expression in the Old Testament[1] or in the Apocryphal books.

We have to note also the negative attitude maintained toward the system of sacrifice by the great Israelitish teachers. The pre-exilian and exilian prophets, though they insisted on the necessity of the faithful worship of Yahwe, discerned what was superficial and false in the offerings in contrast with true ethical service , and denounced it as hateful to God : "I hate, I despise your feasts, and take no delight in your solemn assemblies ; yea, though you offer me your burnt offerings and meal offerings, I will not accept them, nor will I regard the peace offerings of your fat beasts ; take away from me the noise of your songs, for I will not hear the melody of thy viols" (Amos v. 21–23); "To what purpose is the multitude of your sacrifices to me ? says Yahwe. . . . I delight not in the blood of bullocks" (Isa. i. 11); "Will Yahwe be pleased with thousands of rams, with myriads of rivers of oil ? Shall I give my first-born for my transgression, the fruit of my body for the sin of my soul ?" (Mic. vi. 7); "I spake not to your fathers, nor commanded them in the day that I brought them out of the land of Egypt concerning burnt offerings or sacrifices" (Jer. vii. 22). A similar antagonism or negative attitude, which in the prophetic writings is based on moral grounds, appears in some of the Psalms as the result of a like ethical feeling combined with spirituality of thought : "Sacrifice and offering thou hast no delight in ; . . . burnt offering and sin offering thou hast not required" (Ps. xl. 6). In Ps. l, God's indifference toward sacrifices is based on his exalted position as Lord of the world and on the pre-eminence of his moral functions : "I will take no bullock out of thy house, nor he-

---

[1] We may compare the functions of the guardian angels in the book of Daniel (x. 20, 21).

goats out of thy folds ; for every beast of the forest is mine, the cattle on the mountains ; I know all the birds of the mountains, and the roamers of the plain are in my mind ; if I were hungry, I would not tell thee, for the world is mine and the fullness thereof ; will I eat the flesh of bulls or drink the blood of goats ?" (vs. 9–13). We have here the germ of a feeling expressed in the Epistle to the Hebrews (x. 4) that it is impossible that the blood of bulls and goats should take away sin. But while the author of the Epistle insists on the worthlessness of such sacrifices in order that he may substitute another better sacrifice (quoting, curiously enough, Ps. xl. 6, 7, in support of his position), the prophets and psalmists are only concerned with the insufficiency of this outward act as contrasted with the inward service of the soul. The two movements toward elaboration of the ritual of sacrifice, and direct appeal of the soul to God, went hand in hand, each responding to a need of the human heart. The body of the nation felt that, in its moral weakness, it could not dispense with some intermediary between man's feeble life and the august holiness of God. And on the other hand, there were moments of exaltation for pious souls when this same conception of the divine purity made all bodily intercession seem worthless, and drove the worshipper to cast himself on the supreme attribute of Israel's God, — his pitifulness and lovingkindness. Repentance was indeed demanded as the condition of forgiveness : " Pardon my iniquity, for it is great " (Ps. xxv. 11) ; " I said, I will confess my transgressions to Yahwe, and thou forgavest the iniquity of my sin " (Ps. xxxii. 5) ; " Against thee, thee only have I sinned, and done that which is evil in thy sight " (Ps. li. 4). Such was the condition, announced by John the Baptist and Jesus, of entrance into the kingdom of God (Mark i. 4, 15). These two elements of the Old Testament thought — the inward preparation of the soul through repentance and the outward preparation through intercession — the Christian Church endeavored, with more or less success, to combine in its religious consciousness into a unity.

The extra-canonical books add nothing of importance to the Old Testament ideas. The scheme of temple sacrifices continued as before, only with some small additions to the ceremonial. Still, there are hints that the old mechanical conception of atonement was undergoing a gradual transformation through all the influences that affected the ethical thought of the nation. The books of this period that have come down to us are chiefly the products of messianic or other purely national interest. But the synagogues and legal schools nourished other ideas, spiritual and ethical. The conception of sin as an offence against the absolute right, or against the will of God, held to be identical with the absolute right, shows itself in sayings attributed to the great teachers, and in the Wisdom of Solomon. Atonement for sin was, from this point of view, held to lie in rightdoing. This idea (in which non-Jewish influence is discernible was not definitely formulated, but colors such works as Wisdom and the treatises of Philo, and was doubtless not without effect on portions of the New Testament.

The point of view of Jesus himself was substantially that of the pre-exilian prophets. He recognized the existing system of national sacrifices (Luke xvii. 14; John v. 1; Matt. xxiii. 2, 3), and, according to the First Gospel, declared that he had come not to destroy, but to fulfil, the Law and the prophets, and that no man could without blame ignore one of the smallest commandments of the Mosaic legislation (Matt. v. 17, 19).[1] On the other hand, in defence of a larger

---

[1] Some critics regard this last utterance as belonging not to Jesus, but to a Judaizing editor of the Matthew-Gospel, and intended as a protest against the supposed Pauline hostility to the Law. In any case, it testifies to a profound respect for the Mosaic legislation in a section of the Church of the first century.

interpretation of the Law, he adduced the example of the priests themselves, and cited (Matt. xii. 5, 7) the words of the prophet Hosea : " I desire mercy and not sacrifice" (Hos. vi. 6). But, above all, the pure ethical-spiritual view which he taught (as in the Sermon on the Mount) of man's relation to God contained the germs of the destruction of the mechanical legal-sacrificial system, — a work which, not undertaken by him, was accomplished by the great apostle, who most truly represented and embodied in deeds the spirit of the Master.

The early disciples doubtless followed the example of their Master in maintaining allegiance to the temple-service. This is the impression made by Acts i.–v., where Peter and John go to the temple at the hour of prayer (iii. 1), and Gamaliel's speech (v. 38, 39) does not seem to contemplate a fundamental schism ; and later there is even an account (xxi. 20–26) of Paul's taking part in a purification-offering.[1] This feeling would naturally survive longest among the Palestinian Christians ; elsewhere the bonds which united the Church to the old faith were weakened by distance and by the incoming of Gentiles. The construction of the death of Jesus as sacrificial did away with the old system of animal-offering. This was not a change of the fundamental idea, but only of the nature of the offering. It was still held that the removal of sin and guilt was affected by the shedding of blood. But the greater dignity of the victim corresponded to a deeper sense of the evil of sin ; the conception of atonement was held in a more distinctly ethical way. It is in the writings of Paul (Gal. i. 4, etc.) that we first meet with the statement of the sacrificial nature of the Messiah's

---

[1] It is not intended by this to decide on the general question of the historical trustworthiness of the book of Acts, but only to infer from the passages quoted the existence of a belief that the early Church had not completely broken with the temple-ritual.

death ; and we may suppose that he and others were led to this view by their conception of the exalted function of the glorified Messiah in conjunction with their adherence to the Old Testament idea of atonement. Jesus had departed from the world and been raised to the right hand of God as Saviour, whence he would soon return to deliver his people. What function, in the divine scheme, could be assigned to his death but that of expiation of sin, which the Scripture connected with the blood of a victim ? That the old legal view had a strong hold on a part of the Church appears from the earnestness with which the Epistle to the Hebrews endeavors to prove that Christianity really retained the ideas of the ancient system, only substituting for its forms more perfect forms, merging the type in the antitype.

4. The positive side of the ethical relation between man and God is given in the idea of righteousness ; and we have now to ask wherein righteousness consisted and how it was acquired.

We need not stop to examine special shades of meaning of the various terms employed in the Old Testament to express the idea of moral goodness. They all go back finally to the conception of some standard of conduct which is referred to God as its author. Such is the usage of the Old Testament in the form in which we now have it, as the production of men who lived and wrote in a relatively high ethical-religious atmosphere. In the earlier, unreflective time, a good man was one who conformed to the somewhat rude ethical ideas of the community. He might be a warrior like Jephtha, who was relentless toward his enemies and capable of sacrificing his own daughter in fulfilment of a vow ; but if he fulfilled the moral demands of the time, he was accounted righteous. From the beginning, the accepted system of ethics was identified in a general way with the will of the deity, since God could not be conceived of as requiring anything else than that which the best moral sense of the community called for. There was a double progress: the ethical standard was gradually raised, and at the same time the identification of righteousness with the will of the deity became more and more systematic and conscious. This will was at first announced occasionally and fragmentarily by the priests and the prophets, and then more definitely embodied in legal codes. The elements of the prophetic preaching of righteousness were two: the worship of Yahwe alone, and obedience to the rules of social ethics. This is the controlling view in the Old Testament; it is the necessary product of experience and reflection, and at the same time the simplest and broadest theory of life regarded as a mass of actions. The prophets always treat idolatry in connection with its moral accompaniments; for them it was not only disloyalty to the God of Israel, but also inevitably the occasion of moral offence. It was a sin against the covenant which God had made with his people; it was an alliance with the immoral habits of the surrounding peoples. Their judgment on this point is to be taken with some degree of allowance. There was ground for it in the fact that the Canaanitish worship contained licentious elements; on the other hand, their own writings show that the body of Israelitish sin sprang out of Israelitish society, out of human weakness, independently of the particular form of divine service which was followed. The prophets, however, were guided by a true instinct in their opposition to idolatry on moral grounds. The Israelitish religious genius was to develop a moral code more strenuous than that of their neighbors, and national development in this, as in all other points, was favored by isolation. Idolatry — or, to state it more precisely according to the Old Testament conception, the acknowledgment of any other god but Yahwe — was a confusing and disintegrating fact. From our point of view, it was in itself morally indifferent, though an occasion of moral loss; to the prophets, it was treason against the national idea and the national deity, itself a heinous sin, and the source of all impurities. The introduction of a written code (Ex. xxi.–xxiii., ninth or eighth century, and Deuteronomy, end of seventh century) served to define the moral standard and to make the moral life more precise. Nor is it an accident that along with this more definite expression of ethical-religious law we find the first traces of a more spiritual conception of righteousness in the "new heart" of Jeremiah and Ezekiel. Deeper reflection on the inner experiences of man and the recognition of a higher standard of life led the better religious thinkers to the conviction that true righteousness could not be defined merely as a series of acts of obedience; that it must proceed from a heart whose impulses were in harmony with the divine standard of right. Here, then, we have the two tendencies which from this time on determined the ethical-religious development of Judaism and then of Christianity. Both are founded in human nature, and represent real and necessary elements of the moral life. Each had its period of supremacy; the highest result was gained when the two were completely harmonized in the religious consciousness.

The same conception appears in the Psalms, but intenser and more elaborated. The Psalter is the product of deep national distress. It was in the Greek period, and especially in the second century B. C., that the Jews first felt the poignancy of foreign oppression. They had been contented vassals of Assyrians, Babylonians, and Persians, who recognized and respected their religion. By the end of the third century they had grown into a church; their national existence lost, they clung to their religious faith with a reverence and devotion all the more intense; they lived in the midst of aliens, who oppressed them in person and property and derided their religion. Thus driven into religious isolation, they fell back on God and their own souls; minute outward obedience to the divine commands came more and more to be recognized as the mark of righteousness, but at the same time the conviction grew stronger of the need of inward purity, of the ripeness of the heart toward God. The authors of the Fifteenth and Twenty-Fourth Psalms define the ethical conditions of alliance with the people of God; Ps. cxix. is the Ode of the Law, which is extolled as the perfection of truth and the infallible guide of life and source of happiness; the author of Ps. li., in his deep consciousness of sin and desire of oneness with God, cries out for a new heart, asking nothing less than that God would re-fashion the very spring and essence of his moral-religious life.

Corresponding with this double sense of the nature of righteousness was the twofold view of its source, of the manner in which it was to be achieved. The simpler, earlier view was that it was gained by man's effort, by the free determination of his will. Men were held to differ in the attitude of their will toward right; the final exposition of human conduct was that some men loved and others hated the law of God. The later view, springing from the conviction of human weakness, was that man needed the power of God in his soul. The Old Testament utterances on this point are indeed restricted, being too much controlled by nationalism. The interest of the prophets was centred in the nation as a whole, and the relation of God to the people was one rather of "favor" than of "grace." He was pledged by his choice and covenant to bless Israel with outward prosperity and the knowledge of his will; but individual morality was taken for granted, and the presence of the divine spirit as an illumining and regenerating power in the individual soul was not distinctly thought of. In the period of storm and stress in the second century B. C., though individualism had been largely developed, the nation was still the fundamental unit; righteousness was the condition of citizenship in the Church (Pss. xxiv., ci., cf. lxxxvii.); and while, as we have seen, there were individuals who clung passionately to the divine spirit as the source of life, for the most the essential point was obedience to law secured by right disposition of mind.

The introduction of the definitely formulated Law was a turning-point in the history of Judaism, — the ground at once of its success and of its failure. The Law prepared the way for Christianity, and at the same time repelled the Jewish nation from the Christian reconstruction of the idea of law. Judaism, the Jewish Church, is nomism, the embodiment of devotion to a fixed rule of belief and conduct. Other communities of that time, and especially the Romans, had developed systems of life resting on legal standards; it was only the Jews who identified law with religion. Jewish nomism has two elements, — that which is common to all legally organized societies, and that which springs from the religious genius of the nation acting in conjunction with certain favorable circumstances. The fusion of the civil and religious codes began at an early period : it appears in the law-book of Ex. xxi.–xxiii., then in Deuteronomy, then in the legislation of the middle books of the Pentateuch, and finally in the Talmud. The civil-religious law sprang out of the national life, was built up, generation after generation, according to national needs, and finally, after the time of Ezra and Nehemiah, effected a social-ecclesiastical organization, — in other words, the nation assumed the form of a church. There were internal and external grounds for this movement. The internal ground was the religious instinct of the nation, — that inexplicable necessity which it felt for realizing and defining its relation to God, — an instinct common indeed to all nations, but assuming among the

Jews proportions which we can no more explain than we can account for the genius of Plato and Shakespeare. No other nation produced an order of prophets. The flower of the Athenian mind devoted itself to literature, art, and philosophy; the highest and noblest Jewish thought was consecrated to religion. The prophets passed away, and were succeeded by lyric poets, students of practical life and schools of law; but all these, no less than their predecessors, were inspired by the idea of religion. From the belief that God was the only law-giver, it was but a step to the conviction that the national life was to be absolutely regulated by the divine will. The attainment of this end was favored in a remarkable manner by the outward conditions of the nation. From the Babylonian exile on, they were inured to the idea of political dependence, — they were forced more and more to see that their life as a State was crushed beyond hope of resuscitation, and all the energy which would otherwise have gone into affairs of civil government was given to ecclesiastical organization. It is a proof of the intense vitality of the Jewish people that they did not, like the surrounding communities, succumb to the oppression of foreign political domination. Their energy came from, or was in closest union with, their consciousness of possession of highest truth and their hope of a brilliant future. Thus their political annihilation was favorable to their religious growth; it was an isolation from the great world, which permitted them to sink themselves in religion, like a scholar who retreats to a monastery or a cave in order to give himself up to study. Their freedom from political complications gave them greater liberty in the elaboration of their religious-legal material; they had to consult the interests of no king or noble, the demands of no foreign intercourse, but worked out their scheme in an ideally rounded shape which would have been impossible for a community standing in lively political intercourse with its neighbors. Add to all this the smallness of the territory in which the Jews found themselves after their return from Babylon. Religious centralization was comparatively easy when no inhabitant of the land was more than a few hours' journey from Jerusalem. A rigidity of organization was effected which would have been impossible in a larger community. This state of things gradually changed, it is true, but not before Judea worked out the fundamental principles and methods of the nomistic life.

The Jewish Law was a mass of prescriptions, civil, moral, religious, ceremonial, — an attempt to define all the beliefs and acts of life. What we commonly call the Law is the body of legislation contained in the Pentateuch; that is, the form which the code assumed in the time of Ezra and Nehemiah. In fact, however, the Law came in later times to include much more than this: as the legislation of Ezra was a development of earlier material, so it became the basis for a succeeding development, — courts and schools of law added much by way of interpretation and application, which became as binding as the words attributed to Moses. A dividing line was made, it is true, by the canonical books; the Pentateuch was the text, all else was commentary. But in the feeling of teachers and people, the commentary was no less authoritative than the text. The whole was a lofty attempt to order the social, religious, and political life of a nation, to create an absolute external standard of right. In such an attempt there is nothing necessarily unnatural or wrong. Law is a necessity for human life. The highest effort of individuals and nations is found in the discipline which tends to bring them under the control of a true and high standard of conduct; perfection consists in the harmony of the human will with the perfect law. But the attempt to devise and impose an absolutely controlling external standard is confronted by two difficulties: it is impossible for man to construct a perfect law, and even that which is relatively perfect for one generation is in danger of losing its pertinency for the next; and what is more serious, the law does not in itself supply the motive of conduct, — tends, indeed, by emphasizing the outward standard, to attract the will from that inward love and devotion which is the mainspring of the moral-religious life.

The Jews made the experiment of nomism under most favorable conditions, and with an unexampled fulness of experience. The Law got a hold on the affections of the people of which history furnishes no other instance. Neither Moslems nor Parsees ever exhibited such a thoroughgoing and intelligent devotion to their sacred books and their systems of life as appears for many centuries in the history of the Jews. The One Hundred and Nineteenth Psalm embodies the reverential delight which the pious Jew experienced in the presence of the perfect instruction granted by the God of Israel to his chosen people. The nation embodied this reverence in its heroic resistance to the Greek-Syrian encroachments of the second century. The Maccabean struggle was a religious war waged to maintain liberty of belief and practice, liberty to obey the law given by God to the fathers. The struggle was successful; nor in after times was any combination of circumstances able to alienate the Jew from his law. Foreign oppression, political annihilation, dispersion over the world, social contempt and degradation had the effect only of driving the people to a more passionate love for that which they conceived to constitute their everlasting glory. If ever a nation was faithful to an idea, the Jews were faithful to the conception of legally ordered life; and they enjoyed the fruits of their devotion, good and bad. They reached an unequalled fulness and rigidity of social-religious organization. The sharp-sighted earnestness with which they watched over the details of life, the interest they threw into the discussion and determination of minutiæ of faith and practice may be compared with the metaphysical enthusiasm of the Scottish people. It is not to be supposed that all the individuals of the Jewish nation were equally interested in these questions; it was the select few who were prominent. The masses may often have seemed indifferent, and a Pharisee might even denounce the people as accursed through their ignorance of the Law (John vii. 49); but the leaders gave the tone to the national feeling, — the life of the Jewish nation was ordered by religious law. Thus the people enjoyed those benefits which result from habits of organized study, — intelligence, alertness, definiteness of opinion, decision of conduct; and this training of life moved on a high moral-religious level. The ethical and religious ideals of the Jews were in general superior to those of their neighbors; their God was just and righteous. Their ethics not only included the laws of ordinary social morality, but was moving toward more spiritual principles of sympathy and love, and their religious ideas were growing broader and purer. Such is the bright side of the Jewish nomistic development, — the creation of a self centred, well-balanced, intelligent, and strenuous moral-religious life, illustrated by many shining examples of lofty probity and spiritual piety.

On the other hand, nomism brought its inevitable evils. The consciousness of superior privileges and enlightenment called forth a national and individual pride which was hostile to moral-religious growth. The Jews had a far more definite historical feeling than their neighbors. Their records went back to a remote antiquity, and their history was an embodiment of the fact that the one Supreme God had chosen them from the beginning to be his own, and had without ceasing guided their fortunes toward a glorious future, which was not the less sure because the present was dark. Natural satisfaction in so remarkable a career had grown, by the beginning of the second century B. C., into overweening pride. The world was divided into Jews and not-Jews. The leading minds of the nation cherished a lofty scorn of foreign thought and civilization. A part of the people, indeed, were allured by the splendors of Greek life, and forsook the faith of their fathers; but this partial apostasy only served to intensify the zeal and the unrelenting hate of the faithful. To the pious of the second century the Greeks were the embodiment of everything sensual and devilish.[1] This hatred of national enemies was not new: it appears in exilian prophecies (Isa. xxxiv. 45; Jer. l., li.), and was to appear later in the struggles with the Romans and other peoples. It was in itself a morally injurious attitude, though for the rest one not confined to the Jews. It had the further effect of tending to isolate the people from foreign thought, and in so far of dwarfing their intellectual growth. The isolation was not and could not be complete. The traces of foreign influence on Jewish thought cannot fail to be recognized; but the isolation, so far as it existed, was an evil thing for the Jews. It closed their eyes to the defects of their law, and made them as zealous for the wrong as for the right; and it excluded them from a share in certain better ideas which they might have learned from their neighbors.

A more serious defect of the nomistic scheme — one that entered deeper into the moral-religious life — was the externalism which it tended to produce. The natural result of complete devotion to an external law was the breaking up of life into minute details, the loss of unity and the loss of spirituality. The biblical code was comparatively simple so far as the conduct of daily life was concerned; but the

---

[1] See First and Second Maccabees and the Sibylline Oracles, *passim*. A similar feeling appears in the first chapter of Romans.

application of the principles of the Law, guided by zealous consciences, led gradually to the multiplication of particulars bearing on all the acts of life. The full development of this scheme is found in the Talmud; but we may be sure, on general grounds and from the hints given in the New Testament, that much of it was already in existence at the beginning of our era. The frame of mind of the pious Jew of that period must have been one of frequent anxiety lest he should omit something that was essential to righteousness; for the most unhappy result of this developed scheme of law was the definition which it gave of righteousness as obedience to a mass of precepts. Power of spiritual discrimination and purity of spiritual life were dimmed and dulled. The prescriptions of the Law included duties of the most various kinds, ceremonial, moral, and religious, insignificant details of ceremonial cleanliness standing side by side with most important ethical rules and religious principles. Men became habituated to looking at the Law as a whole. The principle was established that he who offended in one point was guilty of all (James ii. 10). It was inevitable also that the ceremonial side of the Law, because it was visible and tangible, should assume constantly increasing proportions, and tend to cramp or expel broader principles. The human mind is so constituted that, provided an outward show of duty is maintained, men are content to slur over the inner life, the thoughts and intents of the heart, which are invisible to their fellows, and which they cannot be summoned before a human tribunal to account for. It is the history of all religious organizations, only more patent and developed in the Jews of this time.

Casuistry came in as the natural accompaniment of this outward scheme of righteousness. Where there was an intellectual assent to obligation without the full assent of the heart, the temptation would arise to get rid of oppressive duties by an ingenious process of reasoning, by substituting the pleasant for the unpleasant, and explaining away what was disagreeable by the pretence of higher obligation. There is no more sacred duty than care for one's parents; but a man might declare that money which should have been so appropriated was devoted to God, and so withhold it from father and mother, while by an ingenious device he enjoyed the use of it for himself (Mark vii. 10–13). There were similar shifts for dispensing with other acknowledged duties. It was debauching the conscience in the name of religion. It was a phenomenon of the same sort as that which Pascal describes in the "Provincial Letters." Such Jews were in the moral position of school-boys who consider themselves justified in evading the master's rules by any device which is likely to escape punishment. It amounted so far to a paralysis of the moral sense. Fortunately, such tendencies bring their own cure.

Such a scheme tended to depress spirituality. It obscured the fundamental principle of life, that goodness consists in the attitude of the soul toward the right. It metamorphosed God into a list of commands, and life into a chaos of obediences. It was slavery to the letter of the Law. It dwarfed the liberty of the soul by repressing its instinct of love. It took away the ideal of righteousness which the mind of man naturally tends to shape for itself, and substituted in its place a body of rules which could not command the best affection of the heart. It stamped failure on religion. Where there should have been a generous lifting-up of the soul into a self-forgetting purity and love, there was the self-seeking devotion to a mechanical scheme of personal righteousness. The great transforming power of religion, purification from selfishness, devotion to truth for its own sake, was lost in the multitude of cramping details which falsely assumed the name of obedience to God. Righteousness was not the esseuce of the soul, but a garment which could shift its place and be put off and on at the pleasure of the wearer.

But while this is a fair description of the logical tendencies of the Jewish Law, it must not be supposed that its injurious effects were universal in the nation. We must remember that much of the Law is moral, and that no one could fail to feel a spiritual significance beneath its letter. The book of Deuteronomy with impressive eloquence preaches loving obedience as the essence of piety. Alongside of the Law were the prophets and the Psalms, which could not have remained without effect on the religious life of the nation. There is no proof that the excessive insistence on ceremonial details existed in the masses of the people; it was probably confined to the few, — the bigots who formed a separate party and held themselves aloof from the masses. It is the Pharisees that Jesus attacks, — never the people at large. Doubtless the mechanical side of the nomistic system made itself felt everywhere, but it was not necessarily always fatal. It made its appearance in the Christian Church also, was predominant at certain times and in certain places, but in the main succumbed to the higher principle of liberty announced by Paul. We may believe that the germ of this principle existed among the Jews of the two centuries preceding the beginning of our era. It is found in the Psalms and the prophets; it could not have been completely extinguished by the Law. The later Jewish history presents many noble figures, from Mattathias and Judas Maccabæus to Hillel, Gamaliel, Akiba, and Jehuda the Holy. The trouble with Judaism was not the absence of spirituality; it was the inability sufficiently to isolate this principle and make it the controlling power. Toward this end the Christianity of Jesus and Paul took a long step; the Christianity of later times, yielding to the constant pressure of the unspiritual

side of human nature, receded toward the mechanical conception of religion. Jesus found a not inconsiderable body
of the people ready to receive his teaching. The common
folk heard him gladly, — a sign of spiritual receptivity.
The early Church was composed of Jews, who, if not eman-
cipated from the narrow Jewish idea of law, had yet been
able to accept part, at least, of the more spiritual doctrine
of Christ. The germ of spiritual reconstruction lay in the
people.

5. The progress of the Jews in religion, or, what amounts
practically to the same thing, in devotion to the Law, is
marked by the rise of synagogues, parties, and legal schools.

The beginning of synagogal worship is involved in some
obscurity.[1] It is not unlikely that during the Babylonian
exile the captives would meet together to listen to the
exhortations and consolations of the prophets and to pray
for the peace of Jerusalem. Deprived of the temple, the
centre of the old religious service, they would be forced to
devise non-ritual modes of worship, to dispense with sacrifices and address themselves directly to God. There is no
record of such gatherings ; but a hundred years later, in the
prophecy of Malachi, we find a hint that the faithful were
accustomed to meet together and speak one with another
(Mal. iii. 16), doubtless on things pertaining to the worship
of God. (Jewish tradition, indeed, places in the time of Ezra
and Nehemiah the Great Synagogue, a body of men who are
said to have pronounced on all questions affecting the national religion ; but there is positively no evidence for the
existence of this body, — there is no trace of its work in
later times, and it is not mentioned, except in the Talmud.
It is an invention of the tradition, after the rise of the legal-

---

[1] See Hausrath, "History of the New Testament Times," Eng. transl.
London, 1878, pp. 84 ff. ; Schürer, "Geschichte des Jüdischen Volkes im Zeit-
alter Jesu Christi," ed. 2, Leipzig, 1886, part ii. pp. 356 ff.; Herzog, "Real-
Encyclopädie."

scholastic system, for the purpose of referring the beginnings of legal study to the man who is said in the Old Testament to have brought the Law from Babylon.[1] The book of Chronicles knows nothing of synagogues; they are mentioned in the Old Testament only in a psalm (lxxiv. 8) which bears evident marks of the Maccabean period. It is strange that there is no mention of them in Josephus or the Maccabean histories. In the New Testament we find them numerous throughout the Roman Empire, and we may infer that they had been in existence no little time. In the absence of any definite information, it seems most probable that they did not assume their developed form before the beginning of the second century B. C., though the idea may have come into existence earlier. Their influence on the religious development of the Jews must have been enormous. Meeting Sabbath after Sabbath to listen to the reading of the Law and the Prophets, the people became familiar with the sacred writings, and were trained to reflection on religious questions; the synagogues would become the natural centres of religious movements. In the temple-service the people took no active part; the ceremonial was conducted by the priests, — the congregation was the passive recipient of the blessing. But in the weekly meetings of the synagogue each individual felt that he had a share; individual independence and moral-religious strenuousness were cultivated. The custom arose of having addresses to the congregation in explanation or application of the scrip-

[1] Pirke Aboth, i. 1 · "Moses received the Law on Sinai and delivered it to Joshua, Joshua to the elders, the elders to the prophets, and the elders delivered it to the men of the Great Synagogue." Berakoth, 33 a: "The men of the Great Synagogue appointed for Israel the benedictions and the prayers, the formulas of consecration and distinction." The body consisted of one hundred and twenty men (Meg. 17 b), and continued to about the time of Simon the Just, B. C. 219–199 (Pirk. Ab. i 2; Ecclus. L.). The extent of its alleged activity has already been referred to; it was held to have edited various books of the Old Testament, and to have settled the sacred Canon.

tural reading, and liberty of speech was accorded to every one. Thus, while attachment to the Law was strengthened, freedom of discussion was promoted, and it could not fail to be the case that many serious questions of religion should come up for consideration.

So active and intellectual a religious life as that of the Jews of the third and second centuries B. C. naturally produced different tendencies of thought, and called into existence parties which embodied them. It was a stirring and excited time, a formative period, next to that of the pre-exilian prophets, the most striking epoch in Jewish religious history. Before the Babylonian exile, the national growth had been comparatively simple and quiet. The elements of progress were furnished almost entirely by the nation itself; the prophets, as the expounders of the national conscience, were the preachers and establishers of the fundamental principle of ethical monotheism; the priests, aided by the judges, and perhaps stimulated by the example of the Assyrians, were the formulators of the civil and ceremonial law, which arose out of the needs of Jewish society itself. The exile was a time of seething and sifting. The Jews accepted ideas from the Babylonians and worked them up in the spirit of their own institutions; but these ideas were Semitic and in the line of the existing Jewish thought. The result of the whole process was the Pentateuch and the reconstruction of the nation as a church. There followed a century of quiet, during which the new organization was acquiring firmness and adapting itself to the national life; then came the Greek conquest. The Jews, no longer a quiet province of the Persian Empire, found themselves enclosed in a network of Greek kingdoms, and invaded on every side by Greek customs and ideas. There was a gradual infiltration of foreign thought, Persian and Greek; the doctrines of immortality and the resurrection received definite shape; Greek ethical and theological ideas were in the air, and mingled with and colored the old Jewish conceptions. The new ideas were differently received by different sections of the nation. One party planted itself firmly on the existing national traditions and discouraged their further development, while it showed itself kindly disposed toward foreign manners and in part toward non-religious foreign thought. Another party, accepting the Law as the national idea, endeavored to develop it in the spirit of the age. A third party represented extreme national particularism. In a fourth a tendency to mystical asceticism showed itself.[1] There was a strife of warring opinions, full of earnestness and bitterness, for it was held that the true life of the nation was at stake. While these tendencies were slowly formulating themselves, came the series of political events which crystallized them into parties. The Syrian Greeks attempted religious coercion of the Jews; it was necessary to take sides. The Maccabean War secured the independence of the country. In the quiet that ensued in the second half of the second century the great parties assumed definite shape.

When Mattathias retired into the wilderness to make fight against the Greeks, he was joined by a party of men called Asideans (1 Mac. ii. 42 ; 2 Mac. iv. 6), distinguished by their devotion to the national law and customs. They were the *Hasidim* of the book of Psalms, the pious, godly men who stand everywhere in contrast with wicked heathen and apostate Israelites. They seem not to have formed a religious party in the strict sense of the term ; they were rather men of exemplary piety, who would make no compromise in faith and practice. They were a product of the times ; they had

---

[1] On the parties see Wellhausen, "Die Pharisäer und die Sadducäer," Greifswald, 1874, the works of Hausrath and Schürer, the dictionaries of Winer and Herzog, Kuenen's "Religion of Israel," Lightfoot's Commentary on Colossians.

grown, by a natural process of discrimination, out of the con-flicts of heathen opinion. In the Psalms they are intensely national, confident in trust in God, bitter against enemies. The picture given of them in the Psalter corresponds exactly with the social-political condition of affairs in the first half of the second century. It was they that furnished the ma-terial out of which the Pharisaic party was formed.

The Pharisees, as the name imports,[1] were the "sepa-ratists," the party which was marked off from the rest of the nation by its rigid adhesion to the moral and cere-monial requirements of the law.[2] But the essence of their party-character lay deeper than this, — they were the rep-resentatives of nationalism in the broader sense. They ac-cepted the Pentateuchal legislation as the fundamental law of the nation; but they saw that to make it effective, it must be defined in a multitude of particulars, — it must enclose the life of the people in a network of prescriptions. They boldly took the position that this oral, administrative legislation was no less authoritative and binding than the Mosaic Law. From their point of view, they were logical and right. If the true life of the nation depended on its fidelity to the Pentateuchal law, it was necessary to make that law intelligible and real. It was no narrow and ill-considered view that the Pharisees took of the situation. What the nation was it had become, they believed, through the Law; and they held that all prosperity depended on maintaining this absolute standard of right, which alone could train the people into moral-religious vigor. The de-fect and the danger of their view of the national life were such as have been above described: it lacked spirituality, it tended to formalism and pride. The Pharisees did not limit themselves to Old Testament religious conceptions.

---

[1] Aramaic, *parish*, Hebrew, *parush*, "separated."
[2] Jos. Ant. xviii. 1, 3.

Since the days of Ezra and the prophets, the doctrines of immortality and the resurrection had taken shape among the Jews of Egypt and Palestine. These doctrines the Pharisees seem to have accepted as part of the existing national faith ; for we may infer from the literature Wisdom of Solomon, Daniel, Enoch, Second Maccabees) that they were generally believed in the second century B. c.[1] Whatever the shortcomings and the crimes of the Pharisaic party (and they were great), its function and its mission were broad and noble. It undertook to develop the nation on the basis of the absolute divine law. It accepted at home and abroad whatever it could assimilate, and with singleness of view and unswerving resoluteness rejected all else. It was hospitable to foreign ideas so far as these could be made serviceable. The attitude of different teachers toward alien thought might vary ; but this was the predominant consideration. There were rabbis, like Paul's teacher Gamaliel, who were friendly to Greek study ; there were others who dreaded it as a source of religious infection. The Pharisees by no means formed an intellectually closed community. From the notices in the Talmud, we may infer that there was a good deal of liberty of thought among them, which manifested itself in various theological and literary tendencies. Of their contact with Greek ideas we know little. The Egyptian Jews were decidedly influenced by Greek culture ; the proof is found in such books as the Wisdom of Solomon and Ecclesiastes, and in the writings of Philo. But Pharisaism is more particularly a Palestinian development, and in Palestine Greek thought was less prominent and less known than in Egypt. Still, it can hardly be doubted that

[1] On this point see below, Ch. VII. The references to the future life in Palestinian works outside of the apocalypses are very few. None are found, for example, in the sayings ascribed (in Pirke Aboth) to the heads of the legal schools, though this may be an accident, and the genuineness of these sayings, moreover, is not beyond suspicion.

the ethical and religious ideas of the great Greek teachers
had found their way from Egypt, Asia Minor, and Syria to
Galilee and Jerusalem, and had to some extent modified or
directed Palestinian Jewish thought. Josephus describes the
Pharisees as Stoics; and though this may be only a loose
attempt to designate them by a term familiar to his Roman
public, still it suggests a resemblance. The moral strenuousness, the conception of the world as absolutely ordered in all
its details by a supermundane power (fate or providence),
in general the conception of the absoluteness of law, and the
necessity of ordering the life thereby, — these ideas, not unknown to the old Israelites, were not improbably in some
degree defined and shaped by the better elaborated Greek
thought. Pharisaism (and therefore substantially the whole
later Jewish life) may be conceived as an amalgamation
of Greek and Jewish nomistic conceptions, just as in the
thirteenth century Jewish theology, under the guidance of
Maimonides, reposed on a blending of Talmudic and Arabo-
Grecian philosophy. The two constituents were fused into a
unity in Palestine by the overpowering nationalism, as the
exiles of the sixth century B. C. absorbed and assimilated
Babylonian ideas. Hints are not lacking of the presence
of Greek influence in the Jewish schools. Perhaps we may
thus in part explain the saying attributed to Antigonus of
Socho, that men should serve God without an eye to the
reward. The methodizing, codifying impulse which showed
itself in the time of Hillel may have arisen partly from the
same source, as well as the extraordinary glorification of the
Law in the Talmud, according to which God himself was
determined by its content.[1] Be this as it may, Pharisaism
was practically identical with Judaism.

[1] God, when he would create the world, looked into the Law (Bereshith
Rabba, 1), and took counsel with it (Midrash Tanchuma, 1); to its study he
devotes three hours every day (Aboda Sara, 3 b), and to its prescriptions he
conforms himself (Wayikra Rabba, 19, 35). Weber, "System," § 4. This ex-

The rival sect of the Sadducees never had any strong hold on the people. According to Josephus (Ant. xiii. 10, 6), their adherents were found only among the rich, while the Pharisees had the multitude on their side ; and so, he adds, the former, when they became magistrates, were forced to adopt Pharisaic notions because the people would listen to nothing else (Ant xviii. 1, 4). The unpopularity of the Sadducees was no doubt due in part to the character of their religious ideas. They rejected the authority of the traditional interpretations of the Law, and held themselves strictly to the text of the Pentateuch.[1] This is possibly the explanation of their attitude toward the doctrines of immortality and the resurrection, neither of which they accepted (Ant. xviii. 1, 4 ; Matt. xxii. 23 ; Acts xxiii. 8) ; that is, perhaps they held strictly to the negative position of the Pentateuch.[2] But this was out of harmony with the existing views and feeling of the people ; popular feeling had advanced beyond the point of view of the Old Testament, and the cold scepticism of the Sadducees was unacceptable. It seems probable also that the social position and culture of the party kept them aloof from the people. Josephus intimates that it was composed of aristocrats, and the history shows that it furnished many magistrates and high-priests. This fact has suggested

uberantly fanciful representation embodies the feeling that the universe is determined by an eternal law, of which God is the personal and the Torn the written expression.

[1] Nevertheless, it must be supposed that they recognized judicial interpretations of the Pentateuchal code, which were necessary in order to apply it to particular cases (Jos. Ant. xx. 9, 1).

[2] There is some difficulty in the statements of Josephus that the Sadducees believed that souls die with bodies, and of Acts that they accepted neither angel nor spirit. This goes beyond the Pentateuch and the Old Testament generally. Perhaps it is only intended to say that they denied the independent existence of souls and spirits, holding the dead to be confined as "shades" in Sheol, and that they rejected the later post-biblical elaboration of the doctrine of angels. Otherwise we must ascribe to them a doctrine of annihilation which is allied to the Stoic view. In the absence of preciser information these affirmations must be received with caution.

the view that the germ of the Sadducean party was formed by the old priestly families, who for a long time enjoyed political and social supremacy and inherited the religious traditions of the temple-ceremonial. The priests would naturally be a conservative body, holding to the letter of the law and careless of modern innovations of thought[1] Their position did not bring them into close contact with the people, and they would have small knowledge of popular needs and small sympathy with popular ideas. On the other hand, their social traditions allied them with the rich and aristocratic; they would easily adopt foreign habits of luxury and social ideas, while they rejected those new conceptions of the Law and those doctrinal interpretations which were necessary in order to bring it into living harmony with the new generation. Thus they stood outside the line of national progress, and had small effect on the national thought. They seem to represent a petrified conservatism which is not entitled to the name of nationalism. They are of no recognizable interest in the history of Christian thought. Their activity in Palestine was almost exclusively political up to the destruction of Jerusalem by the Romans, when they vanished from the scene to appear as a party no more. Traces of similar negative opinions may be found in later times, but not of such an organization.

The third Jewish party, the Essenes, presents characteristics in some respects more remarkable than those of the other two. When it first took distinct shape we do not know; but as the Essene Manahem was a friend of Herod the Great (Ant. xv. 10, 5), and as the party seems at that time to have been well established, it may be inferred that it arose not later than in the early part of the first century

---

[1] The name "Sadducees" is most probably identical with "Zadokites" (Ezek. xliv. 15), the priestly family which came into control of the temple just before the beginning of the Babylonian exile.

B. C. Its members were found in small numbers in various parts of Palestine, including the cities (Jos. War, ii. 8, 4); a large community was settled on the northwest coast of the Dead Sea.[1] They represented in the first place an extreme legalism so far as ceremonial purity of body was concerned, and in this point may be regarded as an exaggerated form of Pharisaism. Singularly enough, however, their attitude toward the temple-sacrifices was hostile; they refused to take part in them. The ground of their repugnance to the national system of offerings seems to have been not that of the prophets and psalmists, — it was neither ethical nor spiritual. It perhaps connected itself with their second peculiarity, a pronounced asceticism, which reached the proportions of gnostic dualism. They abstained from wine, animal food, and oil, and most of them from marriage. They obviously held that the body, as the seat of evil, was to be repressed and chastised. Whence this decidedly non-Jewish view came, it is hard to say; it has been ascribed to Persian and other Oriental influence, but the data for determining its origin are lacking. Un-Jewish it certainly was, since the nation otherwise never showed any such tendency. The Old Testament heartily accepts and approves the ordinary social life of man; yet a point of departure for such a system may be found in Old Testament ideas (especially in the conception of the weakness of the flesh, in the Nazarite vow, and the Rechabite life), and traces of asceticism appear in the books of Daniel (i. 8, 12) and Tobit (xii. 8). It is conceivable that the Essenian asceticism may have arisen out of

---

[1] Pliny, Hist. Nat. v. 15. For an account of similar communities in Egypt known as Therapeutæ, see Philo, "On the Contemplative Life." According to him, the Essenes represented the practical, and the Therapeutæ (the Healers of Souls) the theoretical side of the deeper, philosophic religious life. Of this Egyptian sect, which may have sprung out of the Jewish-Alexandrine theosophy, we are unable to trace with distinctness any influence on the succeeding Jewish or Christian development of the first century of our era.

this general idea. The turmoils of the time may have led certain persons (there were perhaps five or six thousand in all) to withdraw from the world and seek peace by suppressing the body in order to cultivate the soul ; and it was possibly this conviction, that happiness was gained through inward purity, that produced the negative attitude toward sacrifices.[1] Other peculiarities of the party lead us to suspect Oriental influence: they practised occult arts, were acquainted with medicinal roots and stones, had secret books and mysteries, and made predictions (Jos. Ant. xv. 10, 5, where Manahem foretells the greatness of Herod); they practised a sort of sun-worship, and had a special doctrine of angels. So far as their life was concerned, it was of the most exemplary sort ; they were everywhere famous for piety and virtue.

Though the Essenes did not affect the general national Jewish development, standing as they did outside of its lines of advance, yet it is not likely that they remained entirely without influence on current thought. In fact, there are traces in the New Testament of their two distinctive peculiarities, their communistic morality and their gnostic conception of life and of the world. While the supposition that Jesus was an Essene must be pronounced to be baseless and even bizarre, it is not impossible that he may have been attracted by that self-abnegation which the party so strikingly illustrated. The Essenian practices of non-resistance and abandonment of claim to private property were doubtless well known in Palestine in the first half of the first century, and may have been sympathized with by many persons. Such ideas, which were in the air, Jesus may have in part adopted in the form in which we find them expressed in the Sermon on the Mount; but he combined them with

---

[1] Perhaps also the feeling against the shedding of blood, for which reason probably in part they abstained from animal food.

pure spiritual views and vigorous positive morality in such a way as practically to take them out of the circle of Essenian doctrine. The only other trace of this party in the New Testament is found in the gnosticism which is combated in the Epistle to the Colossians. The similarity between the Jewish-Christian doctrine there opposed and the Essenian views is striking:[1] there is the same asceticism and dualism and the same prominence given to angels. But it is not certain that the Colossian gnosticism was derived from the Essenes; it may have come from similar, but independent, movements of thought in Asia Minor. The historical origin of these early forms of gnosticism is not clear; but it is of great interest to note that similar developments took place in Judaism and in Christianity. And when we consider the wide diffusion of gnostic opinions in the early part of the second century of our era, we are forced to recognize a deep-lying tendency in the Jewish world (perhaps non-Jewish in origin, and numbering comparatively few adherents) to adopt a mystical-philosophic view of the universe, discarding both Jewish and Christian nomistic, Messianic, and sacficial ideas, undertaking on the one hand to bridge over the chasm between God and the world by a series of intermediate intelligences, and on the other hand to lift man into union with God by a process of bodily and spiritual self-culture. The points of contact between this scheme and the Mazdean and Buddhistic conceptions of life cannot be denied; but in the absence of all proof, it would be rash to affirm an historical connection between the Jewish and the Oriental systems. We can only say that gnostic thought has its basis in human nature, and we need not be surprised at its appearance in Jewish circles. Christian gnosticism may have sprung in part from the Jewish thought, but certainly owed its fullest development to other than Jewish influences.

[1] See J. B. Lightfoot's note in his Commentary on Colossians.

Josephus (Ant. xviii. 1, 6) mentions a fourth Jewish party, the Zealots, of which Judas, the Galilean, was the founder, but it was rather political than religious in character. It represented a fanatical nationalism, a rejection of all earthly rulers, an inviolable attachment to liberty, and devotion to the God of Israel as the only Lord. The part played by these men in the revolt against the Romans and the siege of Jerusalem belongs to the civil history.

The Sanhedrin and the great legal schools, though they were influential in the elaboration of the ethical, civil, and religious law, had little to do with the development of religious doctrine. They were the official representatives and expounders of the national nomism, which they received from their fathers and transmitted to their descendants. The earliest mention of the Sanhedrin occurs in Josephus' account of the reign of John Hyrcanus II. (B. c. 47), where Herod is summoned before this tribunal to account for certain murders committed by him (Ant. xiv. 9, 3–5). It is there spoken of as an established institution, and had doubtless been in existence for a considerable period, though the beginnings of its history are unknown There is no proof that it was connected with Ezra ; the form of the name[1] points to the Greek period as the time of its origination. It was doubtless a gradual development out of older judicial institutions. Its membership consisted of seventy-one priests and scribes ; it had two secretaries, and was presided over by the high-priest. It was the supreme judicial and legislative body, having nominally final jurisdiction in civil and ecclesiastical affairs ; but its power was practically limited by the authority of the Jewish kings and the Roman procurators.

The best activity of the nation during the Greek period appears in the legal schools. The class of students called

---

[1] It is the Hebrew or Aramaic form of the Greek συνέδριον.

Soferim, or Scribes, had arisen in response to the demand for
the interpretation and application of the Law. The name is
given to Ezra (Ezra vii. 6); and there was doubtless, from
his day on, a succession of men who devoted themselves to
the elaboration of legal science. The study seems, however,
not to have been definitely organized until the second century B. C. At that time there began a line of teachers, each
of whom gathered around him a body of disciples and expressed his opinions in the form of apothegms. Most of the
sayings of these masters that have been preserved[1] are ethical and legal, and have little direct bearing on the history
of religious thought. Indirectly, no doubt, their influence
was great. The schools cultivated the habit of independent
thought, and introduced into religion an ethical element
which could not fail to counteract the materializing tendency of nomism. So far as there was a scientific development of thought among the Jews of this period, we find
it in the succession of heads of schools.

The saying attributed to Simon the Just expresses the
fundamental idea of Judaism : "On three things the world
rests, — on the Law, on divine service, and on good works."
This is the starting-point of Jewish development proper, —
absolute obedience to the external divine standard, and along
with this kindly deeds toward mankind. It recognizes both
the outward law of the code and the inward law of the conscience. Of the same import is the injunction ascribed to
the early teachers to "make a hedge about the Law," — that
is, to enact and enforce minute ceremonial and other prescriptions so as to define the Law with precision, and secure
its effectiveness.[2]

[1] In the tract Pirke Aboth, and in other Talmudic treatises.

[2] There was probably also in some circles a desire to guard the purity of
the nation by surrounding initiation with difficulties that should deter all but
men of serious intention. The horror of heathenism was great, the fear of
its seductive influences ever present, and isolation was a familiar idea. The

The first of the great teachers whose name has come down to us, Antigonus of Socho (second century B. C.), is credited with the remarkable declaration that men should not serve God for reward, — that virtue is to spring from love of right, and to be accepted as its own sufficient reward, — an utterance which has no parallel in Old Testament or New Testament. According to the tradition, his teaching was understood by some of his scholars as a denial of immortality, whence sprung the party of the Sadducees.[1] That this is not a correct account of the origin of that party, we have already seen. But the Sadducees were credited with a leaning to foreigners, and it is possible that we have here a vague reminiscence of fear of the Greek influence in the school of Antigonus. The probability is that Stoic thought was known in Palestine at that time.[2] It is noteworthy that Antigonus seems to have maintained his position in spite of a dictum which was contrary to the Jewish ortho-

opposite policy of liberality also found favor, if we may rely on the anecdote which represents Shammai as repelling would-be proselytes by the severity of his demands, while Hillel summed up the legal requirements for candidates in the golden rule. Shab 31 a, cited by Jost, "Geschichte des Judenthums," I. 265. Jost remarks (in note) that this conflict between legalism and morality was afterwards transformed into that between legalism (Peter) and faith (Paul).

[1] The name is said in one tradition to be derived from that of one of these scholars, Zadok, but this is probably an invented etymology; already in the Talmud these early times of legal study have a legendary coloring.

[2] Its presence in Palestine is not expressly mentioned, but may be inferred from the general prevalence of Greek thought. The intimate relations between Palestine and Egypt, where it is certain that Greek ideas were hospitably received by Jews, the Greek translation of the law and the prophets, which gradually made its way into Syria; the adoption of Greek customs by a part of the Jewish people in the time of Antiochus Epiphanes, — these facts point to the presence of Hellenic ideas among the Palestinian Jews as early as the beginning of the second century B. C. That Antigonus of Socho bears a Greek name may be not without significance. Greek culture would naturally bring with it Greek philosophy, — Stoic, Platonic, and other systems prevalent at the time. Whether Greek books were then read by Palestinian Jews, we have no means of determining; the documents, absorbed in political and Messianic interests, are unfortunately silent on this point.

doxy of the period; and while we cannot regard him as the founder of the Sadducean party, we may suppose that he represents a direction of opinion which found sympathy and expression in Sadduceism. The Old Testament everywhere connects man's conduct in this life with divine reward and punishment; but, except in the book of Daniel, it has nothing to say of reward and punishment in the future life. A thinker, like Antigonus, especially under the influence of Stoicism, might find the gist of the Old Testament teaching in the doctrine that reverence toward God was the central fact of religious life, and that obedience to him brought not outward prosperity, but that inward satisfaction which constituted the highest happiness. How far such an opinion was held by the later Sadducees, we have no means of determining; our accounts of them come from their enemies. The Talmudic Pharisees could see no good in men who held aloof from what had come to be regarded as the vital principle of the nation, devotion to the ceremonial law. The Talmud was edited, moreover, long after the Sadducees as a party had ceased to exist. Time had stamped failure on them; it was not likely that they would receive justice at the hands of their successful opponents. On general grounds, considering the prominent part played by the Sadducees in the civil and ecclesiastical government, it is likely that they numbered in their ranks not a few men of exemplary, moral-religious character, maintaining the Old Testament standard of faith and conduct, but standing necessarily in a position of antagonism toward popular thought. They were probably neither better nor worse than their adversaries. If the history of the times had been written by them, we should no doubt find in their policy and conduct the usual mixture of good and bad; it was their misfortune that they were out of accord with the Jewish spirit of the age, and vanished from the scene almost without leaving a trace of influence on national opinions. So far as the practical ethics of the time is concerned, it was not determined by the dicta of teachers and schools, but sprang out of the social conditions, to which the Sadducees, no less than the Pharisees, were subject.

The rivalry between Pharisees and Sadducees is in one aspect a struggle between progressive nomism and conservative nationalism. The question was virtually decided in favor of the party of nomistic advance, in the second century B. C. In another aspect this party strife connected itself with the conflict between Jewish and foreign ideas. The historical content of the second century has been described as the victory of nomism over Hellenism. This, however, is a partial statement of the case, true from one point of view, untrue from another. The sharp attack of the Syrian Greeks on the organized Jewish faith was thoroughly crushed by the Maccabean uprising ; the attempt was not repeated by Greeks or Romans. Yahwe, the Lord, was not displaced by Jupiter Capitolinus. The Jewish sacred books were not destroyed. The hold of the Jewish ritual on the national mind was not weakened. Judaism as a religious system remained firm, and Hellenistic heathenism suffered a decisive defeat. But this is only the outward aspect of the question. Judaism, while it had an inward life vigorous enough to repel all such attacks, had also a depth and breadth of susceptibility which recognized the value of certain foreign truths. Notably the great belief in immortality came to the Jews through Greek intermediation. In the Egyptian-Jewish literature there is many a trace of Greek influence in philosophical-religious views of the world and of life, — the conceptions, for example, of the divine cosmos, the divine mediating logos, the divine power of human wisdom and virtue. Palestinian nomism was less affected by such ideas; but in Palestine also we find the doctrine of immortality, and in the legal schools the idea of moral order and individual strict rectitude and justice. All these conceptions passed over to Christianity. From this point of view Hellenism did not suffer a defeat, but succeeded in impressing itself on Judaism. The contact between these two great systems of thought is to be looked on rather as an intellectual-religious conference, in which the more firmly organized religion, while maintaining its general character, accepted suggestions from its neighbor. Judaism, by virtue of all the elements of its past, had a vigor of constitution and a common-sense practicalness which assured it existence and success in the strife of opinions. The strength of Hellenism lay, not in its religious organization, but in its general conceptions of life. Its pantheon and its priesthood were doomed to extinction; but its philosophy was to survive as a permanent element of civilization. The Jews, however, and especially those of Palestine, did not express Greek philosophical ideas in technical terms; the philosophical influence shows itself in the general coloring of the thought. Nor is more than a general coloring to be expected. The Jewish ethics and religion of the second century B. C. sprang out of old Israelitish soil, and were developed largely by Israelitish experiences. But when we compare the utterances of the great lawyers with the purely national tone of the apocalyptic and historical books, we are naturally led to attribute the broad humanitarian and cosmopolitan elements of the former to that breath of foreign influence which we have reason to believe was then found in Palestine.[1] By way of illustration we may cite some of the sayings which are attributed to the centres of legal-ethical teaching.

---

[1] For the extent of Hellenic culture during this period in Palestine, in Judean and non-Judean districts, see Schürer, "Geschichte des Judischen Volkes," II. pp. 9–50.

Simon the Just declared that the world rested on the Tora, on the divine service, and on deeds of kindness or mercy (with possible allusion to Hos. vi. 6, cf. Matt. xii. 7), that is, he puts duty to one's fellow-men on the same level with the obligation to obey the ritual law. The dictum of Antigonus is the exaltation of the pure spirit of devotion to duty: "Be as servants who serve the master without view to reward." The sayings of the succeeding teachers down to Hillel deal exclusively with ethical and legal principles. We cannot conclude from this that they neglected the ceremonial law, but it may fairly be inferred that they laid very great stress on the ideas of justice and probity. X The most important of the heads of the legal schools was the Babylonian Hillel, who belongs to the reign of Herod the Great, the last third of the century before the beginning of our era. A richly endowed and many-sided man, he left his impress on the national development in more than one direction. As a lawyer, he was famous not only for his great learning, but also for his clearness and analytic power. He arranged the enormous mass of the traditional interpretations of the Law into something like a regular code, and thus laid the foundations of the Mishna, and prepared the way for the precise scientific legal study which was to occupy the Jewish mind for the next thousand years. In this way he helped to bind the nation more firmly to the nomistic idea, and to develop more fully all the good and bad that lay in the nomistic scheme of life. On the other hand, his ethical conceptions were characterized by remarkable freedom, breadth, and genialness. He and his colleague, Shammai, stood at opposite poles in the construction of the Law; the latter was stern and uncompromising, the former was mild and liberal. It was to a Gentile candidate for proselytism that he is said to have declared that the whole Law was comprised in one word: "What thou wouldst not have another do to thee, do not thou to another." A similar idea is contained in his saying: "Be of the disciples of Aaron, loving and following after peace, loving mankind and leading them to the Law," where it seems that he regards the Law as the embodiment of order informed by kindness and love. Respecting self-seeking he said: "Who seeks fame loses fame; who does not increase [in learning] decreases; who does not teach is worthy of death; who uses the crown [of learning] for his own ends perishes." In enigmatical fashion he expresses the idea of unselfish self-culture: "If I am not for myself, who is for me? and if I am for myself, what am I? and if not now, when?" Here is both ethical stringency and philosophical subtlety.

In his time the Jewish legal system acquired definite consistency, and after him no important change seems to have occurred. The great lawyers worked out details, but the national conception of righteousness remained essentially unmodified. Righteousness was obedience to the Law. We have already noted the vice of this system, — mechanical and external self-confidence. But we are not to suppose that formality obtained the entire control of the religious life of the period, that the national conception of life was wholly vicious. We know that the national instinct demanded inwardness and spirituality of life. With so great a mass of ethical thought as the Jewish nation then possessed, it was impossible that there should not be some trace of higher and purer devotion to right for its own sake. In the person and teaching of Hillel we have the example of such a nobler conception of religion, and there must have been many who shared his views.[1] But it is true at the same time that this better side of the national religious life was not the controlling one; it was constantly in danger of

---

[1] On Hillel see Jost, "Geschichte," I. 257 ff., art. in Herzog, and Delitzsch's monograph.

being overborne by the ceremonialism which tended to depress or to crush the spiritual independence and freedom of the soul. The Law offered a great religious career to the Jewish people, but only on the condition that along with this external guide there should be also the recognition of the conscience as a divinely enlightened source of truth,—that the impulse to right-living should spring not merely from a desire to keep the mass of precepts, but also from an inward perception and love of divine truth. Hillel had perceived the necessity of a freer element in the religious life, but he had not been able to lift it into a position of control. There was needed a more piercing insight and a more lofty spirituality to convert Jewish nomism into a true spiritual life.

6. It cannot be considered an accident that Jesus of Nazareth and Hillel stand historically so near together. We see in the latter the germ of the religious feeling to which the former gave full shape. The peculiarity of the position of Jesus as religious teacher was not that he rejected the national nomistic scheme, but that he sought to infuse into it the vitalizing principle of independent communion with God.

It appears from the Synoptic narratives that Jesus recognized and accepted the national system of sacrifices and the national law. Lepers whom he healed he sent to make the offering prescribed by law (Matt. viii. 4); he kept the regular feasts (Matt. xxvi. 17); and according to the First Gospel (Matt. xxiii. 2, 3), he declared that the scribes and the Pharisees were authorized expounders of the Mosaic law, and that their prescriptions were to be obeyed. We must therefore conclude that he accepted in full the Mosaic law, with the rest of the Old Testament, as the divinely given guide of life. We need not lay stress on the declaration of Matt. v. 19: "Whosoever, therefore, shall break one of these least commandments and shall teach men so, shall be called least in the kingdom of heaven, but whosoever shall do and teach them, he shall be called great in the kingdom of heaven." From the generally admitted Judaizing character of this Gospel, it is not impossible that these words were added by an editor in the time of conflict between the Pauline and Judaizing parties of the Church, yet there is nothing in the other Synoptics in contradiction of this declaration; it is not the Law, but its abuse, that he condemns. It is quite in accordance with the Synoptic portraiture of him that he should say: "Think not that I came to destroy the Law or the prophets; I came not to destroy, but to fulfil" (v. 17). And if he looked on the Old Testament as the final divine revelation of truth, he might well add: "Till heaven and earth pass away, one jot or one tittle shall in no wise pass away from the Law till all things be accomplished" (v. 18). He seems, indeed, in the Sermon on the Mount, to criticise and modify the Law in certain particulars. The modifications, however, when we examine them closely, are, with perhaps one exception, not an attack on the fundamental principles of the Old Testament. When he declares against the habit of swearing, on the ground that it is irreverent and unnecessary, this does not impugn the moral principle of the Old Testament, which required the performance of oaths made to the Lord; it is rather the utterance of a more developed religious feeling, which perceives the inutility of primitive modes of religious service. So, also, his command not to resist evil is directed against the legal prescription: "An eye for an eye and a tooth for a tooth." But in the old legislation this was rather a rule for the guidance of the judges than an ethical precept; it was a survival of the old system of retaliation, which was no doubt modified by the Jewish judges themselves. He, however, makes it the occasion for affirming the general ethical principle intended to strike at the root of a purely self-ish assertion of one's legal rights. In his injunction to love one's enemies he no doubt not only advances beyond the Old Testament point of view, but also distinctly condemns that hatred of national enemies which is involved in all the Old Testament ethics and is distinctly avowed in the prophetic writings and the Psalms. But these criticisms, whatever their import, are not to be construed as implying a rejection of the Law as the guide of life. There is no hint in the Synoptics that he ever called in question its supreme obligation and authority. He attacked the traditions of the Pharisees, but never the text on which they were based; and his hostility seems to have been directed not against the serious injunctions of the traditional law (Matt. xxiii. 3), but against those trifling observances which interfered with the free moral conduct of life.

It must be held, therefore, that his conception of righteousness was nomistic in so far as it was conceived of by him as obedience to law. The precepts which he gave were intended, not to set aside, but to expound and develop, the existing legal system. He contemplated no fundamental change in the national life; of such an idea there is no trace in the three first Gospels. As far as we can judge, his hope for the nation was that it should continue under the Law, only with a higher spirit of obedience, such as that which is not dimly expressed by the prophets Jeremiah and Ezekiel, and comes out still more clearly in the One Hundred and Nineteenth Psalm. But it is precisely at this point that his conception of righteousness assumes a peculiar and revolutionary tone. His ethical precepts do not express the essence of his idea of religion. That is found in what he represents as the ideal attitude of the soul toward God. He speaks, indeed, of a higher reward for the better spiritual service (Matt. vi. 1, 15 20, 33), a consideration which, though not, strictly speaking, of the highest ethical character, is perfectly legitimate. But he also holds up the divine father of men as the standard of human conduct, and represents the desire to be in perfect harmony with him as the highest motive of life : " That ye may be sons of your father who is in heaven " (Matt. v. 45). The very conception of God as father implies a tenderness of sympathy and a spirituality of relation which involved a new departure in religion. It amounts practically to transferring the devotion of the soul from the outward objective standard of law, and making the conscience itself, enlightened, freed, and stimulated by devotion to a perfect ideal, the arbiter of moral life.

The source of this spiritual righteousness he finds in the soul itself. His exhortations are all addressed directly to man's will, for which he assumes complete independence and responsibility. He speaks of no mediator between God and man, describes no theological process by which righteousness is to be obtained. He pictures man as standing face to face with God and dealing with him alone. The necessary condition of true righteousness is that man should come into a relation of trust and love with the divine father, but this relation is attained by man's own effort. The religious teaching of Jesus may therefore be termed a spiritual nomism, a principle which contained the germ of the destruction of formalism, though the latter has always maintained itself in the Church from the failure fully to appropriate the real spirit of Jesus. The early Church, if we may take the Epistle of James to be a fair exposition of its belief, did not grasp the spirituality of the Master's conception. The righteousness described in this Epistle is marked rather by sincerity than by high spirituality. What the writer opposes is false pretence, disregard of the poor, evil-speaking, jealousy, pride, luxury. So far as regards the source of righteousness, it is in general that of the Old Testament and of the Sermon on the Mount. A spiritual sonship is recognized: "Of his own will he brought us forth by the word of truth, that we should be a kind of first-fruits of his creatures" (i. 18). On the other hand, he throughout regards men as the shapers of their own moral characters, and has nothing to say of a divine transforming power, or of a mediator between God and man. For him, true religion consists in deeds of charity to the afflicted and freedom from worldly impurities (i 27). One may receive wisdom from God if one ask in faith; one is tempted, not by God nor by Satan, but by one's own evil desire. A sinner may be converted from the error of his way and thereby saved from death by his fellow-man (v. 20). It is the conscience that determines moral guilt: "To him who knows how to do good and does it not, to him it is sin" (iv. 17). The relation of Jesus Christ to man's righteousness is scarcely touched on. He was believed in as the Messiah and the Lord, as the source of wisdom and of health of body and mind, and his speedy coming was to be waited for as the consummation of things. This is apparently the essence of the faith which the believer is to exercise toward Jesus, — acceptance of him as the Messiah with faithful obedience to all his precepts. Any other kind of faith the writer rejects with contempt, and indeed appears to make an argument against Paul's conception of the nature and office of faith without works. Such a faith, he says, is dead, — is nothing more than what demons possess, — is in opposition to the Old Testament teaching, according to which Abraham was justified by works. It is obviously the abuse of the Pauline doctrine against which the writer is here arguing; but it is also clear that he himself rejects that doctrine, and looks on a sincere life of thought and deed as the righteousness which is acceptable in the sight of God. This conception does not differ from that of the better Jewish thinkers of the day, as indeed the Jewish portion of the early Church was little more than a section of Judaism which regarded Jesus of Nazareth as the Messiah.

A radical change in the conception of righteousness was introduced by the Apostle Paul, a man who combined in his thought spiritual depth and mystical school-logic in so remarkable a manner that we are at a loss to estimate the bearing and influence of his ideas. He was led by his experience to reject the possibility of obtaining righteousness through obedience to an outward law. A profoundly religious nature, passionately devoted to his ideal of perfectness, and at the same time keenly introspective, he became convinced, soon after (or perhaps before) his acceptance of Jesus as the Messiah, of the futility of man's efforts to achieve perfect righteousness. This is a conclusion which must be reached in a measure by every earnest soul. In Paul's case, the weariness of human works was intensified by the Jewish ceremonial system and the huge mass of scribal ordinances under which he had been brought up. He describes it as a terrible burden and bondage, — a burden imposed by God himself, indeed, for a wise purpose (namely, to develop man's consciousness of sin), but in itself inconsistent with liberty of soul and peace of mind (Gal. iii. iv.; Rom. vii.). He had struggled long to satisfy the demands of law, and the only result was that he was overwhelmed with the bitterest sense of his own moral impotency; yet righteousness was an absolute necessity. What, then, was man to do? How was salvation possible? It seemed to Paul that the perfect righteousness was to be prepared and bestowed by God himself. It could not be of man's working out; it must be achieved by a perfect being to whom God had assigned the task of saving humanity, and this perfect saviour could be none other than the glorified Messiah, Jesus of Nazareth. It is precisely at this point that we wish to know the development in Paul's mind of his conception of Jesus ; but unfortunately specific historical data for this purpose are lacking. He speaks much of his experience in certain points, but his knowledge of Christ he represents as an immediate revelation, and he gives us no details of the mental process by which the person of the Messiah was brought into connection with his consciousness of sin.

Paul's idea, though conceived and developed in an original and thorough manner, is not antagonistic or alien to the thought of the time ; it has connections with both the preceding and the succeeding Jewish literature. The principle of national and social solidarity had never lost its hold on the people ; some of its cruder features had been cast away (see above, pp. 184 f.), but the essence of the thing had remained. In the Old Testament, society is conceived of as a unit in such a way that its good element may set aside the evil, and gain the divine favor for the whole. In a number of particular instances the merits of the righteous are spoken of as transferable to others : Job secures forgiveness for his friends (Job xlii.); Abraham, by his personal interest with Yahwe, gains the promise that Sodom shall be spared for the sake of ten righteous men, if so many can be found in the city (Gen. xviii.) ;[1] for his sake Abimelech is pardoned and Isaac blessed (Gen. xx. xxvi.). The completest statement of the idea is found in Isaiah liii., where the Servant of Yahwe by his suffering and knowledge[2] — that is, in general by his merit — "justifies many," causes the nation to be esteemed righteous by God. Nothing is here said expressly of an imputation of moral character, but some such transference is involved. It is declared

---

[1] See, on the other hand, Ezek. xiv. 12–20; but the idea remained (as appears from the Talmud) in spite of the prophet's protest.

[2] The precise construction and meaning of the Hebrew word so rendered are doubtful; but this does not affect the general sense.

that a certain person designated as "the righteous one" pro-
cures that other persons shall be pronounced righteous in the
divine court.[1] Virtually, therefore, recreant Israel is justified,
not by its own righteousness, but through the righteousness
of the faithful Servant. The same general idea finds expression in some Apocryphal books (Ecclus xliv. 11, 12, 19–21;
Song of the Three Children, 12), and in the New Testament, in the form of intercession, in James v. 16 (cf. Luke
xxii. 32). The Talmud develops the idea of the transference
of merit and imputation of righteousness in a remarkable
manner. A great rôle in the history of the nation is ascribed to that righteousness of Abraham and others which
had procured them favor with God and influence in his coun-
cils, while to the righteous is assigned an almost unlimited
power. In one passage Succa 39, it is affirmed that "the
merit of the righteous is able to free the whole world from
condemnation," and another (Ber. 10 b) ventures the sweeping assertion that in general it is desirable "to rest one's
hopes on the merits of others."[2]

It would thus seem probable that the notion of the imputation or legal transference of moral character and its
merits or rewards was not strange to Paul's generation, especially not to that Pharisaic school to which he belonged.
How the Jewish thought harmonized this idea with the
principle of individual moral independence and responsibility does not appear, but it is clear that the harmon-
ization was effected. Paul, we may imagine, could not be
content with a vague theory of the vicarious efficacy of
merely human righteousness; his sense of sin was too deep.
The peculiarity of his system is his recognition of the
righteousness of the Messiah as the one only moral gar-

---

[1] The verb rendered "justify, make righteous," is a forensic term, meaning "to pronounce righteous."

[2] On the doctrine of the Talmud see Weber, "System," chs xix. xx.

ment which by reason of its perfectness could clothe all humanity with legal purity. In his principle of imputation he is at one with the Old Testament, and especially with that later development of Old Testament ideas which is found in the Talmud; he differs from both in the depth and fulness of his moral demands. How he came to his special view it is impossible to say with definiteness. It was most likely an intuition, — an idea that burst up in his soul out of the mass of material over which he had been brooding; he describes it as a revelation. It brought him unity, order, light, where before all had been darkness and chaos. It may have been that profound prophetic vision of the suffering Servant of the Lord (which he doubtless interpreted Messianically) that led him to connect salvation with the Messiah's righteousness;[1] and it seems to have been in connection with his acceptance of Jesus as the Christ that he perfected his exalted conception of the Messiah's nature and function. He seems to have had little knowledge of the earthly life of Jesus, and for this reason, perhaps, the more readily idealized him into the absolutely perfect Servant of the Lord. He had disappeared from earth, — where could he be but at God's right hand? The disciples had their hopes, but Paul, convinced that he was the true Messiah of God, accepting him as the risen and glorified Lord, was unable to rest in the early Church's limited and undefined idea of the Messiah's moral-spiritual functions. He could not restrict the promised salvation to a political deliverance of the nation, or to a vague happiness to be bestowed at the second coming of the Christ. He looked for a speedy second coming (Thess., 1 Cor. xv.), but he demanded a present deliverance. His moral consciousness assured him that the Messiah had achieved abso-

---

[1] His expression for "justify" is the Greek rendering of the Hebrew forensic verb mentioned above.

lute deliverance from the burden of sin ; for this, he held, was the only true deliverance which the holy God could offer to sin-burdened men. Jesus was perfect ; and his perfect righteousness offered man that ideal perfectness without which the awakened conscience could not be satisfied.

He found also in the Old Testament the hint of the instrumentality by which the righteousness of the Messiah was to be appropriated. It is said (Gen. xv. 6) that Abraham's faith was reckoned to him for righteousness. It is clear from the connection that this act of belief is here represented as part of Abraham's personal righteousness, not an appropriation by him of the righteousness of another. But Paul applies the words without further explanation, and out of their proper sense, to the attitude of the believer toward Christ. There is, indeed, a profound spiritual truth in this conception, as will be pointed out below. But Paul takes it, in the first instance (Gal., Rom.), in a literal and somewhat mechanical way, and develops its consequences with unsparing logic. By faith in Christ, he says (and this faith must be regarded as having a moral-spiritual basis, including desire to be freed from sin), the believer is clothed with his perfect righteousness, stands therefore as just in the sight of God, and for him there can be no condemnation ; he has fulfilled all the divine commands. It follows that man's personal righteousness has no share in effecting his salvation. Whatever its purity and sincerity, it can never be perfect, and is moreover excluded by the very fact that it is the righteousness of Christ which God accepts and puts to the credit of those that believe in him. There is absolutely no place for human goodness in the divine decision respecting man's justification or condemnation.

This doctrine, which is peculiar to Paul, naturally excited grave doubts and opposition, a trace of which we find in the Epistle of James. It was, indeed, theoretically antinomianism of the most thoroughgoing sort. It was an unsparing attack on the Jewish national nomistic scheme of life. It was said by objectors (Rom. vi.) that it necessarily led to license, as indeed it may well have done when embraced by ignorant, unspiritual, or unconscientious persons. If obedience to law availed nothing for salvation, why, it might be asked, should one be obedient?

Paul's reply to this objection gives him occasion to bring out the profoundly spiritual side of his plan of salvation. It is true, he says (Rom. vi. vii.) that the believer is absolved absolutely from obedience to the law, but only under the condition that in accepting Jesus Christ as Saviour he dies to sin; the old sin-enslaved nature is crucified with Jesus on the cross, the believer is buried with him through baptism into death, and rises with him in newness of life. In the act of believing, the man is introduced into a new world, with transformation of desire and will: he has no longer any wish to do what is contrary to the divine will; there is a living spring of purity and obedience in his heart. How is it possible that he should continue in sin, which has become distasteful to him? There were some who supposed that reliance on God's grace for salvation would make men arrogant and defiant, — that, having a pledge of salvation from God, they would with devilish ingenuity and malignity give free rein to their passions, wallow in sin that they might test the stability of God's word and of his power to save. But no, cries the Apostle, indignantly; such a thing is impossible; the existence of such a desire would show the absence of true faith. He who believes not only has no desire to sin, but has intense desire to do what is pleasing in the sight of God, and performs from an inward impulse of love and with gladness of soul what other men wearily toil over, urged on by a mechanical and commercial hope of salvation.

Paul does not develop in detail the way in which this transformation of soul is accomplished, but we may gather his idea with sufficient distinctness from the Epistles to the Galatians, the Corinthians, and the Romans. In the first place, faith for him is not a mere intellectual belief that Jesus of Nazareth is the Messiah and the Saviour. It is a confiding, loving attitude of the soul toward God and Christ, a completely sympathetic acceptance of the divine nature as the object not only of affectionate reverence, but also of intimate communion, whence results an appropriation of and assimilation to this divine nature: "As many of you as have been baptized into Christ have put on Christ" (Gal. iii. 27); "If we have become united with him by the likeness of his death, we shall be also by the likeness of his resurrection" (Rom. vi. 5). It is here left undetermined how this perfect assimilation to the perfect character of Jesus is effected, — whether by the experience of the human soul or by an immediate divine intervention, or by both. But it is clear from the Apostle's description of his own experience (as in Rom. vii.) that he conceived of it on the human side as a radical psychological process, the basis of which was desire to be free from the mastery of sin, and the culmination of which was the establishment of a hearty and intimate friendship with God. It is here that Paul shows his deep insight into human nature. Such friendship could not exist while the heart was full of dread of God as a judge who unsparingly required complete obedience to his minutest commands; such a relation (and this the exaggerated Jewish nomism was) converted man into an anxious, toiling slave. But now through Christ the fear of failure in obedience was done away with, and the soul, reconciled to God (2 Cor. v. 19), might lift itself into a free and frank communion with his goodness.

It was thus the power of an ideal to which Paul appealed. His experience and his reflection led him to see that the mightiest instrument for the transformation of character was the hearty devotion of the soul to a supreme model of truth and holiness; and so he trusts confidently to the power of faith to reorganize and perfect man's nature. This is the highest development of the individual, when he is governed not by a set of minute rules (as was the case in the extreme nomistic scheme), but by his love for an object which included in itself all good. Thus man might attain to that sense of freedom in which the Apostle revels (Gal. iv. v.), — full liberty to follow his own impulses, knowing that these can be nothing but pure, inasmuch as they are called into being by an absolutely pure object. This view furnished the necessary complement to the legal scheme. Obedience to law was indispensable,[1] but it could be secured only by love of the deeper principles of law and of the law-giver. This part of Paul's conception is contained germinally in the Old Testament (as in Ps. cxix.), and more definitely in the Wisdom of Solomon, in which (chs. vii.–ix.) wisdom is really a divine ideal, the breath of the power of God, the brightness of the everlasting light, acquainted with the mysteries of the knowledge of God, and man's guide into all things pure and noble. It is contained substantially in the word of Jesus: " Ye shall be perfect, as your heavenly Father

---

[1] In the Apostle's system the theoretical freedom of the believer is practically controlled in its judgments by the content of the divinely revealed ethical law. The truthfulness of the conscience is tested by its conformity to the existing standard. License is condemned on its face as antigodly. Christian liberty is deliverance from the dogma that salvation is wrought out by obedience, — that is, from external ecclesiasticism, salvation is not in the Church, but in Christ. The obligation to keep the moral law remains; the obligation of the ceremonial law falls away of itself. Such is the distinction that runs through Paul's writings. He assumes, he does not discuss, the eternal significance of ethical principle. This was assumed no less by the Jews, his opponents. Neither party felt called on to establish this universally recognized fact. The conflict was over the ritual law; but it carried with it the deeper question of the relation between spiritual freedom and the perfection of the soul.

is perfect" (Matt. v. 48). But Paul gave it greater definiteness, and it may be said more effectiveness, by identifying it with the more definite person of Jesus and connecting it with his position as redeemer of man.

From another point of view he connects this inward transformation with the presence and indwelling of God in the soul, whereby the spiritual life is called into existence: "God has sent the spirit of his son into our hearts, crying, Abba, Father" (Gal. iv. 6); "Know ye not that ye are a temple of God, and that the spirit of God dwelleth in you" (1 Cor. iii. 16); "We all, with unveiled face reflecting as a mirror the glory of the Lord, are transformed into the same image from glory to glory even as from the Lord, the spirit" (2 Cor. iii. 18); "Ye are not in the flesh, but in the spirit, if so be that the spirit of God dwelleth in you" (Rom. viii. 9). Paul thus seems to regard the whole process of inward salvation as a supernatural one. Compare the conception in Wisdom of Solomon ix. 17, 18: "Thy counsel who has known, except thou give wisdom and send thy holy spirit from above? For so the ways of them which lived on the earth were reformed, and men were taught the things that are pleasing to thee, and were saved through wisdom." The Apostle does not exhibit in a systematic way the relation between the work of the spirit, the work of the Christ, and the faith of the believer. But his view seems to be that the divine spirit is imparted when the man believes. It is in fact simply the Old Testament doctrine of God's universal creative activity which he here adopts: nothing is done except by the divine power, and the spirit is the representative and instrument of the divine influence on the soul. In like manner, Paul adopts the Old Testament conception of God's predetermination (Rom. viii. 28–30), which in the thought of that time was merely a necessary part of the idea of God's absolute control of the world.

The instrument or condition of man's salvation, in Paul's view, is the death of Christ: men are justified by his blood, saved from wrath through him, reconciled to God through his death (Rom. v.). God condemned sin in the flesh by sending his own son in the likeness of sinful flesh and as an offering for sin (Rom. viii. 3). This representation of the Messiah as a sacrifice for sin originated, as far as our information goes, with Paul; it is not found in the words of Jesus, nor in the speech of Stephen, nor in the Epistle of James. Its germ may be found perhaps in Isaiah liii., a passage which was early regarded by the Jews as Messianic (Targum of Jonathan, cf. Acts viii. 32, 33), though the idea of an atoning death seems not to have entered into the current Jewish theory of the Messiah.[1] Paul doubtless reached his position by the combination of the two ideas that the Messiah was to achieve complete salvation, and that there could be no salvation without offering for sin; yet it is to be noted that he lays comparatively little stress on the death of Christ, and in general on his humanity (Gal. iv. 4). He accepts the atoning death as a necessary condition of salvation, but looks with preference to the risen Saviour, whose present glory was both the type and the pledge of the supreme blessedness reserved by God for the believer: "If we died with Christ, we believe that we shall also live with him, knowing that Christ, being raised from the dead, dies

---

[1] Weber, "System," cap. xxii. The Targum of Jonathan does not see in Isa. liii. the vicarious suffering, but only the intercession of the Messiah. The later Jewish theology, perhaps under the pressure of Christian doctrine, evoked a subsidiary Messiah, an Ephraimite, whose death was to have atoning efficacy. But of such a rôle for a Messiah there is no trace in the existing pre-Christian Jewish literature. It is natural to suppose that it was the deep sense of the sinfulness of sin that forced the idea on the mind of Paul; it was for him and for that age the profoundest explanation of the death of the Messiah. An historical connection might be sought between this view and the old-Semitic conception of the death of the man-God (as in the Adonis-cult). If this latter conception was a familiar one in the first century of our era, it may have helped to shape the Christian doctrine.

no more, death no more has dominion over him. The death that he died, he died to sin once for all, but the life that he lives, he lives to God; even so reckon ye also yourselves to be dead to sin, but alive to God in Christ Jesus" (Rom. vi. 8–11, cf. iv. 25, Phil. iii. 10). It was the living Jesus to whom he looked as the source of spiritual life, and he could call his preaching the gospel of the resurrection.

We may sum up Paul's doctrine of saving righteousness as follows: its legal condition is the sacrificial death of Jesus Christ; its ethical content is the personal righteousness of Christ; its source is the power of the living, glorified Christ committed to him by God and exercised through the spirit; its human condition is the humble and grateful recognition of Jesus as the perfect ideal, through whose presence the soul is transformed. Thus we may see the difference between Paul's teaching and that of Jesus: for the latter, the ideal is God; for the former, Jesus as the glorified son of God. The latter accepts man's personal righteousness, only purified by spirituality; the former rejects human righteousness, which seems to him necessarily impure, and substitutes for it perfect righteousness of the Christ, with the condition that the soul in the act of believing is quickened into free, ethical activity. Jesus thinks of an inward transformation wrought by the communion between man's will and God's; Paul demands a new divine creation. Jesus brings the soul face to face with God; Paul interposes the person of the Christ as reconciler.

The subsequent development of the idea of righteousness in the Pauline school variously combines the elements of Paul's thought. The Epistle to the Ephesians represents the sacrificial death of Christ as the cause of the reconciliation of God and man (ii. 13; v. 2; ii. 16); believers are raised with him (ii. 6), and he dwells in their hearts through faith (iii. 17); the new inward nature of man is created by God in righteousness and holiness (iv. 24), and Christ is the ethical standard of growth (iv. 13); salvation is not of works, but the believer is created in Christ Jesus for good works (ii. 9, 10). We here recognize the essential points of Paul's doctrine, without the systematic development which he gives. Faith secures to the believer the benefits of Christ's death, and there is the Pauline indefiniteness as to the precise relation between the function of this death and the transforming power of God. Substantially the same view is given in Colossians. Believers die with Christ (ii. 20), are raised with him (iii. 1), their life is hid with him in God (iii. 3). A modified view of the effect of Christ's sufferings is given (i. 24) by the statement that believers fill up by their own afflictions what is lacking in the afflictions of Christ. The conception is that the earthly life of Jesus, with all its elements, is the ground of the salvation which he accomplished; the significance of his death as a single act becomes thus relatively less important. In the conception of salvation stress is laid on the inward transformation of soul and union with Christ, and faith does not play the prominent part which Paul assigns it. Though Christ is said to blot out the legal ordinances which are hostile to the soul (ii. 14), yet we find no trace of Paul's thoroughgoing rejection of law and works. Very similar is the idea of righteousness given in the First Epistle of Peter (i. 19; ii. 24; i. 3; iii. 21; iv. 1, 13); but in declaring that believers are priests whose sacrifices are acceptable through Christ (ii. 5), and that they purify their souls in obedience to the truth (i. 22), the author withdraws from Paul's technical position, regarding righteousness rather as the act of the soul, though its possibility is conditioned on the death and resurrection of Christ.

Still farther removed from the Pauline point of view is the position of the Epistle to the Hebrews, whose doctrine is substantially that of the Old Testament with certain modifications of detail. Christ, as offering and priest, is the author of salvation (v. 9); he is intercessor (vii. 25), the mediator of the new covenant (viii. 6 ; xii. 24), and attained his position at the right hand of God by despising the shame and enduring the suffering of his earthly life (xii. 2, 3). Faith is not belief in Christ whereby we are freed from the Law, but confidence toward God (vi. 1 ; x. 23, 36–39 ; xi.), — the Old Testament scheme of righteousness, with the substitution of Jesus Christ for the old sacrifices and priesthood.

The First Epistle to Timothy, while it regards Christ as Saviour (i. 15 ; ii. 5, 6), takes a distinctly un-Pauline view of the law, which it regards as good and necessary in itself if it be used lawfully (i. 8), and made not for the righteous, but for the wicked ; that is, the law furnishes the standard of moral conduct, being herein identical with the " sound doctrine " of the Gospel.[1] Its more universalistic view is shown not only by its ignoring the idea of the imputation of Christ's righteousness, and laying stress on man's own moral effort, but also by its representation of God as the Saviour of all men (ii. 3; iv. 10). Second Timothy, an earlier production, has substantially the same view as First Peter (i. 10 ; ii. 11 ; iii. 15), and Titus approaches nearer the Pauline type by the rejection of works as the ground of salvation (ii. 11, 14 ; iii. 4–7).

The Fourth Gospel, ignoring the details of human ethical effort, conceives of righteousness as a necessary accompaniment of entrance into the world of light. The historical condition of this entrance is the sacrificial death of Christ (i. 29) and faith in him and in God (iii. 16 ; v. 24). He frees from sin (viii. 26) ; life is the abiding in him (xv. 4) ;

---

[1] Paul also regards the moral law as good in itself (Rom. ii. vii.), but treats it as helpless and obstructive, so far as regards salvation (vii. 9), while for First Timothy it is a normal and beneficial element of religious life.

sin is the rejection of him (xvi. 8). At the same time, it is a new birth of the soul which ushers one into the kingdom of God (iii. 3, 5). It is the divine interposition which divides mankind into the two masses of light and darkness; and while it is declared that they who do truth come to the light (iii. 21), yet they only can come whom God leads. Righteousness means the possession of the light-nature, which manifests itself by the acceptance of Jesus as the Son of God, the spiritual food and drink of man, the only way to God, the absolute truth, the essential life. The same conception of union with Christ as the source of righteousness is found in the First Epistle of John (iii. 6). The Epistle, however, emphasizes the human activity more than the Gospel: forgiveness is obtained by confession (i. 9), and the world is overcome by the love of God (ii. 12–17).

This conception of righteousness connects itself with that view of the world which in the prologue to the Fourth Gospel has the Logos for its centre and explanation. The world had been created through the divine Word; yet it lay in darkness, the darkness of sin, the origin of which is not explained. The world was his own, yet it knew him not. The reign of the Jewish Law belonged also to the period of darkness; the darkness was dispelled by the manifestation of grace and truth through Jesus Christ, in whom was the manifestation of God himself. The divine influence affects the individual soul. No process of moral regeneration is described; there is a new spiritual creation (iii. 3) parallel to the physical creation in the beginning. At a moment in the past God through the Word had called the world into being; now, at the appointed time (after ages of unexplained darkness and doubt), the Word had appeared in human form, bringing divine light and eternal life. Every vestige of nationalism has here disappeared; the relations of God are primarily not with the Jews, but with humanity.[1] In the moral-spiritual history of the world the author sees the divine creative activity. He thus expresses substantially the thought of Jesus, that human perfection lies in communion with the divine father, only the thought is clothed in the form of the Jewish-Alexandrian philosophy.

The history of the idea of righteousness in the New Testament involves the interplay of three conceptions: the Old Testament idea of personal goodness, Paul's scholastic scheme of imputed righteousness, and the transformation of the soul by union with Christ or by the direct power of the Holy Spirit. The first of these maintained itself throughout, more or less modified by the conviction (which is found also in the Old Testament) that true goodness is the gift of God. The Pauline idea of imputation, devised by a logical mind to meet a specific Jewish objection, seems to have faded away with the crisis which gave it birth. It appears in not very prominent shape in Second Timothy, Titus, and First Peter, and at a later time virtually withdrew from the field. The more simple ethical conception of righteousness as personal thought and conduct is found particularly in Hebrews and First Timothy, and to a greater or less extent in all the other Epistles; it is in fact too obvious and necessary a conception of life to be got rid of except in transient moments of fanaticism. The profounder conception of inward transformation is especially prominent in Ephesians and Colossians (union with Christ), and in the Fourth Gospel and the First Epistle of John (renewal of heart); and whatever the particular scheme of righteousness and salvation, the appeal of all the New Testament writers is to the consciousness and will of men.

---

[1] The statement in John iv. 22, that salvation is from the Jews, is not, rightly considered, in opposition to this universality of view. Out of Judaism, indeed, had come the manifestation of salvation; but the author of the Fourth Gospel everywhere assumes a hostile attitude toward the Jews, and

Thus Jewish national nomism, which had successfully withstood the assaults of Hellenism, succumbed to a spiritual force which sprang from its own bosom. It was superior, as an organized religion, to the religious thought of the Greeks; it had more definiteness and intensity, greater control over the moral-religious life, and it was in completer harmony with men's growing unitary conception of the world. While, therefore, it was not averse to accepting a certain Greek coloring, it maintained its organized existence over against Hellenism unimpaired. Its own life had, however, called forth needs which it was powerless as a system to satisfy. Increasing moral-religious experience and reflection had awakened in the Jewish consciousness more definite demands for self centred and complete moral power, for inward purity and harmony with the divine will. The Jewish Hellenizing philosophy and the great legal schools endeavored in one direction and another to realize in life the higher ideals which became distincter with every generation. But the national ritual, which had been growing for centuries, and had interwoven itself inextricably with the moral-spiritual consciousness of the people, stood grievously in the way of a satisfactory isolation of the higher ideals. The necessity for getting rid of the mass of ceremonial and other external details became more and more evident, and Christianity came forward to achieve this end. The founder of Christianity responded to the needs of his times and of humanity by announcing the two universal and eternal principles of inward truthfulness and harmony with the divine father of men. He did not attack the national system as such, but he laid down a scheme of life which struck at the roots of nationalism and laid the foundations for a righteousness sufficient for all times and places: the

the antithesis which he presents is not between Judaism and Gentilism, but between light and darkness, belief and unbelief.

conscience as subjective standard and guide ; God, the moral ideal, as objective law and aim ; outward and inward absolute purity and sincerity. To these all-embracing principles he added nothing ; he said nothing further of the details of moral reconstruction and development. The elaboration of the details was effected by the great theologians who followed him. His person became the centre of a new conception of moral-spiritual life. The secret of salvation was sought not in his teaching, but in himself, — in himself not as an ideal and inspiration, but as the divinely endowed creator of spiritual life and happiness. Paul, looking at the problem from the Jewish national point of view, in despair at man's moral impotency, cast away human righteousness, and substituted for it the righteousness of the Christ, made available by his death, and accompanied by an inward transformation wrought by the divine spirit. The author of the Fourth Gospel, following Alexandrian Greek-Jewish ideas, thought of the Master as the divine Word, manifesting the moral glory of God in the world, bringing an atmosphere of light and life, in the midst of which dwelt, transformed and saved, those who were chosen and led by God. Unlike Paul, he takes no account of the national legal scheme ; he takes refuge alone in the absolute manifestation of the divine goodness and power, within which is life, without which is death. It may be added that an approach to a purely ethical scheme of righteousness is found in that circle of Christian thinkers which is represented by the Epistle of James ; not the Stoic system, but the old Hebrew prophetic conception, wherein, general provision for sin having been made by a divinely appointed sacrifice, the righteousness acceptable to God is manifested by obedience to his moral precepts. Later Christianity endeavored, with varying fortunes, to combine these different points of view into a single system of theology and life.

Christian antinomism grew out of Judaism, but was not embraced by the Jewish people. Christianity speedily passed into the hands of the Gentiles; the Jews retained their national system. Nomism included the sacrificial ritual and the every-day legal-ceremonial prescriptions of personal purity and obedience. The sacrificial system vanished when the temple was destroyed, but Judaism clung to the rest of the ceremonial as the law of its life. It distinctly rejected the innovations of Christianity, — the Messiahship of Jesus of Nazareth, the atoning efficacy of his death, his exaltation to the right hand of God, the substitution of his righteousness for the righteousness of obedience, the expectation of his reappearance on earth to usher in the dispensation of blessedness. But its severance from Christianity does not imply that it remained morally and religiously stagnant. Its ethical code was substantially the same as the Christian; its ethical development, like the Christian, was determined by social conditions. Neither in the early centuries nor in the Middle Age nor in our own times is it possible to discover any marked ethical difference between Jews and Gentiles; Shylock and Antonio are on a par in this regard. In the sphere of religion, also, Judaism, like Christianity, has taken its tone and coloring from the changing phases of social growth. The national nomistic idea, to which the Jews remained faithful, has been modified from time to time, notably by Maimonides, and then more radically by Moses Mendelssohn. These modifications have been in the direction of greater spirituality and ethical distinctness. Christianity and Judaism may be looked on as parallel developments, starting from the same general material, seeking the moral-spiritual ideal by different paths. Their lines of advance have been determined by the elements of civilization which entered into their lives. It is the intense nationalism of the Jews which, by isolating them more or less from the general European thought, has rendered their peculiar development possible.

In our discussion of the idea of righteousness the distinction between nomism and antinomism has been sharply drawn, in order to bring out more clearly the contrast between the two conceptions of life. It must, however, be borne in mind that this distinction has had no such clear historical embodiment. Judaism has never been all nomistic, nor Christianity all antinomistic. Each of these systems, while following a definite general path, exhibits movements in other directions. There is a substantial agreement between the Old Testament, the Jewish Alexandrian literature, the Palestinian legal teaching, and the New Testament. These must all be regarded as products of the combination and interplay of two conceptions : inward spiritual regeneration, and conformity to divinely given external law, both of which are essential constituents of religious life, and can never vanish from the human ideal. Judaism, in maintaining its national law, did not forget the inward reconstruction which is taught in the Old Testament. Christianity, in rejecting the Jewish sacrificial ritual and traditional ceremonial law, substituted a nomism of its own. The Church has always had its systems of prescriptions, obedience to which it regarded as a necessity. What Christianity did was to deliver to the Gentile world the pure and lofty Jewish ethical monotheism freed from the burden of Jewish nationalism. It thus gave freer play to moral-spiritual forces by divorcing them from the restrictions of particular nationalities. Christianity represents the greatest effort of the world to impose the necessary restrictions on nomism, — to combine that inward purity, without which virtue is mechanical and lifeless, with that obedience to law apart from which conscience must always be an unsafe guide.

The doctrine of the sacrifice of the exalted Christ, the Son of God, embodies the highest and final conception of an external satisfaction for sin. It sprang out of the ideas of the first century, Jewish and perhaps Gentile. Viewed at first simply as a substitute for the old national sacrifices, the death of the Messiah was afterward variously explained by Christian theologians. By its majestic and awful character it represents, as has been said, a deeper sense of the terribleness of offence against the divine law. All advance in the intensity of plans and methods of salvation depends on increase of the seriousness with which men look on the moral problems of life. What a contrast between the simple joyousness of Deuteronomy and the terrible seriousness of the Epistle to the Romans! The interval between these books is marked by constant ethical progress ; the idea of righteousness becomes higher and higher, the sense of sin more and more profound. The culmination of outward method is reached when God is conceived as giving his own Son to achieve forgiveness and righteousness for man. There is only one thing higher, — that is the method of Jesus, — the transformation of the soul by communion with the absolute ideal of holiness.

CHAPTER V.

TO the foregoing discussion of what was held to constitute righteousness in the sight of God we may append a brief account of the historical development of the content of the ethical code. We need not stop to inquire into the philosophical grounds of Hebrew ethics. For such an inquiry there is little material. Abstract psychological and social investigations do not belong to the mental habits or the aims of the biblical writers, who are concerned only with practical morality. The question of the nature of conscience and the origin of men's judgments concerning right and wrong is not discussed in the Bible. There is no speculation respecting determinism and indeterminism ; man's practical freedom is everywhere assumed. There is no coercion of the will by God, demon, or man ; every man is held responsible for his deeds, and the inner history of his will is not further investigated. Joseph's brethren "could not" speak peaceably to him because their malice got the better of their kindly feeling Yahwe hardened Pharaoh's heart ; but Pharaoh also hardened his own heart. Evil spirits enticed prophets ; but the prophets were of their own motion false. Satan tempted David and Judas, and the king and the betrayer were none the less held guilty. The heathen, says Paul, are worthy of death for acting according to that reprobate mind to which God gave them up; and unbelievers. blinded by the god of this world, perish in their unbelief. The wretchedness of the natural life, exclaims the Apostle, lies in the conflict of impulses, the passions doing what the better judgment condemns. So in respect to the rules of good conduct: these are regarded in the books of the Old and New Testaments, with perhaps one exception (Ecclesiastes), as resting solely on the commands of God, and the motive which is urged for well-doing is the desire to obtain divine rewards or escape divine punishments. It is a purely practical interest that controls the ethical thought of the Bible. The question before it is: What is the conduct that pleases God? In point of fact, the Jewish ethical code, like that of other peoples, changed with the changing social conditions and the consequent rise of new ideals. To follow this history in minute detail would require a treatise; all that will be attempted here is a short outline of the historical progress of the code and of the circumstances which determined its line of growth.

1. The Jewish moral code of the fifth century B. C. (contained in the prophets and the Law) was a broad and noble one, worthy to be compared with the best of the time. Within the limits of the nation it recognized not only the administrative duties of honesty and justice but also the gentler virtues of kindness and love, to the poor and distressed and to all one's brethren. This appears to be the acme of the purely Jewish national ethical development. In spite of contact with other peoples, the nation had up to this time maintained the old social isolation. In the early days there had been amalgamation with the Canaanitish tribes, out of which was formed the Israelitish nation. Once formed, the people worked out its life substantially in its own way, down to the Greek conquest. Intercourse with Babylon and Persia, though influential in the suggestion of ideas, yet left the old national unity unimpaired. The ethical growth during this period may thus be called national.

There was no outlook beyond home-bounds; the international sentiment had not been distinctly cultivated; there was no distinct recognition of the full rights of aliens; the social conditions had not pressed this conception on the moral consciousness of the people. The later purely national books,— most of the Psalms, for example,— while they maintain the high administrative standard, are full of bitterness toward enemies. Jewish morality, in a word, like other ethical systems of the time, bears the impress of national isolation.

2. The new social conditions which the Greek conquest forced on the Jews are well known. Not only were they brought into closer contact with individuals of other nationalities, they were compelled to enter into a confederation of peoples, and were thus led more and more to recognize a bond of brotherhood among all men. Their experience in this regard was the common experience of the Græco-Roman world; its results were seen in all the moralists of the time, whether Greek, Roman, or Jewish. Human nature remained much the same; there were good and bad men everywhere, — Hillels and Herods, Johns and Judases; but the social code was gradually assuming a new tone. The ethical reflection of the new conditions is found in a portion of the Jewish literature of the two centuries before the beginning of our era. The Psalms are, by their nature, the expression of national feeling. Profoundly religious, they do not rise above the level of the old prophetic morality; they illustrate the law, of which there are so many other expressions, that the paths of growth and stadia of development of religion and morality are not always the same in the same community and the same period. On the other hand, in Proverbs, Wisdom of Solomon, Ecclesiasticus, and in the sayings of the great lawyers, we find a distincter recognition of individual social relations and of the law of kindness; exhortation to heal differences between neighbors (Prov.

xxv. 9); to admonish in kindness those who offend us
(Ecclus. xix. 13–17); to cover transgression by friendly for-
getfulness or guidance (Prov. xvii. 9); to be helpful, to lend
and give alms freely (Ecclus. xxix. 2, 12, 20; Tobit iv. 7);
to forgive injuries in hope of being forgiven (Prov. xv. 1;
xxiv. 29; Ecclus. xxviii. 2–5); to be good to enemies (Prov.
xxiv. 17; xxv. 21, 22). We find also injunctions against
swearing (Ecclus. xxiii. 29), and a description of the blessedness of the persecuted righteous (Wisd. of Sol. iii. 4). In
Tobit (iv. 15), and in a saying of Hillel, we have the golden
rule in negative form.

Most of the works above cited belong to that class of productions (the Hokma, the literature of wisdom) which shows
least of the characteristic nationalism of the time, and it
is natural to ascribe their cosmopolitan spirit in part to
the broadening influence of international intercourse. Tobit,
though a national book, shows traces of foreign contact. We
have seen reason to believe that the legal teachers were
not unaffected by the current Greek thought. On the other
hand, the Jewish national feeling was strong, and the national life and culture issued from that past which was
represented by the prophets and the Law. We are led,
therefore, to conclude that the higher Jewish morality of
the period was a true national growth, only broadened and
deepened by all those conditions that acted favorably on
the life of the people.

3. Such was the ethical system in the midst of which
Christianity arose; and it is obvious that it does not differ substantially in details from that of the New Testament. In both we find as controlling elements self-mastery,
self-sacrifice, justice, and love to others. Nevertheless there
is a difference, which meets us at the outset, — a new energy, vividness, enthusiasm. The Sermon on the Mount and
the other sayings of Jesus in the Gospels contain a cer-

tain higher something, — a completer recognition of the positive side of individual obligation and of the inward element of goodness. The ethical falseness of certain ceremonial practices of the time (Mark vii. 5, 9–13); the necessity of sincerity (Matt. vi. 2, 5, 16) and of thoroughgoing conscientiousness (Matt. v. 33–37); the declaration that sin and goodness lie in the thought and in the soul (Matt. v. 21–32; xv. 18); exhortation to self-denial for duty's sake Matt. xvi. 24); the complete identification of ourselves with the interests of others, and the obligation to sacrifice ourselves, if need be, for the sake of others (Matt v 38–42, 43–48; vii. 12); the exhortation to let one's light shine (v. 16), that is, not to limit one's self to passive endurance of wrong, or to occasional bodily help, but to recognize the fact that each man is set to be a guide to his fellows, and must therefore so purify and ennoble himself that he shall lead them not into error, but into truth:[1] here are gathered up all the elements of the highest ethical character, — perfect self-control, enlightened self-development, and complete sympathy with our human surroundings. While the substance of these precepts is found in preceding Jewish and non-Jewish literature, they are here given with a fulness and symmetry which we see nowhere else. The ethical-spiritual

---

[1] The doctrine of non-resistance in the Sermon on the Mount may fairly be understood simply as a protest against selfish and unreasonable assertion of one's rights. A law of absolute non-resistance may very well have been the ideal of Jesus, but it cannot be asserted, from the details of his life known to us, that he did not mean it to be modified or interpreted by a wise regard for the interests of the individual and of society. An unrestricted rule of submission must apply as well to nations as to individuals, and perhaps to men in their relations as well with beasts as with men. It is the law of an ideal society in which justice and kindness are the ruling principles of a very large majority. The hostility to the rich expressed in Luke vi. 24 can hardly be taken in a spiritual sense, but it may be doubted whether Jesus held such a sentiment which accords neither with the body of his teaching nor with his conduct. He taught the equality of all men before God, independently of worldly conditions, and he numbered among his friends rich as well as poor.

insight of Jesus laid hold of what was necessary for the complete development of man's moral nature.

The purity of the ethical teaching of Jesus has been supposed to be marred by the religious sanctions which he holds up. It is said that he represents love of one's fellows and denial of one's self as valuable not so much in themselves or for the maintenance of human rights as for the future rewards they bring (Matt. vi. 1). Here, however, we must distinguish between the ethical ideal and the religious motive. Whatever prominence may be given to the latter (and it is very prominent in the teaching of Jesus), this does not impair the realness of the former. The supreme obligation of human brotherhood is recognized; and this is the essential point for human conduct. Further, though the Sermon on the Mount does not say in so many words, " Follow after justice and love, because they are the eternal right," though it identifies them with the will of God and thence derives their authority, it yet remains true that the ultimate ground of the ethical judgment is a social one: it is the perception of human rights springing out of the feeling of human needs, and it cannot vitiate an ethical principle to identify it with the ultimate moral basis and ground of the world.

Jesus gives no speculative system of morals. The golden rule is, strictly speaking, inaccurate in expression, since it makes one's own desire, instead of absolute justice, the guide of conduct toward others. But it is, in the first place, the best practical safeguard against selfishness; and in the second place, interpreted largely as the appeal to an enlightened and tender conscience, it is practically the safest guide in man's dealing with man. New social conditions are constantly creating new moral problems. There are many modern questions which are not considered in the teaching of Jesus, the detailed answers to which must be worked out by

modern experience; but no ethical principle has yet been discovered more satisfactory than the self-forgetting love which
is enjoined in the Sermon on the Mount.

4. The ethics of the Epistles, so far as the content proper
of the code is concerned, offers nothing in addition to what
has already been mentioned. James has the morality of the
Old Testament (and with his description of wisdom, iii. 17,
cf. Wisd. of Sol. vii. 22, 23). The other books are more distinctively Christian in tone. It is unnecessary to specify
the particular moral duties they enjoin. They emphasize
the gentler qualities, — humility, kindness, love. In 1 Corinthians xiii. Paul rises to a pitch of loftiest inspiration.
It is noticeable that the golden rule in the form in which
Jesus gives it is nowhere quoted. James ii. 8) cites the
"royal law" from the Old Testament : "Thou shalt love
thy neighbor as thyself;" and the content of Jesus' word
is given substantially by Paul (1 Cor. xiii.; Rom. xii. 13).
It is possible that Paul and the author of the Epistle of
James were not acquainted with this saying of the Master. It is also to be noted that the duty of kindness and
love is generally mentioned in connection with intercourse
between Christian brethren. A negative demeanor is enjoined toward them that are without, — soberness, cautious-
ness, forgiveness ; and a general prohibition of vengeance
is quoted by Paul (Rom. xii. 19, 20) from the Old Testament (Prov. xxv. 21, 22); but there is little exhortation to
exert positive influence on unbelievers, to seek to win them
by kindness, to practise systematic beneficence toward them
(Gal. vi. 10). The explanation of this omission is probably
to be found in the social conditions of the time, the social
separateness of Christians and others. Paul, indeed, set the
example of wise self-adaptation to other men (1 Cor. x. 33 ;
ix. 19–22).

Broader cosmopolitan points of view may perhaps be

found in the New Testament; as, for example, the conception of a universal commonwealth (Rom. xii. 5; Eph. ii. 14–19). Such an idea might be referred to Græco-Roman sources. But it is to be observed that these passages deal solely with the Church, and are not properly cosmopolitan; they speak of a community in Christ, not of a brotherhood of humanity. They break down the barrier between Jew and Gentile as such; and this was an important step forward. Similarly the barriers between nationalities were broken down by Roman citizenship. In each case there is a unity based, not on simple recognition of human fellowship, but on an external religious or political condition; yet each represented a step toward the idea of human solidarity, — each was the product of the social conditions. The Christian idea may have issued directly and solely from the Christian doctrine of a universal salvation, or it may have been in part suggested by Greek philosophy and the Roman state.

5. It is remarked above that speculative questions respecting the origin and nature of man's moral consciousness and judgments are not considered in the Bible. It is equally true that there is no recognition of a purely earthly and human end and aim of life. The object everywhere held up is the gaining the favor of God as the means of securing one's own happiness. The prophets and the Law enjoin obedience to divine commands as the condition of national prosperity; the Psalms anticipate fulness of joy in God's presence and unending delights through his power; Proverbs commends wisdom as the bestower of long life, riches, honor, and peace; the Sermon on the Mount enjoins the laying up of treasures in heaven, walking in the narrow way of life, and building one's house upon a rock; the Epistles urge the working out of one's own salvation; and in Hebrews (xii. 2) the motive of Jesus'

endurance is said to be "the joy that was set before him."
Devotion to the interests of humanity for humanity's sake
is nowhere distinctly announced as the chief aim of life.
The end of life is declared to be one's own eternal happiness, and the condition of happiness to be obedience to
the will of God. So far this scheme of life may be called
religious egoism.

But on this point two remarks must be made. So far
as regards the existence of an egoistic motive, this neither
can nor should be got rid of, for the perfection of humanity
involves the perfection of one's self as a part of humanity;
obligation to sacrifice or neglect one's moral perfectness is
inconceivable. The real question, therefore, is twofold: first,
what is the nature of the self-perfection (and this must be
identical with the nature of the perfection of humanity)
which is sought? and secondly, how far are the two aims,
the perfecting of self and the perfecting of humanity, combined into a harmonious unity? As to the first of these
points, the self-perfection considered in the New Testament
(which in this respect completes the Old Testament thought)
is not merely happiness; it is moral union with God as the
moral ideal, which is the highest conception of self-culture,
and is therefore a legitimate egoism. As to the second point,
devotion to the interests of others, though not a definitely
formulated maxim, is a practical aim in the higher New
Testament scheme of life (more vaguely hinted at in the pre-
Christian Jewish literature). Jesus spent his life in doing
good, and died rather than surrender a principle which he
believed to be of prime importance for men; Paul consecrated himself unreservedly to what he held to be the highest human interests. The New Testament idea of duty
involves doing good to all men, not separating one's own
well-being from the well-being of others.

The ethical defect of the New Testament is therefore

speculative rather than practical. The ethical idea is not distinguished from the religious; the perfecting of life is defined to be an everlasting salvation which is to be secured by certain divinely appointed means. Human duty involves the attempt to bring this salvation to all men. The principle of devotion to humanity is not lacking; but it is true that attention is fixed less on the present life with its multifarious social needs, and more on that impending crisis (the new era to be ushered in by the Messiah or else by death) which was to settle the question of human good. The more definite isolation of the whole of earthly life as the object of ethical effort was reserved for a later time.

6. The distinctive characteristic, however, of the New Testament ethics is not so much its content as its spirit. In contrast with the philosophic, self-centred calm of Stoicism and Epicureanism, and the sober-minded indifference of Ecclesiastes, it is permeated by warm sympathy, by a glow of ardent, natural life. Its secret is that it seeks perfection not immediately in self-culture (though this it does not neglect), but in positive self-abandonment to a higher will. It derives its impulse from the sentiments of duty to God and gratitude and devotion to Christ as Saviour. It is free from wearing thought concerning results; these are in the hand of God. Man's only care is to ally himself with God and Christ in sincere, loving beneficence, secure in the conviction that his present and his future are watched over and guided to a blessed end by the hand of the divine father. The elevation of this higher spirit to the distinct position of guiding principle must be ascribed to Jesus. His moral consciousness seized on and blended into a vital unity those great ideas of love and justice which the national experience (and all human experience) had been slowly working out for centuries. Respect your fellow-coun-

tryman's rights and love him·as yourself, say the prophets and the Law; extend this rule of reciprocity to all men, say the Wisdom books and the lawyers; inform it, says Jesus, with a glow of tenderness, with the recognition of all men as sons of one divine father. This he made the central principle of conduct toward others.

It may be added that the form of faith which took shape under the hand of Paul was better fitted to stimulate the ordinary ethical feeling than the moral code given in the Sermon on the Mount. The latter appealed to human love of perfection and to the reward which would come from the favor of God; all else it left to man's own conscience and will. The former presented a grand theological scheme in which the details of salvation were set forth, the central figure of Jesus at once presenting the idea of redemption in definite, tangible shape, and offering a model for ethical imitation. It was the prime defect of Greek systems of philosophy, so far as regards their effect on the masses, that they produced no theological organization, no church in which the warm human life might be appropriated, fostered, stimulated by a definite hope of complete happiness; and the same remark applies in less degree to the religious reform instituted by Jesus, who also contemplated not a church, but the purification of the national spirit. What was needed for the people was the embodiment of the best ethical law and spirit in an organization which by its work and its sanctions should stimulate human effort to the utmost. This result was achieved mainly by the Apostle Paul; or, it may be more accurate to say, the work of church-organization, begun by the first disciples, received a mighty impulse from him. Certain peculiarities of his scheme were gradually dropped, but the organization itself was maintained and developed in succeeding generations, and the Church took its place as a powerful ethical lever, imposing its morality on the world, and supporting it by all those motives of gratitude and hope of reward which are most effective in the life of man.

This is not the place to attempt to state, even in merest outline, the actual influence of Christianity in moulding the ethical life of the world. Such questions are very complicated and difficult. But without undertaking to define the particular elements of the new moral order of things, and recognizing the slowness of its growth, it may be said that the ethical outcome of the Christian teaching was the more definite isolation and formulation of certain controlling principles of conduct, and the implanting of them in the general life of men as an effective everyday power. They were intelligently and vitally accepted only by the higher souls; but they secured public recognition as the basis of the ethical code, and thus entered with fresh vigor on their task of coercing the baser principles of human conduct. The public conscience was enlightened, life became ethically simpler, and the higher maxims more and more demonstrated their truth by the practical evidence they gave of conformity to men's noblest instincts and best interests.[1]

---

[1] On biblical ethics, see the commentaries, works on the philosophy of religion (Pfleiderer and others), works on Old Testament theology (Schultz, Oehler, etc.) and New Testament theology (Immer, Weiss, etc.), articles in encyclopædias (Herzog-Plitt, Lichtenberger, etc.), and general remarks in works on general and Christian ethics (Dorner, Gass, Martensen, Martineau, etc.). On the relation between Greek and Christian ethical ideas, see O. Pfleiderer, "Moral und Religion," 1872; F. Jodl, "Geschichte der Ethik," 1882; C. E. Luthardt, "Die antike Ethik in ihrer geschichtlichen Entwickelung als Einleitung in die Geschichte der christlichen Moral," 1887, and "Geschichte der christlichen Ethik vor der Reformation," 1888. On the ethics of the Gospels, see J. R. Seeley, "Ecce Homo," 1886; W. M. Salter, "Ethical Religion," 1888; J. A. Broadus, "Jesus of Nazareth," 1890; O. Flügel, "Die Sittenlehre Jesus," 1888 (which I am sorry to have been unable to consult). A good bibliography will be found in the "Theologischer Jahresbericht."

CHAPTER VI.

THE KINGDOM OF GOD.

THE conception of the kingdom of God is a marked characteristic of Jewish religious thought, — perhaps its most distinctive peculiarity. It is the idea of a social organization in which the divine and human shall be perfectly blended, the social ideal being complete conformity to the divine will and complete interpenetration by the divine guiding and moulding presence. Such a conception may be said to exist to some extent in all communities, inasmuch as the supremacy and control of the supernatural powers is everywhere recognized; but among no other people has the idea been so definitely grasped as among the Jews. Elsewhere the main stress has been laid on conquest, government, literature, philosophy, or art; and the theocratic idea, the feeling of the direct and complete dependence of the community on God, when it has been recognized, has played only a secondary rôle. It is only in a few cases that the attempt to embody it in an historical form has been at all successful; and among these it is to the Hebrew theocracy that the first rank, in precision and practical efficiency, must be assigned.[1]

[1] Next to the Jewish, the most successful theocratic system was that of Islam, especially under Mohammed and the Medina califs, less under the first century of the Bagdad califate. Still less definite were the attempts at theocratic organization under the Buddhist Asoka (third century B. C.) and the Sassanian Zoroastrians (from third to seventh century A. D.). Traces of the conception are recognizable in ancient Egypt, in modern China, and in a peculiar form in the first century of the New England colonies. It is note-

The Jewish theocratic idea has a noteworthy history extending over many centuries. Beginning with a merely external political form, it grew finally, under Christian influence, into a predominantly moral-spiritual system, in which comparatively little of the external remained. It is this development which we are called on to trace. We are concerned not so much to mark all the differences of detail of the Jewish ideas on the subject in the Old Testament and the New Testament as to note the increasing control which was obtained by the higher elements of the religious life.[1]

Four stadia may be recognized in the history of the Jewish-Christian theocratic idea: the early unconscious period of mere non-ethical nationalism, the prophetic or ethical nationalism, the apocalyptic conception of special divine external interposition, and the higher New Testament thought in which the ethical-spiritual predominates.

Nothing in the history of the Jews is more remarkable than the hope which they continued for a long period to cherish of a definite and brilliant future. Other peoples have been patriotic, have shown themselves capable of heroic effort for freedom and of resistance to foreign pressure. The Persian kingdom of to-day is a striking example of the maintenance of national life through many centuries of depression and subjugation. Persia has lived through the domination of the Parthians and of the Arabians, and grown finally into an organization which, with modifications that have come in through the centuries, may be regarded as an

worthy that we find little or no trace of a theocracy in any ancient Semitic people except the Jews, though this may be due in part to the scantiness of our information.

[1] It does not belong to our subject to follow the history below the New Testament, but it may be noted that the same sort of moral-spiritual growth has gone on within the bounds of Judaism. There is a large section of modern Jews which retains only the ethical-spiritual side of the Messianic idea.

historical continuation of the Achæmenian times. History
offers other, though less striking, examples. But the Jewish
experience differs from all these. It is not merely patriotism ; it is the patriotic imagination quickened and organized
by religious feeling ; it is the national sentiment exalted into
glowing fervor and unswerving confidence; it is the completest organization that the world has ever seen of patriotic-
religious hope.

The origin of this hope may be traced, as far as such
things are traceable, to certain elements of the Hebrew character and development. In the first place, we have to recognize in the Jews an extraordinary power of persistence.
Their whole history shows an uncommonly great development of individuality, ability to maintain their own personality against opposing influences, a toughness of fibre, the
like of which may be seen in some other nations, but perhaps nowhere else so marked as in the Jews, — at least, no
other people has had such opportunity to show it. Their
experience during the Middle Age in Europe is sufficient to
prove their enormous power of self-maintenance. Their survival is no doubt to be attributed to a combination of circumstances ; but whatever else there may have been, it is
evident that no small part of the result is due to their
innate resisting and persisting power.

In close connection with this quality is the religious side
of their history. As far back as we can trace them, their
attitude toward the national deity was peculiar, — a very
pronounced and controlling theological particularism. The
later Babylonians had a decided preference for Marduk above
other gods ; the Moabites seem to have been devoted chiefly
to Kemosh ; but the Israelites, with still greater devotion,
through all their long dallyings with other deities, clung to
their own Yahwe, whose sole worship was made by the
prophets (that is to say, by the controlling intellect of the

nation) the central point of religion and politics. At the same time, the remarkable religious organizing power of the people showed itself; a series of religious institutions, destined ultimately to transform the nation into an ecclesiastical organization, began before the exile. Religious ideas were worked up with fulness and roundness. The relation of the people to their god took very definite shape: he belonged to them, and they to him; they were under obligation to honor and serve him alone, and he under corresponding obligation to help them against all their enemies. These ideas crystallized in the prophetic thought into a conception of a covenant between God and the people; a covenant was the necessary expression of alliance. It was held that Yahwe had chosen Israel from among all nations in the earth, and had promised it his continued blessing on the condition on its part of obedience and loyalty

This is only the developed form of a very early set of ideas, and one not peculiar to the Hebrews. A clan, or tribe, at a certain stage of growth, enters into a specially close relation with a deity who is its kinsman and fast friend, its ally and patron, and entitled to its special devotion; at a later stage such a deity may become a national god. With such an origin agree the first details we have of the relation between Yahwe and the Israelitish tribes.[1] In the period of the Judges he is to Israel what Kemosh is to Ammon (Judg. xi. 24). The relation is here one of external worship and protection, and so remains substantially down to the

---

[1] Of the origin and meaning of the name "Yahwe," and of the beginnings of the Yahwe-cult among the Hebrews, we have no definite information. One tradition (Ex. vi. 3) states that it was unknown till after Jacob's time, and apparently ascribes its introduction to Moses, while another (Gen. iv. 26) refers it to the earliest times of the human race. For discussions of the name see Friedrich Delitzsch, "Wo lag das Paradies?" Leipzig, 1881, and S. R. Driver, in "Studia Biblica," Oxford, 1885; and on the origin of the cult, the histories of Kuenen, Wellhausen, Grätz, Stade, and Renan.

time of Ahab and Jehoshaphat (early part of the ninth century B. C.), whose attitude toward Yahwe is about the same as that of the Moabite king Mesha toward Kemosh.[1] The idea of an agreement or covenant between deity and people is primitive. The peculiarity of Israel is that, in accordance with its general power of religious organization, it so clearly defined and expressed the idea, and wove into it its highest religious thought, — absolute justice in God, spirituality in man. This highly developed idea appears already in the earliest of the writing prophets (Amos iii. ix).

Out of this conception of the covenant flows all the succeeding history. The nation continued its particularistic development ; it elaborated more and more its ceremonial law ; it attempted to isolate itself. The thicker its misfortunes, the more it wrapped itself up in its own ideals. All its experiences were interpreted in the light of the covenant : prosperity was regarded as a fulfilment of the divine promise ; adversity was accepted as a chastisement for unfaithfulness and a preparation for coming blessing. Whatever the situation, the leading religious thinkers explained it in the interests of the nation. The national imagination, embodied in prophets and seers, looked to the near future for the realization of boundless hopes, and most of all in times of suffering. The picture of the future was based upon the present, and changed from age to age with the changing circumstances of the nation. The Messianic history is a series of shifting views. The essential thing was the enlivening, stimulating hope ; the historical shape which it assumed was an accident of the times.

The history of the national hope is the history of the national thought ; whatever elements entered into the one showed themselves in the other. So long as the nation

<hr>

[1] See the inscription of the Moabite Stone in Ginsburg's edition, London, 1871, or " The Records of the Past," vol. xi., or Stade's " Geschichte," I. 534.

preserved its political independence and its comparative isolation in the midst of small nationalities, its conception of
the future was similarly restricted; when it became a part
of great world-empires (Persia, Greece, and Rome) and entered into closer association with other peoples, the picture
assumed a more cosmopolitan shape. At the same time the
eschatology became more definite; the doctrines of immortality and resurrection took shape and naturally colored the
view of the future. The modifications in the ethical ideas
of the nation necessarily showed themselves in the forms of
the Messianic hope; the individual assumed greater prominence in accordance with the general ethical development;
the idea of self-culture and self-denial became more important; the general tendency, especially among the nobler
minds, was to exalt and make prominent the element of ethical spirituality. With all these modifications, however, the
original, central idea remained unchanged, — the righteous
nation was to be delivered from enemies and ushered into
an era of prosperity. A brief review of the portraiture of
the national future, beginning with the pre-prophetic period
and coming down through the prophets and the apocalyptic
books into the Jewish and the Christian literature of the first
century, will exhibit both the local coloring of the thought
and the growth of the ethical element.

1. We find no outlook into the future before the eighth
century. Up to that time the nation was engaged in the
ordinary struggle for existence; its thought centred on the
present. It had not come to political or moral self-consciousness. Gideon, Jephtha, Samuel, David, and Solomon
represent only the ordinary national ambition. There was
a certain religious unity (as in all ancient and modern nations), and there was a certain general hope in God, vague,
non-ethical, not yet advanced to the rank of an article of
the national faith. As far as we can judge from the docu-

ments, no prophetic voice had, as late as the tenth century, announced a definite relation between righteousness and prosperity.[1] Time naturally brought about a change in the nation's inner life; political complications and reverses forced it to think of its future, and the development of the moral consciousness introduced an ethical element into its self-analysis. This progress had doubtless been going on in an unconscious way during the ninth century (Elijah and Elisha); but it did not take shape until the eighth century, when the Syrian and Assyrian powers began to be oppressive, and in the Northern kingdom the shadow of the final catastrophe became visible to the more keen-sighted of the religious statesmen. The suffering of the nation, said the prophets, was a chastisement from God for the national sin; but there should follow political and moral regeneration, the maintenance of the existing form of government with the triumph of the religion of Israel.

2. The pre-exilian prophets looked to the defeat or subjugation of surrounding nations, including the Assyrians, and the perpetuity of the Davidic dynasty. For their sins, said Amos (c. B C. 770), Israel should be carried into captivity beyond Damascus, the land should tremble, the people should be sifted among all the nations, yet not the least grain should fall to the earth, the sinners of the nation should die by the sword[2] (Am v. 27; vi. 14; viii. 8; ix. 9). Hosea (c. B. C. 750–730) describes the long-suffering, faithful love of Yahwe: he would betroth the nation to himself in

[1] The books of Samuel and Kings are in many passages, notably in the portraitures of Samuel, David, and Solomon, colored by Deuteronomic ideas; examples are 1 Sam. xv., 2 Sam. xii, 1 K. viii.

[2] The genuineness of the references in Amos and Hosea to the establishment of the Davidic dynasty may be doubted. Amos ix. 11–15 appears to be colored by experience of captivity, and in Hos. iii 5 the words "David their king" seem out of place, since the prophet is there concerned with Israel alone.

righteousness and faithfulness; the earth should yield its increase. Israel, after abiding many days without political and religious organization, should seek Yahwe, their God; strange gods should be put away; the divine anger should be turned into love; the beauty of Israel should be as the olive-tree, and his fragrance as Lebanon (Hos. ii., iii., xiv. 1–7). A deeper and sadder conception of the national life appears in Isaiah (B. C. 740–700), who lived in the midst of the Assyrian invasions and the fall of the Northern kingdom: the gross conscience of the people should not respond to his appeal; the land should be wasted, but a remnant should be left, sacred to the God of Israel, governed in righteousness by a Davidic king, when the Assyrian should have been driven away (vi. 9–13; x. 20, 24–27). Here we have merely an ethical-religious organization of the nation, on the old political lines, but with a thorough-going demand for righteousness. Isaiah's younger contemporary, Micah, has left us no word of hope, but only a prediction of punishment (i.–iii.).[1] Nahum (c. B. C. 634) utters only an exulting cry over the approaching fall of Nineveh; the destruction of the great world-empire of Assyria was doubtless then a part of the national hope. Zephaniah, somewhat later, sees in the coming "day of Yahwe" not only the desolation of Nineveh, but also the chastisement of Jerusalem (i. ii.).[2] In Habakkuk (c. B. C. 605), who looked to the punishment of the Chaldeans, there is the larger expectation (Hab ii. 14) that the whole earth shall be forced to recognize the glory which belongs to the God of Israel by virtue both of his moral perfection and of the power which he manifests in

---

[1] The remainder of the book of Micah (perhaps intended to supplement the prophet's meagre utterances) is later than the eighth century, and will be referred to below. Chapt. vi. may belong to the seventh century, but contains no outlook into the future

[2] Chapt. iii. differs in tone from the preceding, appearing to have in view a different condition of things; its similarity to Mic. iv. 6–13 is obvious.

the deliverance and maintenance of his people. Jeremiah's attitude toward the Chaldeans is different from that of Habakkuk; he is decidedly friendly to Nebuchadnezzar,[1] whom he regards as God's instrument for chastising recreant Israel. The nation shall go into captivity for its sins, but shall be restored to its own land and live prosperously under the righteous rule of its own princes, with the maintenance of the complete national organization (Jer. xxv. 8–11; xxx.; xxxi. 1–30); and God, says some prophet of this time, will make a new covenant with his people, writing his law in their hearts, forgiving their sins, and establishing them in moral purity (Jer. xxxi. 31–34).[2] Ezekiel, who was in Babylonia, and showed no less kindly feeling toward Nebuchadnezzar and his people than Jeremiah, looks likewise to a political restoration in Canaan, a new spirit of hearty obedience, a resuscitation and moral regeneration of the people, the final victory to be preceded by a combined attack of certain Northern peoples on Israel; and he gives in the form of a vision a complete political-religious constitution for the restored nation (Ezek. xxxvi.–xlviii.). The expectation of the exilian Isaiah is substantially the same, only he idealizes Israel into a divinely appointed instrument for the enlightenment of all the nations. The restoration to Canaan was to be marked by a regeneration of all things, the creation of new heavens and a new earth wherein Jerusalem was to be the centre of strength and hope and joy, and Israel should remain forever holy and blessed in the sight of God (Isa. lx.–lxvi., especially lxv. 17–25, lxvi. 19–24). Here probably

---

[1] The prophet's friendliness toward the Chaldean king is so marked and persistent that passages ascribed to him which breathe a different tone (such as xxv. 12, l., li.) may be set down as coming from another hand.

[2] It seems doubtful whether xxxi. 31–40 belongs to Jeremiah; or rather, the style and the attitude toward the ritual make it probable that the passage is from another hand; but it in any case belongs to the period of Deuteronomy, Jeremiah, and Ezekiel, and illustrates the thought of the time.

belongs Mic. vii., where the prophet looks to deliverance from exile and foreign oppression, and the exaltation of the nation, basing his hope on the incomparable pardoning mercy of Yahwe. To the exilian or a somewhat later period we may also perhaps refer Deut. xxviii–xxx., 1 Kings viii, passages in which the perpetuity of the national life is anticipated, but conditioned on obedience to the divine law.

3. The exile exalted the hopes of those Israelites who cherished most ardently the national feeling. After this terrible blow, the God of Israel, they felt sure, would raise his people to an unexampled height of happiness, of which the elements were political independence and prosperity, fidelity to the worship of Yahwe, and moral uprightness of life. Whatever was necessary to secure these ends, that they believed God would do. When Cyrus, in accordance with his general policy of restoring the exiled peoples in Babylonia to their homes, gave the Jews permission to return to Canaan, a portion of the Israelitish colony gave themselves up to the most unbounded joy and expectation,[1] the expression of which is found in the exilian Isaiah. This was the culmination of the prophetic hope, which on the political side was never fulfilled, though it was a true instinct which foresaw the triumph of Israelitish religious thought.[2] The little band of patriots, about forty thousand in all,[3] returned to Canaan and found little or nothing that the

---

[1] It is not a matter of course that all the real patriots returned to Palestine. Opinions probably differed as to the wisest policy; and it is certain that at a later period a very decided national feeling showed itself among the Jews who remained in Babylonia.

[2] It was about the same time (second half of the sixth century B. C.) that the foundations were laid in India, Greece, and Rome for three other great movements of human progress.

[3] The number given in Neh. vii. 66 (42,360) is described as that of the "men" (verse 7), according to which the whole population would have been about 200,000; but the number of servants of both sexes (7,337) and of asses

great exilian prophet had predicted. Steady toil was necessary to gain their daily bread, and it was with great difficulty that they found means to rebuild the temple. It
was to this last end that the prophets Haggai and Zechariah (Zech. i.–viii.) devoted themselves; yet they also, in all
the pressure of the time, cast a glance into the future.
Zechariah predicted a righteous, political success, and Haggai the exaltation of the temple; the desirable things of all
nations should come and fill the new house with glory (Zech.
viii. 1–15; Hag. ii. 6–9). Half a century passed; Palestine
was a Persian province, and there was no prospect of political independence. The ritual-religious organization had been
steadily growing, and the hope of the best men lay in obedience to the Law. The prophet Malachi (c. B. C. 460) predicted the appearance of a messenger of God, who should
purify the Levites, separate the evil element of the nation
from the good, and unite the hearts of the people in the fear
of Yahwe; after him should come the great and terrible day
of Yahwe, the divine intervention which was to strike dis-
may into the souls of the evil-doers, and establish Israel in
ethical and Levitical uprightness (Mal. iii. iv.).

Other ideas, however, than the predominantly legal-ritual
existed in the fifth century, if we may here place the prophetic sections, Isa. ii. 2–4 (nearly the same in Mic. iv. 1–5),
xix. The first of these stands out of connection in its present position, and has a quiet tone wholly different from the
vigorous, intense polemic of Isaiah. It has a more defined
conception of law than Isa. lxi. (which it in other respects
strongly resembles), and less ritualism than Zech. xiv. It
is a definite anticipation of the universal acceptance of the
worship of Yahwe, the accompaniment of which shall be

(6,720) suggests not more than 8,000 families, or a total population of 40,000,
and this number agrees with the feeble condition of the colony as described
in Ezra and Nehemiah.

the prevalence of universal peace. It is the vision of the
ethical-religious triumph of Israel, the national life and independence being assumed, but not emphasized.[1] There is a
similar universality of hope in Isa. xix. 18–25,[2] set forth
under the form of the anticipated religious unity of Egypt,
Assyria, and Israel, all of whom Yahwe, it is said, will
regard with equal affection. Here is a cosmopolitan spirit
that reminds us of Ps. lxxxvii. It seems to have been born
of that ethical-religious largeness of view that came into
existence after the breaking up of the national life. It is
the older conviction of national permanence illuminated by
a distincter moral-religious ideal.

4. Prophecy was now dying out, giving place to the orderly
study of the Law as the national guide of conduct. More
than another century passed before a new prophetic word
was heard (or, to speak more precisely, no prophecy of this
intervening period has been preserved). Joel and the Second
Zechariah (Zech. ix.–xiv.) seem by their historical references
and the pronouncedly legal-ritual character of their religious
thought to belong to the Greek period. Their expectation is
the same as that of the earlier prophets. Joel sees the hostile nations assembled and judged, while Judah and Jerusalem abide in their own land forever, free from the presence
of strangers and secure in the protection of Yahwe (Joel ii.
28–iii. 21); Zechariah's picture includes victory over Greece
under the lead of a righteous king, the reconciliation of Jerusalem and the rural districts (which had been at variance),
the overthrow of hostile nations, and the complete triumph

---

[1] Verse 5 of the Micah-passage (with which compare Isa. ii. 5) introduces
a general national particularism which seems to be at variance with the uni
versality of verse 2, and may be an addition by another hand.

[2] Verse 18, with the reading "the city of the sun," was cited by Jews in
support of the proposal of Onias to build his temple in the Heliopolitan
nome; and some modern critics have hence been inclined to refer this passage to that period, but the absence of a distinct reference to a temple seems
to make this view improbable

of the religion of Yahwe, so that all the families of the earth should go up to Jerusalem to worship (Zech. ix. 9–17; xii.–xiv.). Zechariah's ritualistic conception of holiness (xiv. 20, 21) marks one line of the progress of the national thought: the perfection of the people is held to be inseparably connected with the strict maintenance of the temple-service. A somewhat similar view of the future is given in the little detached section, Isa. iv. 2–6.

The occasional mention of a king who is to be Yahwe's instrument for the final establishment of the nation does not add to or modify the essential elements of the prophetic thought. The king is an all but necessary part of the body politic, — the natural head of the nation and leader of its fortunes. His presence at the final catastrophe, when the great divine blessing is to come, is assumed, but not spoken of in the pre-exilian prophecies;[1] it is the nation, as the chosen of Yahwe, that is the object of interest. This may be called specially the period of national solidarity. We have already seen that an era of more defined individualism and institutionalism began just before the exile, and the blow which destroyed for the time being the political and ritual organization aroused a keener interest in the offices by which it was represented. Thus Ezekiel, when the fate of Jerusalem was decided, cheered his people with the promise of the perpetuity of the Davidic dynasty (xxxiv. 23, 24; xxxvii. 24, 25) as well as of the Levitical priesthood (xliv.

---

[1] As pre-exilian may be regarded Amos (except the last section), Hosea (omitting a few verses), Isa. i., ii. 6–22, iii., iv. 1, v.–x. (except ix. 6, 7, and perhaps several of the preceding verses), xiv. 24–32, xv.–xviii., xx., xxii. 15–23, xxviii.–xxxi., xxxvii. 21–35, Mic. i.–iii., vi., Nahum, Zeph. i., ii., Habakkuk, Jeremiah (except x. 1–16, xxiii. 5–8, xxxiii. 14–26, l.–lii., and perhaps xlix.), Ezek. i.–xxxii. and part of xxxiii. (that is, the utterances of the prophet up to the time when news came of the fall of Jerusalem, though all his prophecies were given in the land of captivity). The omitted parts suggest an exilian or post-exilian origin by their style, historical references, or ritual tone.

15 ; xlviii. 11, 35). To the same effect are Jer. xxxiii. 14–26 (cf. xxiii. 5–8), where the Davidic prince is called a "right-eous scion,"[1] and 2 Sam. vii., where it is declared that the throne of David shall be established forever. A more par-ticular application of the term "scion" is made just after the exile by Zechariah (vi. 12), who gives this title to his contemporary the Davidic prince Zerubbabel, the builder of the temple, associating him in a sort of dual government with the priest Joshua. It seems to have been in the suc-ceeding period, when Palestine was merely a province of the Persian empire, that the longing for deliverance and na-tional organized and independent life was embodied in the portraiture of an ideal king. So long as the regular govern-ment existed, the king was taken for granted. The time of political dissolution recalled the glories of David and his suc-cessors. A people without a head thought of a royal leader as the natural saviour. Such appears to be the feeling that prompted the utterance of Mic. v. 2–6 (*Heb.* 1–5) : Jacob is scattered among the nations (vs. 7, 8), and the seer hopes for a military deliverer in the person of a scion of the ancient royal house of Bethlehem.[2] Elsewhere we find the ethical element predominating in the description of the king. The main function of the Davidic scion of Isa. xi. 1–9 is wise and just care for the interests of the "poor" and "meek" of the land. These are the epithets by which the book of Psalms everywhere designates the Israelites who, true to the law of their God, were oppressed by foreign potentates (Per-sian or Greek) or by apostate or unscrupulous countrymen. The seer embodies his idea of perfect national happiness

---

[1] The expression "scion" (or "sprout") is used in Isa. iv. 2, apparently of the nation, or rather of the righteous remnant as a branch of the original stock. The close relation between people and king makes it equally appli-cable to both.

[2] The Tigris-Euphrates region is here called by the old name "Assyria," as in the post-exilian Zech. x. 11.

in the statement that there shall be no hurtful power in the world, and he connects this blessed condition of things (apparently following Hab. ii. 14) with the universal recognition of the religion of Yahwe. We have here almost the germ of an apocalypse, and, as in the pre-exilian predictions, it is the welfare of the nation which the prophet has in mind; the prince exists for Israel. The author of Isa. xxxii. 1–8 describes the future ethically constituted Israelitish community, of which king and princes are only a natural incident. A fuller governmental description, like that in Isa. xi., is given in Isa. ix. 6, 7 (*Heb.* v. 6). The preceding verses speak of a great national affliction to be followed by a glorious victory like that of Gideon over Midian. The national saviour is a Davidic king, whose reign is to be characterized by justice and peace, and whose dynasty is to continue forever. On this glorious deliverer the seer bestows the most exalted epithets. He represents the presence and power of Yahwe in the midst of the nation (like the child Immanuel, "God is with us," of Isa. vii. 14), and, as Israel (Hos. xi. 1) and the king of Israel (2 Sam. vii. 14; Ps. ii. 7) are called "son of Yahwe," so he receives as surnames titles which express the divine presence. He is wonderful (or divinely mysterious), like the angel of Judg. xiii. 18, wise in counsel, like the king in Isa. xi. 2, a hero, like the king in Ps. xlv. 3 (*Heb.* 4), everlasting father or head of a perpetual dynasty, prince of peace.[1] Finally, we have a

---

1 The expression *el gibbor*, commonly rendered "mighty God," is difficult; it occurs naturally of Yahwe in Isa. x. 21, but seems inapplicable to a man. Some attach *el* to the preceding word, and render "counsellor of God," which is possible, but not natural; and there is the same objection to "counsellor of the mighty God." *Gibbor* would then stand separate in the sense of "hero," as in Ps. xlv. 3 (4). Some take *el* as adjective, meaning "mighty;" but we should then expect the reverse order, *gibbor el*. No satisfactory emendation of the text has been suggested. The word *el* can be employed of men, according to Old Testament usage, only in the sense of "mighty." The text may originally have expressed some relation of the king to the "mighty God."

simple picture of a peaceful monarch in Zech. ix. 9 ; but it appears from verse 13 that peace is to be gained by a victory over Greece. In this prophetic anticipation (the latest of those that deal with the re-establishment of the kingly government) the hope is the same as in the others, — national prosperity, secured by divine aid and conditioned on obedience to divine law.

This prophetic-patriotic hope, ennobled by the demand for righteousness, may be traced far down in the succeeding literature : in Ecclesiasticus (xxxvi. 1–17; xxxvii. 25; xlvii. 11; l. 23, 24), Wisdom of Solomon (iii. 8 ; v. 1), Baruch (ii. 27–35 ; iv. 36 ; v. 5–9), Tobit (xiii. 12–18 ; xiv. 7), 1 Maccabees (ii. 57), 2 Maccabees (ii. 18 ; xiv. 15), Psalms of Solomon. In the prophetic scheme of the future the only definite trait is the establishment of the nation in peace and prosperity in its own land. The hope is distinctively national ; Israel is the centre, the sole object of the divine care. Other nations are subordinated to the chosen people, and their future is variously described, according to the point of view and feeling of the writer. In the earlier prophecies those who are hostile are to be destroyed or severely punished ; at a later time (especially in the Second Isaiah and the Second Zechariah), they are represented as attaching themselves to the religion of Israel. Their happiness is conditioned on their submission ; they are always aliens, and such blessings as they receive come through the intermediation of Israel. The object of God's intervention is his own glory and the exaltation of his own people. But along with this particularistic national feeling there is the moral earnestness which demanded righteousness as a necessary element of the national good. If this righteousness was in part ceremonial and dogmatic, it also included ethical perfectness according to the best standards of the time ; and this redeems the prophetic hope from the imputation of mere national narrowness; this lifted the national consciousness up to a noble ideal, and gave it universal significance for men. The prophets did not attempt to fix the details of the great deliverance; theirs was a free, spontaneous, national feeling. They speak from time to time of some individual deliverer; but it is an ideal king, vaguely expected in the near future. No one actual personage stands out with controlling prominence. Their picture concerns this world only. The judgment of God is temporal; the doctrine of immortality had not been established in the national consciousness.

5. The Greek oppression (beginning about 200 B. C.) introduced important changes, political and religious. The national sense of suffering became distincter than ever before. The iron entered into the soul of the people; the hand of the stranger weighed heavily on their most sacred rights and sentiments. The fulfilment of the divine promises seemed long delayed; an intense desire of deliverance took possession of the Jews. From the time that they had fallen under Greek control they had been learning more of the history of the world, and had gained the idea of the succession of empires. Their thought had passed beyond this life; in place of the old Semitic conception of Sheol, the gloomy abode of life-in-death, had come the hope of immortality. Scribes and lawyers began to devote themselves to a study of the sacred books, to formulate their doctrines, to search them for indications of the future. Out of all this material grew up a new literature, different in tone from the old prophetic writing, called forth by the needs of the times and expressing the current feeling; the prophet was replaced by the apocalyptic seer.

The first apocalyptic work produced by the Maccabean struggle was the book of Daniel, the only book of this class which gained entrance into the Canon. It was composed in the midst of the stirring career of Judas Maccabæus.

Antiochus Epiphanes, the mighty successor of Alexander
the Great, and the representative to the Jews of the Greek
world-kingdom, had attempted to crush the religious liber-
ties of the people. The little band of the faithful, led by
the heroic Judas, had withstood his efforts, defeated his
armies, and captured and cleansed Jerusalem and the temple. It seemed to some pious souls that this was God's
time for final intervention for his people. Our author, in
the form of visions ascribed to the seer Daniel, supposed
to be living in Babylon during the whole of the captivity,
describes the fortunes of four empires, — Babylon, Media,
Persia, and Greece. That this is the ground over which he
goes is evident from the fact that his four visions, chapters
vii. (with which that of Nebuchadnezzar in chapter ii. is
identical), viii, ix., and xi., xii., give the same history, and the
terminus ad quem is stated in chapter viii. to be the reign
of one of the successors of Alexander, who can be no other
than Antiochus. The picture of the future is of the most
general character; it includes only the triumph of Israel
and the establishment of God's everlasting kingdom. The
personage described in vii. 13 as "like a son of man" is
explained in verse 27 to represent the Jewish people, or
more particularly the pious kernel of the nation, the saints
of the Most High. The final victory is to be preceded by
a time of great tribulation (cf. Ezek. xxxviii., xxxix.); the
angel Michael will be the patron of the people; many of
the dead will arise, some to honor and some to shame; the
wise shall shine as the brightness of the firmament, and
they that turn many to righteousness as the stars for ever
and ever (xii. 1–4). The future of the nation is thus connected with the doctrine of the resurrection which the Jews
had recently adopted. The resurrection would be confined
to Israelites, but should be a blessing only for the righteous;
that is, those who remained faithful to the national religion.

The apostates should be overwhelmed with contempt. The abode of the new congregation was to be on the earth, but under what local conditions is not said; it was sufficient that there should be victory and happiness. It does not appear whether the writer supposed that all other nations were to be set aside, so that the earth should be the possession of the Jews alone; into details on this point he does not enter. There is a judgment (vii.) which overthrows all enemies, and gives the kingdom to the saints;[1] but the picture is vague. We do not know the precise nature of the resulting world-society. The ethical element in the life of the restored nation is the same as in the prophets. No earthly leader is named; there is no Messiah; the regenerating influence is in the body of the pious. One would expect reference to Judas; the book was perhaps written by one of the Hasidim or saints who regarded themselves as the true life of the national struggle (between 167 and 164 B. C.). The writer expects the consummation in a short while (xii. 11–13). He is explicit and detailed in his statements up to near the death of Antiochus, after which he becomes general and vague (xii. 9). The book is therefore simply the expression of the hope that God was about to endow his people with the happiness promised in the prophets.

Two things are especially noticeable in this picture of national reconstruction. One is the character and function of the body of the righteous who are to constitute the new national life. It is the idea of a remnant which is found in Isa. vii.–x., but with a more definite and prominent statement of its ethical perfectness; the righteous are wholly righteous, altogether approved by God. They suffer; but there is no explanation of their suffering. It is not puri-

---

[1] Here apparently (vii. 27; ii. 44) is the germ of the expression "kingdom of heaven," or "kingdom of God," which afterwards came to be the name of the Messianic era.

fying, as in Isa. xl., or vicarious, as in Isa. liii.; it is accepted as a fact without inquiry. The writer's eye is fixed simply on the coming reward, and his conception of righteousness is the legal-ritual one which had grown up since the fifth century. The second point is the author's indifference to the political idea. Of course he says nothing of civil liberty; this was a question into which the Jews never entered. It was left to Greece and Rome to develop this side of social life; Israel dealt with religion only. Nor does the author think of the form of government any more than did prophets, psalmists, and apostles. The one thing for the nation, in his view, was national independence and exaltation over other peoples, which should carry with it the supremacy of the national law. For the welfare of other nations he is not concerned; his is that intense devotion to one idea that was so important an element in the success of the Jews.

It is a little later that we must put the prediction in the Sibylline Oracles (iii. 652–794), in which substantially the same picture is given as in Daniel : foreign kings attack the land and the temple ; they are judged and crushed; there are signs in heaven ; terror prevails over the whole earth ; the people, delivered from enemies, dwell in peace ; other nations adopt the worship of the God of Israel ; the world shares the blessings of the chosen nation ; there is to be universal freedom from suffering ; Greece is exhorted to pray submissively to God, who was about to establish an everlasting kingdom of peace. The allusion is most probably to the Maccabean struggle ; but the Sibyl differs from Daniel in looking for a king who should rule in the fear and by the help of God,—a trait taken from the prophets, and especially suggested, perhaps, by the existing Maccabean rulers and the writer's familiarity with Greek kingdoms. The king has no supernatural endowments : he is simply one of the people. He is not the Messiah in the later significance of the word. There is the same ignoring of the political problem proper as in Daniel, but more recognition of the personality of foreign peoples, that is to say, of the one alien people with which the writer was in contact, — a difference that came from the more cosmopolitan spirit of the Egyptian Jewish colony. As to the hope of an independent Jewish state, this was made possible and was doubtless suggested by the innumerable strifes between the various Greek kingdoms of Asia and Africa. The Maccabean movement had succeeded, and might sustain itself. Jewish enthusiasm has always ignored seemingly insuperable difficulties. It is nevertheless remarkable, when from our point of view we survey the historical situation, to find this political vitality in a tiny fragment of the Græco-Roman world, while at the same time the scribes were building up a compact and powerful ethical-religious organization.

A further step in the elaboration of the picture of the future is taken in Enoch xc. 16–38, a passage which belongs to the same general period as the one above cited. The author gives a review, couched in symbolical language, of the history of Israel, and comes finally to the time when the people were devoured by the Greeks. He describes the rise of the Hasidim, and the appearance of a great, victorious leader, who is probably Judas Maccabæus (but held by some to be John Hyrcanus the First; the difference in time is not important for the idea). Then comes the final general attack of the enemies of Israel, their overthrow by God, the judgment of the angels and of the unfaithful Israelites, and the establishment of the new Jerusalem grander and more beautiful than the old. Then the Messiah appears, one of the people, not a supernatural personage, yet wielding authority over all the nations. The advance in the thought is the greater prominence given to the person of the Messiah, who, however, is not the author of the deliverance (that is effected by God), but comes forward after its completion. The ethical element is the same as in the Sibyl, but the greater prominence is given to the political deliverance. It seemed to the writer that the old glories of the Davidic kingdom might now be renewed, and other nations might share the blessing by submitting to Israel.

In addition to this purely national expectation, Enoch has the representation of a general judgment (i.; xxii. 11; lxxxiv. 4), the result of which shall be the destruction of evil and the constitution of the just into a blessed congregation for the worship of the one only God. In the chapter quoted above, also (xc., there is a judgment of evil angels and renegade Jews (20–27), while the heathen oppressors are converted to the worship of the God of Israel (33). Whether these two judgments are identical is not clear; the first seems to be held on Sinai (i. 4), the second in Palestine (xc. 20). Nor is anything said in the second account of judgment of a punishment to be inflicted on human enemies.[1] There is the same vagueness here as in Daniel. But the general result, according to both books, seems to be that at a certain moment God intervenes, destroys all opposition to his people, and establishes them (restoring the dead to life) in security in Palestine, making Jerusalem (a new Jerusalem, according to Enoch) the centre of religious worship for the world. It was a wave of Messianic feeling produced by the apparently brilliant outcome of the Hasmonean uprising.

---

[1] We have here probably nothing more than a repetition of the prophetic pictures. Isa. lx. represents kings as coming to pay homage to the glorified Israel; of a judgment on them nothing is said. Other prophets, as Joel (followed by Daniel and the Sibyl), think of a sentence of condemnation and destruction passed on alien nations. The details of the future were differently construed by different seers; the main thing was the triumph of Israel.

The hopes excited by the first Maccabean successes gradually vanished amid the experiences of a petty kingdom. So long as the Hasmonean dynasty retained its position, the dream of independence might seem to be realized, and Sadducees and Pharisees were content to struggle with each other for the control of affairs. For nearly a century the Jews were absorbed in internal and external political and religious dissensions, and we hear nothing of apocalyptic visions. With the approach of the Romans under Pompey the cry for deliverance made itself heard again. In the Psalter of Solomon (c. B. C. 48) we find the prayer that God would raise up Israel's king, the son of David, Christ, Lord, to destroy his people's enemies, to reign over all the earth, to make Jerusalem the centre of worship for the whole world (Ps. xvii.). Here for the first time the deliverer is called the Anointed, the Messiah, the Christ. It is the old prophetic hope without apocalyptic details.

A passage in the Sibylline Oracles (iii. 36–62), which appears to belong to the time of the Second Triumvirate (B. C. 43 or 42), announces the speedy establishment of the kingdom of God. A much more developed view is given in the Parables of the book of Enoch (xxxvii.–lxxi.), especially in the second Parable (xlv.–lvii., omitting the Noachic interpolation, liv. 7–lv. 2), which, from the mention of the Parthians (lvi. 5), probably a reference to the Parthian invasion of Palestine, may be put near the year B. C. 40. Here the general judgment is committed by the Lord of the spirits, the Head of days (Dan. vii. 9), to the Messiah, who is called, after Daniel, the Son of Man, but is more commonly styled the Chosen One. The judgment is directed against the kings and other potentates who oppressed Israel, herein following the prophets, and differing from the earlier part of Enoch. The situation had changed during the past century. Israel triumphant and hopeful might be magnan-

imous; crushed and weary, it would naturally be severe.
There is to be a general resurrection. Glory and honor
are to accrue to the holy and just (that is, faithful Israelites), and they are to dwell on the renovated earth. The
most striking point in the description is the apparent ascription of pre-existence to the Messiah. His name was called,
it is said, and he was chosen and hidden before the world
was made; and he will continue to exist forever. It is not
clear, however, whether this pre-existence was real or ideal.
The idea of prenatal calling is not foreign to the Old Testament: the prophet Jeremiah was set apart to his work before he was born (Jer. i. 5, and cf. Isa. xlix. 5); and we may
have here the conception of the later Jewish theology, that
the Messiah existed indeed from eternity in the divine purpose, but came into real being only when he was manifested
to the world.[1] With this view would accord the statement
of the Parable (xlviii. 7), that the wisdom of God revealed
the Messiah [in the day of judgment or divine intervention]
to the holy and just, in order that their portion might be
preserved. The epithet "chosen" may have been suggested
by such a passage as Isa. xlii. 1 (as the whole of the section
xlii. 1–17 seems to have furnished material for later Messianic systems), and represents in general an idea familiar
to the Jews. The conception of pre-existence, thus stated
ideally, prepared the way for the more definite view of Paul
and the Fourth Gospel.[2] In other regards the Messianic
scheme of the Parables agrees substantially with that of the
earlier books. Nothing is said of atonement. There is no

---

[1] For the Targumic and Talmudic references see Weber, "System,"
§§ 78, 79.

[2] For the discussion of the question whether this part of the Parables is
of Christian origin see Drummond, Scholdde, Schürer. On page 65 I say
that the rôle assigned the Messiah seems to point to a Christian source;
but further consideration has led me to change my opinion on this point. A
Christian writer would probably have made his statements more definite.

feeling of international comity. The kingdom of God is understood in a purely national way; and while the whole view of the future involves the ordinary ethical elements, the Messiah is in himself not specifically an ethical power.

The remaining literature of the pre-Christian period presents no new elements of the Messianic hope. The Assumption of Moses (x.), written about the beginning of our era, represents the kingdom of God as about to be established, heralded by signs in the heavens and on the earth, and Israel victorious and honored. The Book of Jubilees, half a century later, has only a very general picture of deliverance (i.). A little earlier, Philo in two passages already cited (ii. 435, 421–428) describes the political and moral redemption of the people under the leadership of an eminent man who cannot be the logos, but may be the Messiah. Philo apparently knew nothing of Jesus, whose contemporary he was, and he has very little to say of the fortunes of his people; yet it appears that to him also, immersed as he was in philosophical speculation, the idea of national deliverance was not wanting.

In estimating the elements of the national hope, we must, however, not lose sight of the moral progress which is to be traced in the non-apocalyptic writings,— in the Wisdom-books, and the teachings of the schools. The apocalypses undertook to define the religious-political future with more or less distinctness; and though their specific predictions were set aside from time to time by the march of events, their general expectation of national deliverance was doubtless shared by the body of the people. Antiochus Epiphanes died; the Hasmonean princes ruled; but there was no realization of the dream of a world-kingdom. Judea remained a petty province, felt the weight of the Roman power, and passed into the hands of an Idumean king. The people continued to hope against hope. Meantime the intellectual-religious life went on, the moral consciousness of the nation gathered force, and formed part of the national hope. The dream of political independence was never abandoned, but it could not be divorced from that moral ideal which had arisen out of all the experiences of the past centuries.

To sum up the Messianic material in pre-Christian literature: the fundamental element is the destruction or coercion of Israel's enemies, and the establishment of the people in Palestine in political independence and prosperity, sometimes by the immediate act of God, sometimes by means of a king or other leader, a man sprung from the people, but raised up by God and endowed with all the qualities necessary to secure success; at the same time the worship of the God of Israel receives universal recognition, and Jerusalem becomes the religious centre of the regenerated world, the new heavens and earth.

The condition of membership in the new community is twofold: national and religious. It is, first of all, Israelites who are entitled to the blessing, but only faithful Israelites. The stress is laid on devotion to the national faith; general obedience to the laws of morality is assumed, but not emphasized. Others than Israelites may become sharers in the advantages of the new dispensation by accepting the national Jewish religion. To these the same sort of moral test is applied as to Jews.[1] If, however, they do not sub-

---

[1] Proselytism was an anticipation of this procedure. It seems to have begun in the latter half of the first century B. C. (John Hyrcanus's forcible conversion of the Idumeans was a purely political measure, but may be regarded as the indication of a tendency). Judaism was one of several Africo-Asiatic religions that then attracted the Græco-Roman world. Though it repelled by its local and oppressive ritual, it attracted by its moral-religious purity and strenuousness, and by the hopes it held out for the future. Judaism thus took one step toward denationalizing itself. Hillel (and probably one section of the Egyptian Jews) was very liberal in the construction of the terms of admission. Under favorable circumstances, it seemed, Judaism might throw off its local character and become a world-religion; and this it actually did become in the form of Christianity.

mit they are to be punished.[1] As to whether they will submit or prove obstinate, this is variously decided; and the question is complicated by the introduction of the conception of a judgment and a future life. This judgment, represented sometimes as held by God, sometimes as held by the Messiah, ushers in the Messianic era, and the chosen people dwell on the earth. But the conception of the future life was in process of formulation, and the mode in which the heathen are to be dealt with is not stated precisely. In one point, however, all shades of opinion agree: there is to be endless triumph for the people of Israel and their religion.

In the New Testament we find mention of several points in the popular belief, which do not appear in the Jewish literature, such as that the Messiah was to be born in Bethlehem (Matt. ii.); that when he appeared no one would know whence he came; that he would work miracles; that he would be preceded by Elijah or Jeremiah or some unnamed prophet (Matt. xi. 3, 10, 11; xvi. 13, 14; xvii. 10, 11; John vii. 27, 31, 40–42). It is evident, from Dan. ix. as well as from the New Testament, that the pious and the scribes had for some time been searching the sacred books for predictions of the great deliverance. As soon as the idea of an individual Messiah was established, ardent men would see a reference to him, a description of his person or of the circumstances of his coming, in many a passage of the Scripture. Doubtless many such Messianic allusions were current among the people that do not appear in the New Testament.[2] That Bethlehem was to be the birthplace

---

[1] The same thing in Islam. Mohammedan preachers still continue, in the Friday mosque-service, to invoke the divine vengeance on the unbelieving oppressor.

[2] The Talmud contains all this material and much more of similar character, part of which probably goes back to the first century of our era. See Weber's "System," Edersheim's "Life and Times of Jesus the Messiah,"

of the deliverer was inferred from Mic. v. 2 (1); that his
appearance was to be mysterious, perhaps from Mal. iii. 1;
his power of working miracles might be suggested by such
passages as Isa. xxxv. 5, or might be regarded as a necessary accompaniment of his exalted mission, since the prophets Elijah and Elisha and others were endowed with this
power; Mal. iv. 5 (iii. 23) seems to say that Elijah would
be the forerunner of the grand catastrophe; the great rôle
assigned to Jeremiah appears from 2 Mac. ii. 1–8,[1] xv. 13–
15; and the important parts played by him and other prophets (as Isaiah) in the old history may explain the position
given them in the current Messianic theories.[2] It appears
also from the Gospels that the Messianic hope was generally diffused among the people and excited lively interest. The same thing may be inferred from the local political revolts which took place from time to time during the
first century of our era. There must have been an under-
current of deep Messianic feeling in Palestine. The social-
religious life went for the most part quietly on. The people
bought and sold, the scribes worked out the minutiæ of
the law, the priests officiated in the temple ; but under
this outward acceptance of the Roman rule there was in

Drummond's "Jewish Messiah," Duschak's "Biblisch-talmudische Glaubenslehre"

[1] The author refers vaguely to earlier material for the source of his legend
of Jeremiah, a story which, thus accidentally preserved, suggests that there
were others of the same sort which have been lost.

[2] Neither in the pre-Christian Jewish literature nor in the earlier Targums
is there any trace of a suffering Messiah. The idea of a non-expiatory suffering, which appears in the Talmud, and is attributed to the Jews by Justin
Martyr (Trypho, lxviii. lxxxix.), may have existed as early as the first century or earlier. The conception of an expiatory suffering of the Messiah,
which might naturally be suggested by Isa. liii., is found in later works, but
was foreign to the reigning Jewish thought, and has never taken hold of
Jewish feeling. On the other hand, that the righteous may turn away the
divine wrath from their friends and from the nation is an idea familiar to
the Old Testament as well as to the Talmud. Weber, "System," chs. xx.
xxii., Schürer, "Geschichte," pp. 464 ff.

the first century, as there had often been before, an eager hope, a latent expectation that God was about to interpose, that the man would soon appear who should lead Israel to glory.

6. But there was more than this. The materials for tracing the history of Messianic thought during the fifty years preceding the birth of Jesus are scanty. We have a few psalms, a few somewhat vague verses in the Sibylline oracles, the Enoch-Parables, and some detached ethical-legal sayings of prominent lawyers. The country was in a state of unrest; the reign of Herod was marked by conflicts without and disorders within. Quiet was restored by the banishment of Archelaus, and the final incorporation of Palestine into the Roman Empire under a procurator; but it was only an external and partial quiet. The people were wearied and sore at heart. It was not a time for literary production; yet during this period the seeds of a great religious revolution were germinating. In the absence of specific historical information, we can only conjecture the causes which produced in the more serious minds a profounder view of the political-religious situation. One of these we may judge to be the recognition of the hopelessness of a struggle against the power of the Roman Empire. There had been for a long time in the higher circles of Jewish society a pronounced aversion to political revolt. The Sadducees were content with their position as aristocratic representatives of the old religious order, especially as they freely adopted the broader social ideas and habits of their cultivated neighbors; the Pharisees were absorbed in the elaboration of the Law on its ceremonial and ethical sides, holding this to be the real life of the nation, anxious mainly for the quiet necessary to do their legal work, willing to accept any government which left them in peace. One result of this recognition of the existing order

of things we may suppose to have been an enfeebling of the desire for political sovereignty, and in so far a modification of the old Messianic scheme.

In addition to this, there was the recognition of the necessity of moral reform. It is likely that this feeling of the ethical shortcomings of the nation, handed down from the prophets, had never been entirely wanting. There was a time, indeed (as we see from such writings as Ps. xliv.), when there existed in certain circles a consciousness of national righteousness; but this was mainly the expression of Israel's devotion to the one true God and his law, in contrast with the idolatry and lawlessness of neighboring nations. No serious mind could fail to perceive the ethical defects of Jewish society. We need not suppose that these exceeded the bounds of ordinary human weakness. Then, as now, there was enough self-seeking, untruthfulness, hypocrisy, oppression, to call forth the severest condemnation of moral-religious teachers. Perhaps the disorders of the times intensified the feeling of ethical dissatisfaction. The assiduous study of the prophets forced on reflecting minds the conviction that an inward change was necessary before the people could receive the long-promised divine blessing. The first condition of God's aid, it might naturally be felt, was a moral-religious reform. One other step might have been taken. To a profounder spiritual soul it might seem that the essence of the divine salvation would be faithful obedience to the law of God. This was, indeed, the new covenant of Jeremiah and Ezekiel; and this was the characteristic of the ideal Israel, which, according to the exilian Isaiah, was to be the bearer of truth and light to the world. Such a view would not necessarily exclude (as in the prophets it did not exclude) the conception of a special divine interposition in the future; but it would transform the scheme of God's earthly kingdom from a political sovereignty to a society organized on moral-religious principles. Such thoughts as these may have floated, more or less vaguely, in the more serious and reflective minds in the century preceding the birth of John the Baptist. There are hints that such an ethical view of the situation, though doubtless feeble and indistinct, actually existed among the people. Of this nature was the expectation, derived from the conclusion of Malachi's prophecy, that Elijah, in the rôle of moral reformer, would precede the final interposition of God; and according to John iv. 25, there was a belief that the Messiah when he came would solve all religious problems. We may point also to the moral earnestness of Hillel's reported sayings, to the profound desire for personal purity which was embodied in the Essene organization, and in general to all those moral elements in the idea of the kingdom of God which are mentioned above.

If such a feeling existed in Palestine at that time, we cannot be surprised at the appearance of a man like John the Baptist. Of his antecedents we know nothing; he appears suddenly in Judea as a preacher of repentance and a herald of the approach of the kingdom of God. More than this he did not claim to be. He rebuked the sins of all classes of society (Mark i., Matt. iii., Luke iii.); he met his death by his denunciation of the immoral conduct of King Herod (Mark vi. 17–29). His silence is as significant as his utterance. In his reported words he says nothing of a political kingdom, he draws no detailed picture of the future; he confines himself to moral exhortation. For him the kingdom of God seems to be simply the purification of the national life. How far he shared the prevailing views respecting this kingdom it is perhaps impossible to say. The sober report of his preaching in the Synoptics may be due to a process of sifting by a later generation when Christian ideas prevailed. But it is still noteworthy that he by no word suggests other than a moral-religious rôle for the Messiah, and that no record connects him or his followers with any political movement.[1]

He was the last of the prophets. He had the thorough-going, uncompromising decision and fearlessness of Elijah, whom he seems to have taken as his model in dress and demeanor. Like Elijah, he worked only for present reformation within the bounds of the national religious organization. He hoped for a coming kingdom of God, but he did not cherish the brilliant anticipations of the writing prophets. He did not think of himself as the person destined to introduce the new dispensation of things. He felt that while he was a preacher of righteousness, a stronger arm than his was needed to establish the perfect divine society. He spoke of a successor, who should complete what he had begun, who should baptize[2] not with water but with the Holy Spirit.[3] Who this successor was to be he seems never to have known. After he was thrown into prison by Herod, he heard of the new teacher whose fame had spread throughout the land, and sent messengers to him to ask if it was he that should come, or whether they were still to expect some other. The tone of the question implies ignorance on John's part of the

---

[1] What Josephus says of him agrees substantially with the statements in the Gospels.

[2] Schneckenbürger and others hold that the baptism of John was a new ceremony, not borrowed from the Jews, and I took the same position in an article on proselyte-baptism in " The Baptist Quarterly " (1872); but it now seems to me that the facts favor the opposite view.

[3] The incident recorded in Acts xix. 1–7 seems to show that a theory of immediate divine influence did not exist among the disciples of John. If in verse 3 we are to translate, " We have not even heard whether there is a Holy Spirit," it must be concluded either that John said nothing about such a divine power, or, as is more probable, that these particular disciples had failed to receive the proper information. It seems unlikely, however, that any disciple of John could be ignorant of the existence of the Spirit of God, — a common Jewish idea of the time, — or without the hope of that outpouring which was promised by the prophets (Joel iii.). The alternative rendering, " whether the Holy Spirit is " (harsh, but not impossible), would imply only that these disciples did not know of the pouring out of the Spirit.

person and purpose of the young master, who had indeed been baptized by him, but had been undistinguished in the crowd.[1] For answer Jesus simply pointed to what he was doing (Matt. xi.). It is not said what conclusion John drew from this response. Jesus expressed his own opinion of John in a very decided manner. According to the First Gospel, he declared that John was more than a prophet; that no greater man than he had yet appeared in the history of Israel; and at a later period, when the Pharisees demanded the source of his authority, he replied by asking whether they looked on John's mission as deriving its authority from men or from God. They were unwilling to commit themselves to a definite answer, and he therefore declined to answer their question; but he evidently placed himself in the same category with John so far as the authority of his mission was concerned (Matt. xi. 7–19; xxi. 23–32).[2]

John died without having witnessed any great forward movement in the people. His disciples continued to exist in the form of a sect for a considerable time (Acts xix. 3), but apparently without exerting any considerable influence on the community. They had little to affect the popular imagination, or stir to action. We should suppose that they all would have taken Jesus for their teacher after the death of John; yet they not only retained their separate organization, but according to Matt. ix. 14, in certain customs, as fasting, they were nearer to the Pharisees than to the disciples of Jesus.[3] They seem to have represented little more than a somewhat dull moral reform. Perhaps they were also looking for a Messiah; but if so, their expectation was undefined, and stirred no great hopes among the people. John's

---

[1] The incident mentioned in Mark i. 10, 11, is an addition of the later tradition. If John had witnessed it, he would not have sent such a message.

[2] Cf. Maurice Vernes, " Histoire des Idées Messianiques," Paris, 1874.

[3] From this fact it may reasonably be inferred that John had said nothing of Jesus to his disciples, and was unacquainted with the ideas of his successor.

movement was completely swallowed up in that of Jesus, and left no traces, as far as we can perceive, in the development of the nation. It was a real response to the demand of the times, but not strong and deep enough to furnish all that was needed. It was the last attempt of the old prophetic thought to guide the religious life of the nation, and it proved a failure. The body of the nation continued its nomistic development, while the disciples of Jesus threw off the Law. The Johannites neither attained to any deep spirituality nor affected the growth of the nomism to which they continued to cling.

John may be called, in a peculiar sense, a Jewish product, the outcome of the national development. Of pure, unmixed nationalism, indeed, we cannot speak, for the Jewish thought of the time, as we have seen, was all colored more or less by foreign influences. But John seems to represent particularly a circle which held to the traditional moral-religious ideas. His was a sturdy, outspoken ethical system. He lashed the vices of the time; he denounced the leaders of orthodoxy as a brood of vipers. He had the moral insight of a true reformer, and he had further the power of genius or the skill to separate the local from the general in the prophetic teaching. He is even reported (Matt. iii. 9) as anticipating the Apostle Paul in discarding the national and hereditary claim to the divine favor, and looking, as it seems, in part, outside of Israel for the membership of the kingdom of God.[1] In so far his work was an attempt to convert Judaism into a universal religion. He lacked enthusiasm for humanity, tenderness of sympathy, breadth and depth of ethical principle. He seems to have aroused interest in all classes of

---

[1] The partial rejection of Israel is an old prophetic idea (Am. iii. 2 ; Isa x. 22), and a certain sort of incoming of Gentiles was early looked forward to (Isa. lx.). Whether the word ascribed to John is simply a repetition of this old prediction (cf. Mark xii. 9), only in a more definite way, or the reflection of a later time, it is difficult to say.

Jewish society (Matt. iii. 5–7), but he was overborne by the current of the times. He is a witness to a definitely Jewish demand for moral reform.

The desire for reform was, however, not confined to the Jews, but made itself felt throughout the Græco-Roman world. This is not the place to describe in detail the intellectual-moral condition of society in the Roman empire at the beginning of the first century of our era.[1] That a notable current of ethical feeling then existed in the western world appears from the writings of Cicero, Juvenal, Persius, Plutarch, Seneca, and others. These men not only attack the grosser moral evils of their time, but set up a high moral standard, and embody the striving after an ideal which they are conscious has not been reached by society. This deeper moral sentiment was practically the same all over the empire, expressed under different social and religious conditions and in different ways, yet looking everywhere to the one end of the purification and ennobling of life. Juvenal is a sort of Roman John the Baptist; Seneca has noteworthy points of ethical agreement with Paul. The Roman world was in an important sense a unit, — full of diversities, indeed, but informed by a great common body of moral feeling which was fed by streams from all the great civilized communities. The various ethical tendencies had sprung out of the social conditions of various independent nations, and had come to form one mass of opinion through the series of events which, beginning with the Assyrian, Babylonian, and Persian conquests, had finally, through Greece and Rome, impressed political and social unity on a huge congeries of communities. The essential oneness of human moral experience had shown itself in the ethical results achieved by

---

[1] It is described in the works of Baur, Schürer, and Hausrath, and in Döllinger's " Heidenthum und Judenthum " (Eng. transl. " The Gentile and the Jew ").

these various peoples, and one of these results was the establishment of a higher ideal. In order to discern clearly why a special ethical-religious movement should have set in just at this time, we should have to make a minute examination of the moral phenomena of the age, — an inquiry too large for our present purpose. But two great and generally recognized facts present themselves distinctly in the history of the period, and furnish a not unsatisfactory answer to our question. One of these is the wide and intimate intercourse between members of different peoples, which had helped to break down artificial barriers between men and promote the sense of human brotherhood; the other is the rupture which had taken place between the common-sense of the Græco-Roman world and the old mythologies, driving men back on fundamental principles of religion and morals. We must content ourselves here with the bare mention of these facts, without attempting to illustrate them by examples or trace them to their origin.

Reform, it may be said, was in the air. Reform is, indeed, a constant element of a healthy community; but there are special movements in special directions, as in this case. Different nations moreover, differ in methods and capacity of reform. Especially does the power of organization vary in different communities. The organized force of Greece expended itself in literature and philosophy, that of Rome in politics and law, that of Israel in religion. Greece specially affected ethics through philosophy, Rome through government. The Jews had organized religion, and their religion became constantly more ethical; Hillel surpassed Isaiah in distinctness of moral view. The conception of a society organized on the basis of ethical religion was peculiar to Jewish thought. The idea had been developed by prophets and lawyers continuously from Elijah and Amos to Hillel and John the Baptist. This was the advantage that Israel had over Greece and Rome at the beginning of our era: it was not that its ethical principles and life were essentially purer, but that its capacity for ethical-religious organization was greater. It was able to employ in the most effective way the universal motives of religion as an ethical lever. Having a simple and elevated religion, it could unite religion and ethics into a harmonious and powerful principle of life. John the Baptist endeavored to carry out the prophetic idea of reform under the conditions of his own time, but the result showed that he was not equal to the task he assumed. He definitely impressed neither his own people nor foreigners; at most he produced in Judea a moral excitement which prepared the way for his successor. A deeper conception of life and a stronger personality were needed to create a new starting-point for the religious-ethical forces of the world.

Jesus apparently began his career as a disciple of John. But while he was well acquainted with the Baptist's conception of the kingdom of God, he seems to have had no intimate personal intercourse with him. He began his own preaching after John's arrest; and it was in prison that John's attention was for the first time directed to the work of the new teacher. Jesus' idea of the divine kingdom was substantially the same as that of his predecessor. Both laid the chief stress on moral reformation within the Jewish nation; both contemplated the maintenance of the national organization and the perfecting of the nation into an instrument for the establishment of the kingdom. But if the two men started together, their paths soon diverged. The profounder spirituality of Jesus led to an independence of thought and teaching which overshadowed and obliterated the work of the older man. Jesus himself retained the deepest respect for John, though he came to regard his work as preparatory and temporary (Matt. xi. 7–19). The defects of

John's teaching will be apparent from the statement of the characteristics of the work of Jesus.

The movement which Jesus began was distinctly and predominatingly a moral-spiritual one. From all his utterances we may infer that he held the one need of the times to be ethical regeneration, and that he conceived this regeneration from a religious point of view as resting on a friendly relation of the soul with God. From the beginning to the end of his career, he insisted almost exclusively on sincere love of goodness with single-minded regard for the approbation of the heavenly Father. He exposed with a word the moral sophistries of the scribes; he made clear the distinction between the ethical and the ceremonial; he denounced hypocrisy and time-serving; he pointed out the weakness of imperfect moral principle, and he held up to view those fundamental principles which were capable of deciding all moral questions over against the perversions of custom and casuistry and the feebleness of the human heart. His ethical teaching may be regarded as summed up in the Sermon on the Mount; and the Sermon consists of ethical-religious thought pervaded by the sentiment of loyalty toward God, or rather of perfect trust in him and communion with him. If a man so live, says Jesus, he shall be cared for by the heavenly Father in this world and the next: "Seek ye first his kingdom and his righteousness; and all these things shall be added" (Matt. vi. 33). Jesus regarded the essence of the kingdom of heaven as consisting in the moral-spiritual life. He differed from John in the emphasis which he laid on the inner life, on complete oneness of spirit with God, out of which naturally flowed the outward manifestation of good works. This combination of the outward life with the inward spirit is ultimately the same with Paul's conjunction of faith and works, and with the conception in the Fourth Gospel of regeneration of soul whereby one enters into the kingdom of light. Only the idea of Jesus is simpler than the others. He speaks of no theological or other unusual revolution, but only of a new attitude of soul into which the man comes by his own decision.

We are not here concerned, however, with the details of Jesus' ethical-spiritual teaching. The point of interest is to note that it is the summing-up of all that we find in Old Testament and New Testament. The prophets had announced the moral basis of the true Israel, and the Epistles portray the high ethical life as the fundamental characteristic of the Church. In a few words Jesus has comprised all that is essential in moral principle, and held it up as the one necessary condition of perfected human society. Even where he does not offer direct solutions of social-moral questions which have arisen since his time, he furnishes the principles which contain the solution. His teaching stands apart from the political and ecclesiastical relations which we find elsewhere in the Bible. This last point, though hardly a fundamental one, may be exhibited a little more in detail.

We have already seen that the political element is prominent in all pictures of the kingdom of God in the Jewish literature from Daniel to the end of the first century of our era. The nation was conceived of as a political unit, and nothing but the maintenance of its political life was dreamed of. The Messiah, it was held, would rule over a nation happy in freedom and prosperity; and, according to one view, it was he who should hold the final judgment which was to settle the destiny of all things. It is a fair question whether or how far Jesus sympathized with this circle of ideas; and the records of his life, though not free from the coloring of later generations, seem to yield a probable answer. As a Jew and a man of his times we should expect him to share the Messianic opinions of his people, and there are indications that this he did in certain points.

But, on the other hand, it is evident from his words (taking only those that are commonly agreed to belong to him) and from the historical outcome of his work that he stood above his times in the sense that he recognized and organized the best elements of the world's current thought. If he did this in the sphere of pure morals and religion, it is quite possible that he avoided the grosser part of the Jewish national Messianic faith, and isolated and gave life to its essential spiritual core; and this is the conclusion to which several sets of facts seem to point. In the first place, as is remarked above, his teaching, according to the records, is predominatingly ethical-spiritual. The impression made on us is that it was this side of life that most deeply interested him. He is intensely concerned to stimulate men to moral-spiritual broadness and strenuousness. Such overweening interest in the higher aspects of the individual and the national life might be expected to carry with it indifference to the lower. This is, however, only a presumption, not a conclusive argument. It is conceivable that along with this exalted conception of human capacity and function he might have held to the current view of the national deliverance. But we have from him, further, some tolerably specific utterances on this point, especially in a series of sayings contained in Mark x. (and Matt. xix. xx.). These are, indeed, not entirely accordant one with another, and their precise meaning is not in all cases plain; but their general drift may be recognized. He declares that the kingdom of God must be received, not with warlike ardor, but with the docility of a little child. Wealthy adherents are usually welcomed by a political leader; but he simply says in an indifferent tone that it is very hard for a rich man to enter the kingdom of God. Exactly what is meant by the saying attributed to him, that those who had made sacrifices in his cause should be amply compensated with friends and worldly possessions, it is not easy to decide, especially as persecution is included in the list of things to be expected, and the "present time" is distinguished from the "coming age," in which everlasting life is to be the portion of the faithful; but, in any case, it seems to be not a political reward of which he is speaking. Finally, he declares that eminence among his followers is to be of a character wholly distinct from that of ordinary civil lordship, its condition being humility and service. It is true that there are other reported sayings of different import, particularly Matt. xix. 28, where it is promised that, when in the new order of things (the "palingenesis") the Son of Man should be enthroned as king,[1] the twelve disciples should exercise a quasi-regal judgeship over the twelve tribes of Israel. But this is so distinctly contradictory in spirit of that other saying, "To sit on my right hand and on my left is not mine to give" (Matt. xx. 23; Mark x. 40), that it may reasonably be regarded as a gloss or interpretation put into the mouth of Jesus by a writer who did not understand his words. Rewards in this life he may have promised; but they seem to be not the gifts of a worldly king, but the favors which (as in Matt. vi. 33, and in the Old Testament) God bestows on them that trust in him.

The public entry into Jerusalem, though apparently suggested by the word of the prophet Zechariah, "Thy king comes to thee," etc. (Zech. ix. 9), was obviously not meant by Jesus to have political significance. It was intended as an assertion of his Messianic office, and he followed it up by entering the temple and driving out the money-changers,

---

[1] The same phrase occurs in Enoch xlv. 3, in the description of the judgment which is to usher in the final period of blessedness. The expression was probably familiar to Jesus and his disciples as part of a current conception of the Messiah. The question is whether it is likely, from the testimony of the documents, that Jesus employed it of himself. To the generation that followed him such employment would seem perfectly natural.

a procedure in which he acted not as king but as prophet. It is quite possible that the people had another idea, and thought of him as a political leader (Mark xi. 8–10; xv. 1–20; cf. John vi. 15). But he gave no encouragement to such a scheme. To the very end he held aloof from the employment of physical force. When Judas came to seize him, one of Jesus' friends drew a sword and struck the slave of the high-priest; but this was his own act, and had no consequences.

It seems clear, also, that he was looked on by the authorities, both Roman and Jewish, as politically unimportant. It was a restless, excitable time. There had been several up-risings (Acts v. 36, 37), and the Romans would be ready enough to take note of signs of revolt; but Pilate, who was not slow to employ military force, treated Jesus as a harmless enthusiast, and with easy indifference ordered his execution as a convenient means of pleasing the multitude, with whom he was not in good odor. The Pharisees also appear to have feared him, not as a political Messiah, but as an enemy of the Mosaic law (which they believed to be essential to the true life of the nation) and of the order of things from which they derived their consideration. An attempt was made by the Pharisees and the Herodians to entrap him into an expression of disloyalty to the Roman government. We know, said they, that you are concerned only for God's truth. Is it lawful to pay tribute to the Roman government or not? It was the burning question of the time. Should the Jews acknowledge this foreign domination, or should they rise in revolt against it? Jesus, it is true, knew that these men were not friendly to him, and only wished an opportunity to catch him. If he had had political designs he probably would not have expressed them on this occasion; but his answer, though entirely non-committal in form, could only be understood as recognizing the lawfulness of obedience to the existing government. He pointed to the emperor's image on a coin, and declared that it was right to render to the Roman government and to God the obedience which was the due of each. This is the tone of a man who wished to hold himself aloof from political complications. After his death his disciples occupied the same position. Their presence in Jerusalem gave neither Romans nor Jews anxiety on political grounds. There is no sign of political hopes or schemes among his followers in Jerusalem or elsewhere. The natural explanation of this is that he gave no ground for such hopes in his teaching; that he taught only the moral regeneration of society through the announcement of ethical-spiritual truth.

It is harder to decide whether he intended his teaching to be limited to the Jews; that is, whether, in harmony with the old prophets and the body of the later literature, he regarded the Jewish nation as the necessary intermediary between God and the rest of the world. Something like this we should naturally infer from the story of the Syrophœnician woman (Mark vii. 27), to whom he is reported as saying that it was not meet to take the children's bread and cast it to the dogs. In the First Gospel, when the twelve disciples are sent out to teach, they are charged not to go to Gentiles or Samaritans, but only to Jews (Matt. x. 5, 6); but this limitation is not found in Mark or Luke, and we may suspect that it is the addition of a Judaizing editor. On the other hand, he seems not to have confined himself to Jewish territory, but went wherever he had opportunity (Mark vii. 24, 31). The baptismal commission, indeed, containing the command to preach to all the nations, does not belong to his teaching proper, but represents the idea of the succeeding generation. Of the same nature, perhaps, is the saying reported in the First Gospel, that many should come from the east and the west to sit down with Abraham, Isaac, and Jacob, while the sons of the kingdom should be cast forth (Matt. viii. 11, 12); yet this may be interpreted as meaning, in the sense of the old prophets, that members of other peoples should accept the instruction of Israel, while a portion of the chosen nation should be rejected. And here, probably, we find a suggestion of Jesus' position on this point. His mind filled with the prophetic thought, which conceived of Israel as the centre of enlightenment for the world, it would be natural for him to regard Jewish territory as the starting-point for the religious reconstruction of society. Such was the view of the Old Testament and of the succeeding literature. Salvation was held to be of the Jews (John iv. 22), only through the Jewish nation as intermediary was it thought possible that other nations could obtain the knowledge of saving truth. Such an opinion all the conditions of his training would lead him to hold; and that this was really his view may with some probability be inferred from the position of the disciples just after his death, among whom the idea of preaching directly to the Gentiles did not easily find entrance. If he had expressed himself in a universal way, if he had habitually or often spoken of the immediate appeal to the non-Jewish world, these men who had been for several years in intimate association with him would have caught some of this spirit. Their Jewish prejudice was no doubt at the beginning intense; but it would have yielded to repeated instructions on the part of the Master whom they revered as a heaven-sent prophet. At the outset they showed not the slightest trace of any such idea. It was Paul, the man who had had no association with Jesus, and in his writings almost ignores his life and teaching, who completely idealized the person of Jesus from a theological point of view,— it was this outsider, as he may be called, who conceived and carried out the idea that the announce-

ment of the Gospel to the Gentile world was to be made
a direct object of effort. This idea he seems not to have
got from Jesus.

Yet it is conceivable that the Master chose not to burden his disciples with instructions for the far future, holding that his immediate mission was to Israel. We must
believe, indeed, that he expected the ultimate complete triumph of the kingdom of God: such is the teaching of the
prophets. But whether he looked to a gradual process of
moral leavening by the proclamation of the truth, or to a
physical divine intervention, which should coerce alien nations, this we have no means of determining with absolute
certainty. We can only say that if he conceived of the universality of the Gospel in the Pauline sense, it is strange
that they so completely misunderstood him, and that it
afterward required so long and hard a struggle to establish
this idea in the Church. It seems more probable that his
conception of direct reformatory work was limited to the
Jewish nation.

It is in harmony with this statement of his position that
he attempted no separate organization of his disciples. He
preached to the multitudes wherever he had opportunity,
and welcomed all who came to him with serious purpose.
He selected a few of the more receptive and earnest, and
attached them closely to his person. There is no sign of
real distinction between esoteric and exoteric teaching in
his life;[1] but his intercourse with the inner circle of dis-

[1] Such a distinction seems, indeed, to be affirmed in Mark iv. 11, Matt.
xiii. 11, but the "mystery" which is there subsequently expounded is not
remarkable either morally-religiously or historically. That is, the ethical part
of the explanation of the parables does not differ in spirit and content from
other sayings (as the Sermon on the Mount) which appear to have been
addressed to the people at large, and what relates to the gradual development and final establishment of the kingdom of God was neither difficult to
understand nor strange to the current ideas of the time. There is a difference between the reports of this group of parables in Mark and in Matthew;

ciples was naturally freer and fuller than with the others, and to them, we may suppose, he confided more of the content and spirit of his doctrine. They all remained simply members of the Jewish people, professing faith in Moses and practising all the requirements of the Law. He never spoke of his disciples as forming a sect or party, never established separate synagogues nor held separate religious meetings, never appointed officers nor suggested that they be thereafter appointed. After his death, the disciples were gradually forced into a separate organization; but the book of Acts gives no hint that they derived the details or the idea itself from him. The word " church " does indeed occur twice in the First Gospel, but in passages which appear to be later additions. The declaration that the Church is to be founded on Peter (Matt. xvi. 18) is not given in any of the other Gospels, and appears to be an insertion introduced for the purpose of exalting the authority of Peter. It is not quite in accord with Jesus' attitude toward Peter elsewhere in the Gospels. The provision made for dealing with a perverse brother (Matt. xviii. 17), who, if he refuse to listen to the Church, is to be treated as a heathen and a publican, stands so completely isolated, and is so much out of harmony with other teachings of Jesus, that it also may be regarded as the insertion of a succeeding generation. It is noteworthy that the Synoptic Gospels have nothing to say of baptism in the ministry of Jesus. He himself is said to have been baptized by John; but there is no mention of the ceremony's having been performed by himself or by his disciples, and in the Fourth Gospel (John iv. 2) it is said that Jesus himself did not baptize, but left this work to his

Mark is simply ethical, Matthew largely eschatological. But even such a parable as that of the tares (Matt. xiii. 24–30, 37–43, which looks like an eschatological recension of Mark iv 26–29) finds a parallel in Enoch xlv.–liv. Jesus appears to have spoken freely to the people on the highest things, and his parables are said (Mark xii. 12) to have been intelligible to the Pharisees.

disciples. Considering the importance which was afterward attached to this ceremony as the rite introductory to membership in a church (the fact embodied in the baptismal commission, Matt. xxviii. 19), it is strange that it should be entirely ignored by the Synoptics if Jesus had really thought of establishing a new ecclesiastical organization, initiation into which was announced by the ceremony of baptism. We have to conclude that he looked to a reformation within the body of Judaism, whence other nations were to be ultimately won over. He had faith, it would seem, in the possibilities of the Jewish nation. It would be hard to surmise what the result would have been if his disciples had continued his work in his spirit. Such was not to be the case. The increasing prominence given to the spiritual and non-nomistic elements of his teaching, and the conversion of Gentiles who had no sympathy with the Jewish national feeling, forced his disciples to assume an independent position. If they had remained simply members of the Jewish nation, they might have done much in the way of moral-spiritual reform; but it is, to say the least, very doubtful whether Judaism could ever have been fashioned into an instrument for reconstructing the world. National particularism was too deeply ingrained in the Jewish life to permit the emergence of a purely religious principle of universal character. It was necessary that the spiritual should be violently severed from the national-ceremonial; and this was effected, not by Jesus himself, but by the course of events after his death. He announced the spirit and the ethical content of a new world-religion; it was left to later needs, embodied chiefly in the person of Paul, to isolate this spirit and this content from local-national life, and so to fix it in a theological framework and an ecclesiastical organization that it might commend itself to all the world. But whether Jesus contemplated a Church is a question of secondary interest; the main thing is that he laid hold of the highest ethical-spiritual thought, extricated it from disturbing formalities, and clothed it with a powerful spirit of consecration to God and to humanity. Out of this the Church naturally sprang.

If, then, Jesus did not contemplate a political kingdom, and did not attempt to form an ecclesiastical organization, what was his conception of the final outcome of his movement? And first, what was his conception of his own position? Did he regard himself as the promised Messiah? and if so, what was the function which he assigned himself? That the people and the disciples looked on him as the Messiah may be inferred from a number of incidents given in the Mark-Gospel (Bartimæus, the public entry, the trial, x. xi. xiv.), and from the testimony of the two men in Luke xxiv. He made no protest against this assumption, and is said (Mark xiv. 62) to have answered with a decided affirmative when officially asked by the high-priest if he laid claim to such a character. According to the Synoptics (Mark viii. 29; Matt. xvi. 17; Luke ix. 20), he did at a certain point in his career definitely announce himself to his disciples as the Christ. He first asked them as to the current opinions about him. They replied that some held him to be John the Baptist, some Elijah, and others Jeremiah or one of the prophets: whence we may infer that his person and work had produced a great impression on the popular imagination, so that he was taken to be some important personage, but not the Messiah. His bearing did not correspond to the popular conception of the great deliverer. When he turned to the disciples and asked whom they took him to be, Peter, apparently acting as spokesman for all, answered that he was the Christ. Jesus accepted the answer, charged them that they should tell no one, and proceeded to open their eyes to the fate which awaited him.

He was to be rejected, he said, by the leaders of the people, and finally to be put to death. Such a communication was naturally surprising to these men, and Peter began a violent protest against such a Messianic scheme; but his outbreak was sternly repressed by Jesus, who pointed out that Peter spoke from an earthly point of view, and from ignorance of the true nature and demands of the new dispensation.

There seems to be no reason why we should not accept this narrative as giving substantially Jesus' final view of his own career. Whether or not this particular incident happened just as it is reported, it doubtless presents the gist of what the Master said at various times. From it we may conclude that there was a definite moment when he was formally recognized by his disciples and by himself as the promised Messiah, and when at the same time he felt that his construction of the Messianic mission was very different from that which prevailed among the Jewish people of all classes. We should also naturally infer that previous to the announcement at Cæsarea Philippi nothing had been said of a Messianic claim on his part. Either he had made no such claim even in his own mind, or, holding himself to be the Messiah, had remained silent till the disciples should be able through his instructions to receive the surprising and revolutionary announcement which he had to make. The former supposition seems the more probable. He is represented as always speaking very freely to his disciples; and it does not appear why he should have kept back the statement of his claim. It could not have been in order to wait till they were ready, for when he at last spoke they were utterly unprepared for the idea of the Messianic work which he announced. Further, in the accounts of his ministry preceding the incident at Cæsarea Philippi, he is represented as a teacher and healer; and there is no indication that he thought of himself otherwise than as a moral-religious reformer. The probability is, then, that he came gradually to think of himself as the deliverer promised by the prophets. His meditation on the promises of the Old Testament and on the existing moral-religious lacks of the nation, combined with his consciousness of spiritual insight, with the conviction that he had laid hold of the great life-giving principles of religion, might lead him to believe that God had chosen him to initiate the new era of spiritual purity and salvation. His reflection would also lead him to see that the rôle of the deliverer could not be one of physical force; and above all, the portraiture of the servant of Yahwe in Isa. liii., where the path to triumph leads through suffering and death, might have forced on him the conviction that such was to be the nature of his career. After a while, indeed, his own surroundings would suggest something of this sort. The hostility of the religious leaders of the people became constantly more pronounced and more bitter, and he knew that if he remained faithful to his convictions he should antagonize the representatives of Mosaic orthodoxy more and more. He would come to feel that there was a profound and irreconcilable antagonism between his spirit and the spirit of the times. Such a feeling he more than once expressed (Mark viii. 31; ix. 12; x. 45).

It is doubtful in what light he looked on his own death, — what significance he attached to it. The fifty-third chapter of Isaiah represents the death of the servant of Yahwe as vicarious and expiatory in the general sense that God accepts the life of his pure and perfect servant in lieu of the punishment which would naturally fall on his erring people. Such may have been the view of Jesus; such is the general meaning of his declaration (Mark x. 45) that he came to give his life a ransom for many. He had a lofty consciousness of power; he may have felt that the sacrifice of his life was an essential step toward the establishment of his doctrine. But it would be only in a general sense that he would regard his death as expiatory, — the sense in which suffering in general is looked on in the Old Testament as an atonement (as in Isa. xl. 2); and from the meagreness of the data, we must remain in doubt as to the precise nature of this feeling. The saying quoted above is the only one given in the Gospel of Mark in which he refers to this point. In the connection he is speaking only of service as the mark of greatness for his disciples; and he adds, in order to set them an example, that he himself came not to be ministered to, but to minister. The concluding clause, "and to give his life a ransom for many," is not quite in the line of the preceding remarks. It may have been uttered by him as the expression of the culmination of his ministry, or it may have been added at a later time, when the belief in the expiatory character of his death had become fixed. No such view is hinted at in the Sermon on the Mount. If Jesus really held it, it did not belong to his earlier teaching, but was reached by his later reflection called forth by the continually thickening dangers that surrounded him, and his prevision of his tragic end.

Another conception of his mission is perhaps given by the title "Son of Man," by which he preferred to designate himself. This expression occurs first in the book of Ezekiel. It is the prophet's standing name for himself. The Hebrew term means simply "human being;" and the prophet's purpose seems to have been to express his conviction of his own littleness and weakness in the presence of the Almighty God. He at the same time thus sets forth the feebleness of humanity in general; but his primary feeling apparently was that he himself, called by God to announce his will, was in himself only dust and nothingness and entitled to recognition only as the messenger and mouth-piece of the Most High. In Dan. vii 13 the "Son of Man" means (as in Ezekiel) merely humanity, and represents the nation Israel, conceived of as the prophet or human interpreter and representative of God, the favored bearer of the divine truth, and inheritor of the divine blessing. The nation, or rather the faithful part of it, is thought of as morally and religiously pure; but the ethical side of the picture is obscured by the eschatological. In the Enoch-Parables it is a title of the Messiah, doubtless derived from Ezekiel and Daniel, especially from the latter, of whose text (Dan. vii.) the description in Enoch xlv.–xlviii. is an interpretation. The Aramaic dialect, which was probably the language of Jesus and his disciples, employs the same expression for "human being." Jesus may have used it in the moral sense which Ezekiel attaches to it, — to represent himself as the envoy and spokesman of God, by whose authority he acted, without whose aid he was nothing. It would thus be the expression of the feeling both of weakness and of power: of weakness, inasmuch as humanity in itself is weak; of power, inasmuch as humanity inspired by God is strong. Though primarily the synonym of human impotency, it embodies also the profound sense of oneness with God and the appropriation of the divine potency. It is possible, however, that it had become at this time (through Daniel and Enoch) a specific and technical title for the Messiah,[1] and that Jesus so uses it of himself. In that case, that it is put into his mouth (Mark ii. 10, 28) before his declaration of his Messiahship to his disciples (Mark viii. 27–30) may be explained by the fact that it later became a familiar name for him, and might be proleptically ascribed to him

---

[1] If so, it would have a peculiar significance in such utterances as Mark ii. 10, 28, viii. 31, which might then be regarded as defining the Messianic function in general.

even at the beginning. The content of the term, as employed by him, must of course be defined, not simply or chiefly by the preceding or current usage, but by his own words.

Thus far we have noticed only the moral-spiritual elements of Jesus' consciousness and of his construction of the kingdom of God. That kingdom he conceived to be primarily the sincere righteousness of the soul based on and identical with loving trust in God and imitation of him. His mission on earth he believed to be the announcement and exemplification of the new moral-spiritual order of things. The forces to which he appealed were ethical and religious; the consummation to which he looked was moral perfection. What, then, was his conception of the historical unfolding and completion of the new dispensation, or in other words, his idea of the destiny of the world? Did he think merely of a gradual development of society under the control of moral-religious forces, or was there in his view an historical culmination which was to set a limit to the world's moral history? And if there were such a culmination, did he think of it as far off or near, and what position therein did he assign himself? If we are to follow the Synoptics, we shall have to believe that he looked for a speedy judgment, whereby he himself, invested with supernatural power, should usher in the completed and everlasting kingdom of God. According to this view, there were two stages of this kingdom, the one belonging to the present, the other to the future. These are elsewhere in the New Testament designated as "this or the present age or world," and "the age or world to come." The work of the present age would then be considered as merely preparatory, the period of the growing crop; the future judgment was the reaping, when the wheat should be separated from the tares, and perpetual stability guaranteed to the society of the elect servants of God. This conception existed in the time of Jesus, for it is found in Enoch and the Sibyl, and more fully in the New Testament Apocalypse. It is given substantially in the Second Gospel : " Whoever shall be ashamed of me and of my words in this adulterous and sinful generation, the Son of Man also shall be ashamed of him when he comes in the glory of his Father with the holy angels. . . . There are some here of those that stand by who shall in no wise taste of death till they see the kingdom of God come with power " (Mark viii. 38 ; ix. 1). The necessary inference from this passage would be that Jesus expected to come in person, attended by angels, to establish the new dispensation of things in final form. The same conclusion would follow from the parable of judgment (Matt. xxv. 31–46), where a separation is made between the righteous and the wicked of all nations, the former being sent away into eternal life, the latter into eternal punishment. The ground of distinction between the two classes is devotion to the person of the judge, only this devotion is shown by care for his people in this world. The historical consummation is definite and permanent ; the fate of men is decided at once and forever. The present kingdom of God passes into the everlasting world of the future, and good and bad moral qualities, with their retributions, are permanently fixed without possibility of change.

It is difficult to decide whether Jesus taught this doctrine in whole or in part. Though it certainly does not belong to the same stratum of thought as the ethical teaching of the Sermon on the Mount and similar passages, it does not necessarily exclude such ideas.[1] The conception of a final judicial determination of the fate of men has been held from the days of the old prophets till now, in conjunction with the recognition of individual moral development and responsibility. The belief in a divine judgment which was

---

[1] A judgment is suggested in Matt. vii. 22, 23.

to close the existing order of things and introduce the era of Israel's blessedness was well established in the first century of our era. It is found in Daniel, Enoch, the Sibyl, Second Maccabees, and the Psalter of Solomon. In some of these writings, as we have seen, it is God, in others it is the Messiah, that is to be the judge.[1] There was nothing in the intellectual conditions or the beliefs of the time to make such a conception of himself impossible or difficult for a great ethical teacher. It might be supposed that such an one would then have to think of himself as more than human; but this was neither necessary nor probable. He might be chosen and his name called by God before the world was created; so say the Enoch-Parables (xlviii. 3, 6) and the Talmud (Ber. Rab. 1). Such an idea was suggested by such passages as Mic. v. 2 (1), Isa. ix. 6 (5), Ps. lxxii. 17. He might be appointed to come in power and glory to judge the world (so Enoch and the Talmud). But God, it was held, could endow a prophet with such powers and functions; and Jewish monotheistic thought seems always to have conceived of the Messiah both as completely subordinate to the Supreme Being and as an Israelite in origin and nature. It is thus in itself neither impossible nor improbable that such a statement as that of Mark viii. 38 (that the Son of Man should come in the glory of his Father with the holy angels) should represent the real idea of Jesus. Even the declaration of the next verse (Mark ix. 1), that this glorious coming should take place in that generation, cannot be said to be impossible for him, however much we may feel disposed to reject it as out of accord with his moral

---

[1] God himself is judge in Mal. iv. (*Heb.* iii. 19-21), Joel iii. (*Heb.* iv.), Ps. xcvi. xcviii., Dan. vii, Enoch xc., Sibyl iii. 669 ff., 56, Psalms of Solomon, *passim*, 2 Mac. vi. vii.; the Messiah in the Enoch-parables xlv. li. lxix. The latter view seems thus to have come into existence shortly before the beginning of our era. The Talmud also appears in some passages to regard God, in others the Messiah, as the judge. Weber, "System," § 88.

elevation; his ethical purity and greatness are independent of all such local opinions. The subsequent history of his disciples does not prevent our attributing such views to him. The account in Luke xxiv. describes their expectations only in the most general terms. They hoped that it was he that should redeem Israel. Their conduct after his death shows that they were at first grievously disappointed by that event, and the belief that he would speedily appear as judge seems to have been general in the first century (1 Thess. iv. 15–17; 1 Cor. xv. 51, 52; Jas. v. 8; 1 Pet. iv. 7). How, it may be asked, can we account for these statements of the Gospels and Epistles except on the supposition that they rest on a true tradition of his sayings? It may be supposed that such utterances belong to the latter part of his career. Beginning, like John, simply as a moral-religious reformer and proclaimer of the coming kingdom of God, he may, as his conviction of his Messianic character became stronger, have appropriated the current ideas of a Messianic judicial parousia. In the Gospels the discourses delivered after the announcement at Cæsarea Philippi have a decidedly distincter eschatological tone than those which precede.

On the other hand, this pronounced tone may be satisfactorily accounted for by the supposition that utterances of the Master of a general character were afterward interpreted, expanded, and colored in the light of subsequent events. The date at which our present Synoptic Gospels were put into shape (after the destruction of Jerusalem) was late enough to allow a considerable growth of legendary material. The person of Jesus was gradually idealized. At first prophet and Jewish Messiah (Mark viii.; Luke xxiv.), he became the Lord (Jas.), set forth by his resurrection as Son of God (Rom. i.), soon to come as judge (2 Cor. v. 10), destined to reign in heaven till all his enemies should be subdued, then to deliver up his delegated authority to God (1 Cor. xv. 24–

28). If such a conception of Jesus had become general in the Church by the year 70, it would be natural that it should appear in the Gospels. The pictures of his royal and judicial functions in Epistles and Gospels belong to the same circle of ideas. They differ in certain details, but not more than we should expect from the diversities of different sections of the Church. In one point they all agree, — that the coming of the Lord would not be delayed. The details of his coming might have been supplied from current Jewish ideas. There may have been a basis in his words for the later accounts. He may have spoken of a coming age of blessedness, which he as Messiah should introduce, and of a judgment to be held by God. Out of such material, the general sense of which would remain distinct in the memory of the disciples, the later tradition might then have built up the discourses in the form in which we now have them.

To many persons it may seem that the atmosphere of the discourses in question is rather that of the Epistles than that of the life of the Master in the simplest form in which the Synoptics give it. If we follow him along the line of his ethical-religious teaching from the beginning till his death, we have a picture of lofty moral simplicity and devotion which may appear to be marred by the introduction of these details of judgment. The moral-spiritual orderliness and profound sobriety of his ideas would, it might be supposed, put him out of sympathy with the mechanical side of the current conceptions respecting the kingdom of righteousness. It has already been pointed out that such considerations cannot be decisive from either the historical or the psychological point of view. These mechanical conceptions were held by his contemporaries, and afterward by his disciples, and may have been held by him. It does not seem possible to determine from our data whether he held them or not. The acceptance of such ideas carried along with it the supposition of something supernatural, not necessarily in the person of the Messiah, but certainly in his history. This also was in consonance with the beliefs of the age, and need not have been repugnant to him. In fine, the opinions of that time concerning the historical setting of the moral-spiritual kingdom of God must be put into the same category with the opinions respecting the material of what we call the sciences. Their relation to moral clearness and purity was of the same sort as that of the current ideas of geography, astronomy, and biblical exegesis. The power of the founder of Christianity was in his moral personality and his conception of a thoroughly spiritual society, just as the power of the prophets lay in the religious purity of their ideas, in spite of their vain hopes of political sovereignty. The local setting of the ideas respecting the perfect society has changed from age to age ; the moral essence remains. The Church of to-day has given up the special historical hope of the Church of the first century. The moral spiritual teaching of Jesus, resting on his past and reflecting the best thought of his contemporaries, has maintained itself to the present day without having found its realization in social life.

A word may be said about the eschatological discourses in the Synoptics (Matt. xxiv. ; Mark xiii. ; Luke xxi.), which seem to give a date for the final consummation. That they were not delivered by Jesus in the form in which we now have them may probably be inferred from the consideration already mentioned, — that the disciples for some time after his death show no knowledge of their contents. The occasion of the main discourse is the remark of Jesus that the temple should be so destroyed that not one stone should be left on another. His disciples ask when that should be. Jesus replies by giving the premonitory signs of the catastrophe : there were to be false Christs, wars and rumors of wars, earthquakes and famines ; his followers were to be persecuted, and his gospel was to be preached to all the nations. The sign of the end is the desecration of the temple ; after which the heavenly bodies should be darkened, and then the Son of Man would come in clouds. The allusion to the destruction of Jerusalem by the Romans is evident ; and this brief apocalyptic discourse seems to have been written at a time when it was supposed that the coming of the Lord would not be greatly delayed after the fall of the holy city. It belongs also, we may infer, to the period when the principle that the gospel was to be preached to the Gentiles had been widely accepted, — a conception foreign to the thought of the first disciples. It is also to be noted that the redaction of the discourse in Matthew shows certain differences from the accounts in Mark and Luke ; and though these are not very important, they suggest the work of different hands.[1] It is possible that Jesus said something about the future, — some brief word out of which these discourses were expanded. This supposition is, indeed, not necessary to account for their existence. It was a time of apocalypses. Nothing would be more natural than that some disciple should set forth his idea of the end, and should put it into the mouth of the Master, just as similar predictions had been assigned to Daniel, Enoch, and Moses. It was not lack of reverence for these men that led writers of that period

---

[1] Verse 20, the "Sabbath" indicates an observance of the Jewish ceremonial law ; verses 26–28 are minutely descriptive of the manner of the Messiah's appearance (and at the same time give hints of current opinions as to the place at which he would show himself) ; verse 30, "All the tribes of the earth shall mourn" recalls various Old Testament passages, such as Amos viii. 8 ; ix. 5 ; Hos. iv. 3 ; Jer. iv. 28 ; and cf. Sibyl iii. 558, "All souls of men shall deeply sigh." The details of verses 37–51 differ considerably from the corresponding passages in Luke and Mark. The recension of Luke also has its peculiarities : in general it is marked by more literary finish and less regard for details.

to make them mouthpieces of their own reflections. On the contrary, the desire was to gain the authority attaching to their names. We have, in all probability, in these Synoptical pieces, opinions of a later generation. It must be left undecided whether and how far the discourses are built up on real words of Jesus. He may or may not have said something looking to a temporal definition of his coming.[1] In any case, the present form of the discourses seems to be late.

Little need be said of the succeeding history, during the first century, of the Christian conception of the kingdom of God. It was soon practically absorbed in the general advance of Christian life, and ceased to have definite influence. After the death of Jesus, his speedy coming was looked forward to as the relief from present suffering and the introduction to perfect blessedness (James v. 7, 8). A more developed view of the parousia is given in the Second Epistle to the Thessalonians (i. 6–10), a picture which agrees almost exactly with that of the Synoptics : the Lord Jesus is to be revealed from heaven in flaming fire, rendering vengeance to unbelievers and rest to the saints. Substantially the same conception is found in First Corinthians (xv. 23–28, 51–55). The succeeding Epistles of Paul have less definite references to the coming of Christ, nor is it elsewhere prominent in the New Testament except in Second Peter and Revelation. Everywhere it is looked forward to as deliverance from the present distress, and is used as the occasion of ethical exhortation. The coming of the Lord, it was believed, would end the existing dispensation, and introduce the reign of the saints. But meantime life went on, and

---

[1] The statement (given in Mark and Matthew, but not in Luke) that the day of the coming was known neither to angels nor to Messiah, but only to God, is difficult, since the rest of the discourse shows accurate knowledge of the time. Such a statement is more suitable for one who, looking confidently for an impending event, is uncertain of the precise day, than for one who is making a definite prediction a considerable time beforehand.

the expectation of this speedy change in no wise led to a relaxation of moral rules, but rather incited men so to live that the Lord at his coming might find them faithful and worthy to be members of his righteous kingdom. The coming of the kingdom was something to be hoped for and prayed for. Every day the petition was to be put up, "Thy kingdom come;" and this was synonymous with the other petition, "Thy will be done." Few details are given in the New Testament. The old Israelitish conception of the temporal kingdom of Israel passed gradually away; it was swallowed up in the larger idea of the redeemed people of the kingdom of God of all nations ushered into a spiritual blessedness which was not bounded by space or time.

There were attempts in the first century to define with precision the time of the second coming of Christ. We have already seen that the great apocalyptic discourse in the Synoptics looks to the destruction of Jerusalem by the Romans as the turning-point in the history of the world. This discourse must have been composed or finally redacted about the time of the fall of the holy city. Important events of this sort have in all ages excited the imagination of pious men and led to theories of the final consummation of things. Another great fact which before this had seemed to many to give the clew to the mystery was the Roman Empire. At first indifferent, the Roman government had come to be a persecutor. The frightful barbarities of Nero had lifted him to the bad eminence of an anti-Christ. The Jews had a similar feeling. In the Talmud, Edom, the bitterest and most hated enemy of the old Israel, stands for Rome (Weber, "System," § 81). In the New Testament Apocalypse, the Empire is represented by Babylon, whose haughtiness, cruelty, and appalling destruction are celebrated in glowing words in the Old Testament.

The destruction of Rome is the point to which the author looks forward as the immediate introduction to the establishment of the kingdom; the latter event follows immediately on the former (Rev. xviii. xix.). The destruction of the city is preceded by the appearance of a beast (xiii.), who blasphemes God, makes war on the saints, and is worshipped by all that dwell on the earth except those whose names are written in the book of life. This beast is afterward explained (xvii.) to be a Roman emperor, the eighth in the line, yet of the seven first. The reference is most probably to Nero, the fifth of the series, counting Augustus as the first; and the representation proceeds on the supposition that Nero, though dead, will live again. There is reason to believe that the reappearance of the dead emperor was expected.[1] Apparently, therefore, the scheme of the author of this portion of the book of Revelation is that the Emperor Nero was to return to power, exalt himself as an object of worship, and inflict great suffering on the saints; and then the great city was to be destroyed and the kingdom of Christ established (xix.). Such seems also to be the conception of the enigmatical passage in Second Thessalonians (ii.), in which the coming of the Lord Jesus Christ and the gathering of his people are spoken of. The Lord's coming is to be preceded by an apostasy and the revelation of the man of lawlessness or sin, — a mysterious person who exalts himself against all that is called God or is an object of worship, and by his signs and lying wonders deceives those who love not the truth. The portraiture here corresponds so exactly to that in the Apocalypse that we may with probability suppose the man of lawlessness to be the Emperor Nero. But there is something that restrains his appearance

---

[1] For the evidence see Renan, "L'Antechrist." The number 666 assigned to the beast (Rev. xiii. 18) has been variously explained, usually from some name or epithet of Nero, sometimes as symbolical. See the commentaries.

that must be removed before the son of perdition can be manifested. What this restraining thing was we do not know. The author of the Epistle speaks in a mysterious undertone. He had told it to the brethren when he was with them, and they, he says, are acquainted with it. It is of no great importance for our purpose to determine what this restraining thing or person was; the main point is that the consummation is connected with the fortunes of the Roman Empire, and that it is to be expected speedily. The Lord Jesus is to slay the lawless one with the breath of his mouth. It is the opposition of Christ and anti-Christ, germs of which are found in the Old Testament. It was a natural feeling that the evil must go on increasing in intensity, and that then, when it reached its highest point and seemed intolerable, the interposition and deliverance should come.[1] How far this particular view, which connected the parousia with the fall of the Roman Empire, was held in the early Church, it is hardly possible to say. After the destruction of Jerusalem, when Nero did not appear, and the Empire showed only increasing strength and prosperity, other points of view had to be sought. The Church did not cease to cherish the hope of the Lord's coming, but it was less anxious to fix a definite date,[2] and rather devoted itself to the cultivation of social virtues and the perfecting of its organization. It gradually accepted its mission to dwell in the world as a life-giving influence. As its membership increased, its energies were absorbed in the care of the numerous interests which it had gathered about itself. It was the old temporal kingdom of Israel, with an invisible king and a body of citizens who belonged to all the nations of the

---

[1] So in Ezekiel, Daniel, and Enoch. The Antiochus of Daniel may have suggested the Nero of the New Testament Apocalypse.

[2] So much we may infer from the literature of the first century. Since that time there have always been chiliastic or millenarian tendencies (notably A. D. 1000) but they have not been controlling points of view.

earth. Its conquests were of souls, and its aim was the salvation of the world.

The change in the principle of membership was the most important characteristic of the outward organization of the Church. It was the sign of the advance from a national to a universal form of religion. As we have already seen, it is hard to say how far Jesus himself contemplated such a broadening of membership in the earthly kingdom of God. If we are to judge from the procedure of the disciples for twenty years after his death, his attention was fixed mainly, if not exclusively, on his own people. To the parent church in Jerusalem it seemed a self-evident and fundamental principle that entrance into the Christian community was possible only through Judaism. We read indeed (Acts x.) of a special vision and revelation by which Peter was taught that no man was to be called common or unclean, and in consequence of which certain Gentiles to whom he preached and who received the Holy Ghost were baptized and recognized as Christians without having been circumcised. But it is impossible to reconcile this account with subsequent proceedings. The long fight which preceded the admission of the right of Gentiles, as such, to membership in the Church is unintelligible if Peter received so open and decisive a declaration from heaven, and Paul knew of no mission of Peter to the Gentiles (Gal. ii. 7-9). We must regard this narrative as the elaboration of a later tradition, which, after Gentile membership had been fairly established, sought to gain for it the authority of the name of the greatest of the strictly Jewish apostles. The ground of the radical change in the constitution of the Church is to be sought in the circumstances of the times. A violent persecution drove a number of the disciples out of Palestine into the neighboring countries of Phœnicia, Cyprus, and Syria. Here they preached the new faith, but at first to Jews only. At

Antioch, however, as it would seem, they were drawn into addressing themselves to Greeks also, many of whom believed. How the question of admission into the Church was at first solved in Antioch we are not informed; but to this city Paul was brought by Barnabas, labored there for a year, and thence went out to proclaim the new faith in Asia Minor. It was in another Antioch, in Pisidia, that Paul and Barnabas took the decisive step of turning from the Jews and addressing themselves directly to the Gentiles; and it was the entrance of a large body of Gentiles into the Church which decided the question of the terms of membership. Should these persons be forced to submit to the initiatory rite of Judaism before they could be esteemed worthy to be baptized into the faith of Jesus Christ? Paul faced the problem boldly, and with the practical judgment and fearless decision which so eminently characterized him, determined that their faith in Jesus gave them of itself full claim to the privileges of the Church. This was the decisive step; Christianity thus ceased to be a Jewish sect, and became an independent religion which offered itself to all men without distinction of nations. The detailed history of this revolution has unfortunately not been preserved. That there was a sharp conflict we know from Paul's letters (Gal. ii. iv.; 1 Cor. i.) and from hints in the book of Acts (xv.). By the extreme conservatives, who insisted on circumcision as a necessary preliminary to membership in the Christian Church, Paul seems to have been looked on as a traitor to the national faith. He persisted, however, in his more liberal policy, and has himself described (Gal. ii.) how he went up to Jerusalem with Barnabas and Titus, met the chief men of the mother-church, and there in spite of opposition obtained the indorsement of the great apostles, James, Peter, and John, and the recognition of the right of Gentiles to enter the Church without first becoming Jews. And Paul was not content with this admission; he employed his sharp dialectic to show that the insistence on circumcision for the Gentiles was incompatible with true faith in Christ, was a practical denial of the completeness of Christ's redemption and of the sufficiency of the grace of God, — was, in a word, the abandonment of the spiritual religion of divine grace, and the advocacy of the dead and deadly idea of salvation by works. Thus he elevated universality of membership to the rank of a fundamental principle of spiritual religion.

It has already been remarked that Paul gave to the new faith that framework of religious dogma which was essential to its continued existence and efficiency. He connected salvation definitely with the glorified person of Jesus as the Messiah. In detaching it from Judaism and securing it independent organization, he provided the other essential for a world-religion. It is in this sense that Paul may be called the founder of Christianity as the organized embodiment of the ideal kingdom of God. In the higher sense that title belongs only to Jesus. Jesus laid the foundations of a practically universal religious community; Paul narrowed the conception in a dogmatic way. Jesus announced certain fundamental principles which must always and everywhere determine the attitude of the soul toward a personal God; Paul attached these principles to a mass of dogma which essayed to define and explain them theologically. From the whole body of religious thought which the Jewish people had worked out in the long course of its religious experience Jesus selected that part which was independent of national relations. He said little or nothing of the Jewish code. He accepted it as a fact, not undertaking to abrogate or even modify it, but casting into its midst a body of spiritual religious truth which was independent of all codes, and which, if accepted and acted on, would annul the evil of a formal code. Thus, in one sense, as has already been pointed out, his scheme of life was nomistic, in so far as it accepted the Mosaic law as the rule of faith and practice. But on the other hand, the exclusive prominence which he gave to spiritual doctrine might be relied on, if it were sincerely accepted, to establish a new method of moral-religious life. The difficulty was that men would be slow to accept it. So much are men creatures of routine, so much under the domination of mechanical rule, that it is always to be feared that the outward will coerce and repress the inward. Spiritual truth is dimmed and enfeebled by the presence of a great mass of prescriptions. There is indeed no perfect escape from this danger. Whatever the purity and force of the spiritual truth which is committed to men, they will always do what they can to enclose it in a framework of unspiritual dogma, and in the conflict between the spiritual and the unspiritual human weakness always gives the advantage to the latter. The history of Christianity abounds in illustrations of this tendency. The Church has at various times built up a structure of beliefs and practices which for intricacy and crushing power may fairly be compared with the traditional law of the Jews. Even in the first century, within two generations after the death of the Master, the Church had grown into a partially petrified organization. We are not to regard the transition from Judaism to historical Christianity as the substitution of a perfect for an imperfect form of religion, but as an advance from an imperfect to a less imperfect form, — to one which permitted that moral-spiritual truth which is the germ of all religions to assert itself with greater freedom and exert its true influence more completely. For the Jewish scheme of obedience to a mass of precepts Paul substituted faith in Jesus as Redeemer, — a vastly higher and freer conception;

yet even this, especially in its concomitants, speedily became mechanicalized.

Christianity was a Jewish development; but it was much more. The conception of the earthly kingdom of God, as a human organization, was, as we have seen, almost peculiar to the Jews. Elsewhere it is found only in germinal form; but its essential elements are universal. It means the due recognition of all the factors and relations of life, human and divine, — the highest refinement of ethical and religious feeling and action. It must include the best thought of the world, and can come truly into existence only by the co-operation of all peoples and races. It is not exclusively Jewish or Greek or Roman, but more than all this. The ultimate aim of the world's life is the fusion of its highest ideas into a harmonious practical unity; and it is the great merit of Christianity to have taken a decided step in preparation for this end. In the first century already the Church showed an intermingling of Semitic and Hellenic conceptions, both ethical and religious.[1] In the divine there was majesty, justice, and love; in the human there was the recognition of the supremacy of conscience and the power of sympathy and sweetness. This was in itself a great advance; it was the partial fusion of two great masses of human thought. But this is not all. The service that Christianity did was so to strip religion of local and anthropomorphic elements that all the Western world might in a substantial way unite in working out the truly religious life. The Old-World deadly isolation was done away with (Eph. ii. 11–22), — not completely and absolutely, but so substantially as to mark an epoch in human history. There remained localisms and anthropomorphisms whose removal was to be left to the slow-moving moral forces of society;

---

[1] The Semitism, moreover, had already been affected by Persian thought. Whether the Hellenism had felt the influence of Hindu ideas is doubtful.

but the path was marked out, and the greatest obstacles taken out of the way. Political unity had been achieved, but complete harmony was impossible without religious oneness. Christianity offered what all could accept. By furnishing a practical bond between nationalities it effected what the Hellenic and Roman religions had proved themselves unable to effect. It was the fruit of a noble and powerful eclecticism carried on by lofty spiritual thinkers. It had its roots in the far past, but its special impulse came from Jesus of Nazareth.

CHAPTER VII.

ESCHATOLOGY.

THE eschatological ideas of the New Testament offer very little that can be considered an advance on the current Jewish conceptions of the period. Such ideas by their nature belong not to the spiritual kernel of religion, but to its external dogmatic framework. From the point of view of pure religion they are among the least influential and the least interesting of religious facts. They are of importance, however, as showing how much of the existing dogma Christianity felt called on to accept in order that it might become effective for that generation as well as for many succeeding generations. We have to consider the beliefs respecting immortality, resurrection, and the new dispensation. The last of these is closely connected with the doctrine of the Messiah, and has already been touched on. Some points not before brought out may be here referred to. It is probably true of this whole circle of beliefs that only certain current phases of faith are mentioned in the New Testament and in the immediately preceding literature. It is hardly possible to give a complete history of the eschatological ideas of the age, nor is this necessary for our present purpose. They are interesting for us in so far as they illustrate the moral-religious life of the time; that is, in the first place, as contributing an ethical factor, and then as supplying what was regarded as a necessary framework for religious life. It will be sufficient to refer to certain prominent facts in the current belief.[1]

[1] In spite of a number of excellent works, German, French, and English, a critical history of Jewish and Christian eschatology is still a desideratum.

1. Let us first notice the fuller sketch of the fortunes of the earthly kingdom of God which is given in the Apocalypse. The main point of this sketch is the double judgment. The destruction of the Roman Empire is followed by the imprisonment of Satan for a thousand years and by the first judgment. Those who had been beheaded for the testimony of Jesus and had not worshipped the beast — that is, had not acknowledged the religious authority of the Empire — are restored to life (the first resurrection), and reign with Christ a thousand years. At the end of this millennium Satan is loosed from prison, and advances at the head of the innumerable hosts of Gog and Magog to attack the camp of the saints and the beloved city. Fire descends from heaven and devours the antigodly army; the devil is cast into the lake of fire along with the beast and the false prophet (the political and religious enemies of the faith), and there they are to be tormented for ever and ever. Thereupon follows the general judgment, where every man is judged according to his works, and whoever is not found written in the book of life — that is, is not a believer in Jesus — is cast into the lake of fire. Then the first heaven and the first earth pass away, a new heaven and a new earth come, God makes his dwelling with men, and from the eyes of his people all tears are wiped away. There is a city, a new Jerusalem, which shines with an everlasting divine light, and a life radiant with everlasting divine blessedness.

It is evident that the body of this description is taken from the books of Ezekiel, Isaiah, and Enoch. Ezekiel (xxxviii. xxxix.) describes the great invasion of Gog, the Prince of Magog (in the Apocalypse Gog becomes a nation), which precedes the final blessed establishment of Israel in its own land; Isaiah portrays the blessedness of the new heavens and the new earth which God will create for his people, where weeping shall be no more heard, and God will dwell with them forever (lxv.); Enoch gives a picture of the general judgment which is substantially the same as that of the New Testament book (li. lxii. lxiii. xci.). How the conception of two judgments arose it is less easy to say. Perhaps the author of this passage of the Apocalypse, following Ezekiel, regarded the conflict with Magog as the final struggle of the enemies of the people of God,[1] while at the same time he was convinced that the fall of the Roman Empire was in a decisive way to usher in the kingdom of God. In order to reconcile these two views he may then have conceived of an interval between the two events. The first judgment was to introduce a real reign of the saints, — a period in which peace was secured by the imprisonment of the devil,[2] but during which earthly affairs in general went on as before. Then comes the final judgment, the destruction of death and Hades,[3] the final imprisonment of Satan, the removal of all sinful elements from life, and the establishment of a permanent existence of happiness for the righteous.

Whether in this scheme and others of similar character we are to see the coloring of Persian ideas, it is hardly possible to decide with certainty. The resemblances between the Jewish and Persian eschatologies are striking, and the general possibility of Persian influence is proved by the Jewish and Christian angelology and demonology; but the

---

[1] A Messianic interpretation of the invasion of Gog and Magog is given in the Talmud (Weber, "System," § 87). By some it is held to precede, by others to follow, the reign of the Messiah.

[2] The number 1,000 of the years of Satan's imprisonment was perhaps suggested by Ps. xc. 4, or it may be merely a natural expression of a long space of time (cf. Ezekiel's employment of the same unit, Ezek. xlviii.).

[3] So in 1 Cor. xv. 23–28. Here death is the last of the enemies that Christ is to subdue when he shall come. Paul adds that the Messianic reign will then come to an end, swallowed up in the reign of God. A similar view seems to be given in Rev. xx. xxi.

late date of the present form of the Persian eschatological writings (some centuries after the beginning of our era), though they doubtless rest on earlier beliefs, makes it precarious to assume that these ideas affected the Jews so early as the second or first pre-Christian century, when Jewish Messianic systems first make their appearance. Further, the Jewish development would seem to be satisfactorily accounted for from the native material. On the other hand, it is possible to suppose an influence in the opposite direction, of Judaism and Christianity on Mazdeism. The data seem insufficient to decide the question. If the existence of the Bundehesh scheme in the second century B. C. could be made probable, we might suppose that it colored the Jewish Messianic ideas somewhat as the Mazdean dualism colored the idea of Satan. So far as regards the machinery of the New Testament Apocalypse, — the dragon, the beast, etc., — this may be explained out of Jewish material and the historical conditions of the first century. In any case, the moral-religious ideas involved in the Messianic eschatology are thoroughly Jewish and Christian.[1]

The details of the picture belong to the thought of the times. As a history of the future blessedness of the saints, this passage has always awakened the interest and excited the curiosity of the Church. By the author and many others of that generation, doubtless, the fulfilment of the prediction was believed to be imminent; but generation after generation passed, the Roman Empire remained as before, and the time of fulfilment was deferred. So ever since in every age there have been those who expected the speedy coming of the Lord and the introduction of the final dis-

---

[1] On the Persian eschatology, besides the works above mentioned, page 172, see the discussions of Roth, and compare works on the Jewish doctrine of the Messiah. On the supposed composite — Jewish and Christian — constitution of the Apocalypse, see the treatises of Vischer, Sabatier, and others. A comparative history of Messianic ideas in all religions has yet to be written.

pensation of blessedness. The historical interpretation of the various characters and events of the apocalyptic visions has varied with the mutations of history ; but the confidence as to the issue has not lessened among those who regarded this book as a divinely revealed picture of the future. The effect of this faith on the life of the Church has not been great. It was an inheritance of Christianity from Judaism. For the Jews it had a national-political significance, and it was a transfer of the idea of earthly order to the scheme of the universe. There was to be a final settlement, an enforced peace and stability, like that which a conqueror imposes on subject lands. In no other way could that age conceive of the triumph of truth ; and the Christianity of the first century naturally appropriated this mechanical governmental view. The king of the Apocalypse rules with a rod of iron ; and Paul conceives of the reign of the Messiah as a warfare, — he must reign till he has put all enemies under his feet. Still, even in the first century this aspect of the kingdom of God is gradually modified. The spiritual gradually replaces the external ; the hope of the Lord's earthly coming is more and more swallowed up in the larger hope of heaven, — the individual hope, the fulfilment of which death brought to every believer. The expectation of Christ's coming has been mainly a moral element in Christianity. It has not affected the properly religious dogma or the organization of the Church. It has sustained men in adversity ; it has produced enthusiasm or fanaticism. It has not quickened thought, or promoted real social-religious progress. For the first century it was probably valuable as an outward support for the struggling and feebly founded faith (Jas. v. 7 ; 1 Thess. iv. 13–18 ; v. 1–11 ; 2 Thess. i. 3–12 ; 1 Cor. xv. 19 ; xvi. 22 ; 1 Pet. iv. 7–19 ; Rev. *passim*).

Its significance has become less and less ; that is, the stress laid on the particular outward form has been gradually diminishing, and Christian feeling has tended more and more to emphasize the spiritual content of the idea. The Church more and more holds itself to be the visible kingdom of God on earth, its struggle and life to be spiritual, its aim the regeneration of humanity; and this result, it holds, is to be effected by the employment of ordinary ethical-spiritual agencies. The Church feels that its function is not to sit passively waiting for the Lord, but rather to conquer the world for him. The germ of this conception is found in the Old Testament; it is the prophetic exhortation that Israel shall make possible the Lord's intervention by obedience and trust, by the attainment of moral perfectness. This ethical conception was set in the political framework which belonged to the ideas of the age. Christianity received it from Judaism with certain modifications; and the progress of Christian life has consisted in part in cutting away this framework and returning to the simplest conception of moral regeneration. The reign of Christ signifies the reign of ethical purity and true religion, the establishment of moral order. The Church is more concerned with the end than with the means; or rather, it recognizes the fact that the burden of responsibility rests on itself. And this, it would seem, was the idea of Jesus: the regeneration of humanity brought about by individual purity and faithfulness, — the love of God and the love of man the two factors which were to raise human life to its full proportions of purity and majesty, and bring it into intimate union with the complete and everlasting life of the divine father.

2. Christianity received from Judaism the doctrines of immortality and resurrection. They appear in the earliest of Paul's Epistles, and it may be assumed that they formed a part of the material of Christian thought in the middle of the first century of our era. The history of their genesis must be sought in the Judaism of the preceding centuries.

The first distinct announcement of immortality, in our sense of the word, is found in the Wisdom of Solomon, a work which belongs not far from 200 B. C. The Old Testament, if we except the book of Daniel, takes no hopeful view of the future life. Everywhere we find the old Semitic conception of a colorless existence in Sheol : a gloomy underworld with gates and bars, tenanted by joyless shades, whose existence runs a gray, uncheckered course, unilluminated by the ordinary emotions of men, unstimulated by their ordinary aims and hopes, severed from the life of the great world above, and cut off from living communion with God. In the early times it was believed that by magic arts the dead might be brought up to tell the secrets of the living. Samuel rises to crush the unhappy Saul by a prediction of defeat and death. Necromancy was rife in Isaiah's time (Isa. viii. 19). But the better minds of Israel deplored and opposed this remnant of paganism. Why, said they, go to the dead in behalf of the living ? The appeal, they felt, must be to the divine law as spoken by the prophets (Isa. viii.). If the people refused this only lawful means of instruction, it was because they had no true religious light in them. Necromancy was in those times inseparably connected with rude, debasing beliefs and rites. The struggle of the prophets was to banish all other worships but that of Yahwe, and to lead the nation to look to the prophetic word alone for all guidance in life. Thus opposed to the genius of Israelitism, the practice of consulting the shades fell gradually into disuse. The dead were left in their nether abode, forever isolated from the genuine life of upper earth, and excluded from the sympathies of the living except in so far as they furnished examples of good or evil, or were the foundations of divine promises which underlay the development of the nation. Abraham, Isaac, Jacob, and David lived in the memory of the pious ; were the bearers of divine messages and hopes, but only as denizens of the upper world. They lived in the past; their present in Sheol was forgotten or unregarded. At least, this is true so far as the records go. Never is there reference or allusion to them as still truly alive in Sheol, never a hint that they are supposed to follow with intelligence and interest the fortunes of their fellow-countrymen. Jacob shows no interest in the history of his twelve sons; David is unconcerned about the political prosperity of his realm, and Solomon indifferent to the career of the temple. Only once in the Old Testament is there any hint of emotion in the shades of Sheol: when the proud king of Babylon, overthrown and slain, descends to the realms below, the inmates greet his arrival with a cry of malignant satisfaction. Thy glory is departed, they say; thou art become as one of us (Isa. xiv. 9, 10). It is as if all their life was compressed into one gloomy consciousness of failure and nothingness, their only joy coming from the spectacle of others' misery. It is the only approach in the Old Testament to the later conception of a future place of torment.

There are some passages in the Old Testament which have been supposed to contain the hope of immortality; but these all, under careful examination, appear to regard the presence of God only in this life. The declaration of the Sixteenth Psalm — "Thou wilt not abandon me to Sheol nor suffer thy godly one to see the pit; thou wilt show me the path of life; in thy presence is fulness of joy, in thy right hand there are pleasures forevermore" — sets forth the writer's complete satisfaction and security in the divine presence and protection. "Yahwe," says he, "is my portion, is at my right hand; wherefore I am glad, since he will not give me over to death, but will keep me in life, his presence securing all safety and joy." It is the present, the earthly life, of which he is thinking, and the deliverance from that premature death which was the portion of the wicked (Ps. ix.

17), and was esteemed the greatest misfortune. In like manner we must understand the concluding verse of the Seventeenth Psalm. The writer, confident of his own integrity (verse 3), asks for protection against the prosperous wicked. They, he says, are filled with treasure ; and then, contrasting his own situation, he adds : "As for me, I behold thy face in righteousness; I am satisfied, when I awake, with thee." He means that over against the present worldly prosperity of the wicked he himself is satisfied to have God on his side, secure by this fact of ultimate success and happiness in this life. The expression, "when I awake," cannot refer to the resurrection after death ; so important a fact would not be mentioned in this incidental manner, and the point under discussion is earthly well-being. The psalm may be an evening or morning hymn. The writer seems to have in mind the night (verse 3), or he may mean to say, in general, that when he awakes every morning, he is perfectly satisfied to have with him, not the power of his wicked enemies, but the presence of the God of Israel, in whose hand man's might is as nothing.[1] The strong expression of Ps. xlix. 15 (*Heb.* 16), "God will redeem me from the hand of Sheol," is identical in meaning with the similar expression in Ps. xvi. The hope expressed in Ps. lxxi. 20, "Thou who hast showed us many and sore troubles shalt quicken us again, and bring us up again from the depths of the earth," is shown by the context to relate to the restoration of earthly comfort and greatness. It seems equally clear that the striking passage in the Seventy-Third Psalm (verse 24),

---

[1] The expression "awake" is used of resurrection in Dan. xii. 2, and this psalm might belong to the same period (middle of second century n. c.); but Daniel plainly affirms the rising from the dead, while the thought of the psalm points in another direction. Further, Daniel contemplates a new life on earth, while the psalm-expression, if held to refer to the resurrection, would seem to involve the far more advanced conception of dwelling, probably in heaven, in the presence of God.

"Thou shalt guide me with thy counsel and afterward receive me to glory," refers only to the present life. The author has been deeply moved by the spectacle of the prosperity of the wicked. It was too painful for him, he says, until he went to the sanctuary of God and saw their latter end, — how they were consumed and cast down to destruction. He deplores his own ignorance and thoughtlessness in thus misconceiving the problem; yet, he adds, he is continually with God, upheld and guided by him, taken by him into a position of glory and happiness. In the heavens among the gods and on earth among men, he desires no helper but the God of Israel. They that are far from God shall perish (with earthly destruction); but as for him, he draws near to the Lord and makes him his refuge. Here it is still the present life of which the author is thinking. The precise meaning of the familiar passage in Job xix. (verses 25–27) is obscured by the corrupt character of the text. It is almost impossible to give a satisfactory translation of verse 26, and difficult to render verses 25 and 27. If we follow the guidance of the immediate context, we shall be inclined to hold that Job has in mind here only the earthly life. Why, oh, my friends, he exclaims, do you persecute me? Oh, that my words were written in a book, that the grounds of my defence against my accusers might be known; yet I am sure that my vindicator will at last appear; and do you, if you purpose still to persecute me, be afraid of the sword. There is a judgment for evil-doers!

Regarding these passages, then, as at least not decisive, it may be said that the Old Testament elsewhere (except in Daniel) persistently ignores the underworld as a motive for the present life. It is always with a tone of sadness that it speaks of Sheol. The dead cannot praise thee, exclaims the pious soul, lifting itself in supplication to God; the living, they shall praise thee. The psalm of thanksgiving ascribed to King Hezekiah (Isa. xxxviii.) is the expression of complete hopelessness in regard to the other life; similar representations are found in the book of Psalms. Everywhere a long life is esteemed the greatest of blessings, and all beyond this world is ignored; punishment consists not in pains in Sheol, but in the fact of the termination of earthly life, which is the cessation of all joyful and productive activity. The sanctions of the Mosaic law are wholly temporal. Not once does it urge men to obedience by the portraiture of future happiness or misery.[1]

It is the old Semitic conception of the other life. The Babylonian-Assyrian literature which we possess is as reticent as the Hebrew respecting the future as a moral element of the present life. Penitential psalms, where if anywhere we might expect a reference to the other life, confine themselves altogether to this world. The poem which describes the descent of the goddess Ishtar to Sheol gives indeed a striking picture of the underworld and its gates and bars and its presiding goddess, but has nothing to say of rewards and punishments for earthly lives. The case is the same with such fragments as remain of older Phœnician literature, and with the pre-Islamic Arabian poetry. The silence is all the more remarkable when we compare it with the full and varied declarations of the Egyptian ritual. For the Egyptian the world below was a completely organized kingdom; divine judges scrutinized each man's life and meted out to him his fit portion of reward or punishment. The future was ever present in men's minds as an incentive to good living; there was the hope of entrance into the blessed abodes and of assimilation to the gods themselves, and the fear of degradation and suffering. From time immemorial this elaborate scheme had existed in Egypt; and

____

[1] An ingenious but unwarranted turn is given to this fact in Warburton's "Divine Legation of Moses."

that the Israelites remained so long strangers to it is proof that they were never in lively intellectual intercourse with their Southern neighbors till the Greek conquest established a Jewish colony in Alexandria. There was in this regard a great gap between the Egyptian and Semitic races. We may perhaps refer the silence of the Semites on this point to their lack of constructive imagination. The divine, indeed, was ever present to them as a main factor in life. God forced himself on their notice in all the phenomena of nature. They felt in extraordinary degree the pressure of the out-ward powers, — powers which determined the actual course of their daily lives, which shaped their fortunes and demanded their reverence. As practical men of the world they felt the necessity of recognizing and propitiating the divine. But this very practicalness of nature led them to ignore that unseen world which could not force itself on their attention by any visible or tangible phenomenon. The result of their cool judgment was that the nether realm, to which all men indeed must descend, stood apart from the present life, in-capable in any perceptible way of influencing its issues. Their imagination recoiled from the effort of solving its mysteries. A similar lack of constructive power among the Semites is visible in other departments of thought. They have no drama, no metaphysic. With immense power of dealing with current facts (especially those relating to com-merce and religion), they have never succeeded in the organi-zation of conceptions. Imagination they have, but only in the sphere of the actual and practical. For them the under-world was too remote to tempt them to the invention of a nether organized community. This is part of the explana-tion of the enormous success of the Jews in practical life. They concentrated their efforts on the present. Here on this earth in the clash and conflict of this life, they served God and their age after their fashion, and looked for rewards and punishments. And that high spirituality may go along with such a negative conception of the future is abundantly proved by the glowing spiritual utterances of the Old Testament.

We have already observed a general and gradual increase of spirituality in the pre-Christian Jewish literature, a distincter sense of the vital ethical relationship between God and the human soul. This feeling of the dependence of man on God, the longing of the heart for friendly intercourse, might very well exist without belief in immortality; it might and doubtless often did spring partly from a profound sense of ethical weakness and desire for ethical perfectness, and partly from the non-ethical feeling of the need of protection;[1] it might have its roots in sentiments which belonged wholly to the present life. But it also naturally connected itself with another human instinct, — the desire for continuance and permanence. There is little indication, as has already been remarked, in the Hebrew feeling of the Old Testament times, of a projection of such hope beyond the grave; yet we can hardly doubt that many a man of those times looked curiously across the gulf that separated the present from the future and asked himself what it was that the God of Israel had in store for his people; to many a one there would come perhaps a glimmer of hope, or a more or less distinct demand of the soul. This demand and this hope would be heightened by the increasing spirituality of the conception of the relation between God and his people. The devout soul, conscious that its life was in God, would more and more recoil from the prospect of banishment from him; intense desire might lift itself into the form of belief. There had long been faith in national immortality; the prophets think

___

[1] These two elements must be carefully distinguished in the Psalms. Not every appeal to God is spiritual. There is much religiousness that is unethical, — a mere selfish desire for aid, which is a feeling common to man with the lower animals. It is not sufficient that God be invoked; there must be the effort to attain communion of soul with him as the ideal of holiness.

of the people as continuing forever. As the sentiment of individuality became more sharply defined, the pious soul, one might expect, would be less and less satisfied with this communal continuance of life, and would assert its rights to its own individual permanence in and by virtue of its relation to God. And of this forthreaching of the soul toward everlasting life, there may be indications in the psalm-passages quoted above,—not distinct declarations nor certain hopes, but dim surmises and longings. Such feelings could hardly have been general; the tone of the Old Testament respecting immortality is too distinctly negative to permit such a supposition. Perhaps a few gifted souls passed beyond the limits of the current thought; there was possibly a definite desire which might be the germ of a doctrine of immortality. But a defined doctrine there was not. Up to the beginning of the second century B. C., there was no such conception of life beyond the grave as furnished moral support and stimulus for the present life. Job, Psalms, Proverbs, the books, in which if anywhere we should expect to find the best outcome of thought in this direction, still occupy the old Semitic point of view.

It is in a book written under Greek influence that we find the first distinct declaration of a real doctrine of immortality. About the beginning of the second century B. C., three books were composed by Jewish writers, who sought to set forth a finished conception of wisdom,—that wisdom which was esteemed to be the highest quality of man, the broad and high conception of life, which was held to lift man above its ills, to ally him with its highest powers, and endow him with its greatest blessings. Of these books, that which is most decidedly negative in tone (reflecting probably the Greek sceptical philosophy of the time), Ecclesiastes, was received into the third Jewish canon, on grounds which are discussed above. It not only completely

ignores the future life, but treats the present as something
which offers no high hope; it defines wisdom as a large
and genial economy of resources, a pleasant, forbearing,
sceptical, and catholic moderation. The second work, Ecclesiasticus, which resembles in form the canonical book of
Proverbs, was apparently composed in Palestine, and certainly under the control of old Jewish modes of thought.
Though modern and fresh in its material, and full of striking
and suggestive remark, it has no word to say of the future
life. In marked contrast with the other two, the Wisdom
of Solomon, which shows unmistakable signs of the influence of Platonic and Stoic ideas, treats immortality as an
established fact, as one of the main elements of the present
life. The old question which so troubled and indeed discouraged and staggered many Jewish thinkers — he interpretation of the sufferings of the righteous and the prosperity
of the wicked — causes our author no anxiety. He does
not even discuss it; he assumes the solution to lie in the
life beyond the grave, where the inequalities of the present
life shall be equalized, where righteous and wicked shall
receive their just compensations and take their true places
in God's world.

One might then suspect that it was in some Alexandrian
Jewish circle, tinged with Greek thought, that the doctrine
of a true, everlasting life took distinct shape. Yet it is
not easy to find the Greek thought of that period which
might have suggested or determined such a faith. Ecclesiastes was written by a man who had tasted the Hellenic culture of his day; but the point which he reached was as far as
possible from the confident, joyous tone of belief in immortality. It may be surmised that it was from the school
which had established itself at Cyrene that he took the
hue of his conception of life; he has the cool scepticism
and good-natured indifference of the earlier Cyrenaic philoso-

phy, which might often be combined with strict ethical principle and exemplariness of life. It was not here that the author of the Wisdom of Solomon got his inspiration. It was rather, if we are to look to a Greek source, from some current of the old Platonism which survived the dissolution of the original systems of philosophy. In the third century B. C. men began to grow weary of metaphysical speculation and to seek for practical schemes of life.[1] Stoicism and Epicureanism split up into various schools, which all tended toward the same ethical result and toward the same metaphysical negations. But in Alexandria there was something which might quicken afresh the hopes concerning the future. The Egyptian people maintained their faith in the life beyond; their literature and their art, which could not remain wholly unknown to Jews and Greeks, kept the reality of this life prominent before men's eyes. The whole of Egyptian thought was so permeated and colored by a living faith in the tremendous importance of the future existence that no thoughtful foreigner could fail to be impressed by it. It was seed which might find favorable soil among both Jews and Greeks; for both these peoples there were lines of hope or belief going back generations to honored names, which might impel certain minds to look with intense interest on the spectacle of a nation which thus realized and honored the life to come. It was, perhaps, from a fusion of these lines of thought that the well-defined theory of immortality came into the world. The Greek, trained in habits of philosophic reflection, might find himself disposed to adopt the essential ethical content of the Egyptian scheme, while he rejected the local mythological machinery. But for him it would still be only a philosophical opinion. The Jew, seizing on this Egyptian hope, purified by Greek philosophy, could raise it to the

[1] On the history of Greek philosophy after Plato, see Zeller.

dignity of a religious dogma. When once it had commended itself to his mind as the solution of the highest problems of life, he would find hints or demonstrations of it in his own Scriptures, in the lives of the patriarchs, in the translation of Enoch and Elijah, in the words of the prophets, in the spiritual longing of the Psalms. Such was the method of Philo a couple of centuries later, and such seems to have been the method of the author of the Wisdom of Solomon; at least one would be inclined to infer that the review which he gives of the Israelitish history at the close of his book is regarded by him as an illustration of the doctrines of immortality and wisdom with which he begins. The Jews, like other nations, have always found in their Scriptures suggestions or proofs of beliefs which they from time to time adopted.

There is no complete documentary proof of the view above suggested. But it appears that while the national development of the native Jewish thought had not up to the beginning of the second century led to a belief in immortality, the doctrine is announced by a Jew who, while an orthodox and fervent adherent of his own national religion, was yet materially influenced by foreign ideas. We are thus naturally led to refer the origin of the doctrine to a fusion of the Jewish and non-Jewish elements.

3. In like manner the closely related idea of a bodily return from the underworld is probably to be accounted for by the influence of foreign thought. The doctrine of the resurrection of the dead appears for the first time toward the middle of the second century B. C. The germ of such a belief has been supposed to exist in purely Jewish parts of the Old Testament, in Ezekiel's vision of the dry bones (Ezek. xxxvii.), in Isa. xxvi. 19, in Job xix. 25–27, and in some of the Psalms (Ps. xvi. 10; xvii. 15). One might even be disposed to say that the dimness of the old Hebrew con-

ception of the underworld would naturally lead to the idea
of the resuscitation of the dead. So strong was the hold
which the earth and earthly life had on the Jew, so intense
his conviction that the enjoyment of God, whether bodily
or spiritual, pertained to this present worldly existence, that
if his religious instinct should demand a perpetuation of
happy life, he would, it might be supposed, naturally think
of its sphere as mundane, and its conditions as those which
belong to man's present and visible activity; it would be the
man of body and soul whom he would naturally imagine as
the bearer of truth and the recipient of blessing from the
divine hand. Yet however natural such an idea might seem
to be, there is no trace of it in Jewish literature before the
second century B. C. We have already seen how vague was
the conception of the future life in general; and there is
little reason to suppose a development of the idea of resurrection while the Sheol of that day remained unquestioned.
The passages above cited have really nothing to do with the
resurrection; the prophet Ezekiel himself explains (xxxvii.
11–14) that in the vision of the revivification of the dead
bones he means to give a symbolical prediction of the restoration of Israel to its own land. It was not that the individual should live again after death, but that the nation,
though crushed and shattered and politically dead, should
not perish, but should be lifted into an everlasting political
life. The reference in Isa. xxvi. 19, as appears from the
whole course of thought (see verses 15 and 20), is to a similar
national restoration. The passage in Job, so far as can be
gathered from the corrupt text, declares that the sufferer
shall see God, not in his flesh, but apart from it. The Sixteenth Psalm is a profession of satisfaction and delight in
Yahwe, not in the future, but in the present life; and the
"awaking" of Psalm xvii. refers, as the context almost certainly indicates, to this present life of ethical-religious prob-

lems, in which the psalmist purposes to attain to trust and tranquillity in spite of the rampant prosperity of the wicked. The translations of Enoch and Elijah are not examples of resurrection, but exceptional cases of removal from earth without the ordinary process of death, — a survival of the primitive belief, according to which heroes were elevated to positions in the abode of the gods.

It is apparently to non-Jewish sources that we must look for the formulation of the doctrine of the resurrection. The conception of the bodily re-clothing of man after death had been in the world a long time before it appears in Jewish books. It is found in rude forms in primitive faiths, and had survived, in developed shape, in various religions, though the Semites, with their unimaginative scepticism, seem to have rejected it altogether. In the form of transmigration of souls it was held by the Egyptians and the Hindus. There is, however, no indication that the Jews of this period came into contact with the religious thought of India; and the Egyptian doctrine seems not to have been distinct or impressive enough to suggest what we find in the Jewish belief of the time. It is probably to another point that we have to look. The book of Daniel, which contains the first statement of the resurrection in the Old Testament, shows considerable acquaintance with Babylonian and Old Persian history, and points to a connection with the Tigris-Euphrates region. The author writes like a man who, dwelling in what had formerly been the native land of Cyrus, had there met with a real though apparently not perfectly correct historical tradition, and had come into contact with the ideas of the place. Certain traces of Persian influence in the book have already been referred to; the angelology has obviously a Persian coloring, and it would seem that we must seek in the Persian eschatology the origin of the author's doctrine of resurrection.

Our information respecting Persian religious beliefs of this period is unfortunately very meagre. The inscriptions of the first Achaemenian princes, the earliest extant Persian documents, are concerned mainly with political affairs, and their religious utterances are naturally brief and indirect. If the date of the Avestan writings, in the form in which we now possess them, could be definitely fixed, we should be able to speak more advisedly of the Persian dogmas of the fourth and third centuries B. C.; but the best Avestan scholars regard the data as insufficient to determine the chronology with exactness. All that can be said is that Magism (probably a Median form of faith) obtained a firm footing in Persia during the fifth century B. C. So much we may infer from the description of Persian customs given by Herodotus (I. 131–140), in which the Magi appear as the only official priests Herodotus says nothing of the Magian-Persian doctrine of the future life;[1] but the details given by Theopompus (fourth century B. C.), as quoted by Plutarch (Isis and Osiris, 47), lead us to suppose that a doctrine of the resurrection existed in his time. At the end of the contest between Oromazes and Areimanios, says Theopompus, Hades will be abandoned, and men will be happy, neither needing food nor casting a shadow; that is to say, they will be endowed with new spiritual bodies. The supposition that the Magian-Persian religion recognized the bodily resurrection as early as the fourth century B. C. is not at all opposed to what we otherwise know of the persistence of the Zoroastrian dogma. If, as seems probable, the Avestan writings existed substantially in their present form some centuries before the beginning of our era, it is likely that this doctrine, connecting itself, as it does, so naturally with the whole Zoroastrian scheme, had already assumed definite shape as early as the Greek conquest. It

[1] But cf. Herod. III. 62.

might have come to the knowledge of Alexandrian Jews through such Greek writings as those of Theopompus, while it would linger in the Persian population still found in the Tigris region, and there, as has already been suggested, find its way to the Jewish colony which was at that time marked, as we have good reason to believe, by eager intellectual activity. The Jews have ever been willing borrowers of other nations' opinions; and such an idea as that of the resurrection of the body would harmonize with one side of Jewish thought and be absorbed by Jewish theology. The idea of the permanence of the national life had always been cherished by Israelites, and at a time when the hope of deliverance was keen, and the interposition of God was looked for, the suggestion that the nation's dead would be called back to earth to share in the nation's life might meet with welcome reception from ardent Jewish thinkers and believers. Its progress might be slow; a couple of centuries might elapse before it would be generally accepted. It would naturally be adopted slowly and cautiously by the leaders of Jewish thought, with such modifications as the old Jewish national faith suggested. The books of Psalms, Proverbs, and Ecclesiasticus know nothing of it, and the Mosaic law is equally silent. The doctrine seems never to have been received by the Sadducees (Matt. xxii. xxiii.), the priestly representatives of the old Mosaic orthodoxy. At first, as might be anticipated, the bodily resuscitation seems to have been limited to Israel; such appears to be the idea in Daniel (xii. 1–3). Israel alone, it was apparently supposed, was worthy of the supreme blessing of the everlasting perpetuation of the earthly life. Other peoples might be left to endure the inanity of the shadowy existence in Sheol; they had no covenant with God; there was no reason why they should be lifted again into the struggle of earthly life. Indeed, it might have appeared necessary for the peace of the chosen people that they alone should possess the earth, though on this point there was probably indefiniteness and difference of opinion. Daniel recognizes two classes of Israelites, one of which should awake to everlasting life, the other to shame and everlasting contempt. Here is the germ of the conception of a moral distinction among those who were raised from the dead. In process of time the doctrine of bodily resuscitation connected itself with that of final judgment, and with it approached the form of universality. This development of the doctrine seems to have been formulated not long before the beginning of our era. The second book of Maccabees (vii. 9, 14, 23), a work of uncertain date, possibly to be put about 100 B. C., apparently affirms resurrection only of Israel. One of the seven brothers says to the king: "It is good, being put to death by men, to look for hope from God to be raised up again by him. As for thee, thou shalt have no resurrection to life." On the other hand, the Parables of the book of Enoch appear to speak of a general resurrection. "In those days," says the writer, "the earth will return that intrusted to it, and Sheol will return that intrusted to it, which it has received, and Hell will return what it owes," — apparently a declaration that all men, good and bad, will rise from the dead.

How far the doctrine of a general resurrection prevailed during the first century of our era is not clear. It is found in the Fourth Gospel (v. 28, 29), and apparently in the Apocalypse (xx. 12). These books probably vouch for its prevalence toward the end of the century. But in the Synoptics and the writings of Paul and his school, though there is much about immortality and judgment and the resurrection of believers, no stress is laid on the rising of all men; it is even doubtful whether it is affirmed. Paul, in his argument for the resurrection (1 Cor. xv.), treats the rising from the dead as a purely Christian hope belonging to believers by virtue of their union with Christ.[1] Rom. ii. 1–16 and 2 Cor. v. 10 speak only of judgment, and in the latter passage it is not certain that the "we" includes any but Christians. He everywhere lays stress on the resurrection of Jesus in such a way as to show that he regards the raised body of the Redeemer as the pledge and the centre of the future blessed bodily existence of believers, as, therefore, offering no hope to the world at large. The ground adduced in the First Gospel (xxii. 31, 32) for the resurrection relates only to the chosen people: "I am the God of Abraham and the God of Isaac and the God of Jacob; God is not the God of the dead, but of the living."[2] The parables of the tares and of the net, and the great assize (Matt. xiii. xxv.), affirm not a general resurrection, but only the separation of the righteous and the wicked at the end of the age. We might thus be led to suspect that the doctrine in its general form did not establish itself till toward the end of the first century, when Christianity had with some definiteness separated from Judaism. Such a view would find support in the fact (Weber, "System," § 88) that the Talmudic-Midrashic literature recognizes only a resurrection of Israelites, holding it to be a part of the reward of the righteous. In truth, the restoration to bodily life is generally treated in the New Testament as a reward of Christian faith. For unbelievers there was no risen Redeemer, no definite centre of activity in the coming life. It might have been felt that for them

---

[1] Though he introduces two general considerations, — one (ethically low), that without hope of the future there would be no sufficient reason for well-doing (verse 32), the other based on the analogy of plant-life (verse 36), — he does not make a general application.

[2] The argument, as stated, goes to establish not resurrection, but immortality; but it seems that the former was regarded as included in the latter, a proof that the idea of resurrection was thoroughly ingrained in the popular belief. The Old Testament passage cited (Ex. iii. 6) contains, in the intention of its author, no hint of immortality, but merely the declaration that God would be faithful to the promises made to the fathers.

it was enough that they were abandoned to an endless existence of suffering. We must then suppose that the broader
idea of the Enoch-Parables (li.) did not for a long time obtain general recognition,[1] and was finally established through
the social intercourse that promoted belief in the equal
moral responsibility of all men. On the other hand, it is
possible that the idea existed, and is only not made prominent or distinctly brought out, because interest was concentrated on the Church. In fact, the conception of a general
resurrection seems allied to that of a general judgment. In
any case it appears that resurrection is treated practically
in the New Testament (and this is true largely even in the
Apocalypse and the Fourth Gospel) as a reward of believers. Its psychological basis is the desire for the continuance of human life, of which the body was regarded
as a necessary element, though this body might be thought
of as perfected into a fit dwelling-place for the regenerated
soul (1 Cor. xv. 44).

4. Hand in hand with the three just mentioned the doctrine of a last judgment advanced to its final formulation,
proceeding from a national to a universal form. The general notion of a divine decision respecting human conduct,
with appropriate rewards and punishments, belongs to the
essence of the conception of the deity. It is found loosely
expressed in primitive faiths, and in developed religions is
more definitely embodied in persons, in the Egyptian Osiris,
the Hindu Indra, the Persian Ahuramazda, the Babylonian
Shamash, the Greek Zeus, and the Roman Jupiter.[2] The

---

[1] It is open to the critic to suggest that the Enoch-passage in question
has been touched by a Christian hand. Otherwise it is not easy to account
for its ineffectiveness. The paucity of data makes the history obscure.

[2] It may be left undecided whether or how far the Jewish development of
the idea was affected by foreign influences At Alexandria the Egyptian
elaborate apparatus of underworld-judgment and the Athenian opinion (Plato,
Apology 32) would be well known. But the form in which the Jewish idea

progress of the idea was along three lines : the ethical element become more and more prominent ; individualism took the place of nationalism ; and the judgment, from being a purely earthly procedure, came to be regarded as the boundary between this life and the next. The history of the Jewish-Christian movement may be traced in general outline, though the data leave much to be desired in fulness and precision.

The ethical progress is tolerably well indicated in Old Testament, Apocrypha, and New Testament. There is steady advance in the standard of individual morality. In the Jewish scheme, however, the moral judgments attributed to God, though otherwise pure and high, are never quite free from the taint of nationalism. From the eighth century B. C. on, Yahwe is a just God within the national limits, punishing unsparingly the sins of his own people; but foreign nations are judged mainly according to their relations of friendliness or unfriendliness with Israel.[1] To be hostile to Israel was itself a crime; and this non-ethical standard of judgment clung to Judaism down to the times of the Talmud. Christianity did not wholly escape a similar limitation. Though the Sermon on the Mount declares that God will judge men simply according to the moral character of their conduct, the followers of Jesus put the Church into the place of the national Israel, and made acceptance of Jesus as Messiah the basis of the divine decision (2 Thess. i. 8; 1 Cor. xvi. 22;

is worked out (Daniel, Enoch, etc.) does not suggest Greek influence, and may be accounted for from native materials.

[1] See, for example, Amos i. ii., Isa x., Nahum, Obadiah, Joel iii. (*Heb.* iv.), and the very different estimates of Babylon given by the prophets of Nebuchadnezzar's time (Jer. xxv. 9; xxix. 7; xxxviii. 17; Ezek. xxix. 17–21) and those who lived when Cyrus' approach was expected (Isa. xiii. xiv. xlvi. xlvii.; Jer. l. li). Jeremiah and Ezekiel have not one unkind word to say of Babylon, because it was, in their opinion, the protector of Israel; but the Babylonian kingdom, though its moral character could not have changed materially in fifty years, is denounced so soon as it is regarded as hostile.

1 John v. 10). Men were to be judged by their works (Rev.
xx. 12), but the "works" included belief in the Christ. The
general ethical standard was high, but a controlling non-
ethical condition was introduced.

Nevertheless, there was a gradual recession from the old
nationalistic point of view; that is, the individual came
more and more to be the human unit. The beginning of
this movement is seen, as has already been pointed out, in
such passages as Ezek. xviii., which affirms a moral distinction in the judgments on Israelites. The progress is clearer
in the Wisdom of Solomon and in the sayings of the lawyers, which treat character without respect to nationality.
The mingling of peoples during the two centuries preceding
the beginning of our era led, in the better minds, to a partial obliteration of national lines; the feeling arose that there
was a definite relation between God and every human being.
The individual was no longer swallowed up in the community. It is doubtful, as is intimated above, whether the
divine judgment was ever in the Jewish and Christian developments completely sundered from religious dogma. It
was probably held that character acceptable to God could
never be attained apart from certain religious beliefs peculiar
to Judaism or Christianity. But it was a great point gained
when the conviction was established, as a living principle,
that each man must give account of himself, that the divine
judgment would be meted out to each on his own merits.
This principle, on which the New Testament everywhere
insists, existed indeed elsewhere, but was firmly planted in
society by the powerful agency of Christianity.

The conception of a universal judgment was involved in
the developed Hebrew religion. Yahwe was king and guardian of his people; and in order that he might assign them
their proper position in the world, it was necessary that
other nations should be cited before the divine tribunal and

judged for their offences against the chosen people. In the pre-exilian and exilian prophets God is represented as administering punishment to the enemies of Israel from time to time, as occasion demanded. A more formal judicial procedure is hinted at in Joel, Zechariah (xiv.), and some of the Psalms (xcvi. xcviii.). The apocalyptic books of the second century B. C. introduced more definitely the idea of a summing up of things and the inauguration of Israel's reign by a general divine judgment (Dan. vii.; Enoch i.). In Daniel (xii.) this consummation is not unnaturally connected with the return of dead Israelites to bodily life, — the pious to share in the national triumph, the apostates to suffer merited punishment. God was the judge; and the scene of the judgment and of the succeeding life was on the earth, probably Palestine (Enoch lxxxix. 40).[1] It was a reconstruction of earthly society, with Israel as centre and lord. This was the simple national and earthly idea of the final divine judgment that prevailed up to about the middle of the second century B. C. Two other articles of faith, recently adopted by the Jews, then took their place in the scheme and gave rise to some complication of views, — these were the expectation of a personal Messiah, and the belief in immortality.

It was only gradually that the deliverer, who finally received the title of Messiah, was brought into connection with the judgment. In the prophets he is a Davidic king, employing the usual means of a political leader to secure national success; in Daniel he disappears, and the agent of salvation is the angel Michael; in the original Enoch and the Psalter of Solomon he is a human leader. Up to this point he has nothing to do with the final authoritative reconstruction of the world. But there soon arose a

---

[1] In Enoch i. the place of judgment seems to be Mount Sinai, though this is not clear.

new conception of his person and function ; he was represented as being of a very exalted (though not divine)
nature, and the immediate conduct of the final judgment
was assigned to him. Whether this new function was inferred from the new nature, or the nature from the function, or both arose out of the same conditions, it is not
easy to say. It is in the Enoch-Parables that the higher
idea of the Messiah first appears. Here he is the chosen
one, set apart from all eternity, hidden and then revealed,
who, endowed with all wisdom, sits on his throne, receives
homage, judges powerful kings and all sinners, and dis-
penses rewards and punishments. The same conception of
Messianic judgment is contained in the earliest of Paul's
writings (1 Thess. iv. ; 2 Thess. i.), and perhaps in 2 Cor.
v. 10 ; it is involved in the apocalyptic letters to the
churches (Rev. ii. 23), and is distinctly affirmed in 2 Tim.
iv. 1 and John v. 27. On the other hand, in the apocalyptic
pictures, and especially in the great judicial scene at the
end of the book (Rev. xix. xx.) it is not quite clear whether
it is God or the Messiah who is the judge. The Lamb
opens the sealed book (v.), and all men flee from his
wrath (vi. 16) ; but seals, trumpets, and bowls usher in only
preliminary judgments, and the day of final decision is still
in the future. When that day comes, it is apparently God
before whose throne the dead appear (xx. 11).[1] In the
Synoptics the Messiah appears as judge (as in 2 Thess.)
in the apocalyptic discourse (Mark xiii., Matt. xxiv., Luke
xxi.), and in the judgment-scene of Matt. xxv. According
to the later Jewish view (Weber, "System," § 88), as it
would seem, the final judgment is conducted by God.

[1] The similarity between the royal functions of the Messiah in the Enoch-
Parables and the New Testament Apocalypse is of such sort as to suggest
that the one was taken from the other, or that the two issue out of the same
circle of views. This favors the hypothesis that the Apocalypse contains a
Jewish basis which has been built upon by a Christian hand.

The evidence, with the exception of that of the Enoch-
Parables, points to a Christian origin for the conception of
the Messiah as final judge. In any case this function is
closely connected with an idealization of his person, which
lifted him above the ordinary human sphere, — an exaltation that is explained more naturally from Christian conditions (following on the disappearance of Jesus from earth),
but cannot be said to be impossible for an earlier Jewish
circle of thought. It is possible that Paul's view was
affected by some current opinion like that of the Parables
(the date of which is probably not long after B. C. 40). A
Jewish idealization of the Messiah, arising from reflection on the great rôle assigned him as national deliverer,
may have coalesced with a similar Christian tendency. In
the Old Testament (as in Ps. ii.) the king of Israel is represented as ruling all the nations, whence to his elevation to
the position of judge at God's right hand (see Ps. cx.) it
would be no great step. It is always as God's vicegerent
that the Messiah exercises his judicial functions (John v. 22;
cf. 1 Cor. xv. 24). That the conception of the Messiah as
judge was gradually accepted by the Church of the first century may perhaps be inferred from the infrequency of reference to it in the New Testament. Of the history of the idea
in the period between the Enoch-Parables and the First Epistle to the Thessalonians we have no certain information.

So long as the Jews had no effective and universal doctrine of immortality, the divine judgment was necessarily
conceived of as confined to the earth. Daniel, the Sibyl,
the original Enoch, and the Psalms of Solomon picture the
future in a vague way as the destruction or subjugation
of foreign nations and the establishment of Israel in perpetual peace and prosperity through the protecting presence
of God. The judgment ushers in only a change of earthly
relations; there is a resurrection, but the abode of the

blessed people is still the earth, though the earth transfigured (see Isa. lxv. 17; Enoch xc. 33; cf. 2 Pet. iii. 13).
There appears to be no material advance in the ethical
representation in the Enoch-Parables; the antithesis is in
form a general one, between the just and the evil, but the
evil are the enemies of Israel, and Israel's new place of
abode is the earth (xlv. 5). Throughout the book of Enoch
(x. liv.) judgment is passed on evil angels as well as on
evil men. It is apparently in the Parables that the belief
in immortality first shows itself in connection with the
judgment; the just enjoy everlasting life (xxxvii., lviii.); sinners dwell in endless shame (xlvi. 6). Here is the germ
of a new signification of the expressions, "age to come" and
"kingdom of God," or "kingdom of heaven." The age to
come is essentially the era of social regeneration, ushered
in by the God-appointed deliverer, to endure forever, and
this is the kingdom of God or of heaven. It was originally the happy life of the chosen of God on the earth; the
general effect of the introduction of the full idea of immortality was to transfer it to heaven, and to make the
judgment a formal winding-up of all earthly affairs, with
discontinuance of the present earthly life. But a complete
assimilation of this new element was not effected at once;
the New Testament presents slightly varying views of the
judgment and of the future. Most of the Epistles, absorbed
in the present needs of the struggling Church, content
themselves with looking to the coming of Christ (thought
to be impending) for the judgment which was to introduce
his followers into eternal bliss. Second Peter (iii. 13) regards this earth as the scene of the future life; and the
same expectation is perhaps contained in Rom. viii. 19,
where the outward creation, groaning in the pain of sin, is
represented as looking eagerly for deliverance in the revelation of the sons of God, though Paul elsewhere (1 Thess.

iv. 17) appears to hold a different opinion. In general it seems to be the larger idea of immortality that the Epistles have in view, a state the conditions of which differ from those of earthly life (so also Matt. xxii. 30).[1] The Synoptics give signs of the Messiah's appearance, and describe a final general judgment (Matt xxiv., xxv.). The Fourth Gospel omits all particulars, presenting only the moral-religious conflict of earthly life and the fact of final judgment (v.) The Apocalypse has a series of partial judgments, a preliminary imprisonment of Satan during the millennial reign of the saints, and a final universal judgment (xx.). The kingdom of God is viewed sometimes as present (1 Cor. iv. 20; Rom. xiv. 17), sometimes as in the future (Matt. vii. 21; viii. 11; 2 Tim. iv. 11); that is, it is a constitution of things beginning now and having its culmination and completion in the future. "This age" (rendered "this world" in the English version) is the present condition of things reaching up to the coming of Christ to judgment (Gal. i. 4; Matt. xii. 32; Tit. ii. 12); the final decision is made at the end of the age (Matt. xiii. 40). The "age to come" is the period following the appearance of the Messiah. According to the Jewish view it is still in the future, since the Messiah has not come. In the Christian conception it has a double meaning; it may be historical Christianity introduced by Jesus (Heb. vi. 5; Eph. ii. 7, "ages to come"), or the period following the final Messianic judgment (Mark x. 30; Matt. xii. 32). In Heb. ix. 26 Christ is said to have been manifested and sacrificed "now once at the end of the ages," and with this is contrasted his second coming to judgment (verse 28). The double meaning of the expression was natural; it signified the reign of

---

[1] See 2 Thess. i.; 1 Cor. i. 8; xv.; 2 Cor v 10, Rom. ii 16; Phil. i 6; 2 Tim. iv. 1; Heb. vi. 2; ix. 27; 1 Pet. iv. 5, v 10; 2 Pet. i. 11; Jude 21; 1 John iv. 17. James and First Timothy have only the expectation of the coming of Christ, and Galatians is occupied with salvation and eternal life.

truth, the time of adjustment, when the wrongs of the present should be righted, when the righteous should enjoy the dignity that was properly theirs in a world governed by a righteous God, and the wicked should pay the penalty of their impious defiance and their unnatural worldly prosperity. The first fruits of that blessed time appeared under the Messiah's earthly rule ; the consummation could be reached only when earthly existence was over and men's destinies were fixed in an endless existence beyond the grave. The first phase was introductory to the second; for the individual and for the nation or Church the future blessedness was the continuation and completion of the earthly peace, — a conception that could not assume perfect shape till immortality, heaven, and hell had become familiar ideas.

The Church received the doctrine of judgment from Judaism, and introduced the additions mentioned above without always discarding Jewish local views, which should have been set aside by the spirit of Christianity. This is true of the old belief that the Jewish nation should be permanently established in political independence in its own land. Such in fact is the declaration of the prophets (Ezek. xxxvii. 25 and many other passages). Christianity in general substituted the Church for the nation, and interpreted the prophetic promises as signifying the conversion of the Jews to faith in Jesus,[1] — an interpretation which is exegetically unsound, but, if held, completely sets aside the expectation of political permanence. In spite of this there have always been Christian circles which held after

---

[1] Paul does not entirely escape confusion of thought on this point. After making an argument (Rom. iv., ix. 7, 8 ; x.) from the Old Testament to show that the promises were not to the bodily descendants of Abraham but to all who had like faith with him, he cites similar passages (Rom. xi. 25, 26) to prove that the bodily, national Israel shall all be saved. His exegesis is controlled at one time by his religious-dogmatic feeling, at another by his patriotism.

the dispersion of the Jews to their restoration to Palestine as part of the final divine settlement of earthly affairs.

5. The formulation of the doctrines of immortality and judgment was accompanied by the reconstruction of the theory of the future life. The old Hebrew idea of Sheol as the colorless abode of all the dead gradually gave way to the representation of a place of happiness for the righteous and a place of punishment for the wicked. The growing sense of ethical individuality demanded the future meting out of proper reward to earthly moral-religious character, and the details of existence beyond the grave were gradually worked out. The Egyptians had a well-developed system of rewards and punishments in the underworld, but the idea remained strange to the Semites. The conception of "hell" is not found in the Old Testament;[1] there is no local distinction in Sheol between good and bad,[2] no apparatus of reward and punishment. The reward of the righteous is long life on earth (Prov. iii. 16); the punishment of the wicked is premature death (Prov. x. 27). The first departure from the old conception of the future is found in the book of Daniel (xii. 2) in connection with the idea of resurrection; of those Israelites who are raised to life, it is said, some will be happy and some wretched. Enoch similarly describes the punishment of bad Israelites (xxvii. 2; xc. 26) and of evil angels (x. 6, 14; xc. 24, 25; liv.) at the judgment. In the Parables (liv., lvi.), the punishment is not confined to Jews, but falls on all wicked men. In the early days of the Maccabean struggle it was only Israelites who were included in the scheme of resurrection; later, it was extended to include all men. In Enoch there is an abyss (x.)

---

[1] Abaddon, "destruction" (Job xxvi. 6; xxviii 22, Prov. xv. 11) is simply a synonym of Sheol.

[2] In such passages as Ezek. xxxi. 18; Isa. xiv 9, the point is the overthrow of mighty and insolent enemies of Israel.

or valley (liv.) of fire prepared for the disobedient angels ;
so in Matt. viii. 29, the demons look forward to a time
when their torment is to begin. In the Parables (liv., lvi.),
human sinners (that is, enemies of Israel) are cast into the
valley of fire.

How did the Jews reach the practical conception of rewards and punishments after death? Were they driven to
it by moral-religious feeling, — by their sense of the inequalities and injustices of this life? In that case we
should expect to find hints of the idea in such books as
Psalms and Proverbs ; but there are no such hints. On
the other hand, its first affirmation in the existing literature
occurs in connection with a doctrine which we have seen
reason to believe was developed under Persian influence,
and in Enoch it stands in close relation with the demonology. Are we to see the influence of Persian thought here
also? The data hardly warrant an answer to this question : we know too little of the Persian dogma of that time.
Nor can we look to Egypt. The idea seems not to have
arisen in the Jewish colony in Egypt, nor is there great
resemblance between the Jewish and the Egyptian schemes.
The details in Enoch, such as the valley and the fire and
the chains, may have been suggested by the Old Testament
or by the ordinary imagination. Of the main idea we can
only say that the Jewish moral consciousness was prepared
for it and that it arose out of the conditions of the time.
It was familiar to the Egyptians and not unknown to the
Greeks. Once suggested to the Jews, it would supply what
they had probably been conscious of needing. Attached to
the doctrine of resurrection it would accord with fundamental Israelitish beliefs. Confined at first to members of
the chosen people, it would come, by the growth of ethical
feeling, to embrace other nations.

Christianity took the conception from Judaism. The representation of future punishment in the New Testament is substantially the same as that of Enoch. The specific term for hell is Gehenna (Matt. v. 22 ; Jas. iii. 6), the "valley of Hinnom," the spot consecrated to the old Moloch-worship (2 Kings xxiii. 10 : Isa. xxx. 33 ; lxvi. 24), an abominable place of filth which became the symbol of future torment. Elsewhere " Hades " (in Greek, the dwelling-place of all the dead) is used in very much the same sense (Matt. xi. 23 ; Luke xvi. 23 ; Rev. xx. 13, 14). When specific terms had been devised for the abode of happiness, the general Greek term was applied to the other division of the life beyond.[1] It was conceived of in general as a subterranean place of torment. The tormenters, however, are apparently not Satan and the demons, who are themselves tormented, but the good angels appointed by God to that office (Enoch liii. liv.; Rev. xx. 10). It seems to be intimated by Paul that the saints, the believers in Jesus, are to take part in the final judgment of wicked men and disobedient angels (1 Cor. vi. 2, 3); but it is not said in what relation they are afterward to stand to the lost. In the parable of the rich man and Lazarus (Luke xvi. 19–31) it is declared that bodily communication between the denizens of Paradise and those of Hades is impossible, there being a great gulf between them (verse 26); yet the sufferer appeals to Abraham, whom

---

[1] Except in the Synoptics and the Apocalypse, almost nothing is said of hell in the New Testament. James (iii. 6), looking on it as the locus and representative of all evil, speaks of its setting the tongue on fire; Jude (6, 13) and Second Peter (ii. 4, 17) have mention of the bonds in which the disobedient angels are held in darkness unto judgment (Second Peter calls the place of punishment Tartarus) and of the blackness of darkness reserved for certain false teachers. Elsewhere only general expressions, such as " destruction " and " condemnation of the devil," are employed. This reticence may be explained in part from the practical aim of the Epistles, which are mostly occupied in meeting actual emergencies and building up the life of the Church; it may also be true that the conception of the place of punishment became distincter and more familiar after Paul's time.

he supposes to be invested with authority, and begs him to send Lazarus on a mission of mercy.[1]

As to the duration of future punishment, the general doctrine of the New Testament is that it is to be without end, — it is to endure as long as the blessed life of the righteous (Matt. xxv. 46 ; Rev. xx. 10, 15 ; xxi. 4, 8, 27 ; xxii. 5, 11, 15). Such is the representation of Paul in First Corinthians. The abolition of death (1 Cor. xv. 26, 54) is not the abolition of the suffering of the wicked, but, as is clear from Rev. xxi. 14 and 2 Tim. i. 10, the annulment of all suffering for the righteous and the beginning of the endless torment of the unrighteous. It is doubtful how we are to understand the declaration in Colossians (i. 20), that it was God's purpose to reconcile to himself through Christ all things on earth and in the heavens. From a comparison of other statements in the Epistle (as ii. 15, where Christ triumphs over the principalities and the powers, and iii. 4, where at the manifestation of Christ only the saints are to be manifested with him in glory), we might rather conclude that the writer's intention is to ascribe all reconciliation to Christ, but not to affirm such a pleroma or fulness in Christ or such a summing up of things (Eph. i. 10, *Anakephalaiosis*) as would exclude that retribution for evil doing which everywhere else in the New Testament is assumed to be an essential part of the divine government of the universe. If, however, we are to see here the conception of a final reconciliation between God and his creatures, a blotting out of evil in the sense that it shall be transformed into good, a complete harmonizing of the universe so that neither angel nor man shall be found to set himself against the divine ethical order, then we must hold this view to spring out of a philosophical thought which does not find

---

[1] This, however, may be merely a part of the framework of the parable, introduced simply to bring out the final character of the doom of the departed.

support elsewhere in the New Testament, and which did not afterward meet with wide approbation in the Church.

So soon as the idea of a future life of compensation and happiness for the good was established, the question would arise in men's minds where the abode of the righteous should be. This subject has been mentioned above from time to time. The points may be summed up briefly. There was not unnaturally fluctuation of opinion. The history of the future had to be constructed from such data as were at hand, and the data were indefinite and to some extent mutually contradictory. The prophets of course thought of Jerusalem as the centre of the coming kingdom of bliss (Isa. lxvi.), and this continued to be the national Jewish view. A new Jerusalem, as the capital of the Messianic kingdom, is found in the book of Enoch (xc. 29); in the New Testament this representation is given in the Apocalypse (xxi., xxii.). The earth, according to this Jewish-Christian conception, was to be the home of the saved, but the earth reconstructed, purified from all evil, new heavens and a new earth (2 Pet. iii. 13; after Isa. lxv. 17; lxvi. 22), the abode of righteousness. It was the conviction that man's life is tied to this earth, modified by the feeling that a regeneration of the sin-stricken external world was essential (so Paul in Rom. viii. 18–22). It is doubtful whether the earthly Paradise, the reconstructed Eden of Genesis, was regarded in the New Testament times as the future abode of the righteous. Such an opinion would be not unnatural; it would be a return to the primitive blessedness from which man's transgression had expelled him. The history of the world would then become the record of the divine movement for the subjugation of the powers of evil which had intruded themselves into the first happy creation of God. There is a hint of such a view in the Enoch-Parables (lxi. 12), where the "garden of life" is the dwelling-place of the chosen. The same spot under the name of the "garden of justice" is described in an earlier portion of the book (xxxii.), but without intimation that it was assigned to the chosen as their habitation. The term "paradise"[1] is indeed employed several times in the New Testament to designate the future dwelling-place of the righteous, but the locality which it is intended to mark is left uncertain. In the Apocalypse (ii. 7) it is simply mentioned as the reward of those who overcome; in the Third Gospel (xxiii. 43) it is the abode into which the righteous enter immediately after death ("To-day," says Jesus to the malefactor, "shalt thou be with me in Paradise"); Paul, with somewhat more definiteness, seems to identify Paradise with the third heaven (2 Cor. xii. 2–4). It may be added that the expression "Abraham's bosom"[2] (Luke xvi. 22), while it signifies a state of content and happiness, is not definite as to locality. There is a gulf between the abode of the saved and that of the lost, but whether on earth or in Sheol or in some celestial region is not said. But Christian opinion moved toward the hope of a future dwelling with Christ in some bright celestial place. "We," says Paul, "shall be caught up in the clouds to meet the Lord in the air, and so shall we ever be with the Lord" (1 Thess. iv. 17). "Rejoice and be exceeding glad," we read in the Ser-

---

[1] The word ($\pi\alpha\rho\acute{\alpha}\delta\epsilon\iota\sigma\sigma$) is generally held to be of Persian origin (etymology uncertain), the original sense being "park" (Xen. Anab. i. 2, 7, etc.); so it is employed in the Hebrew Old Testament (pardes, only in very late books, Neh. ii. 8; Eccl. ii. 5; Cant. iv. 13). In the Septuagint it is the rendering of the "garden" of Eden (Gen. ii. 15); thence it easily passed to represent the future abode of the righteous. See Smith, "Dictionary of the Bible," art. Paradise; Friedrich Delitzsch, "Wo lag das Paradies?" Weber, "System," § 75.

[2] The expression is derived from the Roman habit of reclining at table. The existence of the saved is pictured as a feast, where Abraham the father of the Jewish nation, is head and master, and the righteous man, as honored guest, reclines with his head on the bosom of the patriarch (cf. Luke xiii. 29).

mon on the Mount (Matt. v. 12), "for great is your reward in heaven." "When Christ," says one epistle, "who is now seated on the right hand of God, shall be manifested, then believers shall with him be manifested in glory" (Col. iii. 1–4). The person of Christ formed the centre of the Christian picture of the future; happiness was the being with him. But beyond the feeling that there was to be no suffering and no anxiety, the details of the blessed life are not given. The New Testament writers are concerned with practical affairs. All that the Church needed was the support and the stimulus of the transcendent hope of coming blessedness.

The question of the condition of men between death and the final judgment is not fully treated in the pre-Christian literature or in the New Testament. The original Enoch (xxii.) divides the intermediate abode of souls into several[1] compartments. One is for the righteous who (like Abel) suffered injustice on earth, another for sinners who were not punished on earth, another for sinners who were punished on earth, their fate after death being thereby mitigated. The place is described indefinitely as being "in the west," but is apparently in the underworld. The New Testament statements or allusions present a simpler scheme. Paul, at a time when he expected to witness before death the coming of Christ (1 Cor. xv. 51, 52), naturally thought of passing from earth directly into the presence of the Lord (2 Cor. v. 4–8); at a later period (Phil. i. 21–23) he speaks of death as equivalent to union with Christ.[2] The Epistle to the Hebrews (xii. 23) regards the spirits of the just as already made perfect; and in the Apocalypse (vi. 9–11) the souls of the martyrs (like the soul of Abel in Enoch) cry

---

[1] The text says "four," but only three can be clearly made out. The number is not important; the fact of punishment and division is clear.

[2] Yet in this Epistle also (i. 6, 10: iii. 20) he seems to expect the parousia in that generation.

for vengeance on their slayers. In the Lazarus-parable the righteous man and the sinner pass immediately to their rewards, and so the thief on the cross. The reasonable inference is that in the main teaching of the New Testament earthly death ushers men immediately into a new life and fixes their destinies forever for happiness or misery. Such also is the view in Daniel (xii.) and in Enoch (xxii., cii., ciii.; cf. Wisd. of Sol. iii. 10, 19; v.). Neither annihilation nor future probation can be affirmed to belong to the prevailing doctrine of the first century. Annihilation was a conception foreign to Jewish thought. It does not appear in Ecclesiastes, the most sceptical of pre-Christian Jewish writings; it is found nowhere in the New Testament. The terms "destruction" and "death," so often used to describe the future state of the wicked, are taken from the Old Testament, and are obviously intended to express not the annulment of existence but the cessation of happy activity. Good and bad must continue to live after bodily death, and continuing to live, must accept the conditions which the government of a just God imposes. Nor is there any trace in pre-Christian Jewish literature or (with one exception) in the New Testament of a disciplinary and restorative force in future suffering, or of the conception of a moral probation continued after death. The prevailing tone of the Jewish thought on this point is summed up in the word of the New Testament Apocalypse (Rev. xxii. 11): "He that is unrighteous, let him be unrighteous still, and he that is holy, let him be holy still." Such is the representation in the parable of the rich man and Lazarus (Luke xvi.), — there is an impassable gulf between the good and the bad. The only New Testament passage which seems to teach the possibility of repentance and salvation after death is the obscure paragraph in the First Epistle of Peter (iii. 18–20; iv. 6), where Christ is said to have preached, after his death, in the spirit, to the spirits in prison ; that is, as it seems, to those men who, disobedient to the divine command in the days of Noah, were now in bonds in the underworld. The intention of the writer of the Epistle seems to be to represent Christ as preaching the Gospel to these imprisoned spirits that the possibility of believing and being saved might be offered them (a similar view is found in the Talmud). But this passage, if that be its meaning, stands alone; everywhere else death seals man's fate. The decisive impetus to preaching came from the conviction that what was to be done for men must be done in this life. The most dreadful summing up of destiny is found in the words, " Ye shall die in your sins " (John viii. 24).[1]

The idea of moral probation, which runs throughout the Hebrew and Christian Scriptures, being indeed at the bottom of every scheme of life, is modified or controlled by that conception of a final judgment which passed over from Judaism into Christianity. The antithesis is distinctly stated in Acts xvii. 30, 31 : " God commands all men to repent, inasmuch as he has appointed a day in which he will judge the world." There is nothing in man's view of his own nature that should lead him to regard death as putting a quietus on free moral development. Other nations had doctrines of continuous growth and possibility of moral revolution and regeneration in the life beyond ; but the Jewish monarchical scheme of an organized kingdom with God as king, following the analogy of human governments, assumed a final judicial sentence passed on enemies with permanent security for citizens of the kingdom. It was an external, mechanical conception of human life. The soul of man, with its ceaseless ethical struggle, was lost sight of in the picture (grand

---

[1] On the later Jewish view of the condition of men after death see Weber, " System," cap. xxi. The Talmudic doctrine of purgatorial suffering in hell seems to have arisen after the first century.

in itself) of a universe forced into submission to an all-powerful ruler.

Thus Christian thought, following on a long course of Jewish growth, reached the conception of a highly organized kingdom of God beginning on earth and completed in heaven. This conception, resting on an ethical basis (though it also contained non ethical elements), satisfied both the desire for permanent happiness and the demand for moral perfection; it included present holiness and future blessedness. For its content it had drawn on all the available resources of the Western world. It took from Jewish and Persian theology and eschatology and from Greek ethical philosophy what it could assimilate, and rejected the rest. Its guide was the Jewish religious instinct enlightened and broadened by contact with the other great religious systems of the time and the region. It was the Israelitish nation which by all its endowments and training was best fitted to undertake the organization of a religion for the world. But the Jews could not alone have provided all that was required, and but for the social unity created by the Greek and Roman empires would neither have felt the need of foreign help nor been in position to profit by it. Paul, the creative mind of the first great organizing period of Christianity, represents Jewish theology constrained and impelled by non-Jewish surroundings.

The Jewish scheme of national-political supremacy was soon cast away by the disciples of Jesus, and in its place was substituted the hope of the future triumph of the Church. This was the essence of Christian eschatology, and it was this that furnished the main motive power of Christian effort. The New Testament throughout holds up the rewards of the future as the incentive to present holiness. The eschatology necessarily shaped itself out of the ideas of the time, and the task of the creators of Christianity

was to select these so wisely, with such combined liberality
and sobriety, that the result should offer the world of that
time just what it needed for support and inspiration in the
hard struggle of life. How well they chose, time has shown.
But for this distinct and reasonable hope of the future, it
may safely be said, Christianity would not have imposed
itself on the world; it would have shared the fate of Greek
ethical systems, which were philosophically lofty but lacking in fulness of life.

On the other hand, it is evident that the Jewish-Christian
conception of the kingdom of God, though encumbered with
mechanical, soteriological, and eschatological elements, reposed on an ethically practical and strenuous scheme of the
present earthly life. Prophets and apostles are at one in
holding up a high moral standard and insisting that men
are to suffer or enjoy the consequences of their earthly deeds.
No man, they say, can do wrong with impunity. The punishment of evil they refer, it is true, not to a divinely constituted course of nature, but to a specific divine decree:
in any case it is just and inevitable. No one can enter the
kingdom of God except by conforming himself to the ethically perfect divine will; the new man is created in holiness; the essence of the divine kingdom is righteousness;
whatever a man sows, that he shall reap, — such is the burden of all utterances of Old Testament and New Testament.
This has remained a permanent element of Christianity. Theories of atonement, of faith and works, of heaven and hell,
have changed from time to time; the ethical conception of
life has stood fast. Apart from its framework of dogmatic
apparatus Christianity offered the world of the first century
a simple working theory of God and man, — God just and
loving, man free and responsible. By its dogma it was attractive and effective; on its ethical-religious side it was
worthy of its triumph.

CHAPTER VIII.

RELATION OF JESUS TO CHRISTIANITY.

WE have thus endeavored to trace the process by which
Judaism, the religion of a nation, was transformed
into Christianity, a religion for the world. We have followed the progress of the Israelitish faith in its efforts to
formulate ideas, to organize life, to rise to greater spirituality, to reach the breadth which the advancing thought
of the people demanded. At a certain point in its career
a new faith suddenly sprang into existence, which from a
feeble and undefined beginning soon assumed an assured
and vigorous form. It first showed itself as a new conception of that kingdom of God which in one shape and
another had been the dream of the pious of Israel for
many centuries. This new conception was a startling one.
Whereas prophets, psalmists, and apocalyptists had thought
of the ultimate earthly state of blessedness as a moral and
political reconstruction of the nation, — political independence and perfection of national obedience to the Law, —
Jesus made the essence of the new life to be the purity
of the individual soul. The deliverer, who had always been
conceived of as a temporal king, he held to be a teacher
sent from God to show men the spirit of the divine law.
While he said nothing of an abrogation of the Mosaic law
or of the equality of all nations in the sight of God, he
announced principles which by giving paramount importance to the spiritual tended to depress the ceremonial, to

abolish outward distinctions, and to lead to the conclusion that all men stood in the same relation to God. His disciples, at first only dimly apprehending his spirit, but looking after his death for his reappearance as the divinely promised deliverer of Israel, gradually formed themselves into a separate society, which speedily became a church. Into the new organization came Gentiles, — men who stood outside the tradition of Jewish national custom, and valued in Christianity other than its purely Jewish ideas, — and in their interests a further reconstruction became desirable. This was effected mainly by the Apostle Paul, under whose lead a large section of the Church threw off circumcision, the badge of Jewish nationality, dispensed in general with Jewish ceremonial, and made the person of Jesus Christ the ground of salvation and the centre of the religious life. The expectation of his speedy reappearance, becoming by degrees more composed, took its place as part of the Christian hope; preparation for heaven was held to consist in religious-ethical faithfulness. He came to be thought of as the eternal Son of God, and then, under the influence of Greek philosophy, as the eternal Word, the reason, utterance, and agent of God in the physical and spiritual creation and maintenance of the world. In process of time the Church passed entirely out of the hands of the Jews into the hands of the Gentiles, entered the circle of Roman and western European thought, and submitted to those changes which were entailed by the progress of civilization. What is the relation of Jesus of Nazareth to this vast movement of human thought? This question has been touched on in the preceding pages, but we may here attempt, at the risk of some repetition, to answer it more directly and fully.

1. In the first place, it seems evident that Jesus announced those germinal principles of which the succeeding history of Christianity is only a development. The records of his teach-

ing leave much to be desired. His words are not always correctly reported, and there are not a few interpolations from later tradition; nevertheless, it seems possible to gather from the New Testament a fairly faithful idea of the spirit of his instruction.

We have recognized in the pre-Christian Jewish literature the progress which the Jewish mind was making in ethical breadth and spirituality. Various thinkers had reached very high conceptions of the principles of moral conduct and of the nature of religion (Proverbs, Psalms, Wisdom of Solomon, Wisdom of the Son of Sirach, Hillel). There was an earnest effort to grasp spirituality; and this must be set over against the tendency of the extreme Pharisaic party to insist on external details up to the point of forgetting sincerity and spirituality. It was by no means a religiously torpid age; on the contrary, there is reason to believe that there was a well-defined feeling of discontent in the best minds, — a desire for something purer and higher than had yet been attained.

It was Jesus of Nazareth who grasped the situation as no one else did, and in response to the demand of the time came forward with principles which satisfied men's highest moral and religious instincts. He faced at once the burning questions of the day: What is the kingdom of God? What is salvation? Ignoring the ecclesiastical and ritualistic machinery of the Jews, he declared that salvation was trust in God and obedience to him. Obedience he defined to be imitation of the divine perfection, which he summed up in the two qualities of justice and love, or in love alone, which includes justice. Sincerity he assumed as an element of love, and he felt himself obliged, as has been the case with all moral teachers, to denounce the insincerity of the religious leaders and practices of the times. Trust in God he held to be filial confidence in the divine goodness and wisdom, hearty sympathy and co-operation with the divine Father in thought, feeling, word, and deed. In fine, it was oneness with God in spirit which he announced as the controlling principle of the religious life. It was the profound conviction that this was the essence of salvation which enabled him to go his way undisturbed by current practices and ideas. Whatever his attitude toward the transitory opinions of his time and people, he never relaxed his hold on this fundamental and formative principle, — a principle which gave shape to all succeeding phases of Christianity. It may be that he sympathized with a half-Essenian quietism (Matt. v.); but this local coloring soon vanished in the process of development, and the great principle remained. Perhaps his intention was to restrict his direct teaching to the Jews as the chosen people of God (Matt. x. 5, 6); but this was a limitation which could not survive in the presence of the declaration that God's love was bestowed equally on just and unjust (Matt. v. 45). His conception of the future of the kingdom of God may have included some of the outward details of the popular opinion. Something that he said may have been understood by his disciples as meaning that he himself would return to earth to establish the kingdom forever (2 Thess. i. 7, 8; but against this there is the apparent hopelessness of the two disciples in Luke xxiv. 17, 21). But this expectation, so long and so anxiously held by the Church, did not modify the essential life of Christianity, serving rather only to quicken its faithfulness and spirit of obedience.

On the other hand, the silence of Jesus is no less striking than his utterances. It is not indeed to be considered important that he added nothing to the existing idea of immortality. The doctrine of the future life was already clearly formulated, — continued existence, with rewards and punishments corresponding to earthly moral character. The assertion by a comparatively late writer (2 Tim. i. 10) that Christ Jesus "brought life and incorruption [or immortality] to light through the gospel," refers not to the general doctrine of the continued existence of all men, but to the promise of a future life of blessedness for believers in Jesus. In opposing the Sadducean denial of the resurrection of the body Jesus had the concurrence of the scribes (Mark xii. 28); so Paul (according to the account in Acts xxiii. 6–8) on a critical occasion appealed to the Pharisees as the representatives of this doctrine. On this point the Church coincided with the Synagogue, and the teaching of Jesus was in explicit agreement with both. His silence in respect to himself is, however, noticeable. Here we have to rely almost wholly on the Synoptics and the Epistle of James, the Fourth Gospel being so deeply colored by later ideas that it must be used with great caution as a portraiture of the Master. The statements of the Synoptics are not altogether harmonious among themselves, and must be judged by comparison of one with another and by the teachings of the succeeding history.

In the first place, it appears probable that Jesus did not represent himself as a sacrifice for sin. There can be little doubt that he held in a general way the doctrine of the necessity of vicarious atonement. It was part of the current opinion; and he nowhere controverts it, as we may suppose he would certainly have done if he had thought the doctrine wrong. It was the teaching of the Law, and he accepted the Law as a divinely appointed rule of life. He both himself observed its ritual requirements and advised others so to do (Mark i. 44; xiv. 12–16). In thus accepting the sacrifices for sin prescribed by the Law, he virtually declared that no other sacrifice was needed. Paul, in proclaiming Jesus to be men's propitiation and redemption (Gal. iii. 13; 1 Cor. i. 30; Rom. iv. 25), seems distinctly to set aside the Mosaic scheme of sacrifice (Gal. iii. 13; iv.

10, 11 ; 1 Cor. i. 23 ; Rom. iii. 19–31 ; v. 12–21), though his
polemic is specially directed against circumcision. The Epistle to the Hebrews makes a detailed argument to show that
the sacrifices of the Law were in themselves impotent and
were formally abrogated by the death of Christ ; but no
such statements are ascribed to Jesus either in the Synoptics or in the Fourth Gospel. In Mark (vi. 33, 34, 45) he
predicts his death and declares that he came to give his
life as a ransom for many. This last expression, isolated
as it is, cannot in the face of his other teaching be taken
to mean that his death was a substitute for the legal offerings. Vicarious he might have called it in the sense in
which the term is used in Isa. liii., or as the high-priest
Caiaphas is represented (John xi. 50) as employing it in
reference to Jesus himself ; the rather that in the connection in Mark (and so in Matt. xx. 28), the giving of his life
as ransom is mentioned along with the ministering which it
is Jesus' special purpose to describe as a part of the humility that is characteristic of the new kingdom of God. If
the ransoming is not of the nature of ministering (which
is not technically and legally a sacrifice), it is probably an
expression of later tradition. The expression used by Jesus
at the passover-meal, "This is my blood of the covenant,
which is shed for many" (Mark xiv. 24), may be understood in a similar sense ; or it may be that the original form
of the saying was less decided, and that tradition has impressed on it the tone of a later time. Certainly the conception of atonement for sin effected through his blood does
not accord with the tone of the Sermon on the Mount or
with that of his general teaching as given in the Synoptical Gospels. There it is individual conduct that determines men's destiny. Nor can it be said that conduct is
in these passages represented as the outcome of spiritual
power implanted in man in consequence of his atoning

death; the silence of the Gospels on this point (omitting
the two passages above quoted) makes such a view practically impossible. With more reason it might be supposed
that he purposely withheld instruction concerning his death
till the last hour approached, thinking his disciples unfitted
earlier for such teaching, or that he himself did not before
these last days become convinced of the sacrificial nature
of his death. But it would be difficult to reconcile the first
of these suppositions with his distinct statement that whoever did the will of God (Mark iii. 35) was nearest to him
in soul ; and both suppositions are rendered improbable by
the attitude of the disciples just after his death.

Still more decidedly alien to his teaching is the dogma
that justification before the divine tribunal was effected by
his righteousness imputed to the believer. In the Synoptics faith in Jesus is simply confidence in his ability to
cure bodily ailment, or belief that he is the Messiah ; in
some cases the faith is vicarious (Mark ii. 5 ; v. 36). On
the other hand, Jesus makes man's own righteousness the
human condition of salvation, the divine ground being God's
willingness to forgive (Matt. vi. 14). His scheme of life as
given in his reported teaching contemplates no intermediary
between God and the individual soul. He seems, as has
already been remarked, to have accepted the national system of sacrifice ; but from his utterances as they have been
handed down we should infer that he attached little importance to it. Apparently he looked on it as a time honored
framework of popular religious life,. but the essential thing
in his eyes was ethical union with God. He would not
directly combat the existing system ; he would quietly substitute for it a spiritual principle,'— not vicarious suffering
or vicarious goodness, but personal obedience. Other great
Jewish moral teachers of the time did not fail, along with
their insistence on ethical purity, to hold up the Law as the

essence of the religious life. Jesus substantially put aside all systems and apparatus and made his appeal simply to the individual conscience.

Did Jesus regard himself as a divine person or as in any way lifted above the sphere of humanity? It may fairly be said that the general impression left on us by the portraiture of him in the Synoptics is that he lived and acted as other men; that nothing was further from his mind than the desire to be looked on as a superhuman being. In his appeals to the people, in his more familiar intercourse with his disciples, in his arguments with his opponents, in his hours of prayer and of struggle he thought and spoke as a man. He claimed to be only a teacher of righteousness; and certainly this was the impression received by some of his followers, — by the two who went to Emmaus (Luke xxiv. 19–21), and (if we may rely on the account in Acts) by Peter himself (Acts ii. 22–24, 32–36). If he claimed miraculous powers, the same claim was made by many others, prophets and apostles. As to the forgiveness of sins, he himself pointed out that this was no more a divine power than the gift of healing (Mark v. 21–23), and it is represented as belonging also to the disciples (Matt. xviii. 18 ; cf. Luke x. 16). The titles "Son of Man" and "Son of David" do not suggest a superhuman nature, nor according to the Fourth Gospel (John x. 33–36) does a claim to such a nature reside in the title "Son of God." There Jesus is represented as making an argument from the Old Testament (Ps. lxxxii. 6) to show that men might be so called, and (expressly disclaiming divinity) describes himself as one "whom the Father consecrated and sent into the world." Nothing more than this seems to be involved in the declaration (Matt. xi. 25–30) that "no one knows the Son save the Father, nor does any one know the Father save the Son and he to whom the Son wills to reveal him" (where the believer is in this respect equal with the Son). Other passages, in which the "Son of Man" is represented as lord of the angels (Matt. xiii. 41; xvi. 27, 28), seem to imply a power not indeed divine yet more than human. This view of himself, out of harmony with the utterances above mentioned, might be supposed to express a later phase of his inward experience, to be a product of the time when he had come to look on himself as the Messiah and destined to reappear in judgment; but as his disciples do not seem to have expected such a reappearance (Luke xxiv.; Mark xvi. 2–5), it is probable that this announcement was not made by him but expresses the idea of a later time. In the same way we may understand the declarations that he would be with his followers everywhere and always (Matt. xviii. 20; xxviii. 19, 20), unless, indeed, a merely spiritual presence is here intended. With such evidence as lies before us, it seems reasonable to conclude that Jesus laid no claim, in thought or in word, to other than human nature and power. He was conscious of profound sympathy with the divine mind; the formality and folly of the prevailing religion pressed on his soul as a heavy burden that he felt called on to bear; he believed himself to be a prophet sent by God with a message of salvation to men, whom he embraced in his deep and yearning love; yea, in the intensity of his conscious union with the divine Father he knew himself to be the Son of God. But beyond this he did not go. It would indeed be a noteworthy thing that a Jew of that period, with the profound Jewish sentiment of the unspeakable distance between God and man, should have overstepped the boundary, and being in human form, have equalled himself with the divine. For so remarkable a departure from the national thought we naturally demand clear evidence, and such evidence we do not find in the existing records of the life of Jesus.

2. Such was his teaching. What were the fortunes of

the doctrine that he cast forth as seed into the world?
That he made a profound impression on his disciples is
evident from the fact that after his death his name was
the bond of union and basis of organization for them. That
his teaching contained a true response to the demands of
the age is clear from the religious revolution which was
effected by his followers. But was all his teaching accepted
by his disciples, or only a part of it? and was his doctrine
alone the potent element in the Christianity that subdued
the Roman empire, or did it call to its aid ideas to which
he was a stranger? And if this last was the case, what
was his relation to the new ideas thus introduced?

It is commonly said that the disciples just after the
death of Jesus were merely Jews who believed him to
be the Messiah. This is probably true so far as their
religious dogma was concerned. We may infer from the
opening chapters of Acts that they still practised all the
observances of the Law; and Gamaliel's speech, which may
be regarded as embodying a reliable tradition, seems not
to contemplate the new movement as necessarily inimical
to the national faith. Jesus in fact did not announce any
new dogma, and there was no reason why his followers
should not remain Jews in religious belief. But he did
proclaim and illustrate a new spirit in ethics and religion,
and it was this that was destined to overthrow Mosaism
in the Church. How far in the first years this spirit had
gained possession of the disciples, it is hard to say; for
information on this point we are wholly dependent on the
account in Acts, which is certainly not free from the expansions of tradition. Yet so far as we can judge from
the tone of the opening chapters of Acts, there was an
inspiring exaltation of soul in the little company of men
and women who were awaiting the appearance of Jesus.
They had come during his lifetime to look on him as the

Messiah. This was not strange; there were not a few Messiahs, who had each his followers. A more noteworthy thing was that they had retained their faith in him even after his death.[1] Whether this was due to something which they understood to be a promise of return on his part or to the powerful impression made on them by his personality, may be doubtful. It is certain that they believed him to mark a turning-point in the history of Israel, the redemption, perhaps in some not clearly defined way, of the people from all evil. Thus his person naturally became the central point of their religious faith and hope, he would sum up in himself all the promises. This seems to have been the attitude of the infant Church. Its creed in other respects had undergone no change. Salvation was still the reward of obedience to the Law, manifested (as John and Jesus had taught) by repentance and the outward separation by baptism from that crooked generation; but there was the subtle influence of devotion to a pure and lofty personality; the memory of his consecration to his spiritual ideal would leaven more and more the Church's life and thought.

Thus it is not surprising that we do not find in the earliest Christian. records any clear signs of dogmatic reconstruction. The burden of the discourses and prayers reported in the twelve first chapters of Acts (up to the time when Paul began his active work) is simply that Jesus of Nazareth, who had been put to death, was the promised Christ, the prophet foretold by Moses and the prophets, the servant of God sent to turn men from their iniquities. And if he was all this, it was of course necessary that men should believe on him, that is, should accept

---

[1] This fact also, as is well known, has its counterparts in history and especially in other religious movements, as, for example, Buddhism, the Mahdi-form of Mohammedanism, and the Persian Babism.

him as the final teacher and deliverer. The belief early established itself that he had risen from the dead, that he had been received into heaven, there to dwell till the time of his coming, — a belief which may be regarded as a natural pendant to the conviction that he, though he had died, was the Messiah. Such is the doctrine of the Epistle of James, in which, as in the early chapters of Acts, there is no word respecting a sacrificial character attaching to the death of Jesus nor any ascription of divinity to him, — nothing but the exhortation to lead a holy life in expectation of his coming.

It was thus that the early disciples interpreted the teachings of Jesus in the light of their own hopes. From their opinions we may gather what had been the nature of his instruction. We may infer that he had spoken of himself only as the servant of God, sent to announce the new order of things, the essence of which was unfeigned love to God and man. There was here an extraordinary concurrence of favorable conditions : a people with a firmly organized monotheistic faith, and in contact with the best ethical thought of the time; a circle within the people conscious of the lacks of the existing system and anxious to establish a higher spirituality; a general belief that God, in accordance with his ancient promises, was about to introduce a new order of things; a man who by his extraordinary endowments was able to inspire a select circle of followers with a controlling enthusiasm both for his person as the final deliverer sent by God, and, in a germinal way, for those lofty principles of ethical-religious life which he set forth in his teaching and illustrated in his conduct, — these were the conditions of the birth of Christianity, briefly and roughly stated. Those subtle influences which we call the spirit of the age and the spirit of the teacher require for their detailed comprehension fuller literary data than we possess ; but from the existing records and from the succeeding religious development we may infer their general character, and it appears that the early Church was the direct product of the teaching and personality of Jesus.

3. This was the dogmatic position of the Church when Saul of Tarsus entered it. It is unnecessary here to attempt to explain his conversion. From the little bit of autobiography in the first chapter of Galatians it may be concluded that the person of Jesus had made a profound impression on him. We may suspect that to Paul he was from the first more than the risen Messiah who was to restore Israel, that the future apostle saw in him even then the hope of that spiritual regeneration for which he seems to have been long struggling. Unfortunately Paul has left us no full account of his early experiences, only reminiscences which may be colored by his later thought. We know only the dogmatic system which he worked out after many years spent in Arabia and Syria. There he came into contact with Gentiles, whose peculiar position may well have caused him to reflect on the conditions of church-membership, and have helped to lead him to the conclusion that salvation was complete in Christ without the works of the Law. This was equivalent in his mind to affirming that Christ had worked out a perfect righteousness, since without perfect righteousness there could be no salvation, and man's own righteousness was necessarily imperfect. But this imputed righteousness was inseparably connected in his conception with an inward spirit of obedience, an impulse of love, the gift of God through Christ. Such an idea may have been present to him from the moment when the conviction had seized on him that the true Christ was this suffering crucified man of spotless life. Paul seems (such is the impression made on us by the history) to have had a sudden revelation (born of much preceding struggle of soul) that God's promised salvation

was a spiritual one, and that it was embodied in Jesus of Nazareth. Salvation carried with it remission of sins, and remission of sins implied an offering; thus the death of Jesus naturally assumed a sacrificial character. Paul's whole scheme was not only made possible but was forced on him by his conception of the person of Jesus.

We may suppose that it was by some such process of feeling that the Church at large came to interpret as the foundation of salvation that mysterious death which it had at first regarded as an interruption of the divine deliverance. The disappearance of the Messiah from the earth was hard to understand. Surely, said the disciples, he will come again to complete what he has begun. Then with the growth of spirituality in a section of the Church (for one portion of it seems never to have advanced beyond the Old Testament point of view as given in the Epistle of James) came the belief that the end of the divine intervention was deliverance from sin, and Jesus was regarded as the exalted Son of God who had given his life for men. This conception of the Master is found in the majority of the books of the New Testament. In his death that age, looking on sacrifice as an absolute necessity, found a complete solution of the problem of satisfaction for sin. The Jewish ethical-spiritual thought thus created out of the person of Jesus a framework (indispensable for that time) for his higher religious teaching.

The exaltation of Jesus, implied in the title "the Lord Jesus Christ" and in the frequent coupling of his name with that of God the Father, was a natural consequence of the increasing value which was attached to his person and work. Withdrawn from earth, he was thought of as in heaven, and charged with the salvation of men, he was believed to be invested with the universal authority necessary for the fulfilment of his mission. When this feeling first found expression it is not easy to say. That it was not in existence immediately after the death of Jesus may be inferred from the narratives of the Synoptics; but the general impression made on us by Paul's history of his conversion (Gal. i.) is that it formed a part of the apostle's experience at an early stage of his Christian career. The Lord Jesus is thought of as sitting at the right hand of God and controlling the destinies of men. This conception, interpreted as a part of the new-born Christian consciousness, signifies the exaltation of righteousness to the place of honor in the world. In the person of the Redeemer it is made glorious and everlasting. Yet on the dogmatic side this exaltation of Jesus is always in the Pauline period distinguished from deification. He is the Lord, the pre-existent Son of God, but he acts according to the will of God, who sent him forth (Gal. i. 4; iv. 4); he is God's as believers are Christ's; all spiritual life is in him because he has been made by God the source of life (1 Cor. i. 3); iii. 23); all things shall be subjected to him that he himself may then be subjected to God (1 Cor. xv. 28); he is the fulfilment of the promises unto the glory of God, which shines in his face (2 Cor. i. 20; iv. 6); God reconciles men to himself in Christ, and raises them from the dead as he raised Jesus (2 Cor. v. 19; iv. 14); Christ was born of the seed of David according to the flesh and determined to be the Son of God according to the spirit by the resurrection from the dead (Rom. i. 3, 4); and as final judge of men (2 Cor. v. 10) he is the agent of God (Rom. ii. 16).[1] An exalted position not thought of by

---

[1] On Rom. ix. 5, see the discussion by Abbot and Dwight in Vol. I. of "The Journal of the Society of Biblical Literature and Exegesis," (Boston, 1881). The passage must be interpreted in accordance with Paul's unvarying usage elsewhere, and it may fairly be said to be highly improbable that the author of Galatians, Corinthians, and Romans should apply the epithet "God" to Christ.

himself was assigned him; but conceived, as it was, reverently and soberly, it did not impugn the aloneness of God, and practically served to give impressiveness to the fundamental religious ideas of the Master. It was, we may conclude, the natural way in which the age expressed its estimate of his greatness.[1]

To this portraiture of the function of Jesus Paul added the conception of perfect legal righteousness worked out by him and reckoned as a legally justifying fact to every believer. This idea was not embraced by the whole Church of the first century (it does not appear in the Apocalypse, the Epistle to the Hebrews, the Fourth Gospel, or the Pastoral Epistles, or indeed distinctly anywhere except in the four great Pauline Epistles), nor has it ever succeeded in establishing itself firmly in the Christian consciousness. Yet, though its scholastic and apparently mechanical form has often been repellent, it is based, as has been pointed out above, on a profound ethical-spiritual feeling, on the conviction that man's spiritual powers can have full play only when he is relieved from the obligation of an impossible performance and quickened into activity by love. Jesus himself did not hold that the efficacy of the divine love in awakening in man's soul love of holiness depended on the forensic intermediation of an imputed righteousness; but to Paul, with his peculiar training and experience, such an intermediary appeared to be necessary. In general the position of mediator assigned by the Church of the first century to Jesus seems to have been alien to his thought. This departure from his teach-

---

[1] So far as Paul and the early Church are concerned, such an estimate might be held to have grown up on purely Jewish soil, though Greek influence is neither impossible nor improbable. Exaltation of men into the divine sphere was rather an Hellenic than a Semitic mode of thought, and may have been insensibly appropriated by a portion of the Jewish world. Whether this was actually the fact, it is hardly possible to say.

ing is an evidence of his power. The Jew of that period (and the New Testament writers were probably all Jews) could hardly conceive of an immediate friendly relation between God and man; all the past religious development, beginning from primitive times, involved the interposition of some reconciling or propitiating agency. For the Jew it had been the national system of sacrifices. That Jesus took the place of this great mediatorial scheme, which the wisdom and mercy of God, it was believed, had devised for the fathers, shows the enormous significance which was attached to his person, the controlling power of his personality; he, by the impression he made, coerced and revolutionized the religious apparatus of a nation. It is possible, it is even probable, that the disciples never asked themselves whether the Master had practically ignored mediating agency in his teaching. His silence on this point would hardly attract their attention; they would assume that he taught what the Scriptures enjoined. The grafting of a mediatorial doctrine on his conception of salvation was doubtless an unconscious procedure on their part; the doctrine was a part of that framework without which the age seemed unable to appropriate his higher thought.[1]

4. While the Jewish and the Pauline conceptions of Christianity were thus moving side by side, a new tendency of thought was coming into view. The union of Greek philosophical speculation with Jewish theology had produced the Alexandrian doctrine of the logos, the conception of an exalted being nearly allied in nature to God,

---

[1] Here again, in the development of the Christian mediatorial scheme, the possibility of non-Jewish influence must be admitted. Such influence is certain so far as regards the logos-doctrine, which involved the idea of mediation. Whether the Persian conception of intermediation (Mithra) was then in position to be effective is doubtful. The groundwork of the Christian idea was Jewish; the possibility of its extension, as it appears in the New Testament, was probably made easier by the diffusion of Greek (and perhaps of Persian) modes of thought.

the image of the divine glory, the agent in the divine creation, standing midway between God and the world as mediator between the two. This conception, originating in Alexandria (to this conclusion the documentary evidence points), seems to have made its way to Asia Minor, and perhaps to other parts of the Jewish world. At any rate it commended itself to not a few Christians, who recognized its grandeur and relevancy and saw in the description of the mediating image and son of God a portraiture of the person and work of the Christ of God, Jesus of Nazareth. This construction of the divine method of government is expressed in four books of the New Testament, the Epistles to the Hebrews, the Ephesians, the Colossians, and the Fourth Gospel, which may thus be considered to form in this respect a separate group. They agree in ascribing to Jesus the most exalted position in the universe under God. They differ in the terms which they apply to him, and in the way in which they represent his functions in the divine plan of salvation, as well as in their view of the human conditions of salvation ; they differ also so far as regards the circumstances of the circles to which they are addressed. The design of Hebrews (addressed to Jewish Christians by one who felt called on to reconcile the Jewish sacrificial idea with his Pauline-Alexandrian conception of Jesus) is to portray Jesus as the priest and sacrifice of a new covenant made far more glorious than the old by his personality. He, says the Epistle (i. 1–4), appointed heir of all things and agent in the work of creation, the impress of the divine substance, made purification of sins and sat down on the right hand of the Majesty on high, having become by so much better than the angels as he had inherited a more excellent name than they. The author's leading idea is the dignity of the priestly Saviour, whom he identifies with the

Alexandrian creative logos. The Epistle to the Ephesians sets forth against Jewish exclusiveness the sufficiency of the salvation of Christ, presenting him as the consummation of all things (i. 10), lord over the universe and head of the Church by divine appointment (i. 20–23), the revelation of the divine wisdom to the heavenly principalities and powers (iii. 10). The author of Colossians is led to speak more fully of the person of Jesus, his polemic being directed against a current form of Gnosticism (apparently Jewish) which laid stress on angelic intermediaries between God and man and on ascetic observances (ii. 16–19). In opposition to this belief he represents Christ as the image of God, the first-born of the creation, the agent in the creation of the universe, the head of the Church, the possessor of the fulness [the Gnostic *pleroma*, the content of all being], the reconciler of all things to God (i. 15–20), — forms of expression substantially identical with those of Philo. The relation of the Fourth Gospel (in the same category with which is the First Epistle of John) to the Jewish-Alexandrian philosophy has already been pointed out: here Jesus is the logos, head of the kingdom of light and life, himself revealer and source of salvation.

The variety and vividness of these portraitures of Jesus, the activity and enthusiasm of thought they show, is an indication of his wonderful power. His person assimilated all the elements of thought of the time. Into whatever circle his name made its entrance, it there became the controlling factor. He represented purity and salvation, and around him as a centre all systems of life and of the universe arranged themselves. The Church in expanding and embellishing his theology still made him the essence of her theology. With all the variations in other points she held fast to the conception of Jesus as the exalted Saviour. Salvation was inseparably connected with his person, — this was the inspiring idea of Christianity. As to how the salvation was effected — by what acts or experiences of God, of Christ, and of men — there were differences of view. The Pauline theory of imputed righteousness does not appear outside of Paul's writings. Hebrews and First Timothy represent faith as exercised toward God primarily ("God our Saviour," 1 Tim. ii. 3). These, together with Ephesians, Colossians, Second Timothy, Titus, First Peter, and the Apocalypse, refer to the death of Christ as expiatory. The Fourth Gospel and the First of the Epistles ascribed to John further lay stress on the living union of the soul with Jesus, who is regarded as mystically imparting spiritual life or giving entrance into the kingdom of light. But amid all these variations the person of Jesus remains the centre of the religious life. It was indeed this personal character of the Christian faith and hope which both produced or permitted individual differences, and maintained the substantial unity of the Church in spite of them. A great inspiring idea, the idea of salvation, was cast forth into the world, and men held it in such forms as were suggested by their views of God and the world. Thus it was possible that a real catholic church with a catholic faith could exist amid such diversities of national, social, and intellectual relations as the Church of the early centuries showed. It is further true that the ethical teaching and example of the Master determined the ethical creed of the Church. For him salvation was oneness of soul with God, and his followers, though they developed his religious teaching in a theological way and departed from the simplicity of his doctrine, did not forget the spirit of his life. The sweetness of patient, self-forgetting love which entered, like a breath from heaven, into the hardness of the Roman world, was the copy of the daily life of Jesus, strengthened by the belief that his atoning death made manifest the value of the individual soul and swept away the artificial barriers that had hitherto separated men. In a word, the Church was the creation of Jesus partly by his direct teaching, partly by the stimulating and organizing power of his personality.

The formative period of the Church extended over the first century following the death of Jesus. Then came a formulating period of about three centuries during which a number of ideas which in the New Testament books are more or less fluid were put into the shape of propositions and received as dogmas. Each of the great races that embraced Christianity impressed its thought and its personality on the body of doctrine. The faith passed from the Greek and Latin to the Celtic and Germanic communities of Europe. Protestantism threw away part of the great mass of beliefs which the medieval Catholic Church had accumulated, and entered on its own career of transformation. Both branches of Christianity, Catholic and Protestant, have followed the currents of modern thought; there is not a phase of science, philosophy, or literature but has left its impress on the body of beliefs that control Christendom. But in all this freedom of movement the person of Jesus has maintained its place as the centre of religious life. Whatever the particular construction of the theology, whether he be regarded as substantially divine or only as a profoundly inspired man, whether his death or his life be most emphasized, whether Church or Bible be accepted as infallible guide, he is ever the leader and model of religious experience. It becomes more and more evident that the fundamental truths which he announced are as new as they were in his time, and that he alone is in the highest sense the founder of Christianity.

INDEX OF CITATIONS.

OLD TESTAMENT.

Reference	Page
Gen. i.-xi.	160, 195
i.	196
i. 2	161 n.
i. 20, 21	161 n.
i. 26-28	173
i. 26	147, 153, 161
ii. 1	161
ii. 7	173, 175
ii. 15 (Sept.)	409 n.
iii.	157, 167, 194, 195, 199, 204, 209
iii. 21	197
iii. 22	198
iv. 16-24	160 n.
iv. 18	160 n
iv. 26	306 n.
v.	196
v. 18	160 n.
v. 29	196
vi.-ix.	196
vi.	65, 167, 201
vi. 1, 2	159
vi. 2	147
viii. 21	176
ix. 4	174
xi. 7	147
xii. 5	175
xii. 13	175, 194
xv. 4	177 n.
xv. 6	275
xv. 10	107
xvi. 7, 13	91
xvi. 7-13	148
xviii.	202, 272
xviii. 19	147
xviii. 25	81
xx.	272
xxvi.	272
xxvi. 7	194
xxvii.	194
xxvii. 33-37	103 n.
xxix. 14	174
xxx.	194
xxxi. 12, 13	109
xxxii. 24, 30	91
xxxv. 11	177 n.
xli. 8	176
xliii. 30	177 n.
Ex. iii. 6	394 n.
vi. 3	306 n.
xiv. 20	113 n.
xv. 16	107
xxi.-xxiii.	235, 237
xxiii. 21	91, 148
xxxiii. 14	90
xxxiii. 15	148
Lev. iv.	226
v. vi.	226
v. 1	175
xvi.	143, 167, 226
xvi. 17	109
xvii. 7	142
xvii. 11	174
xviii. 18	17 n.
xxi. 11	175
xxiv. 11	91
Num. xxi. 4	175
xxiv. 7	113 n.
Deut. v. 9	185
viii. 3	104, 105
xiii. 3	175
xxviii.-xxx.	312
xxxii. 8	147 n., 151 n.
xxxii. 17	142 n., 155
Josh. v. 1	176
v. 13	148
vii. 24, 25	184
Judg. vi. 11	121
ix. 23	145
xi. 24	306
xiii.	121
xiii. 13, 18	91
xiii. 18	148, 317
xiv. 6	92 n.
1 Sam. ii. 16	175
xii. 23	228
xv.	309 n.
xvi.	168
xvi. 13, 14	92 n.
xvi. 14-23	145
xvi. 23	145 n.
xix. 20	92 n.
xix. 24	170
xxviii.	143 n.
2 Sam. v. 1	174
vii.	184 n., 316
2 Sam. vii. 14	317
xii.	309 n.
xii. 1-14	184 n.
xxiv.	185 n.
xxiv. 1	157
1 Kings iv. 29-34	135
v. 32	135
viii.	309 n., 312
xvii. 21	175
xxii. 19-23	144
xxii. 21	165
2 Kings ii. 9	176
iii. 15	145 n.
vi. 17	149
xiv. 25	134
xxiii. 10	406
1 Chron. i.-ix.	55 n.
xxi. 1	78, 157, 202
2 Chron. xiv. 11	127
xxxii. 8	174
Ezra ii.	55 n.
vii. 6	259
Neh. ii. 8	409 n.
vii.	55 n.
vii. 7, 66	312 n.
viii.	127
ix. 6	161 n.
xii. 11	55 n.
Job i. ii.	147
i. 5	227
i. 6	165
iii. 8	162
iv. 15	145 n.
vii. 17-21	228
ix. 13	162
x. 1	175
xiii. 25	228
xiv. 1-3	228
xix. 25-27	381, 388, 389
xxvi. 6	404 n.
xxvi. 12	162
xxvi. 13	92 n., 162
xxviii.	98, 98 n.
xxviii. 22	404 n.
xxxii.-xxxvii.	98 n.
xxxiii. 23, 24	228
xxxviii. 7	147, 161

	Page
Job xl.	162
xli.	162
xli. 1	161
xlii.	272
xlii. 8	227, 228
Ps. ii.	400
ii. 7	317
ii. 9	120
iv. 2	87
v. 10	206 n.
vi. 1	87
vi. 2	174
vii. 10	176
viii. 5	147
ix. 17	379
x. 6	176
x. 14, 36	80
xiv. 2, 3	206 n.
xv.	236
xvi.	379, 380, 383
xvi. 9	174
xvi. 10	388
xvi. 11	87
xvii.	389
xvii. 3	380
xvii. 15	380, 388
xviii. 20-27	189
xix.	80
xix. 7	175
xxiv.	236, 237
xxv. 4	87
xxv. 7	187, 228
xxv. 11	230
xxvii. 1	87
xxix.	80
xxix. 1	147 n.
xxxi.	187
xxxii.	188
xxxii. 5	228, 230
xxxiii. 6	104
xxxiii. 16	127
xxxiv. 20	87
xxxv. 3	87
xxxvi. 2	206 n.
xxxvi. 10	188
xxxviii. 1	87
xxxviii. 3, 20	187
xxxix. 8, 11	86
xl. 6	220
xl. 6-8	138, 230
xl. 11	87
xliv.	61, 332
xliv. 17, 18	189
xlv. 3	317
xlix. 15	380
l. 9-13	230
l. 16-21	87
li.	187, 206, 236
li. 1, 2	86
li. 3	228
li. 4	230
li. 5	191
li. 10	86, 176
li. 12	92 n.
li. 17	176
Ps. lvi. 4	174
lvii. 4	175
lviii. 1	147 n.
lviii. 2	78
lix. 3	189
lxii. 5	175
lxv.	80
lxv. 2	174
lxvi. 18	176
lxviii.	202
lxix.	187
lxix. 16	87
lxxi. 20	380
lxxii. 13	175
lxxii. 17	357
lxxiii. 18-20	87
lxxiii. 21	177 n.
lxxiii 24	380
lxxiii. 26	177
lxxiv.	61
lxxiv. 8	247
lxxiv. 21	162
lxxix.	61, 223
lxxx.	204, 223
lxxxii.	78
lxxxii. 1, 6	147 n.
lxxxii. 6	422
lxxxiv. 2	174, 177
lxxxv.	223
lxxxv. 1, 2	187
lxxxvii.	237, 314
lxxxix. 48	175
xc. 4	374 n.
xciii.	80
xcv. 5	155
xcvi.	80, 357 n., 398
xcvii. 7	147 n.
xcviii.	357 n.
ci.	237
cii.	80
ciii. 8-10, 12	227
ciii. 12-14	87
ciii. 13	84
ciii. 13, 14	228
civ.	79, 80
civ. 26	162
civ. 29	204 n.
civ. 30	92 n.
cvi. 37	155
cvii.	79
cvii. 20	104, 105
cviii. 4	87
cx.	400
cxi. 4	87
cxvi. 5	87
cxix.	236, 240, 278
cxix. 120	174
cxxxvi. 37	142 n.
cxxxvii.	18, 61
cxxxix. 17	87
cxliii. 2	206 n.
cxlv. 8, 9	87
cxlviii.	80
cxlviii. 5	161
Prov. i.-ix.	58, 100 n.
Prov. i. 10-14	100 n.
ii. 16-19	100 n.
iii. 13-20	99
iii. 16	404
v.	100
v. 11	174
vi. 1-5	100 n.
vii.	100 n.
viii. i.-ix. 6	99
viii. 22, 31	100
ix. 13-18	100 n.
x. 27	404
xiii. 12	176
xv. 1	294
xv. 11	404 n.
xvi. 2	176
xvii. 9	294
xxiv. 17	294
xxiv. 29	294
xxv. 1	135
xxv. 9	293
xxv. 21, 22	294, 297
Eccles. ii. 5	409 n.
ii. 24	175
iii. 21	176
vii. 20	206 n.
vii. 28	210 n.
viii. 12	192 n.
ix. 10	59
x. 3	192 n.
xii. 9-14	59
Cant. iv. 13	409 n.
v. 4	177 n.
Isa. i.	315 n.
i. 10-18	222
i. 11	229
ii. 2-4	313
ii. 5	314 n.
ii. 6-22	315 n.
iii.	315 n.
iv. 1	315 n.
iv. 2	316 n.
iv. 2-6	315
v.	204
v.-x.	315 n.
vi. 9-13	310
vii.-x.	321
vii. 10-12	123
vii. 14	317
viii.	378
viii. 16	69
viii. 18	137
viii. 19	142 n., 143 n., 378
ix. 6	357
ix. 6, 7	315 n., 317
x.	396 n.
x. 18	173
x. 20, 24-27	310
x. 21	317 n.
x. 22	336 n.
xi.	317
xi. 2	317
xi. 1-9	316
xii.	61

Page
Isa. xiii. . . . 396 n.
xiii. 21 155
xiv. . . . . 396 n.
xiv. 9 . . . . 404 n.
xiv. 9, 10 . . . 379
xiv. 24-32 . . 315 n.
xv.-xviii. . . 315 n.
xix. 313
xix. 18 . . . 314 n.
xix. 18-25 . . . 314
xx. . . . . 315 n.
xxii. 15-25 . . 315 n.
xxvi. 15, 20 . . 389
xxvi. 19 . . 388, 389
xxvii. 1 . 162, 162 n.
xxviii.-xxxi. . 315 n.
xxviii. 11 . . . 138
xxix. 4 . . . 143 n.
xxix. 8 175
xxx. 7 162
xxx. 33 406
xxxi. 3 174
xxxii. 1-8 . . . 317
xxxii. 16 . . 92 n.
xxxiv. 14 . 142, 155
xxxiv. 45 . . . 242
xxxv. 5 . . . 330
xxxvii. 21-35 . 315 n.
xxxviii. . . . 382
xl. 322
xl. 2 . . 223, 353
xlii. 1-17 . . . 326
xlv. 7 . . . 146
xlvi. . . . 396 n.
xlvii. . . . 396 n.
xlviii. 16 . . 92 n.
xlix. 1-6 . . . 166
xlix. 5 . . . 326
xlix. 6 . . . 225
liii. . . 166, 280, 322,
330 n., 352, 420
liii. 1-9 . . . 224
liii. 10 . . . 175
liii. 10-12 . . 225
lv. 11 . . 103, 104
lix. 7, 8 . . 206 n.
lx.-lxvi. . . 311
lx. . . 324 n., 336 n.
lx. 10, 12 . . 225
lxi. 313
lxii. 5 . . . 83
lxiii. 3 . . . 120
lxiii. 9 . . 90, 148
lxv. 374
lxv. 11 . . . 155
lxv. 17-25 . . 311
lxv. 17 . . 401, 408
lxvi. . . . 408
lxvi. 19-24 . . 311
lxvi. 22 . . . 408
lxvi. 24 . . . 408
Jer. i. 5 . . . 320
ii. 1 83
ii. 26, 27 . . 143 n.
iii. 4 83

Page
Jer. iv. 19 . . . 177 n.
iv. 28 . . . 361 n.
vii. 22 . . . 229
x. 1-16 . . . 315 n.
xi. 20 . . . 177 n.
xv. 1 . . . 228
xvii. 9, 10 . . 191
xxiii. 5-8 . 315 n., 316
xxiii. 29 . . . 103
xxv. 8-11 . . 311
xxv. 9 . . 396 n.
xxv. 12 . 64, 311 n.
xxix. 7 . . 396 n.
xxx 311
xxxi. 1-30 . . 311
xxxi. 31-34 . . 311
xxxi. 31-40 . 311 n.
xxxiii. 14-26 315 n., 316
xxxviii. 17 175, 396 n.
xlix. . . . 315 n.
l.-lii. . . . 315 n.
l. . 242, 311, 396 n.
li. . 242, 311 n., 396 n.
Lam. ii. 11 . . 177 n.
Ezek. i.-xxxiii. . 315 n.
xi. 19 . . . 173
xiii. 19 . . . 175
xiv. 12-20 . 272 n.
xiv. 14 . . . 64
xvi. . . . 204
xviii. . . . 191
xviii. 2-4 . . 185
xxviii. . . 195 n.
xxix. 17-21 . 396 n.
xxxi. 18 . . 404 n.
xxxiv. 23, 24 . 315
xxxvi.-xlviii. . 311
xxxvi. 26-28 190, 191
xxxvii. . . 388
xxxvii. 11-14 . 389
xxxvii. 24, 25 . 315
xxxvii. 25 . . 403
xxxviii. . . 320, 373
xxxix. . . 320, 373
xl.-xlviii. . 70, 133 n.
xliv. 15 . . 254, 315
xlviii. . . 374 n.
xlviii. 11, 35 . 316
Dan. i. 8 . . 192 n.
i. 8, 12 . . 255
ii. . . . 320
ii. 11 . . . 174
ii. 44 . . 321 n.
iv. 8 . . . 92 n.
v. 12 . . . 176
vii. . 67 n., 320, 321,
354, 357 n., 398
vii. 9 . . . 325
vii. 13 . . . 354
vii. 21-27 . . 64
vii. 27 . . 321 n.
viii. . . . 320
viii. 16 . . 150
ix. . . . 320, 329
ix. 2 . . . 127

Page
Dan. ix. 24, 25 . . 64
x. 13 150
x. 20, 21 . . 229 n.
xi. 320
xi. 45 64
xii. . 320, 398, 411
xii. 1-3 . . . 392
xii. 1-4 . . . 320
xii. 2 . 64, 280 n., 404
xii. 9 . . . 321
xii. 11-13 . . 321
Hos. i.-xiv. . . 315 n.
ii. 310
iii. 310
iii. 5 . . . 309 n.
iv. 3 . . . 361 n.
vi. 6 . . . 232, 264
xi. 1 . . . 83, 317
xiv. 1-7 . . . 310
Joel i.-iii. . . 398
ii. 28-iii. 21 . . 314
iii. 334 n., 357 n., 396 n.
Amos i.-ix. . . 315 n.
i. . . . . 396 n.
ii. . . . . 396 n.
iii. 307
iii. 2 . . . 336 n.
v. 21-23 . . . 229
v. 27 . . . 309
vi. 14 . . . 309
viii. 8 . 309, 361 n.
ix. 307
ix. 5 . . . 361 n.
ix. 9 . . . 309
ix. 11-15 . . 309 n.
Obadiah . . . 396 n.
Mic. i.-iii. . 310, 315 n.
i. 8 . . . 170
iv.-vii. . . 310 n.
iv. 1-5 . . . 313
iv. 2, 5 . . 314 n.
iv. 6-13 . . 310 n.
v. 2-8 . . . 310
v. 2 . . 330, 357
vi. . 310 n., 315 n.
vi. 7 . . 175, 229
vii. . . . 312
Nahum i.-iii. . 310, 315,
396 n.
Hab. i.-iii. . . 315 n.
ii. 14 . . 310, 317
iii. 61
iii. 14 . . . 90 n.
Zeph. i. 11 . 310, 315 n.
iii. . . . 310 n.
Hag. ii. 6-9 . . 313
Zech. i.-viii. . . 313
i. 9 149
i. 12 . . . 223
iii. 148
iii. 1, 2 . . . 91
vi. 12 . . . 316
viii. . . . 63
viii. 1-15 . . 313
ix.-xiv. . . . 314

Page

Zech. ix. 9–17 . . . 315
ix. 9 . . . 318, 343
ix. 13 318
x. 11 . . . . 316 n.
x.i.-xiv. 315

Zech. xiii. 2 . . . 77
xiv. . . . 313, 398
xiv. 20, 21 . . . 315
Mal. iii. iv. . . . 313

Mal. iii. 1 330
iii. 14 80
iv. . . . . . 357 n.
iv. 5 330

APOCRYPHA.

1 Esdras iii. iv. . . 56
2 Esdras vi. 49–52 . 162
vii. 28, 29 . . 67 n.
x. 11, 7 . . . 67 n.
xii. 10–32 . . 67 n.
xiii. 32, 37 . . 67 n.
xiv. 9 . . . 67 n.
Tob. i. 10 . . . 192 n.
iv. 7 294
iv. 15 294
xii. 8 255
xiii. 4 84
xiii. 12–18 . . . 318
xiv. 7 318
Judith ix. 11 . . . 87
Wisd. i. 2 87
i. 6 100
i. 7 . . . . 92, 100
ii. . . . . . 192 n.
ii. 23 . 202, 205, 207, 378
ii. 24 . . 78, 158, 195,
        202, 205, 207
iii. 4 294
iii. 8 318
iii. 10 411
iii. 19 411
v. 411
v. 1 318
v. 5 84
vi. 18, 19 . . . 100
vii.-ix. 278
vii. 22 . . . 60, 297
vii. 23 297
vii. 26 . . 60, 118 n.
vii. 26, 27 . . . 101
viii. . . . . 182 n.
viii. 19, 20 . . . 219
ix. 1 105
ix. 17, 18 . . . 279
xi. 24–26 . . . 60
xii. 1 92
xiv. 3 79
xvi.-xix. 127
xvi. 7 80
xvi. 12, 27 . . . 105
xvi. 26 84
Ecclus. i. 4, 9, 15 . 100
xi. 1–20 100
xvii. 1 205
xix. 13–17 . . . 294
xxiii. 1 84
xxiii. 29 294
xxiv. 100
xxv. 24 205

Ecclus. xxviii. 2–5 . 294
xxix. 2, 12, 20 . 294
xxxvi. 1–17 . . 318
xxxvii. 25 . . 318
xliv.-xlix. . . . 127
xliv. 11–21 . . . 273
xlv. 17 127
xlvii. 11 318
l. . . . . 127, 247 n.
l. 23, 24 318
Baruch ii. 27–35 . . 318
iii.-v. 66
iv. 36 218
v. 5–9 318
1 Mac. ii. 42 . . . 249
ii. 57 318
iii. 18, 19 . . . 127
iii. 48 127
iv. 9 127
2 Mac. i. 9 . . . . 75 n.
i. 20 127
ii. 1–8 330
ii. 8 127
ii. 13 73
ii. 18 318
ii. 23 . . . . . 75 n.
iii. 24 124
iii. 24 ff. . . . 149 n.
iv. 6 249
v. 2, 3 124
vi. . . . . 68, 357 n.
vii. . 68, 128, 357 n.
vii. 9, 14, 23 . . 393
x. 29, 30 124
xii. 40 . . . . 77 n.
xiv. 15 318
xv. 12–16 . . . 124
xv. 13–15 . . . 330
xv. 36 57
Jubilees i. 327
iv. . . . . . 160 n.
As'mpt. of Moses x. 327
Enoch i.-xxxvi. . 203 n.
i. . . 324, 398, 398 n.
i. 4 324
vi. 6 . . . . 160 n.
viii. 143
ix. 143
x. . 143, 160, 401, 404
x. 6, 14 404
xxii. 411
xxii. 11 324
xxvii. 2 404

Enoch xxxii. . . . 409
xxxvii.-lxxi. . . 325
xxxvii. 401
xlv.-lvii. . . . 325
xlv.-liv. . . 348 n.
xlv.-xlviii. . . . 354
xlv. . . . . 357 n.
xlv. 3 . . 65, 343 n.
xlv. 4 65
xlv. 5 401
xlvi. 6 401
xlviii. 3 357
xlviii. 6 . . 65, 357
xlviii. 7 326
li. . 357 n., 374, 395
li. 1 393
liii. 406
liii. 3 . . . . 203 n.
liv. . 401, 404, 405, 406
liv. 5, 6 . . . 203 n.
liv. 8 . . . . 162 n.
lvi. . . . 404, 405
lvi. 5 325
lviii. 401
lx. 162
lx. 8 162
lxi. 12 408
lxii. 374
lxiii. 374
lxix. . . 160, 357 n.
lxxii.-cv. . . 203 n.
lxxxiv. 4 . . . 324
lxxxix. 40 . . . 398
xc. . . . . 357 n.
xc. 9, 37 65
xc. 16–38 . . . 323
xc. 20 324
xc. 20-27, 33 . . 324
xc. 24, 25 . . . 404
xc. 26 404
xc. 29 408
xc. 33 401
xci. 374
cii. 411
ciii. 411
Sib. Or. iii. 36–62 . 325
iii. 56 . . . . 357 n.
iii. 558 . . . . 361 n.
iii. 652–794 . . 322
iii. 669 ff. . . 357 n.
Pss. of Sol. i.-xviii. 357 n.
ii. 30, 31 67
xvii. 325

NEW TESTAMENT.

	Page
Matt. ii.	320
iii.	333
iii. 5-7	337
iii. 9	336
iii. 16	94
iv. 1-11	163
iv. 24	170
v.	418
v. 12	410
v. 16	295
v. 17-19	231, 266, 267
v. 21-32	295
v. 22	406
v. 33-37	295
v. 38-48	295
v. 45	269, 418
v. 48	279
vi.	80
vi. 1	268, 296
vi. 2	295
vi. 5	295
vi. 14	421
vi. 15	268
vi. 16	295
vi 20	268
vi. 23	268
vi. 33	340, 343
vii. 11	211
vii. 12	295
vii. 17, 18, 20	211
vii. 21	402
vii. 22, 23	356 n.
viii. 4	266
viii. 5 ff.	86
viii. 11	346, 402
viii. 12	346
viii. 29	170, 405
ix. 14	335
x. 5, 6	345, 418
x. 20	94
x. 28	177
x. 39	178
x. 41	423
xi.	335
xi. 3, 10, 11	329
xi. 7-19	335, 339
xi. 19	102
xi. 23	406
xi. 25-30	422
xii. 5, 7	232
xii. 7	264
xii 24-32	95
xii. 24	163, 171
xii. 26	163
xii. 31	83
xii. 32	402
xii. 33, 34	207
xiii.	360, 394
xiii. 11	347 n.
xiii. 19	178
Matt. xiii. 24-30	348 n.
xiii. 37-43	348 n.
xiii. 39	163
xiii. 40	402
xiii. 41	152
xv. 18	295
xv. 19, 20	207
xv. 24	83
xvi. 13, 14	329
xvi. 17	177, 350
xvi. 18	348
xvi. 24	295
xvi. 26	178
xvi. 27	83, 423
xvi. 28	423
xvii. 10, 11	329
xviii. 10	151, 153
xviii. 17	348
xviii. 18	422
xviii. 20	423
xix.	342
xix. 28	83, 343
xx.	342
xx. 23	343
xx. 28	420
xxi. 23-32	335
xxii.	392
xxii. 23	253
xxii. 30	152, 402
xxii. 31, 32	394
xxiii.	392
xxiii. 2, 3	231, 266
xxiii. 3	268
xxiv.	360, 399, 402
xxiv. 20	361 n.
xxiv. 26-28	361 n.
xxiv. 30	361 n.
xxiv. 37-51	361 n.
xxv.	394, 399, 402
xxv. 31-46	356
xxv. 31	152
xxv. 41	152, 163
xxv. 46	407
xxvi. 17	266
xxviii. 19	95, 349, 423
xxviii. 20	423
Mark i.	333
i. 4, 15	230
i. 10, 11	335 n.
i. 44	419
ii. 6	421
ii. 10, 28	354
iii. 35	421
iv. 11	347 n.
iv. 15	163
iv. 26-29	348 n.
v. 9	171
v. 21-23	422
v. 36	421
vi. 17-29	333
Mark vi. 33, 34, 45	420
vii. 5, 9-13	295
vii. 10-13	244
vii. 24, 31	345
vii. 27	345
viii.	358
viii. 12	179
viii. 27-30	354
viii. 29	350
viii. 31	352, 354 n.
viii. 38	356, 357
ix. 1	356, 357
ix. 12	352
x.	342, 350
x. 23-31	83
x. 30	402
x. 40	343
x. 45	352
xi.	350
xi. 8-10	344
xii. 9	336 n.
xii. 12	348 n.
xii. 28	419
xiii.	399
xiv.	350
xiv. 12-16	419
xiv. 24	420
xiv. 62	350
xv. 1 20	344
xvi. 2-5	423
Luke iii.	333
iii. 22	94
vi. 24	295 n.
vii. 35	102
viii. 55	178
ix. 20	350
x. 16	422
x. 18	160, 163
xii. 8	152
xiii. 3	206
xiii. 16	163
xiii. 29	409 n.
xv. 10	152
xvi.	411
xvi. 19-31	406
xvi. 22	152, 409
xvi. 23	406
xvii. 14	231
xx. 3, 31	163
xx. 36	152, 153
xxi.	360, 399
xxii. 32	273
xxiii. 43	409
xxiv.	350, 358, 423
xxiv. 17, 21	418
xxiv. 19-21	422
xxiv. 37-39	178
xxiv. 45	179
John i. 4, 5	216
i. 9	284

	Page
John i. 10	218
i. 14	177
i. 18	115
i. 29	283
ii. 11	125
ii. 12-17	284
iii. 3	284
iii. 3, 5	284
iii. 6	284
iii. 16	283
iii. 19	83, 216
iii. 21	284
iv. 2	348
iv. 22	285 n., 346
iv. 24	88
iv. 25	333
v.	402
v. 1	231
v. 22	400
v. 24	283
v. 27	399
v. 28, 29	393
v. 38-40, 46, 47	217
vi. 15	344
vi. 33-63	216
vi. 37	217
vi. 44	217
vi. 63	216
vii 27, 31, 40-42	329
vii. 49	241
viii. 12	216
viii. 24	412
viii. 26	283
viii. 38-44	218
viii. 39, 40	218
viii. 44	163, 208, 218 n.
ix. 2, 34	219 n.
x. 33-36	422
xi. 50	420
xii. 20	86
xii. 27	178
xii. 46	216
xiii. 2	178
xiv. 6	216
xiv. 16, 17	95
xiv. 30	163
xv. 4	283
xv. 18, 19	217
xvi. 7-15	95
xvi. 8	284
xvi. 9	216
xvi. 11	218 n.
xvii. 2	177
xvii. 9	217
Acts i.-v.	88, 232
i.-xii.	425
ii. 22-24, 32-36	422
iii. 1	232
v. 36, 37	344
v. 38. 39	232
vi. 22	129
viii. 26, 29	154
viii. 32, 33	280
x.	366

	Page
Acts xii. 15	153
xii. 23	152
xv.	367
xvi. 16	171
xvii. 28	85
xvii. 30, 31	412
xix. 1-7	334 n.
xix. 3	335
xix. 13-16	171
xxi. 20-26	232
xxiii. 6-8	419
xxiii. 8	253
xxiii. 9	152
Rom. i.	242 n., 358
i. 3	117
i. 3, 4	429
i. 18-32	214
i. 28	179
ii.	283 n.
ii. 1-16	394
ii. 5	178
ii. 6-11	82
ii. 16	402 n., 429
iii. 9-19	206
iii. 19-31	420
iv.	403 n.
iv. 25	281, 419
v.	82, 280
v. 12	208, 209
v. 12-21	208, 420
vi.	209, 276
vi. 5	277
vi. 6	213
vi. 8-11	281
vii.	271, 276, 283 n.
vii. 9	283 n.
vii. 10, 14, 24	214 n.
vii. 18	213
vii. 18, 19	213
vii. 20	213, 214
vii. 23, 25	170
viii.	82
viii. 2	182
viii. 3	280
viii. 4-8, 9, 16, 27	93
viii. 7	213
viii. 9	279
viii. 13	177
viii. 18-22	409
viii. 19	401
viii. 28-30	279
viii. 38	153
ix. 5	177, 429 n.
ix. 7, 8	403 n.
x.	87, 403 n.
x. 10	178
xi.	87
xi. 25, 26	403 n.
xii. 5	298
xii. 13	297
xii. 19, 20	297
xiii. 1	178
xiv. 17	402
1 Cor. i.	367
i. 8	402 n.

	Page
1 Cor. i. 23	420
i. 24	118
i. 24, 30	102
i. 29	177
i. 30	419, 429
ii. 10-13	93
ii. 16	179
iii. 16	182, 279
iii. 23	429
iv 20	402
v. 3-10	179
v. 5	163
v. 7	118
vi. 2, 3	406
vi. 3	153
viii. 6	118
ix. 9	80
ix. 19-22	207
x. 4	129
x. 20, 21	155, 171
x. 33	207
xi. 10	153
xii. 10	126 n.
xii. 14	177
xiii.	207
xiv.	138
xv.	274, 393, 402 n.
xv. 15	181
xv. 19	376
xv. 23-28	374 n.
xv. 23-28, 51-55	362
xv. 24	400
xv. 24-28	118, 358
xv. 24, 54	164
xv. 26. 54	407
xv. 28	429
xv. 44	395
xv. 44, 45	180
xv. 51, 52	358, 410
xvi. 22	376, 396
2 Cor. i. 20	429
ii. 9	118
iii. 17, 18	94
iii. 18	279
iv. 4	163, 164, 213
iv. 6	429
iv. 14	429
v. 4-8	410
v. 6, 10	177
v. 10	358, 394, 399, 402 n., 429
v. 19	277, 429
v. 21	118
vi. 12	177 n.
xi. 14. 15	152
xii. 1-4	126
xii. 2-4	409
Gal. i.	427, 429
i. 4	118, 232, 402, 429
i. 8	154 n.
i. 11-24	126
i. 16	177
ii.	367
ii. 7-9	366
iii.	271

```
                                  Page
Gal. iii. 2, 3 . . . . 178
     iii. 3 . . . . . 182
     iii. 13 . . . . . 419
     iii. 14 . . . . . 94
     iii. 19 . . . . 227
     iii. 27 . . . . . 277
     iv. . . 271, 278, 367
     iv. 4 . . 117, 281, 420
     iv. 6 . . . 94, 279
     iv. 10, 11 . . . 419
     v. . . . . . 278
     v. 17 21 . . . . 213
     v. 19-21 . . . . 178
     v. 24 . . . 178, 213
     vi. 8 . . . . . 213
     vi. 10 . . . . 297
Eph. i. 10 . 119, 407, 433
     i. 20-23 . . . . 433
     i. 21 . . . . . 154
     ii. 1-5 . . . . . 215
     ii. 4 . . . . . 178
     ii. 7 . . . . . 402
     ii. 9, 10 . . . . 282
     ii. 11-22 . . . . 370
     ii. 13, 16 . . . . 281
     ii. 14-19 . . . 208
     iii. . . . . . 215
     iii. 10 . . . 154, 433
     iii. 17 . . . . . 281
     iv. . . . . . 215
     iv. 13, 24 . . . 282
     v. . . . . . 215
     v. 2 . . . . . 281
     vi. 11 . . . . . 163
     vi. 12 . . . . 154
Phil. i. 6 . . . 402 n.
     i. 6, 10 . . . 410 n.
     i. 21-23 . . . . 410
     ii. 1 . . . . 177 n.
     ii. 6-9 . . . . 118
     iii. 10 . . . . 281
     iii. 20 . . . . 410 n.
Col. i. 15-20 . . . 433
     i. 16 . . . . . 154
     i. 20 . . . . . 407
     i. 24 . . . . . 282
     ii. 3 . . . . . 102
     ii. 10, 18 . . . 154
     ii. 11 . . . . . 178
     ii. 13 . . . . . 215
     ii. 14 . . . . . 282
     ii. 15 . . . 154, 407
     ii. 16-19 . . . . 433
     ii. 18 . . . . . 179
     ii. 20 . . . . . 282
     ii. 20-33 . . . . 219
     iii. 1, 3 . . . . 282
     iii 1-4 . . . . . 410
     iii. 4 . . . . . 407
1 Thess. i.-v. . . . 274
     ii. 18 . . . . . 163
     iv. . . . . . 399
     iv. 13-18 . . . 376
     iv. 15-17 . . . 358
     iv. 17 . . . 401, 409

                                  Page
1 Thess. v. 23 . . 181
     v. 1-11 . . . . 376
2 Thess. i. . . . . 399
     i.-iii. . . . . 274
     i. 3-12 . . . . 376
     i. 6-10 . . . . 362
     i. 7 . . . . . 152
     i. 7, 8 . . . . 418
     i. 8 . . . . . 396
     ii. . . . . . 364
1 Tim. i. 8 . . . 283
     i. 8, 9 . . . . . 212
     i. 15 . . . . . 283
     i. 20 . . . . . 163
     ii. 3 . . . 283, 434
     ii. 5, 6 . . . . 283
     ii. 11-13 . . . . 210
     ii. 14 . . 163, 208, 210
     ii. 14, 15 . . . 210 n.
     iv. 10 . . . 80, 283
     v. 21 . . . . 152
2 Tim. i. 10 283, 407, 419
     ii. 11 . . . . . 283
     ii. 24-26 . . . . 212
     iii. 8 . . . . . 129
     iii. 15 . . . . . 283
     iii. 16 . . . . . 128
     iv. 1 . . 399, 402 n.
     iv. 11 . . . . . 402
Tit. i. 15 . . . . 179
     ii. 11-14 . . 212, 283
     ii. 12 . . . . . 402
     iii. 4-7 . . . . 283
     iii. 5-7 . . . . 212
     iii. 8 . . . . . 212
Heb. i. 2 . . . . 60
     i. 1-4 . . . . . 432
     i. 2, 3 . . . 101, 118
     ii. 4 . . . . . 94
     ii. 13 . . . . . 136
     iii. 7 . . . . . 94
     iv. 12 . . . . . 181
     v. 9 . . . . . 283
     vi. 1 . . . . . 283
     vi. 2 . . . . 402 n.
     vi. 4 . . . . . 94
     vi. 5 . . . . . 402
     vii. 10 . . . 177 n.
     vii. 25 . . . . 283
     viii. 6 . . . . 283
     ix. 6 . . . . . 402
     ix. 14 . . . . . 94
     ix. 22 . . . . . 227
     ix. 27 . . . . 402 n.
     ix. 28 . . . . . 402
     x. 4 . . . . . 230
     x. 5-10 . . . . 138
     x. 23, 36-39 . . 283
     x. 29 . . . . . 94
     xi. . . . . . 283
     xi. 35 . . . . . 128
     xii. 2 . . . . . 208
     xii. 2, 3 . . . . 283
     xii. 23 . . . . . 410
     xii. 24 . . . . 283

                                  Page
James i.-v. . . . . 358
     i. 12, 15 . . . . 207
     i. 18, 27 . . . . 270
     i. 21 . . . . . 178
     ii. 8 . . . . . 297
     ii. 10 . . . . . 243
     ii. 19 . . . . . 170
     iii. 6 . . . 406, 406 n.
     iii. 13 . . . . . 211
     iii. 17 . . 60, 101, 297
     iv. 7 . . . . . 163
     iv. 8 . . . . . 211
     iv. 17 . . . . . 270
     v. 7 . . . . . 376
     v. 7, 8 . . . . 362
     v. 8 . . . . . 358
     v. 16 . . . . . 273
     v. 20 . . . 211, 270
1 Pet. i. 3, 19 . . . 282
     i. 12 . . . . . 153
     i. 22 . . . . . 282
     ii. 5, 24 . . . . 282
     iii. 13 . . . . . 408
     iii. 18-20 . . . . 411
     iii. 21 . . . . . 282
     iv. 1 . . . . . 177
     iv. 1, 13 . . . . 282
     iv. 5 . . . . 402 n.
     iv. 6 . . . . . 411
     iv. 7 . . . . . 358
     iv. 7-19 . . . . 376
     v. 8 . . . . . 163
     v. 10 . . . . 402 n.
2 Pet. i. 11 . . . 402 n.
     ii. 4, 17 . . . 406 n.
     iii. 13 . . . . . 401
1 John iv. 17 . . 402 n.
     v. 10 . . . . . 397
Jude 6 . . . . . 160
     6, 13 . . . . 406 n.
     9 . . . . . 163
     21 . . . . . 402 n.
Rev. i.-xxii. . . . 376
     ii. 7 . . . . . 409
     ii 23 . . . 177 n., 399
     iii. 5 . . . . . 152
     iii. 9 . . . . . 163
     v. . . . . . 399
     vi. 9-11 . . . . 410
     vi. 16 . . . . . 399
     ix. 20 . . . . . 171
     xii. 4, 13 . . . . 162
     xii. 19 . . . 152, 163
     xiii. . . . . . 364
     xiii. 18 . . . . 364 n.
     xvii. . . . . . 364
     xviii. . . . . . 364
     xix. . . . 364, 399
     xix. 13-16 . . . 120
     xx. . 374 n., 399, 402
     xx. 1-3 . . . . 160
     xx. 2, 7 . . . . 163
     xx. 10 . 163, 164, 406
     xx. 11 . . . . 399
     xx. 12 . . 393, 397
```

	Page		Page		Page
Rev. xx. 13, 14 . . .	406	Rev. xxi. . . . 374 n.,	408	Rev. xxii.	408
xx. 10, 15 . . .	407	xxi. 4, 8, 27 . .	407	xxii. 5, 11, 15 . .	407
xx. 21	373	xxi. 14	407	xxii. 11	411

PHILO.

Philo i. 4	112	Philo i. 308 . 109, 111	Philo i. 630 . . . 112
i. 5 . . . 107, 112	i. 414 111	i. 653 . . . 109 n.
i. 6 . . . 108, 112	i. 415 . . . 109, 111	i. 655 . . . 110, 112
i. 7 112	i. 427 . . . 108, 109	i. 656 110
i. 8 112	i. 441 128	i. 684 109
i. 56 101	i. 452 . . . . 109 n.	i. 692 128
i. 64 206	i. 456 107	ii. 28 108
i. 66 112	i. 481 206	ii. 46 107
i. 79 . . 203 n., 205	i. 501 112	ii. 154 110
i. 82 107	i. 502 . 108, 109, 112	ii. 163 128
i. 100 206	i. 505 107	ii. 385 102
i. 128 112	i. 511 128	ii. 421—428 . . . 327
i. 202 102	i. 560 111	ii. 423 . . . 113 n.
i. 207 92	i. 561 . . . 108, 111	ii. 435 327
i. 255 92	i. 562 111	ii. 436 . . . 113 n.
i. 256 92	i. 625 112	

JOSEPHUS.

Jos. Ant. i. 1, 4 . 158 n.	Jos. Ant. xv. 10, 5 254, 256	Jos. Ant. xviii. 5, 2 234 n.
xi. 8, 4 . . . 55 n.	xviii. 1, 3 . . 250 n.	xx. 9, 1 . . . 253 n.
xiii. 10, 6 . . . 253	xviii. 1, 4 . . . 253	Jos. War. ii. 8, 4 . . 255
xiv. 9, 3–5 . . . 258	xviii. 1, 6 . . . 258	vii. 6, 3 169

INDEX OF SUBJECTS.

ABADDON, 404 *n.*

Abbot, on Rom. ix. 5, 429 *n.*

Aboda Sara, 252 *n.*

Abraham, in Talmud, 273; faith of, in O. T., 275.

Abraham's bosom, 409.

Abyss, of Genesis, 161 *n.*

Achæmenian inscriptions, 391.

Acts i.-xii., burden of, 425.

Adam, contrasted with Christ, 180; federal headship of, 135 *n.*; in Ezekiel, 195; moral status of, 197; transgression of, in N. T., 208; contrasted with Christ, 209; introducer of sin, 210.

Aeshma daeva, 150.

Age, the present, in N. T., 343, 355, 402, the coming, in N. T., 343, 355, 402; change in meaning of, 401.

Ahriman, 143, 165.

Ahuramazda, 164; as judge, 395.

Alexandre, Sibyl edited by, 66 *n.*

Alexandria, religious amalgamation in, 43; Jewish colony in, 383; as religious centre, 387, 395 *n.*; as centre of logos-doctrine, 432.

Aliens, prophetic treatment of, 318; in Daniel, 321; in the new dispensation, 328, 329.

Allegorical, exegesis, 138; interpretation of serpent, 203.

Altruism in N. T., 295.

Amesha-çpentas, 150.

Anachronisms in religious progress, 12.

Anakephalaiosis, 407.

Ancestor-worship, 143 *n.*

Ancient world. See States, ancient.

Angel of the Lord, perhaps survival of ancient deity, 148; mediating, 228.

Angels, origin of, 91; appearances of, in O. T., 149 *n.*; guardian, of nations, 150; position of, in N. T., 152–154; later organization of, 154; fall of, as dogma, not in O. T., 161; names of, 168; rejection of, ascribed to Sadducees, 253 *n.*; evil, in Enoch, 324; at final judgment, 356; as ignorant of day of parousia, 362 *n.*; evil, judgment on, 401; punished, 405; as tormentors, 406; as intermediaries between God and man, 433.

Animals, lower, mortality of, 204 *n.*

Animistic material, reshaped in N. T., 171.

Annihilation, 411; ascribed to Sadducees, 253 *n.*

Anthropomorphism in conception of God, 87.

Anthropomorphisms in Eden-story, 201.

Anti-Christ, in Paul's writings, 365.

Antigonus of Socho, 87, 260, 264.

Antinomianism, alleged, of Paul, 275, 276.

Antinomism, Christian, 288.

Antioch, in Pisidia, 367; in Syria, 367.

Antiochus Epiphanes, 64, 320, 365 *n.*

Apocalypse, germinal, 317.

Apocalypse, in Synoptics, 363.

Apocalypse, the N. T., conception of divine justice in, 82, 83; moral-religious ideas in, 375; changing interpretations of, 376; resurrection in, 393, 395; final judge in, 399; constitution of, 399 *n.*; whether imputed righteousness in, 430.

Apocalypses, in N. T. times, 361.

Apocrypha, the, patriotic hope in, 318.

Apostasy, preceding parousia, 364.

Apostate Jews, 249, 321.

Apsu, 162.

Apuleius on magic, 169 *n.*

Arabia, Paul in, 427.

Aratus, Stoic poet, 85.

Aristocracy, Sadducean, 253.

Arrested development, only apparent, 3.

Asaph, psalm-writer, 136.

Ascetic view of body, 206 *n.*

Asceticism, whether a Jewish conception, 219 *n.*; Essenian, 255; in Daniel and Tobit, 255.

Asia Minor, logos-doctrine in, 432.

Asideans, the, 249.

Asmodeus, 150, 151, 168.

Asoka, edicts of, 38; theocracy of, 303 *n.*

Assimilation of ideas, how limited, 30.

Assyria, its religious union with Israel anticipated, 314; post-exilian use of, 316 *n.*

Athenian view of future judgment, 395 *n.*

Atonement, by suffering, 222; day of, 226; later Jewish conception of, 280 n.; in Enoch-Parables, 326.
Avesta, date of, 391.
Azazel, 145, 160, 163; etymology of, 144 n.

Banism, Messianic faith in, 425 n.
Babylon, flood-story in, 194; in N. T. Apocalypse, 363; king of, his descent to Sheol, 379.
Babylonian influence on Jews, 248, 292.
Babylonians, evil spirits of, 165.
"Baptist Quarterly," the, 334 n.
Barnabas, 367.
Baur, works of, 337 n.
Beast, in N. T. Apocalypse, 364, 375.
Beelzebub, 171.
Bel, Babylonian, 152.
Berakoth, 247 n., 273.
Bereshith Rabba, 252 n., 357.
Bethlehem, birthplace of Messiah, 329, 330.
Blood, seat of life, 174; atonement by, 226, 420.
Body, representative of sinful nature, 177; pneumatical, 180; psychical, 180; as seat of evil, 206.
Bone, expression of physical structure, 174.
Bowels, seat of compassion, 177 n.
Brain, not in O. T., 177 n.
Broadus, "Jesus of Nazareth," 302 n.
Brotherhood, human, in N. T., 296; Roman sense of, 338.
Budde, "Bibl. Urgeschichte," 205 n.
Buddhism, foreign influence on, 27; broadening of its constitution, 31; its dogma, 38; birth of, out of Brahmanism, 39; Messianic faith in, 425 n.
Bundehesh, the, 375.

Cæsarea Philippi, 351.
Calling, prenatal, 326.
Canaan, restoration to, 311.
Canaanitish worship, 234.
Canonization, grounds of, 69, 72.
Canons, non-Jewish, 68.
Catholicism, affected by modern thought, 435.
Centralization, Jewish religious, 239.
Ceremonial, Jewish, moral effect of, 243.
Chaldeans, in Habakkuk, 310; in Jeremiah and Ezekiel, 311.
Changes in faith. See Religious revolutions.
Chiliasm, in the Church, 365.
China, state-religion of, 42.
Chosen one, the, in Enoch-Parables, 325.
Christ, contrasted with Adam, 203; humanity of, 280; sufferings of, modified view of, 282; reign of, signification of, 377.
Christ, the, in Psalms of Solomon, 325.

Christianity, rise of, in conformity with law, 1; not obscured in Middle Age, 3; influence of, on barbarians, 4; of to-day not inferior to that of fourth century, 5; whether a universal religion, 38; birth of, out of Judaism, 39; the world prepared for it, 40; connection of, with civilization, 45; now spreading, 45; unifying power of, 370, 371; permanent moral element of, 414; conditions of birth of, 426.
Church, the, relation of, to religion, 39; takes place of Israel, 126; the Jewish, rise of, 237; the Christian, mechanical nomism in, 245; early Christian, composed of Jews, 246; not source of salvation, 278 n.; nomism in, 289; how far cosmopolitan, 298; as ethical lever, 301; in First Gospel, 348; diversities in, 359; its hope of the Lord's coming, 365; partial petrifaction of, 369; intermingling of Semitic and Hellenic conceptions in, 370; spiritual aim of, 377; mission of, 377; in place of Israel, 396; passed from Jews to Gentiles, 416; its coincidence with the synagogue, 419; Mosaism in, 424; growth of spirituality in, 428; ethics of, determined by Jesus, 434; creation of Jesus, 435.
Church government, its relation to social-political ideas, 13.
Church of England, progress of, 43.
Church of Rome, progress of, 44.
Cicero, on divination, 169 n.; ethical sentiment of, 337.
Citizenship, Roman, ethical effect of, 298.
Cleanthes, Stoic poet, 85.
Code, Deuteronomic, 70; Jewish, not abrogated by Jesus, 368.
Codification, in time of Hillel, 252.
Colony, the Egyptian-Jewish, 323.
Colossians, conception of Jesus in, 119; logos in, 433.
Coming of Jesus, hope of, 359.
Commission, the baptismal, late origin of, 345.
Communal immortality, 385.
Communism, Essenian, in N. T., 256.
Communities. See Society.
Community, ethically constituted Israelitish, 317.
Conduct, biblical basis of, 292.
Conflict, between will and nature, 214; between light and darkness, 216; between world and believers, 216-218.
Confucius as founder of a religion, 25.
Conquest of world, O. T. conception of, 377.
Conscience, autocracy of, 15; union with God, 15; how viewed by Jesus, 269.
Consciousness. See Religious consciousness.
Cosmopolitan spirit, Jewish, 294; prophetic, 314.
Cosmos in Fourth Gospel, 216, 218 n.

Creation, divine spiritual, 279; spiritual, 284; the, as groaning in sin, 401.
Creation-tablet, Babylonian, 161.
Criticism, biblical, whether practised in first century, 132.
Cults, foreign, adoption of, 29.
Cyrus, his policy toward exiles, 312.
Cyrenaic philosophy, 386.

DAIMON, 155 n.
Daimonion, 155 n.
Daniel, conception of sin in, 192 n.; no mention of Satan in, 202; political element in, 341; "son of man" in, 354; judgment in, 357; anti-godly evil in, 365 n.; resurrection in, 380 n.; Persian influence in, 390; partial resurrection in, 392; retribution in, 404; intermediate state in, 411.
Darius and young men, episode of, 56.
Darmesteter, "Ormazd et Ahriman," 172 n.; "The Zend Avesta," 172 n.
Davidic dynasty, perpetuity of, 315.
Day of Yahwe, in Malachi, 313.
Death, expiatory, in Isaiah, 352; premature, as punishment, 382, 404; abolition of, in N. T., 407; as end of probation, 411; of Jesus, in N. T., 428.
Debility, moral, in man, 214.
Decay of societies, cause of, 3; only relative, 3, 4.
Defect, alleged, of ethics of Jesus, 296; of ethics of N. T., 299, 300.
Defects, ethical, Jewish, 332.
Deification, of Jesus, Paul's attitude toward, 429; of men, whether Semitic, 430 n.
Deities, heathen, late Jewish recognition of, 77, 78.
Deity, tribal, 306.
Delitzsch, "Jesus u. Hillel," 265 n.
Delitzsch, "Wo lag d. Paradies?" 306 n., 409 n.
Demon, 142, 155.
Demoniacal possession, 168, 170.
Demons, as spirits of the wicked, 169; tormented, 405.
Dependence on God, ethical and non-ethical, 384.
Depravity, total, whether in O. T., 190 ff., 196.
Destruction, future, sense of, in N. T., 406 n., 411.
Determinism, biblical, 291.
Deuterocanonical books, 75.
Deuteronomy, ethical effect of, 235; loving obedience in, 245.
Development, ethical, Jewish, 288.
Devil. See Satan.
Dillmann, Enoch-text of, 66 n.
Disciples of Jesus, their hopes not political, 345; Messianic hope of, 358.
Discourses, eschatological, of Jesus, 355–360.

Distress, national, in Psalter, 235.
Divine intervention, two stadia in conception of, 121.
Dogma, unspiritual, power of, 369; as modifying ethics, 397.
Dogma and conduct, complements of the religious sentiment, 20.
Dogmas, Christian, formulation of, 435.
Döllinger, "Gentile and Jew," 337 n.
Dorner, on biblical ethics, 302 n.
Dragon, in N. T. Apocalypse, 162, 375; Babylonian, 195, 200 n.
Driver, in "Studia Biblica," 306 n.
Drummond, "Jewish Messiah," 66 n., 326 n., 330 n.
Duality of man's constitution, 173.
Duschak, "Bib.-tal. Glaubenslehre," 330 n.
Duty, filial, casuistical treatment of, 244.
Dwight, on Rom. ix. 5, 429 n.

EARTH, the, abode of the new Israel, 321; as scene of future life, 401, 402.
Ecclesiastes, date of, 59; doubts as to canonical character of, 74; providence in, 79; conception of sin in, 192 n.
Ecclesiasticus, date of, 60; second prologue to, 73; fatherhood of God in, 84; idea of wisdom in, 100; conception of sin in, 192, 205.
Eden, garden of, 195 n.; whether in N. T., 408.
Eden-story, central idea of, 198 n.; whether borrowed by Jews, 200.
Edersheim, "Life of Jesus," 329 n.
Egoism, alleged, biblical, 299.
Egypt, its religious union with Israel anticipated, 314.
Egyptian doctrine of bodily resuscitation, 390.
Egyptian idea of immortality, 387.
Egyptian influence on Jews, 382, 383, 405.
El, sense of, 317 n.
Elijah, child restored to life by, 175; translation of, 204 n., 390; forerunner of Messiah, 329, 330; as moral reformer, 333; model of John, 334.
Elohim, sons of, 167.
Elohim-beings, 147, 159, 161, 198.
Enemies, national, hatred of, 242; O. T. hatred of, opposed by Jesus, 268.
Enoch, translation of, 204 n., 390.
Enoch, book of, date and character of, 65; why not canonized, 75, 76; quoted in N. T., 76; Azazel in, 143; angelology of, 149, 150, 160, 167, 168; ethical element in, 324; "son of man" in, 354; earthly consummation in, 356; judgment in, 357, 374; calling of Messiah by God in, 357; anti-godly evil in, 365 n.; whether Christian hand in, 395 n.; judgment in, 398; Messiah in, 398; Israel's future in, 400; retribu-

tion in, 404; new Jerusalem in, 408; intermediate state in, 410, 411.

Enoch-Parables, judgment in, 325, 401, 404; resurrection in, 393; Messiah in, 399; garden of life in, 408.

Enthusiasm, ethical, in N. T., 294.

Ephesians, conception of Jesus in, 119; logos in, 433.

Epicureanism, 387.

Epistles, the, ethics of, 207, 341; expectation of Jesus in, 358; judgment in, 401, 402; immortality in, 402; Pastoral, whether imputed righteousness in, 430.

Eschatology, Jewish, 308; of Gospels, 358.

Essenes, origin of, 219 n.; purity of, 333.

Essenism, whether found in teaching of Jesus, 418.

Ethan, psalm-writer, 136.

Ethical element in Enoch, 324.

Ethical feeling, Jewish advance in, 396.

Ethical ideals, formation of, 18.

Ethical ideas, limited power of, 39.

Ethical standard, primitive, 243.

Ethics, religious sanctions of, 19; Jewish, 48; of John Baptist, 336; modified by nationalism, 396.

Ethics and religion, examples of unequal co-existent developments of, 18, 19.

Eve, prize offered her by the serpent, 203; introducer of sin, 210.

Evil, blotting out of, 407.

Exaltation, of Jesus, 428, 429.

Exegesis in N. T, spiritual power of, 139; basis of truth in, 139.

Exile, Babylonian, teaching of, 224; worship during, 246; influence of, 248.

Expiation, pre-exilian theory of, 220, 221; double view of, 222.

External ethical standard, difficulties of, 239, 240.

Ezekiel, his description of Eden, 195 n.; new covenant of, 332; "son of man" in, 353; anti-godly evil in, 365 n.; his vision of revivification, 389.

Ezra, turning-point in Jewish history, 47; and Nehemiah, advent of, 50.

"Face of Baal," title of Tanit, 89 n.

Faith, view of, in James, 270; transformation by, 276; Paul's conception of, 277; view of, in Ephesians and Colossians, 282; in Hebrews, 283.

Faith and works, Paul's conjunction of, 340.

Faith in Jesus, after his death, 425.

Fatherhood of God, 83–86, 269; Jesus' treatment of, 86.

Fetishism, Hebrew, 141.

First Gospel, word "church" in, 348.

Flesh, in O. T., not impure, 174; contrasted with spirit, 178; hostile to spirit, 213; as seat of sin, 219.

Flood-story, different recensions of, 194 n.

Flügel, "Die Sittenlehre Jesus," 302 n.

Folk-religion, Hebrew, 166.

Foreign thought, how regarded by Jews, 242.

Formulating period of Christianity, 435.

Fourth Gospel, conception of divine justice in, 83; spirituality of God in, 88; idea of divine spirit in, 95; date of, 115 n.; treatment of Eden-story in, 207; antithesis of moral power and impotency in, 217; conflict between divine and anti-divine in, 218; prologue to, 284; regeneration in, 340; baptism in, 348; resurrection in, 393, 395; whether imputed righteousness in, 430.

Fravashis, 150.

Frazer, "Totemism," 141 n.

Freedom, controlled by law, 278 n.

Friedländer, "Sittengeschichte Roms," 169 n.

Friedlieb, Sibyl edited by, 66 n.

Fusion of different elements in Christianity, 370.

Future life, in Palestinian works, 251 n.; Sadducean view of, 253, 260.

Galilee, Greek influence in, 85, 86.

Gamaliel, 232, 251; speech of, 424.

Gass on biblical ethics, 302 n.

Gautama, his relation to Buddhism, 26; to his age, 34.

Gehenna, 406.

Geldner, "Zend Avesta," 172 n.

Gen. iii., object of, 197.

Gentile influence on hypostasis of spirit, 96.

Gentiles, incoming of, 336 n.; acceptance of, in prophets, 346; attitude of early Church toward, 346; uncircumcised, received into the Church, 366, 367.

Ginsburg, his edition of Moabite Stone, 307 n.

Glossolaly, 138.

Gnosticism, whether Jewish in origin, 219 n.; Essenian, 255, 256; Jewish, 257, 433; combated in Colossians, 257; Christian, 257.

God, help of, need of, 2; identified with ethical ideal, 19, 183; national life regulated by, 238.

Gods, heathen, in Psalms, 147 n.

Gog and Magog, 373, 374; in N. T. Apocalypse, 373.

Golden Rule, the, 264, 294, 296, 297.

Goodness, personal, in N. T., 285.

Gospel, the, preached to Gentiles, 361.

Government, ideal, 317.

Gratitude, as ethical factor, 300.

Grätz, "Geschichte d. Juden," 306 n.

Greece, victory over, in Zechariah, 314,

318; in Sibylline Oracles, 322; organized force of, 338.
Greek influence, on Jews, 168, 248, 262, 263, 395; in Jewish schools, 252; on Antigonus, 260; on Christianity, 413.
Greek oppression of Jews, 319; in Enoch, 323.
Greek philosophy, its effect on the masses, 301.
Greeks, the, how regarded by Jews, 242.
Growth of society, 2; when continuous, 4.

HADES, destruction of, 374; in Theopompus, 391; equivalent to hell, 406.
Harlez, De, "Des Origines du Zoroastrisme," 150 n., 172 n.; "Avesta," 172 n.
Hasidim, the, 249, 321, 323.
Hatch, "Essays in Bibl. Greek," 180 n.
Hausrath, "N. T. Times," 246 n., 249 n., 337 n.
Heaven, whether referred to in Ps. xvii., 380 n.; as abode of the righteous, 401.
Hebrew language, ceased to be Jewish vernacular, 136.
Hebrew vowel-points, 24.
Hebrews, conception of Jesus in, 118, 119; its conception of Christianity, 233; whether imputed righteousness in, 430; logos in, 432; faith in, 434.
Hell, in Enoch-Parables, 393; whether in O. T., 404; in N. T., 406 n.; in Talmud, 412 n.
Hellenism, alleged defeat of, 262; influence of on N. T., 286, 287; in the Church, 370.
Heman, psalm-writer, 136.
Herod the Great, summoned before Sanhedrin, 258; conflicts in reign of, 331.
Herodians, the, their effort to entrap Jesus, 344.
Herodotus, on Persian religion, 391.
Heroes, antediluvian, 160.
Herzog, "Real-Encyclopädie," 246 n., 249 n., 302 n.
Hezekiah, Ps. of, 382.
Hierarchy, angelic, 153.
High-priest, as representative of logos, 109 n ; president of Sanhedrin, 258.
Hillel, liberality of, 259 n., 328 n.; teaching of, 264-266; moral earnestness of, 333; moral distinctness of, 338; moral e'evation of, 417.
History, later Jewish literary, character of, 52.
Hokma, the, ethical character of, 294.
Holiness, ritualistic, in Zechariah, 315.
Hope in God, Jewish non-ethical, 308.
Host of heaven, 161 n.
Humanity, devotion to, in N. T., 300.
Hypostasis of spirit, incomplete, 94.
Hypostatization, arrested, 90, 91.

IDEAL, religious, of Paul, 277; ethical, Roman, 337.
Ideas in the air, 29.
Idolatry, Jewish, late, 77; how treated by prophets, 234.
Idumeans, the, conversion of, 328 n.
Imagination, Semitic, defective, 383.
Immanuel, 317.
Immer, "Theol. des N. T.", 302 n.
Immortality, accepted by Pharisees, 251; Jewish doctrine of, 319; national, 384, 389; doctrine of, relation of Jesus to, 418.
Imputation, in 1 Tim., 283; in N. T., 285.
Imputation of righteousness, 272.
Incapacity, man's moral, 215.
Inclination to sin assumed in O. T., 197.
Indeterminism, biblical, 291.
India, whether Jews influenced by, 390.
Individualism, controlled by an ideal, 278; Jewish advance in, 396, 397.
Individuality, religious, cultivated by synagogue, 247.
Indra, as judge, 395.
Inheritance, ethical, natural, 185.
Insanity as demoniacal possession, 170.
Inspiration, its relation to law, 23, 24; Philo's view of, 127, 128; N. T. view of, 128, 129.
Institutions, effect of change in, 4.
Intercession, human, 273.
Intermediary, Jewish nation as, 345, 346.
Intermediation, between God and man, Jewish, 421, 431; Persian, 431 n.; angelic, 433.
Inward divine law, idea of, 24.
Isaiah, the exilian, Israel in, 332.
Isaiah, his denunciation of necromancy, 378.
Ishtar, her descent to Sheol, 382.
Islam, influenced by Jews and Christians, 27, 28; simplicity of duties of, 31; simplicity of doctrines of, 32, 38; birth of, out of old Arabian faith, 39; now spreading, 45; attitude of, toward unbelievers, 329 n.
Isolation, early national, 28; Jewish, 242; its ethical effect, 293; done away with by Christianity, 370, 371.
Israel, a mixed nationality, 10; destiny of, 224; prophetic rejection of, 336 n.; organized force of, 338; superiority of, 339; as prophet of God, 354.

JADDUA, 55 n.
James, its view of faith, 270; opposition to Paul in, 275; indorses Paul, 367; view of Jesus in, 426.
Jeremiah, ethical principle of, 184; forerunner of Messiah, 329, 330; new covenant of, 332.
Jerusalem, in Enoch, 323; the new, 324, 373; destruction of, 361, 363; parent church in, 366.

Jesus, the living, in Paul's system, 281;
his relation to Jewish nationalism,
286; his ethical spirit, 300, 301; his
opinion of John Baptist, 335; his faith
in Jewish nation, 349; his freedom of
speech, 351; his subordination to God,
358; words of, later interpretation
of, 358, 359; his simplicity, 359; hope
of his coming, 359; sobriety of his
ideas, 359; source of power of, 360;
coming of, whether defined by himself, 362; founder of Christianity, 368,
369, 435.
Jewish history, noble figures in, 245.
Jewish religion, persistence of, 8; influenced by Canaanites, Assyrians,
Babylonians, Greeks, 26, 27, 28.
Jewish religious instinct, 237.
Jews, in Egypt, 33; in Babylonia, 33;
religious isolation of, 235, 236; vitality
of, 238; faithful to idea of law, 240;
their consciousness of enlightenment,
241; Egyptian, 251; modern, Messianic ideas of, 304 n.; in Middle Age,
305; as borrowers, 388, 392; conversion of, to Christianity, in N. T., 403;
restoration of, to Palestine, 404.
Jinn, 142.
Job, book of, 61; whether national, 73;
description of wisdom in, 98–100;
date of, 98 n., 157 n.; Satan in, 165;
whether immortality in, 381, 385.
Jodl, "Geschichte d. Ethik," 300 n.
Johannites, influence of, 336.
John, apostle, indorses Paul, 367.
John Baptist, disciples of, 334 n., 335;
how esteemed by Jesus, 339.
John, First Epistle of, its agreement with
Fourth Gospel, 433.
John Hyrcanus, I., 65, 323.
John Hyrcanus II., 258.
Josephus, on John, 334 n.
Joshua, priest and governor, 316.
Jost, "Geschichte," 259 n., 265 n.
Jubilees, descent of angels in, 160 n.
Judaism, its dealing with circumcision,
31; how related to Hellenism, 263;
its severance from Christianity, 288;
religious organizing power of, 306;
attraction of, for Græco-Roman world,
328 n.
Judas Maccabæus, 65, 319, 323.
Judas the Galilean, 258.
Judgment, of nations in prophets, 314;
in Enoch, 324; in Synoptics, 355, 356;
in Sermon on Mount, 356 n.; by
God, 357; by Messiah, 357; general,
in N. T. Apocalypse, 373; general,
in Enoch, 374; future, Egyptian, 382;
allied to resurrection, 395.
Jupiter, as judge, 395.
Justice, divine, theological factor in, 82;
taught by Jesus, 417.
Justin Martyr, "Trypho," 330 n.
Juvenal on magic arts, 169 n.; ethical
sentiment of, 337.

Kemosh, Moabite devotion to, 305
King, Messiah as, in Synoptics, 343;
in Enoch, 343 n.; of Israel, as judge,
400.
"Kingdom of God," germ of, 321 n.;
significance of, 370.
Kingdom of heaven in N. T., 208
Kings, Deuteronomic coloring of, 309 n.
Knowledge of God, by believers, 422.
Kohut, "Jüdische Angelologie," 149 n.,
150 n., 172 n.
Korah, sons of, as psalm-writers, 136.
Kuenen, "Rel. of Israel," 249 n., 306 n.

Lang, "Myth, Ritual, and Religion,"
199 n.
Law, the, turning-point, 47; as factor
in Jewish life, 49; its relation to
prophecy, 53; its acceptance, 70, 71;
ethical power of, 186; moral feeling
in, 226; a civil code, 227; its relation
to Christianity, 237; viewed as a
whole, 243; slavery to, 244; spiritual
element in, 245; Pharisaic attitude
toward, 250; glorification of, in Talmud, 252; recognized by Jesus, 266–
268, 419, 421; its great possibilities,
266; criticised by Jesus, 267; in 1
Timothy, 283; replaces prophecy, 314;
observed by early disciples, 348.
Law, the oral, character of, 239; atti-
tude of Sadducees toward, 253.
Leadership, individual, 21–26, 34.
Legalism, extreme, of Essenes, 255.
Legend, in earlier histories, 55, 56; in
Chronicles, 56; in Pentateuch, 56; in
Synoptics, 358.
Lenormant, "La Magie," 142 n.
Levitical law. See Law.
Levitical legislation. See Law.
Liberty of thought, Pharisaic, 251;
Christian, 278 n.; civil, in O. T., 322.
Lichtenberger, "Encyclopédie," 302 n.
Lightfoot, "Colossians," 249 n.
Life, Christian, of first century, 208;
eternal, in Matthew, 356; Christian,
how affected by eschatology, 376;
new, on earth, in Daniel, 380 n.; long,
as blessing in O. T., 382; earthly,
its hold on the Jew, 389; eternal,
on earth, 401; long, as reward, 404;
future, Jewish monarchical scheme
of, 412.
Lilit, 142.
Literature, Babylonian-Assyrian, 382;
pre-Islamic Arabian, 382; Phœnician,
382.
Liver, as seat of life, 177 n.
Logos, the, in Philo, 106–114; internal
and uttered, 110; in Fourth Gospel,
115–117, 119, 218 n.; in N. T. Apocalypse, 120.
Love, as moral guide, 278; divine,
taught by Jesus, 417.
Luke, eschatology of, 361 n.

Luthardt, "Die antike Ethik," etc., 302 n. ; " Geschichte d. christl. Ethik," etc., 302 n.

MACCABEAN STATE, 323.
Maccabean war, 240.
Magic in Roman Empire, 169; Essenian, 256.
Magism, in Persia, 391.
Mahdism, Messianic faith in, 425 n.
Maimonides, 252, 288.
Man, psychical, 181; pneumatical, 181; moral potency of, 191, 213; primitive, capable of earthly immortality, 204; corrupt nature of, 211 ff.; nature of, in O. T., 212; fall of, 218 n.; his need of power of God, 236; moral autocracy of, 270.
Man-god, death of, 280 n.
Manahem the Essene, 254, 256.
Manichæism, failure of, 43.
Manuscripts, early, liable to error, 72.
Mardochæus, day of, 57.
Marduk, Babyl. preference for, 305.
Mark, Jesus as Messiah in, 350.
Martensen on biblical ethics, 302 n.
Martineau on biblical ethics, 302 n.
Masses, Jewish, not bigoted, 245.
Mazdeism, the later, lifelessness of, 38; complicated theology of, 43; whether affected by Judaism and Christianity, 375.
Mediating power between deity and world, 90.
Mediation, human, 228.
Mediatorial scheme, Jewish, 431.
Meek, the, O. T. sense of, 316.
Megilloth, 247 n.
Mendelssohn, Moses, 288.
Mercy of God, 227.
Messiah, the, whether mentioned by Philo, 113 n.; Ephraimic, 280 n.; rule of, 341; popular idea of, 344; as subordinate to God, 357; as judge, in Talmud, 357 n.; as ignorant of day of parousia, 362 n.; end of reign of, 374 n.; as conqueror, 376; as king, 376; God's vicegerent, 400; person of, idealized, 400.
Messianic hope, in Ezra's time, 49, 50; ethical development of, 308.
Messianic thought, history of, 331.
Metaphysics, absence of, among ancient Jews, 58.
Metatron, the, 91 n.
Meyer, "Gesch. d. Alterthums," 172 n.
Micaiah, vision of, 144.
Michael, angel, 64, 152; as patron of the Jews, 320; as agent of salvation, 398.
Midrash Tanchuma, 252 n.
Millennarian tendencies, in the Church, 365 n.
Millennium, the, in N. T. Apocalypse, 373.

Mills, "The Zend Avesta," 172 n.
Mind, equivalent to spirit, 179.
Miracles, ascribed to Jesus in Synoptics, 125; in Fourth Gospel, 125; post-biblical, 126; of Messiah, 329, 330.
Mishna, beginning of, 264.
Mission of Pharisees, 251.
Mithra, as mediator, 431 n.
Moabite Stone, 307 n.
Mohammed, founder of Islam, 26; represented his age, 34; fitted his ideas into the existing system, 40; theocracy of, 303 n.
Monotheism, when established, 47; its nature, 48; effect of, on national character, 78; imperfect, 147 n.; Jewish, 423.
Moral agencies, supernatural, not differentiated, 146.
Moral capability in man, 213.
Moral codes, origin of, 16–18.
Moral crises in life, 21, 22.
Moral earnestness, prophetic, 318.
Moral ideal, Jewish, 328.
Moral order, aimed at by the Church, 377.
Morality of Sadducees, 261.
Morals, pre-prophetic, 184; prophetic, 184.
Moses, his relation to Israelitism, 25.
Mystery, in teaching of Jesus, 347 n.
Myth of serpent, 198–200.
Mythologies, Græco-Roman, decline of 338.

NAKEDNESS, ethical aspect of sense of, 197 n.
"Name of Baal," title of Ashtoreth, 83 n.
Nathan, parable of, 184 n.
National consciousness of innocence, 189.
Nationalism, shades of, 249; Pharisaic, 250; of Jesus, 268; in Fourth Gospel, 284; in Enoch, 324; stress laid on, 328; Jewish, as affecting ethics, 396.
Nations, foreign, their relation to Israel, 318.
Natural law, O. T. idea of, 121, 122.
Nature, tenderness for, ascribed to God, 80, 81.
Nazarites, 219 n., 255.
Nebuchadnezzar, attitude of prophets toward, 311.
Necromancy, 142 n.; opposed by prophets, 378.
Nehemiah, alleged library of, 73.
Nero, as anti-Christ, 363 ff.; as man of lawlessness, 364.
New Testament, claim to inspiration in, 129–131.
Nicolas, "Des Doct. Rel. d. Juifs," 172 n.
Nineveh, in Nahum, 310.

Nomism, control of conception of sin by, 195; two elements in, 237; alleged victory of, 262; of Jesus, 266, 268, 269; its need, 266; Jewish, 277; national, 286; and antinomism, 289.
Non-miraculous view of life in O. T., 122, 123.
Non-resistance in N. T., 256, 257; taught by Jesus, 267; in Sermon on Mount, 295 n.

Ob, 142 n.
Obedience, inability of, to save, 212.
Oehler, "O. T. Theology," 302 n.
Old Testament, idea of divine spirit in, 92; whether word hypostatized in, 103, 104; claim to inspiration in, 129; N. T. view of, 131, 132; authorship of, how decided by early critics, 132–136.
Omnipotence ascribed to God, 79.
Omnipresence ascribed to God, 79.
Omniscience ascribed to God, 79.
Onias, temple of, 314 n.
Oriental religions, whether they affected Jews, 257.
Organization, Jewish religious, 239, 240, 241; social, its ethical effect, 293; ethical-religious, 338.
Orthodoxy, Mosaic, antagonism of Jesus to, 352; its antagonism toward Jesus, 352.
Osiris, as judge, 395.

Palestine, as scene of judgment, 398.
Palingenesis, the, 343.
Pantheism, not in O. T., 175.
Parables, of Jesus, resurrection in, 394.
Paradise, 408, 409.
Paralyzing effect of casuistry, 244.
Parousia, Messianic judicial, 358; in N. T., 362; moral effect of expectation of, 363; moral power of, 376.
Parsee religion, persistence of, 8; stagnation of, 9.
Parthian invasion of Palestine, 325.
Particularism, national, 48; national, Jewish, 349.
Patriots, Jewish exilian, 312.
Paul, as interpreter of Jesus, 35, 38; illogical nationalism of, 81; his idea of divine justice, 82; his conception of divine spirit, 93; his idea of wisdom, 102; his conception of Jesus as glorified Messiah, 117, 118; his allegorical interpretation, 138; treatment of Eden-story by, 207; his doctrine of moral incapacity, 212; assumes goodness in man's will, 214; affirms man's moral impotency, 214; his picture of the Roman world, 214; his view of nature of Messiah's death, 232; purification-offering of, 232; character of his thought, 271; his attitude toward

the Messiah, 271, 272; his feeling toward Jewish ordinances, 271; his expectation of Christ's second coming, 274; his intuition of the Messiah, 274; his moral earnestness, 274; his view of Abraham's faith, 275; his attitude toward ethical principle, 278 n.; his view of Christ's humanity, 280; self-adaptation of, 297; ethical influence of, 301; his conjunction of faith and works, 340; as preacher to Gentiles, 340; his view of the parousia, 362; his conflict with extreme conservatives, 367; his contribution to Christianity, 368; his view of Messianic reign, 374 n.; epistles of, immortality in, 377; his view of resurrection, 393, 394; his conception of Messianic judgment, 399, 400; his view of future of Israel, 403 n.; his view of abolition of death, 407; his view of regeneration of the earth, 408; his view of intermediate state, 410; non-Jewish element in, 413; as Christian leader, 416; his appeal to Pharisees, 419; his autobiography, 427; his attitude toward deification of Jesus, 429.
Perfection, human, in Fourth Gospel, 285.
Persian ideas, influence of, 374, 375.
Persian influence, on Jews, 151, 168, 248, 292, 390, 405, 431 n.; on Christianity, 413.
Persian kingdom, permanence of, 304.
Persian religion compared with Jewish, 172.
Persius, ethical sentiment of, 337.
Person of Jesus, two lines in construction of, 120; idealized, 358.
Peter, church founded on, 348; protest of, against Messiah's death, 351; reproved by Jesus, 351; vision of, 366; indorses Paul, 367; his view of Jesus, 422.
Pfleiderer, "Moral u. Religion," 302 n.; "Religionsphilosophie," 302 n.
Pharisees, attacked by Jesus, 245; recognized by Jesus, 266; their doctrine of imputation, 273; under Hasmoneans, 325; their aversion to revolt, 331; their fear of Jesus, 344; Jesus intelligible to, 348 n.
Philo, his conception of divine spirit, 92; his conception of wisdom, 101, 102; his idea of the logos, 106–114; influence of, on Fourth Gospel, 117; his view of inspiration, 127, 128; makes woman author of sin, 210; "Contemplative Life," 255 n.; exegetical method of, 388; his relation to Colossians, 433.
Philosophy, Cynical in Eccles., 59; Platonic and Stoic in Wisdom, 60; Jewish, 97; Hebrew ethical, 291; Greek sceptical, 385, 386.
Pilate, his view of Jesus, 344.

Pirke Aboth, 247 n., 251 n., 259 n.
Plato, " Apology," 395 n.
Platonism, influence of, on Jews, 97, 386, 387.
Pleroma, in Christ, 407; gnostic, 433.
Pliny, "Hist. Nat.," 255 n.
Plutarch, ethical sentiment of, 337; on resurrection, 391.
Political annihilation and religious growth, 238.
Political idea, the, in Daniel, 322; in the Sibyl, 323.
Poor, the, technical O. T. sense of, 316.
Prayer for the dead, 77 n.
Pre-existence of Messiah in Enoch-Parables, 326.
Prescriptions, as enfeebling spirituality, 369.
Priesthood, of Christ, 283.
Priesthood, Levitical, perpetuity of, 315.
Priests, conservatism of, 254.
Primitive idea of animals, 199.
Prince of this world, 218 n.
Probation, future, 411.
Problem of evil, N. T. solution of, 171.
Prophecies, pre-exilian, 315 n.
Prophecy, view of, in Zechariah and Joel, 54.
Prophet, the false, in N. T. Apocalypse, 373.
Prophetic writings, conception of sin in, 190.
Prophets, the, formulators of monotheism, 47; their treatment of idolatry, 234; interested in the nation as a whole, 236; peculiar to Israel, 238; their conception of covenant, 307; their interpretation of history, 307; ethical reproofs of, 332; their view of Jewish nation as intermediary, 345; rejection of Israel in, 346; judgment in, 356; nationalism in ethics of, 396 n.; Jerusalem in, 408.
Proselytism, origin of, 328 n.
Protestantism, affected by modern thought, 435.
Proverbs, date of, 58, 100 n.; old Semitic eschatology of, 383.
Psalm xliv., date of, 189.
Psalm li., unique conception of sin in, 192.
Psalm cxix., its motive, 240; idea of righteousness in, 268.
Psalms, Babylonian, penitential, 382.
Psalms, the, date of, 61; providence in, 80; conception of sin in, 186 ff.; whether immortality in, 380, 381.
Psalms of Solomon, judgment in, 357; Messiah in, 398; Israel's future in, 400.
Psychological questions suggested by Eden-story, 198.
Ptolemy Energetes, 60 n.
Ptolemy Physcon, 60 n.
Public worship of Ezra's time, effect of, 48.

Punishment, eternal, in Matthew, 356.
Purgatorial suffering, 411, 412.
Purification, national, preached by John Baptist, 333.
Purim, 57.

Rabbis, their attitude toward Greek study, 251.
Ransom, Jesus as, 352, 353.
Rechabites, the, 219 n., 255.
Reconciliation of man to God, 222, 407.
Records, Jewish, antiquity of, 241.
" Records of the Past," 307 n.
Redemption, national, in Philo, 327; popular hope of, 327.
Reform of John Baptist, value of, 335, 336.
Reformation, moral, of Jesus, 339.
Reformers, not always understood by contemporaries, 35.
Regeneration, ethical, as held by Jesus, 340; in Fourth Gospel, 340; of humanity, taught by Jesus, 377; social, era of, 401; of external world, 408; in future life, 412.
Religion, a branch of sociology, 1; social character of, 1; product of national thought, 7; dependent on social organization, 8; tends to coalesce with ethics, 19; and ethics, difference in their points of view, 20; absolute power of, on what dependent, 21; practical power of, on what dependent, 21; force in propagation of, 32; the absolutely universal, 36; how dependent on organization, 39; effect of slavish nomism on, 244; influence of synagogues on, 247; Israelitish, embraced by aliens, 318.
Religions, barbarous, history of, 44.
Religions that have perished, 7.
Religious cause of failure, 5.
Religious consciousness defined, 1.
Religious decay only seeming, 5.
Religious discoveries, liberating effect of, 24, 25.
Religious gatherings in Malachi, 246.
Religious ideas, gradual victory of, 33.
Religious influence, international, extent of, 26.
Religious life, later Jewish, activity of, 248.
Religious necessity of growth, 2, 5, 6.
Religious progress marked by flows and ebbs, 21; from less to more general, 30.
Religious revolutions, how accomplished, 6.
Religious sects, danger of narrowness, 6.
Religious sentiment, its content determined by science and ethics, 20.
Religious thinkers, when influential, 6.
Religious thought, diverse tendencies of, 192 n.
Religious vigor, relative to size of community, 5.

Religiousness, ethical and non-ethical, 384 n.
Renan, "History of Israel," 306 n.; "L'Antechrist," 364 n.
Renegades, in Enoch, 324.
Repentance, prophetic doctrine of, 221.
Restoration, the, religious struggle of, 313.
Resurrection, accepted by Pharisees, 251; of Jesus, 280, 358; in Daniel, 320; as contained in immortality, 394 n.
Retaliation, opposed by Jesus, 267.
Retribution, divine, in N. T., 407.
Retrogression. See Decay.
Revelation, received by Paul, 427.
Reward, divine, in O. T., 261.
Rewards, promised by Jesus, 343.
Righteous, the, 82; in Daniel, 321, 322.
Righteousness, consciousness of, in Psalms, 188; of Christ, 209; prophetic conception of, 235; twofold source of, 236; later Jewish idea of, 243; nomistic definition of, 244; Jesus' conception of, 268, 269; transference of, 272; as held by Jesus and Paul, 281; in Fourth Gospel, 283–285; ethical, 287; and prosperity, 309, prophetic, 318; national, consciousness of, 332; human, as condition of salvation, 421; exaltation of, 429.
Ritual, expression of dogma, 20; debasing tendency of, 186; elaboration of, 230; organization of, 313; Egyptian, 382.
Roman empire, magic in, 169; ethical progress in, 337; as persecutor, 363; destruction of, in N. T. Apocalypse, 364, 373.
Roman religion of first century, lifelessness of, 38.
Roman world, Paul's picture of, 214.
Rome, organized force of, 338.
Roth, on Persian eschatology, 375 n.
Royal law, the, 297.

Sabatier, on N. T. Apocalyps 375 n.
Sabbath, the, observed by Christians, 361 n.
Sacerdotal system of N. T., 48.
Sacrifice, vicarious element in, 226; outward, insufficiency of, 230; Essenian hostility to, 255, 256; Messianic, 280; of Christ, in Fourth Gospel, 283; of Christ, high conception in, 290; of Jesus, in N. T., 428.
Sadducees, failure of, 261; under Hasmoneans, 325; aversion of, to revolt, 331; reject resurrection, 392.
Saints, the, in Daniel, 320, 321; reign of, 362, 374; as judges of the wicked, 406.
Sa'ir, 142, 145.
Salter, "Ethical Religion," 302 n.
Salvation, not in church, 278 n.; super-

natural, 279; advance in intensity of, methods of, 230; through king, 316 ff.; held to be of Jews, 346; how defined by Jesus, 418; as reward of obedience to the law, 425.
Samuel, Deuteronomic coloring of, 309 n.
Sassanians, the, theocracy of, 303 n.
Satan, as angel of light, 152; identification of, with serpent, 158, 202; his fall from heaven, 160; in Enoch, 163; identification of, with Azazel, 203 n.; blinding power of, 213; in N. T. Apocalypse, 373; imprisonment of, 374.
Satisfaction in God, earthly, in O. T., 379 ff.
Scepticism, religious, among early Jews, 53; Sadducean, 253; Semitic, 390.
Schneckenbürger, on baptism of John, 334 n.
Schodde, Enoch, translation of, 66 n., 323 n.
Schools, legal, 231; Jewish, Greek influence in, 252.
Schultz, "Alttestamentl. Theol.," 302 n.
Schürer, "Geschichte," 66 n., 246 n., 249 n., 263 n., 326 n., 330 n., 337 n.
Science, as handmaid of religion, 15.
Scientific views of N. T. times, 360.
Scion, royal, 316.
Scribes, early, qualifications of, 72; as leaders of legal study, 259; doctrinal studies of, 319; concurrence of Jesus with, 419.
Scriptures, public reading of, 247.
Second coming of Christ, 274.
Second Maccabees, judgment in, 357.
Sects. See Religious sects.
Seeley, "Ecce Homo," 302 n.
Self-abandonment, as ethical factor, 300.
Self-culture, moral, obligation of, 299.
Semitic and Hellenic ideas, united in Christianity, 370.
Semitism, in the Church, 370.
Semyaza, 160.
Seneca, ethical sentiment of, 337.
Sensual pleasure, serpent symbol of, 203 n.
Separateness, social, of early Christians, 297.
Sermon on Mount, no mention of divine spirit in, 94; whether Essenism in, 256, 257; ethics of, 294–296; content of, 340; judgment in, 356, 396; heaven in, 409.
Serpent, the, in Genesis, 158, 195; punishment of, 197; animal nature of, 199; allegorically interpreted, 203.
Servant of Yahwe, 225; suffering of, 352.
Seven Brothers, story of, in 2 Maccabees, 393.
Shabbath, 259 n.
Shades, the, consultation of, 378.
Shamash, as judge, 395.
Shammai, severity of, 250 n., 264.

Shekina, the, 90 n.
Sheol, negative character of, 204; existence in, 378; as motive for present life, 381; in O. T., 381; in Enoch-Parables, 393; whether moral distinctions in, 404; whether Paradise in, 409.
Sibylline Oracles, why not canonized, 75; earthly consummation in, 356; judgment in, 357; Israel's future in, 400.
Simon the Just, 247 n., 259, 264.
Simplicity of Jesus, 359.
Sin, primitive view of, 183; religious and ethical sides of consciousness of, 187; O. T. view of nature of, 190; idea of, how controlled by nomism, 193; in O. T. forefathers, 193; in O. T., whether nature or tendency, 193; origin of, in O. T., 193 ff.; initial act of, 196; universality of, in N. T., 206; beginning of, in N. T., 208; N. T. conception of, 220; ethical escape from, 222; relation of suffering to, 223-226; inward, 227; sense of, developed by the law, 227; in Fourth Gospel, 284.
Sinai, as scene of judgment. 398 n.
Sinfulness, not bodily, 174.
Sins of ignorance, 226.
Smith, "Dict. of Bible," 409 n.
Smith, "Religion of the Semites," 141 n.
Society, see Decay, Growth: apparent stagnation of, 3; ethical organization of, 338; perfect, conception of, 360.
Soc. of Bibl. Lit. and Exeg., Journal of, 429 n.
Soferim, the, 259.
Solidarity, ethical principle, 184, 185; national, 272; national, period of, 315.
Solomon, perhaps author of proverbs, 58.
"Son of God," whether claim to superhuman nature in, 422.
Son of man, in Daniel, 320; coming of, 361; as Lord of angels, 423.
Son of Yahwe, as epithet of king, 317.
Song of Songs, doubts as to canonical authority of, 74.
Song of Three Children, 273.
Sonship, spiritual, 270.
Sophistry, moral, exposed by Jesus, 340.
Soul, the, limits of development, 2; equivalent to person, 175; used for dead body, 175; equivalent to life, 178; and spirit, difference between, 181; of Adam, 181; of Christ, 181; Christian view of, 182; schism in, 213; direct appeal of, to God. 230; death of, ascribed to Sadducees, 253 n.
Spiegel, "Eranische Alterthumskunde," 150 n., 172.
Spirit, whether hypostatized in Bible,

92-96; the divine, Philo's conception of, 92; Paul's conception of, 93; Talmudic conception of, 93 n.; use of, by Augustan writers, 182 n.; hostile to flesh, 213; holy, John Baptist's reference to, 334 n.
Spirits, guardian, Persian, 151; evil, Persian, 155; good, no organization of, in Bible, 170.
Spirituality in Judaism, 245, 265; of Paul, 276; of Jesus, 342, 355, 418; as suggesting immortality, 384.
Stade, "Geschichte Israels," 306 n., 307 n.
Stagnation, social, 3.
States, ancient, cause of ruin of, 3.
Stoicism, career of, 41; not a popular religion, 41; idea of spirituality of God in, 88, 89; influence of, on Jews, 97, 886; influence of, on Philo, 112, 114, trace of, in Fourth Gospel, 218 n.; Pharisaic, 252; in Palestine, 260; in Antigonus, 261.
Storm and stress, period of, 236.
Subordination of woman, 210.
Succa, 273.
Suffering, question of, 166; vicarious, 166; atonement by, 222, 353; national, ethical training of, 309; Jewish, religious effect of, 319; as leading to triumph, 353.
Suffering Messiah in Talmud, 330 n.
Sun-worship, Essenian, 256.
Supernatural, the, in history of Messiah, 360.
Sympathy, in N. T. ethics, 300.
Synagogue, the, religious effect of, 87, 88.
Synagogue, the great, 135, 246.
Synagogues, 231.
Syncretism in ancient pantheons, 10; in Islam, Christianity, Judaism, 11.
Synoptics, the, divine justice in, 83; fatherhood of God in, 84; idea of divine spirit in, 94; idea of wisdom in, 102; baptism in. 348; Messianic announcement in, 350; final judgment in, 355, 356; judgment by Jesus in, 355, 356; date of, 358; eschatology of, 360; apocalypse in, 363; resurrection in, 393, 394; Messiah as judge in, 399; signs of Messiah's appearance in, 402; faith in Jesus in, 421.
Syria, Paul in, 427.
Syrophœnician woman, the, 345.

Tabu, its relation to ethics, 16 n.
Talmud, the, hypostatizing tendency in, 90 n., 91 n., 93 n.; its use of O. T., 137; magic in, 142; angels in. 149; demons in, 169; fusion of civil and religious codes in, 237; detailed prescriptions of, 243; imputation in, 273; pre-existence of Messiah in, 326; suffering Messiah in, 330 n.; calling of Messiah by God in, 357; Messiah

as judge in, 357; Gog and Magog in, 374 n.; resurrection in, 394; nationalism in, 396; future probation in, 412.
Tares, parable of, 348 n.
Targum of Jonathan, 280.
Targums, the, suffering Messiah in, 330 n.
Tartarus, 406 n.
Teaching of Jesus, whether esoteric, 347.
Temple-service, ethical aspect of, 190.
Temptation in Eden, 195 ff.
Tenderness, ethical, of Jesus, 301.
Theocratic idea, non-Jewish, 303.
Theol. Jahres-bericht, 302 n.
Theopompus, on resurrection, 391.
Therapeutæ, the, 255 n.
Tiamat, 152, 158, 162, 200 n.
Tigris-valley, as Persian centre, 392.
Timothy, First Epistle to, faith in, 434.
Tobit, book of, evil spirit in, 168; conception of sin in, 192 n.
Tora. See Law.
Torment, future, whether in O. T., 379.
Totemism, Hebrew, 141 n.
Toy, "Quotations," 163 n.; on proselyte-baptism, 334 n.
Tradition, as interpreter of Jesus, 359.
Transformation, moral, in N. T., 285.
Translation, origin of idea of, 204 n.
Transmigration of souls, 390.
Tree of life, 201, 205 n.
Trichotomy, not in Bible, 180-182.
Tylor, "Primitive Culture," 199 n.

Unbelief, the sin of the world, 216.
Underworld, the, in O. T., 381; Babylonian, 382.
Unity, geographical, as condition of spread of a religion, 37; early Jewish, 308; ethical, Roman, 337; effected by Christianity, 371.
Universality, prophetic religious, 313, 314; of Jewish national aim, 319; attempted, of John Baptist, 336; of membership, in the Church, 366.
Uprisings, Jewish, 344.

Vernes, "Hist. des Idées Mess.," 335 n.
Vicarious righteousness, 273-275.
Vicarious suffering, 223; relation of Jesus to, 420.
Virtue, Antigonus' view of, 260.
Vischer, on N. T. Apocalypse, 375 n.
Vision, prophetic and apocalyptic, 63.
Visions, apocalyptic, historical interpretations of, 376.

Warburton, "Divine Leg. of Moses," 382 n.
Water as male and female, 162 n.
Wayikra Rabba, 252 n.
Weber, "System," 91 n., 93 n., 142 n., 149 n., 161 n., 169 n., 198 n., 252 n., 273 n., 280 n., 326 n., 329 n., 330 n., 357 n., 363 n., 374 n., 394, 399, 409.
Weiss, "N. T. Theol.," 302 n.
Wellhausen, "Pharisäer u. Sadducäer," 249 n.; "Hist. of Israel," 306 n.
Wicked, the, 82.
Will, human, how viewed by Paul, 214; ethical power of, 222.
Winer, "Real-Wörterbuch," 249 n.
Wisdom, pre-Christian Jewish conception of, 385, 386.
Wisdom-books, moral position of, 327.
Wisdom of Solomon, classic character of, 52; religious tone of, 60; providence in, 79, 80; fatherhood of God in, 84; man's relation to God in, 87; idea of divine spirit in, 92; idea of wisdom in, 100; personification of word in, 105, 106; conception of sin in, 192, 205; view of body in, 219; atonement for sin in, 231; immortality in, 251; wisdom a divine ideal in, 278; salvation in, 279; immortality in, 378; ethical progress in, 397; ethical-religious elevation of, 417.
Witchcraft, 171.
Wogue, "Histoire de la Bible," 132 n.
Woman, subordination of, to man, 153; rôle assigned to, by Hebrews, 210 n.
World, deadness of, 216; moral corruption of, 218.
World-religion, announced by Jesus, 349.

Xenophon, "Anabasis," 409 n.

Yahwe, name, abandonment of, 32; Jewish loyalty to, 305; his covenant with Israel, 306, 307; as judge, 397, 398.
Yahwe-cult, origin of, 306 n.

Zadok, 260 n.
Zadokites, 254 n.
Zechariah, Satan of, 167.
Zeller, on Greek philosophy, 387 n.
Zerubbabel, Davidic prince, 316.
Zeus, as judge, 395.
Zoroaster, his relation to Mazdeism, 25.
Zoroastrian resurrection, 391.